THE
ALPINE JOURNAL

1988/89

MULLER

1.   *Karakoram. Duncan Tunstall on the upper Biafo glacier. Tilman's 'Sokha La' is the furthest right gap in the ridge.*

THE
ALPINE JOURNAL

1988/89

Incorporating the Journal of the Ladies' Alpine Club & Alpine Climbing

A record of mountain adventure and scientific observation

Volume 93 No 337

Edited by Ernst Sondheimer

Assistant Editors:
Johanna Merz, A. V. Saunders and Geoffrey Templeman

assisted by Marian Elmes

FREDERICK MULLER

in association with

The Alpine Club, London

IN ASSOCIATION WITH THE ALPINE CLUB

Volume 93 No 337
THE ALPINE JOURNAL 1988–89

Address all editorial communications to the Hon Editor direct at:
51 Cholmeley Crescent
London N6 5EX

Address all sales and distribution communications to
Mike Wicks
Century Hutchinson
Brookmount House
62–65 Chandos Place
London WC2N 4NW

Back numbers:
apply to the Alpine Club

First published in 1988 by Frederick Muller in association with the Alpine Club
Frederick Muller is an imprint of Century Hutchinson Ltd, Brookmount
House, 62–65 Chandos Place, London WC2N 4NW

Century Hutchinson Publishing Group (Australia) Pty Ltd
89–91 Albion Street, Surry Hills, NSW 2010, Australia

Century Hutchinson Group (NZ) Ltd
PO Box 40–086, 32–34 View Road, Glenfield, Auckland 10

Century Hutchinson (SA) Pty Ltd
PO Box 337, Bergvlei 2012, South Africa

The Alpine Club, 74 South Audley Street, London W1Y 5FF

Set in Linotron Sabon by Deltatype Ltd, Ellesmere Port

Printed and bound in Great Britain by
Butler & Tanner Ltd, Frome and London

British Library Cataloguing in Publication Data

The Alpine journal.
 1. Mountaineering
 796.522
 ISBN 0–09–173659–5

Contents

Illustrations

THE ALPINE JOURNAL

The Golden Pillar

*The First Ascent of the North-West Pillar of
Golden Peak (7027m), Karakoram*

A. V. SAUNDERS

In the heart of the Karakoram, in the ancient Mirdom of Nagar, lies a little-known mountain. Although the Karakoram Highway passes no more than 30km from it, the peak is not visible from the road. Yet from Nagar the mountain is striking.

On the Skardu side of the watershed, the peak is called Spantik. (This may be a Balti name: I have not been there.) According to some sources the peak is also known as Yengutz Sar: this is clearly erroneous, as the peak cannot be seen from the Burushaski-speaking Yengutz Har Valley ('Valley of the Torrent of the Flour Mills'), and Sar is not a Burushaski synonym for peak; it means pond.

The first Westerners to attempt the mountain were the Americans, Fanny Bullock Workman and her husband Dr William Hunter Workman. In 1906 they climbed the laborious Chogolungma Glacier, taking in the peaks of Chogo and Lungma on the way to the plateau, about 300m below the summit. Their name for the mountain was Pyramid Peak.

The Workmans' effort was not bettered till half a century later, when in 1955 a party of West Germans under the leadership of R Sander made a successful ascent by the Chogolungma Glacier, possibly following the route pioneered by the Workmans. The Germans used the name Spantik and also (presumably in honour of their home town) renamed the mountain 'Frankfurterberg'.

Visitors to the region have a habit of adopting bizarre nomenclature. One Italian expedition in 1954 improved on local usage with Cima Marconi (Sumayar Bar Chish) and Cima Bolzano (Melangush Chish).

On the N side of the mountain a large monolithic pillar catches the evening sun, and gives the peak its Burushaski name, Ganesh Chish, which means Golden Peak.

The Golden Pillar is marble. The rock is crystalline, almost sugary in parts, but often sound. The pillar is the *coup de grâce* of a vertical outcrop of this metamorphic limestone, which leapfrogs the glaciers from above the village of Hoppar. Looking out from high on the pillar we were able to see the cream-yellow rock arcing from glacier to glacier for 25km, like a series of rainbows.

The Golden Pillar is the clear, unavoidable challenge of the mountain: it soars from the glacier for 2200m. The summit is about 300m higher and is set back, perhaps 3km from the pillar.

We saw the pillar in 1984 while attempting to climb Bojohagar Duonasir (7329m), a mountain directly above the Karakoram Highway. Not only did we fail to climb the mountain, but a Japanese walking club made the first ascent while we were there. They used five camps and several kilometres of fixed rope, while we were attempting an 'alpine-style' ascent. In spite of this obvious difference in attitudes, when Phil Butler and I met them on Day 10 of our gruelling 14-day climb, they were very decent. They offered us food and had kind words about our effort.

The 1984 Bojohagar Expedition was an NLMC (North London Mountaineering Club) affair, and it was much the same team that, seeing the Golden Pillar in 1984, knew they would have to return. Even though Golden Peak was on the horizon, it was clear that something remarkable, very nasty even, decorated its N face. At first the pillar reminded us of Cenotaph Corner.

In England, further enquiries revealed a little of the mountain's history. From Poland the encyclopaedic Kowalewski sent us some photographs taken from Kunyang Chish. Nazir Sabir, Doug Scott and Tadeusz Piotrowski (who perished on K2 during the tragic summer of 1986) all kindly donated 'front-on' prints, which all but persuaded us to cancel. At about this time we began to compare the pillar to the Walker Spur, just a little higher, and perhaps a bit harder.

Also during 1986 the team jelled. It was to consist of the Bojohagarites Phil (Lobby) Butler, Mick Fowler, Dr John English and myself, together with two NLMC members new to this sort of thing, Liz Allen and Bruce Craig. George Fowler (Mick's father), Dr Iqbal Ahmed, our Liaison Officer and Rajab Zawar, our Nagari cook completed the expedition team.

We established our Base at a place known to the locals as Suja Bassa (c4000m) on 14 July. The march from the road-head at Hoppar had taken five days, though it could easily have been done in three. The porters had originally wanted to make six days of it, but we compromised on five and a goat. (It is 'traditional' for expeditions to give their porters a goat.) Visitors to this region should note that, whilst the daily rate of pay to the porters is not excessive, the 'traditional' day stages can be as short as one and a half hours. This makes Nagar the most expensive region of the Karakoram for expeditions. We found the Hoppar men honourable: having struck a bargain, they invariably stuck to it.

We made a dump of gear two hours above Base at a place we called Hewitt's Camp. (There was evidence that this Canadian geologist had used the same site in 1986.) Hewitt's was directly across the small Golden Peak glacier from the base of the pillar, at c4500m. From here we could see that the pillar was divided into four sections. First a 400m pinnacle, the First Tower, barred access to the long serpentine Snow Arête. The Snow Arête ended in a small step, which led to the third section, a tiny Hanging Glacier. The fourth part was the point of the exercise: 1200m of wall, like a great spear thrust into the sky.

As climbers we operated in pairs, and I teamed up with Mick Fowler. Mick is a Civil Servant by profession, who has (among other, equally unique, 'achievements') made a speciality of climbing the loose shale cliffs of Devon. I accompanied him once on one of these excursions, and I remember, as I anxiously studied the clutch of insecure-looking ice-screw belays, Mick enthusing wildly about the 'quality' of the route. We were following a crumbling overhang, and, every time we moved, sections of cliff fell away to land in the sea, far below. It was very probably the most terrifying experience of my life.

On 19 July Fowler and I made a preliminary reconnaissance of the approaches to the pillar (it took three days to reach the Hanging Glacier). Meanwhile, English and Allen made a start on the descent ridge. They were stopped by deep snow and indifferent weather, but not before they had climbed the initial 400m prominence, a sort of pyramidal tower. Butler and Bruce inspected the Yengutz Pass, which had not, as far as we knew, been crossed. This initial flurry of activity was followed by a period characterized by various attempts to climb either the pillar or the ridge, which failed in outbursts of appalling weather.

On the evening of 5 August Fowler and I walked up to Hewitt's Camp, knowing that this was our last chance to try the route. Fowler was due back at his desk on the 23rd, and, if we allowed 10 days for the climb, he would just make it.

We had packed carefully after lunch, checking and rechecking each detail. A great sense of fate hung in the afternoon like an impending storm. We packed and repacked our sacks, tidied the tents, laid out our clothes in order, until there were no displacement activities left. Then we shouldered the enormous loads and wordlessly began to walk. The weather was variable in the extreme: there was even a minor snow-storm while we were walking.

During that night we climbed the 1000m to the Hanging Glacier, and spent the remainder of the 6th praying for good weather. On Day 2 we were fortunate and, starting at 4am, we were able to climb 10 pitches of slabs and walls to reach the Amphitheatre by 5pm. It was important to reach this, as there was no possibility of finding a bivouac ledge on the slabs.

We had thought, when we started, that the main difficulty on this day would be the little walls which crossed the slabs, and a larger wall that barred access to the Amphitheatre. In fact we found that the reverse was true: there was no ice on the rock, and the blank-surfaced slabs offered precarious climbing, with no protection. The walls, however, contained cracks which could be cleaned of snow to provide the occasional runner.

On Day 3 the weather was not so kind, and we stopped at midday for a brew which became a bivouac, as it began to snow heavily. We had climbed out of the Amphitheatre by a steep system of chimneys and grooves. This was one of the few parts of the route which we had not been able to examine with binoculars, so from a route-finding point of view we had passed one of the two cruxes. This day also included some of the most technically demanding climbing of the route. The first pitch out of the Amphitheatre was a groove with an overhanging section. Mick managed to place two wobbly pegs above his head, then began to swear loudly and forcibly . . . for a long time. He could not, it seemed, clip the pegs because the sling was stuck under his hood. At the end of the pitch Mick was grinning like a cat with two tails. I thought that he was rightly pleased with his difficult lead, but I was wrong, he was belayed on black shale. Even more disconcerting for me was the shale chimney that continued in the direction we wanted to climb. Mick had begun his damned enthusing again. The chimney looked as if it might be coated in thick ice, but we were deceived. The pitch was horrible (for me), verglas on shale fragments.

Although it snowed overnight, the next morning brought visibility, if not clear skies. As the mists receded we recognized the features that would act as landmarks. It was enough to go on with. We began to follow lines on the right wall of the pillar. By midday we had reached a large flat ledge, the top of a giant jammed block. Here we made tea and relaxed, until it occurred to us to look up. We were surrounded by overhangs, completely blocked in. Fowler led an aid pitch to gain the lowest of a series of ramps, using a technique that had been developed in Europe in the days of Heckmair. I had never seen anything like it, but Mick was not prepared to learn new tricks just then. The lower ramps led to a Shield which was the other area of uncertainty for us. From Base Camp there appeared to be no line round this feature, but a hidden chimney revealed itself at the end of the ramp. It was blank-sided, and there was no belay at the top, so I was forced to belay Mick by wedging my body across the chimney, and asking him not to fall off.

I do not remember ever having had a more miserable bivouac than the one we had that night. We were benighted, something we said we would avoid at all costs, and there was no ledge, nor any possibility of cutting one, on the thin ice. We used the tent as a hanging bag, inside which Mick spent the night dangling in his harness, while I stood in my rucksack. Both methods had their drawbacks. It snowed all night.

The 3.30 alarm was greeted with relief. It was Day 5, and looking up we could see the final ramps. When we reached them they looked easy; as we climbed the truth dawned on us. They were covered in a layer of powder snow, which, when swept off, revealed blank rock, no runners, and the impending side wall pushed you off balance. We had hundred-foot run-outs, and lots and lots of fear. These ramps in turn led to the final corner, a vertical book-shaped corner under an ear-shaped serac. Mick made short work of the difficulties, banging in the pegs with care. (I had asked him not to disturb the serac above us.) And then we found the snow leading to the plateau so deep that we began to have horrible thoughts of being forced back down the way we had got up.

The next day, Day 6, was to be our summit day. At 6am we started out from the tent, leaving all but our clothes and a stove behind. At 12.45pm we stood on top of the Golden Peak. It was 11 August 1987. We could see Bojohagar, Batura, Diran, Trivor and other large peaks, but from Kunyang Chish black clouds were invading the sky. The storm overtook us within the hour. First the electric shocks: we hid, trying to bury ourselves and our axes in the snow; then high winds swept in from the south. We began to have fears for the tent: we could imagine it flying down to Base Camp in advance of us. The winds brought drifting snow and white-out. Our tracks disappeared. We were high on the plateau, surrounded by precipices. We found, after a bit of experimentation, that if we got down on all fours, we could feel the softness in the slope where our tracks had been filled. In this way we crawled down towards the tent.

By the morning of Day 7 the weather had regained its composure. It was clear and very, very cold. Below us, a sea of cloud filled the valleys. This was worrying because if we could not see the descent ridge, we could not be sure where we were to leave the plateau. During the climb we had noted a tongue of plateau stretching out over the ridge. On this tongue lay some ice blocks which we called the 'crumbs' on the tongue. After three nerve-racking hours of crossing the high plateau, with its crevasses large enough to swallow a battleship, we arrived at the top of an ice-fall. There, below us, were the 'crumbs'. The valley fog was receding and the tongue was revealed, but where on the edge of the tongue was the descent? We knew that, if we picked the wrong spot, not only would we miss the ridge, but we would also be abseiling over large seracs into space.

Descending the ice-fall involved making our first-ever snow-bollard abseils; these led to the tongue, where we found the 'crumbs' were 12 metres high. Guessing that the ridge would be near the tip of the tongue, we pitched the tent and waited for the mist to clear down to the valley. We made brew, and dozed. We were feeling mentally tired and needed to get down. At 5.30pm the mist cleared. We had no 'dead men' for snow belays, and so we dug a large hole in the soft plateau. I got as deep into the hole as possible, and we had a 'live man' belay. Mick gingerly stepped towards the edge, then got on his stomach and crawled towards it. It was an easy cornice, and he descended about a metre before coming back to the belay.

'Well Mick, how is it?'

'You try,' was all he said.

A few minutes later I was looking over the edge of the cornice and saw the descent ridge snaking down to the English–Allen prominence. Surely we were going to survive this climb? Already I began to debate the value of it all. What is the point of mountaineering? It seemed to me in that moment that the nature of the goal did not matter. We are driven to reach for goals, but we can learn no lessons from them. There is no pot of gold, only the rainbow.

'I suppose it's because we live in an achievement-orientated society,' I said to Mick. He looked at me as if I had just announced that I was stark staring mad.

In the tent we discussed our plans, should we get down safely. Over to the north I could see the Yengutz Har Pass. I decided that, after a day's rest, I would try with the others to cross that pass. Fowler said that, if we could get down the next day, he would walk out to Hoppar the next morning, take the jeep and bus to Gilgit the following day, and hope to catch his plane to London from Islamabad on Sunday.

'Why the great rush?' I asked.

'Because it means that by Monday the 16th I shall have parked those Civil Service shoes under that Civil Service desk and saved a whole week's annual leave – know what I mean, Vic?' He tapped the side of his nose.

Iqbal, Lobby, Bruce and myself did eventually complete the traverse of the pass. It took us four hard days for the round trip – much longer than we had anticipated. We made the mistake of selling our rope in Hispar, then descending the Hispar Gorge on the wrong bank. We found ourselves soloing across difficult rock-climbing ground above the roaring Hispar River. The other three showed great patience and waited for me to arrive – tired and emaciated.

As for Fowler, I don't know how he got the energy, but he caught the flight. By Monday morning, 9.30 sharp, those Civil Service shoes were under that Civil Service desk.

REFERENCES

1   W H and F B Workman, *Ice-Bound Heights of the Mustagh*. London (Constable), 1908.
2   R Sander, 'Among the Peaks of Chogo Lungma.' *Mountain World 1956/ 7*, 173–190.
3   M Fowler, 'Bojohagar.' *AJ90*, 77–83, 1985.

Karakoram Lessons: the High-Altitude Expedition

The British–New Zealand Gasherbrums Expedition 1987

ROGER PAYNE

This is not a lesson for those seeking to climb in the Karakoram. Rather, it is a non-exhaustive (and probably un-balanced) retrospective based on the lessons I learnt as leader of the British–New Zealand Gasherbrums Expedition 1987.

Plans for this trip started in 1985 with my wife-to-be (at the time) Julie-Ann Clyma and my partner of previous trips and fellow mountain-guide, Iain Peter. There followed a period of changing objectives and team members as advice emerged, options changed, and individuals found their circumstances or motivation altered. Eventually we set our sights on Gasherbrums 2 (8035m) and 6 (7003m) and found that we had become a team of nine. Despite an early application to the Pakistanis, our permission to climb ran into unexpected problems.[1] However, persistent writing to the highest authorities in Pakistan, and an invitation to His Excellency the Ambassador to attend the marriage of Julie-Ann and Roger, eventually overcame these! Eight months prior to departure the real hard work started. Julie-Ann and I had to give up climbing and social activities for the word-processed sponsorship effort, as the bulk of the organizational work fell on us.

Financed, equipped, and rationed, the team were all together on 11 May in Islamabad. Our reception there was simply superb. Further to Iain, Julie-Ann and myself, the expedition members were: Steve Jones, Donald Stewart, Richard Thorns (cameraman), Jean-Pierre Hefti (Swiss), Guy Haliburton (NZ), and Carol Nash (NZ); our Liaison Officer was Eshaan Ullah, a member of the Pakistan Alpine Club. Our main objectives had become: to make a (relatively) straight-forward ascent of Gasherbrum 2 (previously unclimbed by Britons or New Zealanders); to make a ski descent of its S face; to film the climb and ski descent; and to attempt a new route on Gasherbrum 6 (which is probably a virgin peak).

After the two-day journey along the Karakoram Highway to Skardu – and with additions to our provisions and equipment – we started the walk-in from Dusso on 19 May with 84 porters, one sirdar and one cook. The Balti porters were robust and we found them honest and hard-working. They were good companions and in harmony with the mountain environment; with prayer, song and dance they found their way through any hardship. 13 days after leaving Dusso we arrived at Base Camp (c5280m) on the Duke of Abruzzi glacier. Our arrival coincided with that of an American expedition with whom we had caught up (they had been delayed for eight days by bad weather, just three days away from Base Camp!), and later we were to be followed by a West German group; both teams were also aiming for Gasherbrum 2.

The S Gasherbrum glacier is regarded as one of the most difficult and dangerous in this part of the Karakoram. Although this may be true, by careful route-finding we established a safe and relatively straightforward passage. Once beyond the ice-fall we took a line near the true right bank of the glacier towards Gasherbrum 5 because (as we found to our cost, losing a tent) avalanches sweep down from the NW slopes of Gasherbrum 1 across the glacier, endangering any route along the true left bank.

On 7 June, Julie-Ann and I found a route through the upper glacier to a site for Advanced Base Camp. This was at c6000m and at a safe distance from possible avalanche danger from the S face of Gasherbrum 2. By this stage we had seen most sides of Gasherbrum 6 upon which several possible routes were evident. But it was decided to put our initial effort into attempting Gasherbrum 2, completing our film, etc, leaving Gasherbrum 6 for the end of the trip.

In all our time after arriving at Base Camp we did not have a reasonable period of settled good weather (the best spell of weather, six days, actually occurred during the walk-in). Hence, with time lost because of bad weather and conditions, and time needed for load-carrying and filming, it was not until 25 June that we were in a position to start climbing above Advanced Base Camp. Through a combination of factors, including the complication of filming and the presence of fresh deep snow, the whole expedition set off on the original route of ascent: the Moravec SW spur (1956 Austrian).

On 26 June all members of the team climbed the elegant lower spur past the normal site for Camp 1 (c6500m) to camp on a broad shelf at c6650m below some seracs. Next day everyone moved up without difficulty through the seracs and deep snow to the usual site for Camp 2 (7000m) at the foot of a mixed rib which leads to the summit pyramid. From the other two expeditions, five American and two German climbers who were making their summit attempts were spending the night at this camp.

The next day (28 June) started with some indecision. Fresh snow and cloud brought doubts about the weather, our acclimatization to these heights was questionable, and route-finding on the mixed rib or adjacent deep snow proved problematical in the dark. Hence, by midday everyone in our party except Donald, Jean-Pierre and Richard were back at Camp 2. Iain and Steve stayed at the camp but during the afternoon, in poor visibility and avalanche conditions, Carol, Guy, Julie-Ann and I descended to Advanced Base Camp. Meanwhile, in the early afternoon Jean-Pierre reached the summit, followed some time later by Richard (three of the Americans and the two Germans also reached the top). Close to the summit Donald turned back, worried about over-exhaustion. That day, during their ascent, the three had agreed 'not to be influenced by each other's decisions about climbing the peak'. The summit pair were extremely tired from their ascent. Richard, who had carried a super-8 camera, film and batteries to the summit (but did not shoot a single frame), was particularly exhausted and had problems with his vision. At one point during the descent he fell some 300m, luckily without injury. After this incident one of the descending German climbers insisted that Jean-Pierre and Richard should stay together and look after each other. From c7700m Jean-Pierre used skis for his descent. Both summit climbers were helped back to Camp 2 during the last stages by Donald, Iain and Steve.

Jean-Pierre and Richard were exhausted and showed early symptoms of acute mountain sickness. The pair took lasix tablets to reduce risk of oedema and were provided with many drinks to alleviate dehydration. Next day all five set off to descend to Advanced Base Camp. Jean-Pierre used skis for his descent, while the others came down on foot. At c6750m Jean-Pierre decided to traverse off the route which had been used for ascent, so that he could ski down the S face proper. Tragedy struck at this point; apparently losing control of his skis on a patch of ice, Jean-Pierre slipped and fell 700m to the foot of the face with fatal consequences.

Next day, 30 June, Donald, Guy, and I moved Jean-Pierre to a crevasse near where he fell. I have never been so unhappy in the mountains as on that day. When I had finished helping to bury Jean-Pierre, I was struck down with grief. Fate had been unkind indeed; it provided the chance meetings which led to our friendship at a time when it was Jean-Pierre's ambition to ski Gasherbrum 2, and I was organizing an expedition there. It fell to me to find the final resting-place of this modest and thoughtful man. There is no solace in the grandeur of his tomb, the S Gasherbrum glacier, nor in the enduring nature of his headstone, the S face of Gasherbrum 2; but somehow they do not seem inappropriate.

During the following days at Base Camp, Steve (Jean-Pierre's friend of many years) decided that he should leave for Islamabad to initiate the correct procedures and to ensure that the Hefti family were informed of the tragedy as soon as possible. It was also agreed that we should carry on with our attempt on the mountain and complete our film which we wanted to dedicate to Jean-Pierre.

On 5 July the seven remaining members of the team ascended to the usual Camp 1. Next day Richard returned to Base Camp because he was still suffering from the exertions of his summit climb and was hence unable to carry on filming much above Base. The rest of us set off for Camp 2 in the cool of early evening, but we were delayed by very deep snow. Hence Camp 2 was not reached until late that night, with myself and Donald dangerously near to the borders of cold injury. During the ascent I was suffering from severe stomach pains caused by insufficiently cooked dehydrated food which I had eaten at Camp 1. Because of this, on the following day Julie-Ann and I set off later than the other four, and we did not climb for long before turning back. Donald also soon turned back, feeling drained. Iain, Carol and Guy were stopped at c7300m by deep snow and by breathing problems suffered by Carol. Hence, all six of us were back at Camp 2 early that morning. In the afternoon two German climbers arrived; we made room for them in one of the tents and the snow-hole we were using.

On the next day, 8 July, everyone except Carol set off for the summit. As a result of the stomach pains my food and liquid intake was reduced to almost zero. Hence I was now severely dehydrated. As a result of this I was climbing slowly and only with enormous effort. Although not too far behind the others I decided to turn back at 7500m. Julie-Ann, who had waited for me at this height, descended with me. With the two Germans, Iain, Donald, and Guy reached the summit in the late afternoon. Iain was able to use his skis (which he had carried up on his previous attempt) to descend from 7500m, and he arrived at Camp 2 in gathering darkness. During the descent Donald looked after one of the Germans who had become tired and dangerously cold. However, all were safely back soon after dark.

Next day Donald and I filmed Iain as he ski'd down to Camp 1. Carol, Guy, Donald, and Iain (and the exhausted German, now abandoned by his partner) spent the night there, but Julie-Ann and I carried on down to Base Camp. Over the next two days Iain and Donald finished filming the ski descent.

The whole team was back at Base Camp on 12 July. More expeditions were now arriving at Base Camp, with reports of other groups following. Members of our team, now keen to depart, wanted to use porters from the expected arrivals for our walk-out. However, we still had plenty of food and fuel, and Carol, Julie-Ann and I wanted to make another attempt on Gasherbrum 2. At this stage in the expedition we had our biggest fall of snow.

The three of us set off on my birthday, 16 July. A thin veil of cloud held the promise of yet more snow. We did not make good time; once beyond the ice-fall the fresh snow from the most recent storm became deeper. I had hoped that in the last stages of the trip I would be free from the effort and compromise which had been necessary to make the expedition run. But it was not to be; we had only two or three days to climb the mountain before porters would be hired and the walk-out started. By the time we got to Advanced Base Camp it was snowing steadily. Visibility was reduced to only a few metres; we spent the afternoon resting at Advanced Base waiting for the snow to stop. At 4pm Julie-Ann and I had to leave for Camp 1 (we had left sleeping-bags, etc, there after the previous attempt). We set off in better visibility but heavier snow. Carol wisely stayed at Advanced Base Camp.

The snow was deep, and it took five hours to reach Camp 1. Julie-Ann did nearly all the trail-breaking in the occasionally thigh-deep snow. We were both very cold by the time we reached the snow-cave.

Next day the weather was perfect, but avalanche conditions were acute. Descent appeared only marginally less suicidal than continuing upwards. Julie-Ann was bitterly disappointed at going down. She so wanted to climb this mountain and would probably have done so had she not stayed with me when I was not going well. As we descended we constantly triggered small avalanches on either side of the ridge beneath us. Suddenly, to our left, the weight of fresh snow set off an avalanche from the large hanging seracs on the S face. Airborne powder and serac debris raced down the face and exploded across our ascent tracks from the previous day. Before reaching the glacier we had to make the final slope avalanche so that it would be safe for us to descend. From Advanced Base, with Carol, we carried down expedition equipment to Base Camp where porters had already been hired. The walk-out started on the morning of 19 July.

Ours was the first British expedition to climb any of the six Gasherbrum peaks, and we made the first British ski descent of any 8000er. However, the loss of Jean-Pierre and the circumstances which surrounded my final summit attempt make it difficult for me to feel either success or achievement.

I do not wish to draw conclusions, but several important points may be useful to future parties. Thorough acclimatization is absolutely essential, not just from a fitness point of view, but to help ensure clear thinking and correct decision-making. Even then, once at high altitude, an individual's judgement can be severely impaired; good team-work and clear organization help to counteract this, and an attitude of collective responsibility will help to ensure safety and success.

Recent years have seen drastic changes in the style of climbing high-altitude peaks. Team-work born from responsibility has been exchanged for the team-work of convenience. An individualistic approach can facilitate rapid and lightweight ascents in good conditions, but it leaves only the smallest margin for unexpected delays or problems. Climbers arriving at camps without the means to support themselves, or allowing themselves to get into such a condition that others unexpectedly have to help them, are examples of an attitude which, I am sure, has contributed to some recent accidents.

To Edward Whymper's excellent advice to individual climbers,[2] reminding us of the need for prudence in the mountains, and to 'look well to each step', I would wish to add: care for your companions; and climb with those who will care for you.

NOTES

1   We experienced lengthy delays with the issue of climbing permits and had to enlist a lot of support for our application. On arrival in Islamabad the Ministry of Tourism Officials made reference to parties who in the past had 'extended' permits or had simply climbed peaks above 6000m or in restricted areas without permission. Their message was clear: help to make our rules work, and the system will work for you. As none of us had been to Pakistan before, we felt let down by our predecessors. There is a clear responsibility here for those who climb in ranges where restrictions apply.

2   E Whymper, *Scrambles Amongst the Alps*, 6th Ed. Webb & Bower, 1986, p216.

Crossing the Kurdopin

PHILIP BARTLETT

In the nature of these things, the rather grandly named 'Karakoram Traverse Expedition 1987' underwent a number of metamorphoses even before leaving England. Jerry Gore was keen to reconnoitre the N ridge of Latok I; Duncan Tunstall wished to do the same with the N face of the Ogre. At this stage a circumnavigation of the Latok group seemed a possibility – not exactly a traverse at all. However, Stephen Venables had a trick or two up his sleeve, as usual. He wanted to trek up the Biafo, make the first crossing of the Kurdopin Col above Snow Lake and trek out to Shimshal; or possibly do the same via the Virjerab glacier. This appealed to me, as it would certainly not be easy but would be very different from our attempts on Kunyang Chish in 1980 and 1981. Stephen again: could we ascend the Choktoi as being rather more exciting than the better-known Biafo and thus approach Snow Lake that way, sizing up Latok and the Ogre on the way? Or even the Nobande Sobande? But closer research revealed that, with the exception of the Latoks, the peaks bordering the Choktoi are remarkably uninspiring. Furthermore, Dave Potts had on a previous expedition experienced great difficulties trying to cross from the Choktoi to the Sim Gang glacier, experiencing soft snow overlaying bad crevasses, and had been forced to retreat. I argued that the Kurdopin would prove quite challenging enough without the added problems of the Choktoi or Nobande Sobande. At this point Stephen pulled his master stroke: he had heard that somewhere in the endless wastes of the Nobande Sobande there was an ancient undiscovered fort . . . but no, the boring old Biafo it was to be. The final team also emerged: Duncan, Stephen and myself.

Boring is a relative word. The Biafo may be easy but it has a great deal of virgin climbing potential. In an article in *Mountain* 49 Malcolm Howells pointed out some of the possibilities and presented some tantalizing photographs. (I'm afraid you don't get issues of *Mountain* like that any more.) Some of these possibilities, notably the Ogre and its satellites, have since received a lot of attention, but the peaks of the West Biafo wall still seem to be little known. The most notable, Sosbun Brakk, was climbed from the south by the Japanese in 1981 (see Griffin's article on the Sosbun glacier region, *AJ91*, 49–52, 1986). But there is a fantastic N face which would be technically very hard and could be reached by crossing the Sokha La (Tilman's Col) or by ascending the Sokha (Cornice) glacier. The Sokha La is a straightforward snow-slope on both sides, though there is slight serac danger. It is also possible that Sosbun Brakk could be climbed from a point slightly lower down the Biafo, by entering a cwm which drains its SE side, but this cwm appears extremely hazardous to enter.

North and west of the Sokha La a range of ice-smeared rock-spires, only slightly less impressive than Sosbun itself, extends towards the Hispar pass. There is some excellent mixed climbing here. Whilst I relaxed at Base Camp, set up on the moraine at the Biafo/Sim Gang junction, Stephen and Duncan climbed the subsidiary summit of one of these peaks, tentatively named Solu Tower, and found good Scottish Grade 5 terrain. (Later in the summer Stephen also climbed the main summit.)

To the south-east the Biafo wall takes on a different character. It is composed of snow and ice-peaks which look to be of modest technical difficulty, but are nevertheless most attractive. The most desirable prize, magnificent in the evening light, is Gama Sokha Lumbu which filled the view from the open tent door. Altogether I felt quite happy to be doing nothing for a few days.

The Hispar, Snow Lake and Biafo glacier-systems were first explored by Sir Martin Conway in 1892. The Workmans followed. Tilman/Shipton parties explored extensively in 1937 and 1939, covering an enormous amount of ground and clearing up some of the Workmans' more dubious claims. Most of the work in 1937 was based well to the north-east, on the Sarpo Laggo glacier, but at the conclusion of the trip Tilman and two Sherpas reached the Snow Lake/Biafo junction and then crossed the West Biafo wall by the Sokha La. We were able to reach this col ourselves in four hours from Base Camp. In 1939 Shipton and Peter Mott, with their Indian surveyors Fazel Ellahi and Inayat Khan, produced a superb map of the Hispar and Biafo basins, subsequently published in the *Geographical Journal*, July–September 1950. This map extends as far as the N rim of Snow Lake, i.e. as far as the Kurdopin Col, which Shipton, Scott Russell and two Sherpas reached from the south as the finale to the 1939 expedition. But for the outbreak of war they would doubtless have explored its N side and descended the Kurdopin glacier.

The Greenalds' visit in 1959 (*AJ64*, 175–182, 1959) was a significant one, their primary objective being the first ascent of Lukpe Lawo Brakk or Snow Lake Peak (6593m), the dominating mountain which rises immediately west of the Kurdopin Col. However, they found it a bigger undertaking than expected and had to be content with the first ascent of Cornice Peak (5880m). Their sketch map (printed in *AJ64*) is useful but not wholly accurate. The glacier shown as extending between the N Simgang wall and Cornice Peak does not in fact exist – we couldn't see it, anyway! There is a snow-basin certainly, but the topography seems to be more complex than indicated by Greenald. The well-known Polish map (Jerzy Wala, 1973) is more accurate.

More recently, the Snow Lake area has been the scene of at least two tragedies. In 1985 Mike Harber and Mike Morris were lost, it is believed whilst attempting Snow Lake Peak. This mountain is a very fine one, though, considering its relatively modest height, it does seem to attract a surprising amount of bad weather. Weather apart, the problem seems to be that the most convenient means of attack, up the E ridge from the col, looks very hard, whilst the more feasible southern route, that taken by both the 1959 and the 1985 parties, has a long and quite serious approach. Altogether, the mountain is both avalanche-prone and remote, but from a general mountaineering if not from a technical climbing point of view it is outstandingly attractive – and still unclimbed.

Ian Haig was lost in the vicinity of the Kurdopin Col in 1986, attempting a crossing in the reverse direction to ourselves. From what we learnt when we arrived in Shimshal it appeared that he passed through on 7 August, with two experienced men from Passu. In Shimshal he had hired two additional men to carry supplies as far as 'Kurdopin Base Camp', the last hunter's camp in the ablation valley before the Kurdopin ice-fall, and some five or six porter days from Shimshal. This is also the highest point in the Kurdopin basin which trekkers could hope to reach, and then only with competent guides.

Our own crossing of the Kurdopin began on Tuesday, 28 July, after sitting out a three-day storm at Base Camp. By this time we had already carried some 10 kilos of food and equipment, one day's walk across Snow Lake. Our plan now was to make a single continuous push, picking up the cache of gear on the way and reaching Shimshal within 10 days. We abandoned some small articles of clothing, a good deal of rice, dahl and flour, and some Pakistani corned beef about which the less said the better. That left us about 27 kilos each. Weather made a big difference; the tent flysheet, only 1½ kilos when dry, weighed in at 3½ some mornings. Snow-shoes – or lightweight skis – were essential. Mine, 10 years old and plastic, gradually fell apart and only just lasted the course. Duncan's, also plastic but newer, worked well. Stephen, true to character, had a near antique wood-and-twine pair, one of which Lindsay Griffin had discovered on the summit of the Fou. They were, nevertheless, the strongest of the lot.

The first two days, to a camp below the col, were probably the most exhausting physically. The weather was warmish, and Snow Lake seemed endless. The Workmans estimated it at 300 sq miles, reduced by Tilman to a more modest 30, but that's still sizeable. Trudging across and feeling more like porters than porters' employers, we had a look at the Ogre through the clouds. The N face looked easier than I expected, but then I had expected it to be 89 degrees. Snow Lake itself has a quite un-Himalayan feel to it. There are no massive peaks here, and the general impression is more like the Arctic. Crevasse peak with its meringue cornices, and the more striking peak to its immediate east which may still be unclimbed, could have been straight out of the Andes.

At the end of the first day we found our dump of food, but it had been rifled by the ravens. Not only the biscuits had gone, but so had the full stock of tea-bags. Disaster! The following day we continued our adventure with a stand-up argument about whether we were in a position to explore possible routes on to the Virjerab glacier. In the end it was decided that there wasn't time. This was a pity; it did appear that at the NE corner of Snow Lake there was a saddle leading to the Virjerab which might well be possible. It did not look easy, but there is no reason to believe that there is any easy route on to the upper Virjerab. It would certainly be worth someone investigating. The ascent to the top of the Kurdopin was made on the third day with half the gear, thus committing us to a second carry on day four, more or less irrespective of the weather. Meanwhile we were separated from virtually all the food for 12 hours, a situation which both Stephen and I find quite against our natures. Sure enough, a storm blew up and the second carry was made in a white-out. But we were probably incapable of carrying all the stores to the top in one go. The col itself is at just under 5800m, and the climb to it is 450m of 50-degree snow and ice, with some avalanche danger. Once there we retired thankfully into the tent, but late in the day the storm started to clear, and on Day 5 we were able to descend into the high snow-bowl to the north of the col. The mediocre weather had been blowing from the south for weeks and we expected to find windslab. We were not disappointed. There were some nasty shudders and a smallish avalanche set off not far to the left. I was glad to have the rope on and to know that the two behind me were considerably heavier than myself. If anything happened I would hold my trusty bamboo-pole aloft and wait to be rescued.

This upper bowl has some attractive alpine-scale snow peaks, but they are a long way from nowhere. A well-acclimatized party with plenty of spare food and finding well-consolidated snow (which cannot be common) could hope to climb several worthwhile virgin summits quickly. But under heavy snow they would all be very hazardous. To judge by an impressive granite pillar the rock, what little there is of it, is good.

Below the snow-bowl is a superbly positioned snow-plateau at the confluence with a side glacier, dubbed by Duncan 'the cricket pitch'. There were some tantalizing glimpses of Kanjut Sar from here, which we were not to see again for the rest of the trip. My snow-shoes were suffering from terminal plastic fatigue by this time, as a result of which I had been able to secure myself at the back of the rope, following the track so thoughtfully beaten out by Stephen and Duncan. So I could enjoy the magnificence of the view to the full and wonder what was coming next.

Falling from the cricket pitch was the Kurdopin ice-fall – big, tottery, and altogether impressive. It took us the best part of two days to descend it and reach the beginning of the ablation valleys and the camping ground referred to earlier as 'Kurdopin Base Camp'. It was dangerous but extremely satisfying to negotiate it successfully. One section stands out in the memory: a loose and exposed rock-step which Stephen somehow got down without taking his sack off. To me that was a moment of truth: to try and do the same – it was only a few feet – or to take that unwieldy weight off the back and lower it on a rope? I'm glad I did the latter. Stephen, after all, is dangerously good at that sort of thing. It can cloud a chap's judgement.

The sign of tracks in the ablation valley was a welcome surprise – it showed that the rest of the route was at least possible. On the other hand it led us to believe that it would be easy, which was a mistake. In fact it took another three days to reach Shimshal, with an apparently endless series of 'stings in the tail' maintaining interest. To ice-climbing, rock-climbing and glacier work we were able to add abseiling down conglomerate, mud-cliff climbing, river-wading, a tyrolean traverse and some typical Karakoram scree-slopes. Route finding kept up the interest.

At one point we were tempted off the glacier into an ablation valley by signs of sheep pens and a track – not to speak of sheer logic. It *should* have been right. We sauntered confidently down, only to be confronted after a couple of miles by the end of our valley and a steep drop of several hundred feet to a glacier river below. Beyond, the river churned away at the bottom of some very nasty looking screes. At the time it was a baffling impasse, but in retrospect it is clear that the river must have altered its course, perhaps quite recently, cutting into the moraine and destroying the ablation valley. After some thought we retreated and abseiled down the moraine, only to be confronted by the screes. These were quite up to Hispar Gorge standards with stones coming down constantly, but it was either that or the river, so we advanced resolutely to the attack. Stephen got furthest, before a mass retreat was called. I viewed the river with gloom, not being able to swim, but Duncan surged in with Stephen holding the rope. He eventually struggled to the bank and Stephen and I crossed more easily. At the far side was a shore of silt and black mud into which one sank. It was now dusk, and it had been a long day. Standing there frozen, wet and stuck, Duncan holding the rope only six feet away, it crossed my mind – was this really mountaineering? I decided after the shortest of pauses that the answer was gloriously and unequivocally 'yes'. We sauntered past the scree-slopes grinning, and next day crossed back over on a steel hawser.

Duncan, on his first Himalayan expedition, had enjoyed(?) most elements of the 'Karakoram experience' and it didn't seem right that he should be allowed to escape the scree-slopes. However, there turned out to be some exciting ones on the walk-out from Shimshal, where we were both treated to the sight of Stephen squatting at the river's edge holding his sack over his head for several minutes before, with admirable control, peering upwards and then running like hell out of the line of fire. He then watched us doing precisely the same. Luckily we were all as fit as butcher's dogs by then.

We arrived at Shimshal and its newly opened rest-house on 5 August. Here we discovered that the Kurdopin had in fact been successfully traversed – twice – in 1986. Two Canadian geologists, Barry Roberts and Cameron Wake, who were undertaking snow and ice hydrology work in the Snow Lake area, had walked into Shimshal from Hunza and hired two of the best men, Shambi Khan and Rajab Shah. All four had then walked back to Hunza and travelled to Skardu. From there they had traversed the Kurdopin in the same direction as ourselves and arrived in Shimshal in the second week of July. After a few days' rest they had retraced their steps back over the pass to Skardu, and the Shimshali men had travelled back to Hunza by road. We consoled ourselves with the thought that ours was the first crossing made without porters/guides.

When we reached the Karakoram Highway at Passu two days later, it became clear that there was considerable interest in the Kurdopin amongst trekking businesses. We were descended on by people wanting to know the route. One of these had produced a trekking guide to Hunza and he showed us a copy. It seemed to consist of a series of identical sketches with different captions. In the middle of each page was a glacier, surrounded by spikey mountains; with marvellous optimism, a dotted line representing the trekking route went up one side of the glacier, across the top and down the other side. Only the name of the glacier varied. Certainly, some ambitious outings were included: the Malangutti glacier, for example, caused raised eyebrows from Stephen. He had not thought it a stroll when he had been there is 1984. (See 'Autumn in Shimshal and Naltar', *AJ90*, 64–70, 1985.) Seeing it when walking out from Shimshal to Passu, Duncan and I agreed. And the Kurdopin itself: there was the dotted line, going up the true right bank of the glacier to Kurdopin Base Camp, crossing over and descending the left bank. On our own descent of the Kurdopin the left bank had appeared to be one of the nastiest and most difficult glacier banks any of us had seen. There are good business incentives for finding new trekking routes in the Karakoram, particularly super-trekking routes which are still little frequented and which allow a continuous traverse across a watershed. No one likes to come back the way he went up if he can avoid it. But it can lead to some optimistic judgements. For example, the rest-house book in Shimshal recorded the visit of two Germans at the end of June who had set off for the Kurdopin. They seem to have been adventurous trekkers rather than expert mountaineers and had gathered that the Kurdopin was 'easy'. They were surprised to reach Kurdopin Base Camp and find a huge ice-fall blocking their path. They retreated. But they would have done well to note the experiences of the Dutch explorers Dr and Mrs Visser who explored the lower Kurdopin in 1925.

The obvious alternative, which is no doubt feasible, is to hire a number of high-altitude porters and a guide. Perhaps this is what will happen in the future, if the demand is there. For us, sitting in the Passu Inn being quizzed, it was all rather depressing. Unless one has scientific motives, the whole point of such a trip lies in having a small party, completely reliant on its own devices, with no advance knowledge of the route and no guarantee that it will even be possible. The satisfaction lies largely in the decision-making, or so it seems to me. Without that it would deteriorate into little more than a spectacular route-march. My own final thought was thankfulness that I had been able to get in on the act at this relatively early stage. All modern exploration is artificial, I suppose; NASA must have detailed photographs of everything, and you could always take a helicopter. But it felt like the real thing.

Assignment in Lahul

ANDREW BANKES

After several summers of climbing in the Alps, it was time for a change of venue. First choice was the Himalaya, but there was a difficulty in timing. I thought I would just be able to squeeze five weeks' holiday out of my job, provided that this fell around August. This, of course, is a time when the whole of Nepal and much of India is wreathed in monsoon mists. It was Bob Pettigrew who, at the Alpine Club symposium on 'Lightweight Expeditions in the Greater Ranges' in March 1984, told me about Lahul in North India. This region, he said, contains an impressive range of mountains that lies behind the monsoon belt and can therefore be expected to have good weather in August.

A search through the *Alpine Journal* revealed an interesting venture by Fritz Kolb and Ludwig Krenek (*AJ*52, 135–137, 1940; see also *Himalaya Venture* by Fritz Kolb (London, 1959)). They had led a successful Anglo-Austrian expedition to the Mulkila range in the summer of 1939, climbing and exploring amongst an impressive display of rock and ice peaks of up to 6500m. The North London Lahul Expedition had found its destination. Its members, Bert Simmonds, Henry Todd, Maggie Urmston and myself, had pursued a variety of training methods from alpine climbs to weekend ascents of Scottish ice gullies and brick climbing on the wall of the Regent's Canal, Islington.

From Delhi we careered north for three days by bus. First we crossed the humid plains into a rain-drenched Kulu valley. Then, with engines screaming, we penetrated the mists of the Rohtang Pass until suddenly, at the crest of the col, we breathed the clear dry air of Lahul. It was like emerging, blinking, from a tunnel into the sunshine. The journey gave us time to marvel at the Indians' talent for paperwork: for the trip from Simla to Manali by luxury videobus, our tickets each comprised no less than 27 pieces of paper.

In the evening we reached the hamlet of Darcha, just east of Keylong. It was here that the walk-in began. Looking up the valley to the south, we could just see the distant snows of the Mulkila massif reflecting the warm evening light. The noise and clatter and dust of the journey by road were now over, and I became aware of that silence and solitude which is the unique feature of the high mountains. In a field just outside the hamlet we found accommodation in some large canvas tents that were apparently provided by the Indian Tourist Board. The camp organizer was a friendly and helpful Indian from the plains, who described himself to us as 'master of economics, fluent in English'.

The next morning we were introduced by the economist to a Lahuli called Prem, who agreed to transport our equipment to Base Camp with the assistance of four horses. Just before setting off into the hills, I suddenly remembered that I had some letters to post. I was directed to the Darcha post box, an impressive-looking structure, perhaps the size of a small packet of Shreddies. Having committed the letters to the box, I enquired of some locals as to the frequency of the service. There was much laughter and discussion until one of the men dredged from their collective English vocabulary a single word: 'month'.

Two days of trekking up a wide, arid valley led us to what our guide considered an ideal location for our Base Camp. It was immediately apparent that his opinion did not coincide with ours. This spot of his was nowhere near the conventional notion of a Base Camp: the mountains were still miles away – in fact, they could not even be seen. And we were no more than 3500m above sea-level. But Prem had a trump card up his sleeve which he played with consummate skill: beside a rather unhappy-looking patch of turf there stood a large boulder, about 2 m high. Prem made a grand gesture in the direction of its north side, on which I saw a series of carvings left by earlier expeditions. Here was clear evidence that others before us had deemed this site to be suitable, and we were forced to concede that what was suitable for others was suitable for us. And so, with some relief, Prem and his horses departed.

Over the next three days, as we humped large loads up the crumbling moraine of the Mulkila glacier, we lived to regret Prem's departure. The moraine was not ideal terrain for horses, but the discovery of large quantities of manure on the way made it clear that such animals could make the journey. The load-carrying, if dull and monotonous, at any rate increased our fitness, and by 8 August we had established an Advanced Base Camp in an ideal location. I felt relieved and happy in the knowledge that we had at last arrived. We were situated about 6km up the Mulkila glacier, itself about 14km long and leading like a magician's wand into the very heart of the Mulkila massif. This consisted of 10 peaks of between 5800 and 6500m, named with great imagination on our map M1 to M10.

Of those which were visible from our camp, perhaps the most impressive was M8. At 6100m exactly, M8 had been described by Fritz Kolb as formidable. We looked up at the wide N face of the mountain. This indeed seemed formidable, since there were few lines which would not be threatened by hanging glaciers and stonefall. But the north-east end of the long, horizontal summit ridge descended steeply to the Mulkila glacier in an elegant snow ridge with a prominent ice tower at half height. It reminded Bert, who had climbed the Peuterey *integrale* the previous summer, of the upper half of that fabulous ridge. The prospect of climbing up those beautiful white towers proved irresistible, and we decided to make the ascent in two independent teams.

Bert and I set off first, and pitched an eyrie tent at the foot of a bergschrund, which marked the start of the climbing difficulties. From here, we estimated that two days would be required to complete the climb, and we decided to rely for shelter on Goretex bivouac sacks. That night some snow fell; in the morning the mists were slow to clear and we were not ready to start until 9am. We avoided the bergschrund by a short, vertical ice pitch, and threaded our way through further crevasses before climbing a steep snow/ice headwall to reach a col at the foot of the ice tower.

It was 1pm and the heat of the sun was intense. Although plenty of daylight remained, we were reluctant to embark on the tower in this heat. It looked as though there would be some steep and delicate work ahead, which would be easier and more enjoyable in the cool of the morning. All this provided a welcome excuse to bivouac at the col, and we spent a relaxing afternoon preparing endless brews from snow-melt and speculating about the difficulty of the task that lay ahead.

Day 2 of the climb started with an evil concoction of muesli and Build-up (vanilla flavour) at 5am. That provided fuel for six pitches up the tapering arête of the ice tower, where the angle reached 60 degrees. On top of the tower, a knife-edged descent led to a narrow col from which we could contemplate the next feature of the ridge. This looked like another ice arête, slightly less steep than the first, but it had one undesirable aspect which had appeared insignificant from below: a massive, overhung bergschrund which split the ridge on the left-hand side. The previous year, I had encountered a similar feature – measured in centimetres rather than metres – on the ice ridge of the Frendo Spur. We had climbed the French equivalent by a big stride and one hard pull on the ice tools. But this we would have to turn.

With a certain lack of enthusiasm, I tried the right-hand option. This brought me on to the N face of the mountain which was composed of very steep snow of a revolting consistency. I was soon back at the col, congratulating myself on how the mere mention of avalanche risk is one of the many keys to the 'art of climbing down gracefully'. Bert then poked his nose towards the left-hand option and soon disappeared from sight. About 40 minutes later there came a triumphant shout from somewhere above the 'schrund. The rope went tight, and I followed up what was the crux pitch of the climb. A rising traverse left across an ice wall of 70 degrees led to the left edge of the 'schrund, where the ice formed a bulge with a curious hollow structure like a honeycomb. Here, I let my axe and hammer dangle and climbed by pulling on some icicles which formed convenient jug-holds. It was an exhilarating pitch, and one that proved the key to reaching the top of the second ice arête.

Two further pitches up steep snow led to a narrow, almost horizontal terrace on the crest of the ridge. Immediately above was yet another crevasse which spanned the arête. Here was the last significant obstacle that stood in the way of the summit ridge.

It was 2pm and all around us the snow and ice were melting in the wilting heat of the afternoon sun. We were also beginning to feel the altitude. A strong urge to rest and bivouac here overcame us, so we excavated a shelf of about two by two metres. Once we were installed, my imagination began to work overtime on the big upper lip of the crevasse. This was directly above our nest and it seemed to be substantially overhung, like the nose of the proboscis monkey. I questioned Bert as to the consequences of a collapse of the nose. He stated with a degree of relish: 'Well, that will solve the problems of the descent that you've been worrying about.' It was hard to disagree, but I was unable to share his enthusiasm.

The night was clear and there was a sharp frost. My excitement at the prospect of reaching the top was such that I slept little and persuaded Bert to be out of his bag and ready to climb by 3.30am. This was our first pre-dawn start in the Himalaya, and it was not a success. In the darkness, we were unable to find a way round the crevasse. Having wasted valuable calories, we decided to wait for dawn. We then traversed right, on to the N face, where we found crisp névé of 50 degrees which led to the summit ridge. It was about 9am, and the technical climbing, we considered, was over. What lay ahead was a narrow, heavily corniced snow ridge which abutted on the final summit pyramid of rock.

On reaching the rock on Day 3 of our climb, our enthusiasm for the summit reached its nadir. We were both suffering from the effects of altitude, food was scarce, and Bert had developed a sharp cough which was producing phlegm of a lurid and alarming colour. The quality of the rock was disgusting: steep and very shattered, like lumps of sultanas and raisins stuck together. Bert went on strike: 'The best part of the climb is over, and this pile of rubble just doesn't interest me.'

I had a more traditional viewpoint.

'It just happens to be the summit, Bert.'

'You can keep it.'

Nevertheless, he was good enough to indicate that if I wished to proceed, then that was my problem and he would be delighted to wait for me. I made a half-hearted attempt at the sultanas, then slithered back down to rejoin him. Had I tried to go any further, and had Bert been true to his word, he would be waiting still.

We decided to turn our minds to the descent. Hitherto my energy had been sustained by thoughts of the summit. Now, with that out of reach, I slumped into a heap of exhaustion. It was only our last rations – some dried figs – which revived me sufficiently to concentrate on what was a complicated descent: back across the summit ridge, down the melting snows of the N face to our second bivouac, then a slanting abseil over the hard ice pitch, and so on. By mid afternoon we were back on top of the ice tower, where we saw Henry and Maggie, just below us, completing the last pitch.

Not only had they been badly affected by altitude, but it now emerged that there had been serious misunderstanding about the rations which they had expected us to leave them. What little we had left had been contaminated by paraffin. My conversation with Henry soon erupted into a highly charged high-volume high-altitude slanging match. The silence of the Himalaya was shattered. Bert blinked, and immediately turned his attention to finding an abseil anchor. The row was soon over and the four of us, happy to be reunited, abseiled down to the eyrie tent in the gathering gloom of nightfall.

Next day we descended thousands of feet to Base Camp, where we nourished our empty frames with rice rissoles, chupatties and custard. Over dinner we discussed our future. There was time for another ascent. Having, as it were, fizzled out so close to the top of M8, I felt a strong desire to try something else. From the ridge of M8, we had a good view of another peak which rose from higher up the Mulkila glacier. This I identified as M6: at 6280m, its N face supported ridges that had been compared by Fritz Kolb to that of the Liskamm in the Pennine Alps. Here was a handsome objective.

First we had to obtain further provisions from Darcha. Bert and Henry drew the short straws and descended to the village. They were clearly very fit and returned two days later with sumptuous supplies, having met a delightful Lahuli whom we called Ram (despite tuition, we were unable to pronounce his real name). Ram had loaded their rucksacks groaning with provisions on to his two horses, and that night he joined us for dinner, bringing mutton sausages, liver, and quantities of chang. It was a feast. What was more, Ram agreed to accompany us to Advanced Base Camp with his horses. The back-breaking load-carrying of the earlier days was over.

M6 lies at the head of the Mulkila glacier. We intended to climb its E ridge, a long, wavy ice-crest, heavily corniced and with two rock steps. A steep ice-slope guards entry on to the ridge. We estimated that by bivouacking at the foot of the ice-slope, we would be able to climb to the summit and descend in a day. To reach the bivouac involved a long glacier approach which included an ice-fall. We started from Advanced Base Camp at 7am. Bert and I reached the foot of the ice-fall at 3pm and decided to bivouac. That morning, Maggie had felt that she had not recovered enough of her energy to join us, and so had reluctantly decided to remain at Advanced Base. Henry, however, was brimming with energy, and had decided to come with us.

Our one problem now, as we erected the tent at the foot of the ice-fall, was Henry: he was nowhere to be seen. At first I thought he must just have been taking it steadily. But by 5pm I began to doubt whether he would arrive at all. What worried us was why: had he decided to turn back, had he had an accident, or what? We thought the chances of an accident were extremely remote since the terrain we had covered was a dry ice glacier, partly crevassed but not at all steep.

I felt uneasy, however, and so, while Bert brewed, I descended to search the crevassed section of our route. No sign of Henry. Back at the bivouac, we debated what to do. We were faced with two alternatives: one was to descend to Advanced Base Camp so as to see with our own eyes that Henry was safe, in which event the time would be such that we would not be able to return to M6. The other was simply to make an assumption, based on the various bits of evidence at our disposal, that Henry was safe, and to proceed on our climb. In stating now that we chose the latter option, I attempt no justification of our decision. What it shows is the extraordinary hold that the mountains had over our minds.

The next day, Bert and I climbed up the ice-fall and established a tent at the foot of the E ridge. We watched a glorious sunset spread over the distant peaks. Nearer at hand, the stove roared and the pot bubbled. Such was my optimism that I imagined us, the following morning, soloing up the ice-slope to the col in an hour or so.

The reality, at 5.30am the next morning, was rather different. First, there was an awkward bergschrund to cross, which made me grasp for the security of the rope. Above, the ice-slopes steepened to 60 degrees, and it took seven pitches, and two and a half hours, to reach the col at the foot of the ridge. The slope at the other side of the col was overhung by vast cornices, and we had to traverse to our right in order to reach the crest of the ridge at some rock gendarmes.

It was 8am. I looked down the N side, still in shadow, and marvelled at the isolation of our position: the only sign of life, our tent, now appeared as a tiny raft in an ocean of white. We turned our attention to the ridge. At first, we tiptoed along a narrow ice crest. We then encountered a series of double

2. *Golden Pillar from Melangush.*

3. *Belay beneath the monstrous 'ice ear'.*

4. *Near the top of the 'slabs'.*

5.   *Summit Plateau. Ultar and Batura on the horizon.*

6.   Mick Fowler.

7.   *Girgindil Chish (c. 6000m), from the Golden Pillar.*

8. *A temporary camp on the S Gasherbrum glacier. Gasherbrums 4, 3 and 2 in the background.*

9. *Masherbrum from the Baltoro glacier.*

cornices and our hitherto rapid progress became a crawl. Higher up, the ridge steepened into rock steps which provided easy climbing on sound, dry rock. Then we saw a thin white triangle above us, which looked like the summit. At 3pm we broke through a small cornice to reach the top.

The air was quite still and there was room to sit down and relax over some chocolate and dried figs. It was at least half an hour before we summoned the discipline and energy to tear ourselves away. There were exactly three and a half hours of daylight left. We reached the col as the last glimmer faded from the snows. Meanwhile, a firework display was in progress on the southern horizon as tall monsoon clouds struggled to surmount the Rohtang Pass. We clipped headtorches to our helmets to illuminate our progress as we abseiled down the ice-slope. I was tired, and fumbled with the clip. Suddenly, the torch sprung off the helmet and I watched, fascinated, as it cartwheeled hundreds of metres down the slope, soon to disappear into the mouth of the bergschrund. I was almost too exhausted to mind, although the absence of the torch made our descent considerably more difficult. In due course, we arrived at the upper lip of the 'schrund. As I jumped across the yawning gap I detected – far below me – a lonely beam of light.

By 10pm we were back at the tent, swallowing soup and reliving some of the great moments of the day. When sleep came, the body was utterly still but the mind was still up on the ridge, dancing across its cornices and crests and rocks.

When morning came, we raced back to Advanced Base Camp. Now that the climb was over, I felt more than a stab of anxiety about Henry. It was with the greatest relief that, four hours later, we found a note at camp from Henry and Maggie informing us that they had set off to climb M10.

The next day we watched two small dots move towards us across the glacier. We prepared pints of tea for our friends' return from what had been a successful and enjoyable ascent. We immediately enquired what had befallen Henry on the approach to M6. He had stopped for a long rest, and lost sight of us. Then, unable to see our footsteps on the dry ice of the glacier, he had followed a tributary of the main glacier which turned out to be a dead end. Understandably angry at our conduct in failing to wait for him, he had then descended to Base Camp.

That night we built a fire and, over steaming bowls of rice and lentils, we debated into the early hours the rights and wrongs of our course of action. Despite mistakes and misunderstandings, however, we agreed that we had all immensely enjoyed the past three weeks. We had all taken part in two ascents, one unsuccessful and the other successful. We had been lucky enough to have excellent weather, and we had found the Mulkila range to contain endless challenges and opportunities. As we sat around and watched the last embers die, I felt that each of us was as committed to our sport now as we had been in the initial enthusiasm of our arrival in Lahul.

Mulkila, Mulkila

MARGARET URMSTON

There was a point on the glacier when I thought of white lace, the English countryside and fainting at an open window as I inhaled the spring air. My small feet, though firmly wedged by strong boots, still would not brace themselves against the battering angles and edges of the boulder-field. There was not a thing to see in any direction except boulders – brown ones, pink ones, white ones, grey slaggy ones and icy-blue ones, rising and falling like the peaks and troughs of a giant scarred battlefield.

This was the romance and heroism of the Himalaya. It is impossible to skirt the male-dominated legends that pave the way for female endeavour. Of course, we too can be strong and hearty, bare our bottoms at Base Camp, fart and make rude jokes and declare how ridiculous we all are. But at that moment, alone and exhausted on the boulder-field, all I wanted was to be holding a bag of clothes pegs, a bundle of clean washing and putting the items on a clothes-line blowing in the wind. This was definitely a case of Cinderella and The Three Musketeers. Well, girls will be boys, so let the story begin.

Late one afternoon in June, Bert, in his usual laconic style, was mumbling abstractedly about some plans to go to the Himalaya in July. No one was sure about anything, least of all who was going, where they were going or, indeed, when. But in the inimitable style of the North London Mountaineering Club, somehow, three weeks later, an expedition materialized and met at London Airport complete with team, tickets, equipment and supplies, a name and a destination: North London-Lahoul, Andrew Bankes, Bert Simmonds, Maggie Urmston and Henry Todd.

A few words in passing about the team members, to set the tone for later developments: Andrew and Bert formed a climbing partnership of long standing and considerable alpine expertise. Henry had had one season some years previously in the Alps, and I had never even set eyes upon a glacier, let alone set foot upon a mountain. Henry and I had spent an intense summer rock-climbing together, and had barely met Bert and Andrew when the plan to go to India was conceived. However, although strangers to each other, Andrew and Henry could both lay claim to previous intimate knowledge of the sub-continent – a factor that contributed to much amusement later on as each vied with the other over their authoritative acquaintance with local customs and *mores*.

The intensity of my climbing partnership with Henry reached a climax just before we left England when I had decided to do a crash course in fitness training by walking the 14 peaks with Lyn Allen. I use the word 'intensity' advisedly, since it was the 'intensity' of life at Base Camp that drove Bert into the hermit-like seclusion of his own tent. Henry, generous and willing to a fault, had bowed to my 'indomitable' will and agreed against his own, not only to climb in Wales the weekend before departure, but to meet Lyn and myself at the finish of our marathon. Lyn and I unfortunately failed to meet our deadline and arrived some two hours overdue to find Henry apoplectic with rage. His retelling of this tale, with his brilliant flair for high comedy, had us all aching with laughter as we stumbled under the weight of endless kilograms of muesli, Trailmix, tents and hardware on to the aeroplane.

The subject of food must have its place on any expedition, and this one had its dubious beginnings with me having been given responsibility for 'catering' (a woman's role?). I have to lay blame, at this point, squarely where it's due. My efforts to consult team members as to their preferences failed dismally but, needless to say, I was later castigated for not having provided everyone with their favourite goodies. (Lyn – I still want words with you about sugar-free diets for mountaineering.) Bert said he didn't care what he ate; Henry said he never ate anyway – except for digestive biscuits which he would provide himself. And Andrew – I must give him his due – said he wanted Trailmix, got it, and did his damnedest to eat the lot, much to Henry's disgust. Bert compensated for his own oversight by buying as much jam and sugar as he could lay his hands on in Simla. The evening before departure there was a touching scene, with myself and Maria up to our elbows in buckets of roasted trail – mixing it (it had been specially prepared for the Himalaya: suitable, apparently, for cold and altitude).

I must acknowledge my debt to Maria without whose untiring en-couragement and support I would never have got myself together to step so uncompromisingly into the unknown. A typical sign of my own naïvety, I had amused myself earlier in the season with one of my feeble jokes – 'Hornsey Today, Himalaya Tomorrow'; little had I expected it to become a self-fulfilling prophecy. No women's expedition should ever set forth from the NLMC without Maria's guiding hand.

No one can arrive in India from the British Isles without carrying a host of images and assumptions about what the journey will entail. The object of any climbing party is to get through and clear of the heat, dust and disease as quickly as possible. But even with this overriding concern, one can't help but stand aghast at the sheer novelty of being 'in the East'. Whatever particular political prejudices or sympathies one has, there is a Felliniesque visual onslaught of incongruous, colourful and incessant life; at one and the same time idle, chaotic and aimless, and frenetic, busy and purposive.

I am getting to the mountains – and so were we. The further north we travelled, the more bizarre life became. After an overnight journey by bus which could only be likened to 'The Night of the Long Knives' – all of them digging into us and crushing our kidneys to pulp – Bert left his bag containing all his documents on the bus. We had a tense but, fortunately, successful journey by a proverbial veteran Morris Minor with one and a half gears in sporadic pursuit.

Then came the first moment of High Drama. It may seem an oversight at this stage, but the expedition was, in fact, still in search of an 'objective' (women, I fear, will have to find less militaristic language for their 'hits'). To compound this difficulty, Andrew had been struck down with salmonella and was in his bed losing colour from his face and other things from elsewhere.

Obviously well-trained in how to deal with an emergency, Henry jumped into the breach and, over the candle-lit remains of the contaminated rice, he reassuringly laid out his plan before Bert and myself.

'It's all right,' pronounced Henry, with a masterly flick of the hand, the one he must have used in an earlier age to dismiss the waiting servant, 'leave everything to me. I will go ahead with Bert and get the food and porters and have everything ready for when you and Andrew arrive.'

'Well, Henry. This sounds quite admirable. But how will you know when we are going to arrive?'

'It doesn't matter. I will meet all the buses.' Some statements in life are final and brook no disagreement. This was one of them.

'Quite.'

Andrew and I had much laughter at Henry's expense as we bumped our way along the precipitous mountain-pass towards Keylong and the waiting caravanserai. Our giggles broke into hysterical sobs as our eyes fell on two whirling dervishes in shorts and T-shirts making frenzied contorted gestures at us as we tried to descend from the bus. For the next hour or so utter confusion reigned. With just cause, I am happy to say, for no less a personage than Mrs Gandhi herself (God rest her soul) was arriving the next day. I felt as though Henry had some mystical hand in all this. After all, if he hadn't managed to get the porters, he would have needed a jolly good excuse.

So it was that we found ourselves, later that night, huddled in a British Army tent bargaining over the price of horses to carry our equipment (and probably me) up to Base Camp. There is plenty of scope for linguistic confusion generally, but a particular word of warning here. What the visiting climbers have in mind when they say Base Camp and what the locals mean by it are two depressingly different things – as we were shortly to learn to our cost.

Above the mountain pastures there is the glacier – as clearly mentioned in our photocopied sheets of the *Alpine Journal*. But between the mountain pastures and the glacier there lies the boulder-field – as mentioned at the beginning of this report. Base Camp turned out to be what the locals meant by it – and on the wrong side of the boulder-field. Such an error of interpretation cost me several hours of mournful agony and presented me with my first 'encounter of the worst kind' – you know, the kind where you start becoming seriously deranged and, as you sink once more in utter exhaustion to your knees, you start asking metaphysical questions like 'Am I going to get off here alive?' and 'Will they find me before dark?' and 'Will they find me at all?'

Of course, such moments of doubt have no place in the harsh world of climbing, as I soon learnt when, on arriving at Advanced Base Camp several hours behind the others, I was greeted by the warm tones of Bert's 'Ah! Here comes Speedy Gonzales.' As if this wasn't brutality enough, on the walk-out some days later, he followed this up with 'I can't understand why you are so slow.' I was too polite then to reply, having only just been initiated, or (more likely), too short of breath, so now, retrospectively, I will take this opportunity to say 'F . . . off, Bert.'

It comforts me to say that the boulder-field claimed Henry as a victim too. Eager as ever to make an early start, Henry had set off from Base Camp at dawn the day after our arrival there. When we met up with him the following day we found him clasped around and under a boulder in the dual attempt apparently to avoid being swallowed up by the creaking jaws of the glacier or burnt to a frazzle by the scorching sun. (For those who like a life of extremes, I cannot recommend too highly climbing in the Himalaya).

We eventually made a summit attempt – and, if this article appears a little short on climbing relative to everything else, I assure you that that is what it was like. After a succession of relays and dumps (overall I calculated that we must have crossed that bloody glacier six or seven times, and walked some 30-odd miles up and down the whole dreaded moraine) I think somewhere in all this hideous toil we did manage to do some climbing.

Lagging way behind Andrew and Bert, Henry and I eventually arrived on a snow-slope above the glacier – which we had crossed in our innocence without roping up – no wonder that we experienced delayed shock when, on the descent, this time roped-up, we each in turn sank up to our waists into crevasses through soft snow-bridges.

But we were not quite to make it to Camp 1 that night – which was unfortunate, since Andrew and Bert had the food with them – a pattern which was to be repeated at a later stage. Henry and I bivvied below the bergschrund and felt horrible. I got headaches and what felt like the Maginot Line opening fire on the back of my eyeballs. The next morning we took about three hours to move – I think we were moving – some 300 yards, egged on only by the ever-receding small dots of Bert and Andrew gaining more and more height. To give us our due, we made it to, and up, the first of the ice-walls (itself a respectable route by alpine standards) – after a second bivvy and more headaches and confrontations with ourselves. Confrontations with each other came later, in the climax to this magnificent effort when, just as we had almost reached the top of the wall, we met Andrew and Bert on their way down! Henry, at that point bent double with fatigue, let out an almighty yell and bellowed some very rude things at Andrew, all about food, and waiting, and not getting to the summit which he would have done if he had waited . . .

Well, this was hardly the place for a diplomatic incident over climbing tactics, so the dispute was deferred until we were back at the civilizing influence of Advanced Base.

After this ignominious defeat, it was no small comfort as we abseiled on to a now vertical boulder-field to hear Bert's prophetic voice like some Greek chorus chanting 'Welcome to the most dangerous place on earth.' Predictably, the prophecy was self-fulfilling, and no sooner had we evacuated this stop-over than the boulders began a downward journey all of their own.

This first climb had left everyone a little in need of rest and recuperation; me more than the rest. So, after four days, the Three Musketeers set off again. I gratefully settled into good books and plenty of sleep in my tent. You can imagine my astonishment when the following afternoon I heard the crunch of gravel outside my tent. It was Henry looking like a swarm of locusts after a heavy rainfall.

'Henry! How unexpected. Whatever is happening?'

'I'm going to Delhi.'

Something had obviously gone wrong.

And indeed it had. Andrew and Bert had done their disappearing act again, this time taking Henry's boiled eggs with them, and had left Henry stranded on the glacier. Fortunately, he met a stranded member of the French team and spent the night at their Camp 1.

I myself was beginning to feel a little stronger and more ambitious – after all, there was an inexhaustible supply of Mulkilas to climb. But the memory of Wales hovered like a boxer's bruise on my brow, and I wasn't going to risk upsetting Henry by imposing my will on his generous nature, especially when he was feeling so low. I remained silent while he talked at length about his forthcoming train journey through India. But, as he dozed off to sleep with the tinkle of rolling-stock in his ears, I murmured the relevant mantra gently . . . mulkila . . . mulkila . . . mulkila . . .

The next morning Henry awoke, obviously refreshed from his sleep, and spoke in a determined and enthusiastic tone.

'I think we should go and climb Mulkila 10.'

'Oh, Henry! What an excellent idea.'

And so we did.

EPILOGUE

Andrew Bankes died last year after a long and courageous battle against cancer. But for Andrew my climbing career might have ended as suddenly as it had begun. It was his love of mountaineering that encouraged me to continue what he had given me the chance to begin. It was in the North London Mountaineering Club Hut that he admonished me with the words: 'What's this I hear about you not going to the Alps because you haven't recovered from the Himalaya? Of course you're going to the Alps. You can't stop, now that you've started . . .' This is the spirit of Andrew that will always accompany me on any route.

A Note on Kinnaur

HARISH KAPADIA

Kinnaur conjures up memories of unknown and inaccessible valleys; of the Hindustan-Tibet road; of the gorge of the Satluj and strange customs. It was a well-known district to which Rudyard Kipling's *Kim* travelled on his famous mission. But things have changed drastically since the time of Kim. The obnoxious 'progress' has taken over. But not everything about it is obnoxious. It has opened many advantageous possibilities for trekkers and mountaineers. While it previously took about two weeks of trekking to reach Kinnaur, now National Highway 22 runs along the Satluj and is kept open throughout almost the whole year. One can take advantage of this to trek and climb in this beautiful district.

The earliest travellers-explorers to Kinnaur were the Gerard brothers in 1818[1]. Few others passed on the Hindustan-Tibet road. All the early writings are on how to reach Kinnaur and on dangers along the road.[2] It was left to Marco Pallis in 1933 to bring these valleys to the notice of mountaineers by an article[3] and a book.[4] He climbed Leo Pargial and travelled on the Hindustan-Tibet road into the Baspa valley, crossing the Lamkhaga pass on the way to Gangotri. There were many pilgrims who went around the Kailas massif, clockwise, from the Tirung valley; over Charang Ghati to Baspa and back. The tradition continues even today. The army and the Indo-Tibet Border Police (ITBP), who were the only ones allowed to this restricted area until recently, made many climbs.

Kalpa, situated in the centre of Kinnaur, is the district headquarters. It has one of the finest views one can have whilst enclosed in a comfortable bungalow. 'From the forest bungalow at Chini, 9400 feet above sea-level and 145 miles from Simla along the Hindustan-Tibet road the Kailas massif is seen to advantage. The snow-fields are so close that in spring the reflected light from the snows is painful to the eyes, while during the monsoon the sound of falling avalanches can be heard all day long.'[5]

Incidentally, the old name 'Chini' was hastily changed to Kalpa, just in case the Chinese had other ideas! About 750m below Kalpa is Rekong Peo. It is developing as the central bazaar and administrative town. There are many buses along the Hindustan-Tibet road; from Simla to Wangtu (where the inner-line begins), Karchham (bifurcate here SE for Sangla, 17km), Powari (for Rekong Peo, 6km, and Kalpa in the north, 13km), Akpa (for Morang and Tirung valley in SE), Kanam (for the Gyamthang valley in SE), Shi Asu Khad (for Ropa valley in NW), Puh, Leo and Chango (for Leo Pargial in the east). The motorable road goes ahead to Kaurik and Sumdo to enter Spiti and to reach Kaja.

An afternoon bus from Kalpa will reach Shimla on the same day and Chandigadh the next morning. These developments have opened up many possibilities for the local people, and these valleys are now far more accessible to mountaineers. And, luckily, they have not taken a heavy toll of the forest cover, culture and peace.

Much has been written on the cultural aspects of Kinnaur. An almost total fusion of Hinduism and Buddhism exists. Every village has a temple and gompa, and all worship both. Various primitive traditions, beliefs and superstitions survive. Legends are held in awe. Though a large population is educated, and many serve in the army, you may be fined a sacrifice of a goat if you sit on a temple parapet with your shoes on! Human sacrifice was offered to the goddess in earlier times, and one can see a special square built for the purpose. Now animal sacrifice takes place regularly.[6]

Kinnauri architecture is a thing of beauty to behold. Perched on a hillock, Kamru Fort or some exquisite gompas and temples make one breathless. There are many fruit orchards, and the valleys are rich and hospitable.

For such a large district, where people have travelled for years, the mountain and mountaineering history cannot be recorded exhaustively. What is attempted here is a brief resumé of possibilities in different valleys, important recorded history and updated information about approaches. This is based on recent travels, treks and climbs.

The Satluj literally cuts through the Himalayan chain near Shipki La and then runs through Kinnaur in the centre. There are four major valleys to its south-east and east.

Baspa valley

Captain Conway called this '. . . the most lovely of all the Himalayan valleys'.[7] Many would agree with this. Many have visited this valley; for it is connected by famous passes to its south with Garhwal. The important passes are:

(a)	Buran Ghati	:	Sangla to Pabar gad
(b)	Rupin Ghati	:	Sangla to Rupin gad
(c)	Nargah Ghati	:	Sangla to Nargani khad
(d)	Singha Ghati	:	Mastarang to Supin gad
(e)	Khimloga pass	:	Chhitkul to Supin gad
(f)	Borasu Ghati	:	Nagasti to Harki-dun
(g)	Lamkhaga pass	:	Upper Baspa valley to Harsil.

All these passes offer possibilities for trekking, small peaks and grand views. They have been crossed from time immemorial.

There are also two major passes which lead to Tibet. The famous one is the Yamrang La (5570m), and a little to its south is the Gugairang pass.

For mountaineers the upper Baspa valley offers many shapely peaks. Generally they are all around 5600–5900m, with about five peaks rising above 6000m, and the highest 6227m. Many have passed through this valley but, perhaps because of the lack of higher peaks, the climbing history is brief.

Col Balwant Sandhu led an expedition here in 1976 which climbed Pk 6215m and another peak north of Sui Thatang.[8] Other visitors were: Jack

Gibson on two trekking visits,[9] the Yamrang La visited in 1978[10] and Soli Mehta across the Lamkhaga pass in 1966.[11]

The ITBP has been in the area for many years, and some officers have written warmly and authentically about it.[12]

The ITBP has reported two climbs in the Baspa valley. These are on the three high peaks north of Dunthi. But unfortunately no accurate or written record is available, and only local units confirm the climbs.

A good motorable road branches off at Karchham to Sangla, 17km. It has been extended further to Rakchham, 14km and Shushung khad, 4km short of Chhitkul, 13km. Buses ply regularly as far as Sangla, and most of them further up to Shushung khad. In a year or two the road will reach Chhitkul.

Tirung valley (Tidong)

This is a valley north of Baspa. It has close connections with the Baspa valley across the Charang Ghati (5242m). It runs in the east to the Khimokul la (Gunrang La) and to Tibet. A jeepable road leads from Morang to Thangi. Ahead, the road is being extended to Charang.

Thangi has been used as a starting point for attempts on the peaks in the Kinnaur-Kailash range. It also gives access to Phawararang (6349m) which has been climbed a few times.[13] North-east of Thangi lie two shapely peaks, both awaiting climbers. Sesar Rang is 6095m and an unnamed peak 6248m, both on the Tirung-Gyamthang divide.

Kinnaur-Kailash range

This is the best-known range in Kinnaur. But perhaps it is also the most misunderstood. The locals and maps are very clear that peak Kailash is 6050m, seen near a 'pillar' from Kalpa. This peak is Kailash, and the pillar is worshipped as the holy Kinnaur Kailash, being in the form of Shivling. The highest peak, Jorkanden (6473m), is to its south-east and is generally confused with Kinnaur Kailash.

Jorkanden has received various attempts and ascents. After the recce by P R Oliver in 1931,[14] it was attempted four times by the Indian army.[15] The first ascent was made in 1974 by the ITBP,[16] followed a month later by the army.[17] Since then it has again been climbed by the Indian army, on 13 June 1978, led by the late Major Kiran Kumar,[18] and on 27 August 1987 by an HP Police team.

Gyamthang valley (Nisang)

This is an unknown valley to the north of the Tirung valley. It leads to the Raniso pass (for Tibet) and has one peak of note, 6063m above Gangchha. On the same ridge further to the east lies Gang Chua (6288m). This was climbed in 1974 by an army team from the Hojis Lungba valley in the north.[19] The valley is approached from Kanam. To the north of this there are no mountains of great height to the Shipki La and the gorge of the Satluj and its meeting with the Spiti river north of Puh.

Leo Pargial (Hangrang valley)

This peak at 6791m is a high landmark north of the Shipki La. Situated on the Tibetan border, it has attracted mountaineers for many years. It was reported to have been recced by the Gerard brothers in 1818, and was first climbed by Marco Pallis and Charles Warren in 1933. The army at first attempted it several times, and climbed it in 1967, 1975 and 1980.[20] The ITBP made the third ascent in 1971.

The peak was many times attempted by civilian parties, and was climbed twice in 1982.[21] The principal approach was from Nako, and another was recced from Chango.[22]

There are numerous peaks around it, from 6173m to 6816m (Leo Pargial II). There were discussions about its correct name and height,[23] all laid to rest by the latest Survey of India map (1975) which has adopted the above spelling and height.

North-west Kinnaur

To the north-west of the Satluj lie the other parts of Kinnaur. These gentle valleys lead to a divide with the Pin valley (Spiti). It has numerous passes which would afford many pleasurable trekking routes, but none climbing higher than about 5900m. The important passes are:

(a)	Tari Khango pass	:	Bhabha valley to Pin-Parvati pass.
(b)	Larsa Way pass	:	Larsa Garang (Taiti Garang) to Pin valley
(c)	Ghunsarang pass	:	Ropa valley (to north-west) to Pin valley
(d)	Manirang pass	:	Ropa valley (to north) to Pin valley

The best-known pass, for the trekkers, is the Tari Khango over which the Indo-New Zealand Himalayan Traverse Expedition passed in 1981.[24]

Historically, Manirang Peak (6593m) was climbed by the SW ridge, on 12 September 1952, by Dr J de V Graaff, Mrs Clare Graaff and Sherpas Pasang Dawa Lama and Tashi. The ITBP repeated the climb in 1976.[25] The only other peaks climbed in the area are Manirang South in 1982[26] and 1986[27], and an unnamed peak (6223m) to the north of Manirang in 1973.[28] There are numerous peaks around 5500m to 6000m in the area which have not been touched. It is evident from this brief description that in Kinnaur many trekking and climbing opportunities await mountaineers. There are many side-valleys, peaks and passes which are inviting, unexplored and certainly unrecorded. With the development of roads, the valleys of this beautiful district are one night away; of course one will have to solve the problems of inner-line permits, lack of porters and lack of information. But then, no paradise is gained easily. Even Kim had to hustle with Hurree babu to gain access here.

REFERENCES

(HJ = Himalayan Journal, HCNL = Himalayan Club Newsletter.)
1   W E Buchanan, 'In the Footsteps of the Gerards.' HJ2, 73–80, 1930.
2   Major D G P M Shewen, 'The Way to the Baspa.' HJ1, 67–74, 1929.
3   Marco Pallis, 'Gangotri and Leo Pargial.' HJ6, 106–126, 1934.
4   Marco Pallis, Peaks and Lamas. London (Cassell), 1939.
5   H M Glover, 'Round the Kanawar Kailas.' HJ2, 81–86, 1930.
6   P C Roy Chaudhury, Temples and Legends of Himachal Pradesh. Bombay (Bhartiya Vidya Bhavan), 1981.

7   Capt C W W S Conway, *Sunlit Waters*. Bombay (Thacker), 1942.
8   Lt Col Balwant Sandhu, 'Kinnaur – 1976.' *HJ35*, 224–228, 1976–78.
9   J Gibson, *As I Saw It*. New Delhi (Mukul), 1976.
10   *HJ36*, 193–195, 1978–79.
11   *HJ28*, 55–62, 1967–68.
12   D S Malik, 'Land the Ogress Stalked I – Kinnaur. ' *ITBP Bulletin*, July–
     Sept 1975.
13   *HJ36*, 99–102, 1978–79; *HJ42*, 177–179, 1984–85.
14   *HJ4*, 147–148, 1932.
15   1964, 1967 and 1972: Major A B Jungalwala; 1973: Col D K Khullar
     (*HJ32*, 105–112, 1972–73).
16   Led by D S Malik; on 26 May 1974.
17   Led by S S Kalhan; on 19 June 1974.
18   Major K I Kumar, *Expedition Kinner-Kailash*. New Delhi (Vision
     Books), 1979.
19   *HJ34*, 75–78, 1974–75.
20   1967: Col D K Khullar (second ascent); 1975: Brig J Singh; 1980: Major
     K I Kumar.
21   1982: P Dasgupta (Bengal) and U Sathe (Maharashtra).
22   *HJ38*, 95–102, 1980–81; *HJ39*, 195–198, 1981–82.
23   *HJ6*, 106–126, 1934; *HJ27*, 182, 184, 1966; *HJ38*, 102, 1980–81.
24   G Dingle and P Hillary, *First Across the Roof of the World*. Hodder and
     Stoughton, 1982.
25   *HCNL33*, 27, 1980.
26   *HCNL36*, 24, 1983.
27   *HJ43*, 63–67, 1985–86.
28   *HCNL30*, 13, 1975.

Kharcha Kund North Ridge Expedition

ROBIN BEADLE

The Gangotri has been visited by a number of British parties recently, and there is ample information available for the prospective visitor. The major summits have been climbed, but there are still many good routes awaiting an ascent. These facts, coupled with the relative ease of access and the scale of the mountains (6000–7000m in height) made the area attractive to us as Himalayan first-timers.

We were a four-man team (Robin Beadle, Bobby Gilbert, Rob Tresidder and Pete Scott, all of the Oread Mountaineering Club), planning an alpine-style ascent of Kharcha Kund's N ridge, an objective brought to our attention whilst viewing Neil McAdie's excellent slides of the area. From the photos the ridge appeared long, sustained and committing, so, in addition to the usual gear carried on this type of ascent, we took along some extra rope and a bolting kit. This was intended for fixing rope to facilitate retreat around the many pinnacles, should it become necessary. The bolt kit was, however, deemed too heavy to carry, and was left at Base Camp.

We were much more fortunate with weather and conditions than previous teams who had attempted the ridge. The monsoon itself never materialized, so the rock pitches were completely clear of snow. We encountered conditions ranging from unconsolidated powder to very hard ice, but on the whole the snow was good.

The sky was generally clear during the day, although cloud built up early behind the ridge at the end of the glacier, and poured over it as the day progressed. Nights were also clear and cold. On the mountain the minimum night-time temperature was −15°C, but generally it was −7°C. The worst weather we experienced was an afternoon of mist and light snow showers at the N col.

Base Camp was usually warm and sunny enough for sunbathing, but night-time temperatures were also low here (generally −5°C).

September, then, is perhaps the optimum time to visit the area. The monsoon has passed, and the cold weather and snow experienced later in the year are also avoided.

We made two reconnaissances before embarking on the route. The first was a foray from Base Camp to assess conditions, and to observe the ridge from both sides in order to plan the route. The second involved a pair of us ascending the ridge to the Five Pinnacles, carrying only day-sacks. We thus established the route past the first major difficulties and left ropes on the hardest pitches. These preliminaries ensured that we had acclimatized quite well before starting on the route. Also the sheer length of the ridge meant that we gained height gradually:

we had made six bivouacs between 5000m and 6000m before our summit day (18 September 1987).

The initial difficulties, on rock, were encountered in reaching and traversing a group of five pinnacles. This provided a number of good pitches of standard up to Grade V. Subsequently, difficulties were encountered on both ice and rock, and were separated by much easier stretches on snow. A detailed route description follows.

Route description: Kharcha Kund North Ridge

Alpine rock grades and Scottish winter grades have been allocated to rock and ice pitches respectively. 120m of 7mm rope was carried by the expedition and fixed where stated to facilitate retreat, had it been required. Five rock pegs were also left.

Base Camp was at Sundaban (4700m), and from there the mountain was reached by crossing the Ghanohim Bamak. On a reconnaissance we discovered a comfortable bivouac at the foot of the ridge, at an altitude of 4925m.

Scree slopes on the W side of the ridge were climbed to meet the ridge at a notch, at the start of the difficulties. The first bivouac was made here. The same point could be reached by scrambling up the ridge itself for about 250m, as on the reconnaissance, but this alternative was found very loose.

The ridge was followed with no great difficulty (III) for about 250m until a short crack led to a 6m traverse across a slab (IV, fixed rope). A short descent was made to scree-covered ledges which were followed leftwards. (These ledges lie at the top of a couloir falling to the foot of the ridge on its left-hand side.) Unprotected, loose rock (III) was then followed diagonally up leftwards, to a point on the ridge ahead above the first tower (Robin's Flake).

The right arête of a slab above (V, fixed rope) was taken to a dièdre. An exit on the left by a short, steep corner crack (V) led to an excellent platform on the crest of the ridge. The compact boss of rock ahead was surmounted (IV), and the ridge then followed easily for a pitch. A line keeping to the left of the crest was followed until an icy gully was reached. Here we found it easiest to move back right on to the rib, and continue upwards until a 6m leftward traverse led to a snowpatch (III).

The snowpatch was climbed (50m). This led to a steep section of rock from which a leftward exit led to a shoulder on the ridge (V). A sentry-box was climbed to a belay. A flaky crackline followed (V, 50m), leading to the top of the first of five pinnacles (at 5500m). This pinnacle was descended by abseil, as was the second (fixed ropes). The third small pinnacle was crossed with no difficulty, and a bivouac made on a ledge system on the eastern side of the fourth.

A descent on the eastern side bypassed Pinnacle 5 to reach the foot of a snow-slope. This was climbed for two rope-lengths to a rockband which was passed by a leftward fault (Scottish III), giving access to the upper snow-ice wall. The wall was climbed for 250m to the right of a large serac band. An excellent bivi site is available at the top of this wall. The snow-ice arête, conspicuous from the glacier, was taken easily to its end on top of a pinnacle (5874m). A scramble and abseil (fixed rope) were made down the back of this pinnacle, and a steep

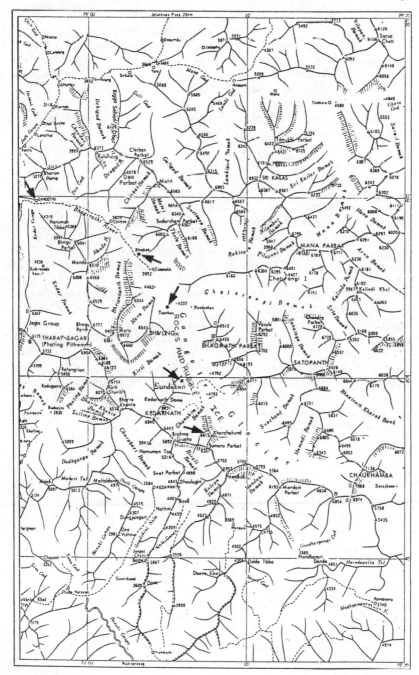

snow-slope on the immediately following 'Bifurcated Pinnacle' was ascended. We passed through the gap in this pinnacle to reach the eastern side, traversed some flakes and made a diagonal abseil (fixed rope) to bypass the bulk of the pinnacle. A short climb up a dièdre (10m) regained the ridge, and the third bivouac was made at the col behind the pinnacle (5840m).

A steep snow-ice crest was climbed, almost to the foot of the next impressive rock buttress, Longland Buttress. A traverse left on soft snow gained mixed ground on the east of this buttress (Scottish IV). From here, a steep snow-slope was ascended diagonally back right to gain a corniced ridge. This gradually steepening ridge was followed to the foot of the initial pinnacle of the Great North Tower (GNT), where a traverse right led to a good belay. Two excellent ice-pitches (Scottish IV) on the right of the pinnacle regained the crest of the ridge. The ridge was then followed for three pitches towards the main part of the GNT (rock move IV, mixed move Scottish IV). At a large bergschrund, a leftward traverse across snow was made to the eastern edge of the tower. Here a system of grooves led for one pitch to a snow-patch on the summit of the tower (VI, A1 3 points of aid). We made our fourth bivouac here (6085m).

From the snow-patch the crest of the GNT was climbed for two pitches. It was blunt at first, but after a notch it became a classic knife-edge ridge (III/IV, 1 rope move). Two 50m abseils were made into the unknown down the impressive S face of the GNT, to arrive at the N col inf (5957m). From the col a steep ice-slope was climbed up leftward for two pitches, followed by a difficult traverse left on ice, bypassing a gendarme on the ridge (Scottish V). This gained a cave below a chimney (V, A1 2 points of aid) and led to the very summit of the Tower in the col (6068m). One abseil was made down the far side of the tower, and poor snow was climbed and traversed for one pitch (Scottish III/IV) to a notch before the next small pinnacle. Here the fifth bivouac was made in a 'V' between ice and rock on the crest of the ridge (6020m).

The traverse along the ridge was continued for 10m, and a 20m diagonal abseil was made on the E side to a snowy ledge (where we left a jammed abseil rope). A traverse on poor snow (25m, Scottish IV) was made to the N col sup (6000m). We bivouacked here in a snow-hole, but a rock-ledge is also available.

Easy snow-slopes were climbed to the summit (6612m, approx 3 hours).

Descent description: Kharcha Kund West Ridge

From the N col sup the big steep couloir to the west was descended. This was achieved by 10 to 12 awkward abseils, keeping to the rock on the north of the couloir to avoid the heavily crevassed centre. Fixed ropes led to a snowfield, which was crossed to a shoulder and our seventh bivouac.

From the shoulder a second ice couloir was easily descended until the crest of the W rib could be gained. This was descended (scrambling, some fixed ropes/abseils) until a snow-slope on the N flank was reached and descended to the Ghanohim Bamak.

10. *Muztagh Tower from the Baltoro glacier.*

11. *Gasherbrums 4, 3 and 2. The Moravec route (SW spur) is picked out by the sun, traverses under the summit pyramid and climbs the final ridge from the R.*

12. *Mitre Peak from Concordia.*

Topo of Kharcha Kund North Ridge

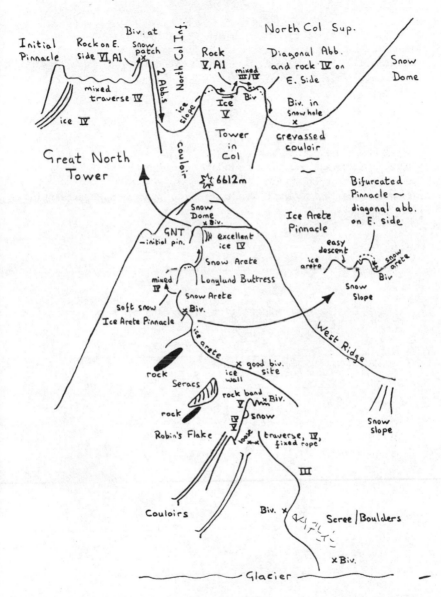

The expedition thanks for their generous support: the Mount Everest Foundation, the British Mountaineering Council, Derbyshire County Council, the Oread Mountaineering Club, Air India, Allcord Ltd, Berghaus Ltd, Burtons Biscuits, Faces, Phoenix Mountaineering Ltd, RAB Down Equipment, Snowdon Mouldings, and J W Thornton Ltd.

REFERENCES

M Moran, 'Views on the Gangotri.' *AJ91*, 57–64, 1986.
Mountain 84, 22–27, 1982.
R Lindsay, 'The Scottish Garhwal Himalaya Expedition 1982 Final Report',
AC Library.

MAPS

Garhwal-West, 1:150,000, Swiss Foundation for Alpine Research. (BMC may
supply a photocopy on request.)
Mountaineering Maps of the World, p217, has a Japanese map, excellent for
identifying peaks.

The First Winter Ascent of Cho Oyu (1984–1985)

ANDRZEJ ZAWADA
TRANSLATED BY INGEBORGA DOUBRAWA-COCHLIN

In the autumn of 1981, after I had been invited by the Canadians to undertake a lecture tour about the Polish expeditions to Everest, a collaboration began between the Polish Alpine Association and the Federation Québécoise de la Montagne. Our first idea was to climb K2 in winter but, since the Pakistani Government refused permission for such a climb, our Canadian partners agreed to a change in our plans. We decided on a winter climb of Cho Oyu. In the spring of 1984 I went to Pakistan to submit application papers for a future attempt on K2, and I then went on to Nepal to obtain permission both for our own joint Polish-Canadian expedition to Cho Oyu the following winter and for the Polish Gliwice Club for their attempt on Dhaulagiri.

Cho Oyu, which lies 28km NW of Everest, has two official heights. The most popular among climbers is 8153m, but the Nepalese authorities maintain that it is 8201m. These differing heights place it as either the sixth or the eighth highest peak in the world.

The first photographic records of the peak were made by British climbers on the 1921 Everest Reconnaissance Expedition. The summit is fairly easy to reach from the west and six expeditions have successfully reached the top in summer. As a result, Cho Oyu has not been considered a particularly difficult mountain. Although the almost impossible SE precipice wall had been attempted by eight expeditions, only one, in 1978, had actually reached the top, and this via the route through the middle of the E wall.

Nobody before us had ever attempted to climb Cho Oyu in winter. You cannot really count the Italian-German expedition of 1982 as a true winter climb, since they had finished by 19 December.

The permit for our climb arrived on 6 September 1984 and, by the end of November, all our luggage had arrived safely in Nepal. These trouble-free preparations were only made possible by the co-operation between our two countries. In our contract the Canadians agreed to pay for everything that required foreign currency. They also undertook to supply ropes, a radio-telephone and solar batteries, 30% of the food and 50% of the medicines. We agreed to provide the remainder of the food and medicines, the tents for Base Camp, clothing for the Nepalese members, and down sleeping-bags for the Canadians. We also bore the total cost of transporting our equipment and supplies to Nepal – by ship from Canada to Poland, by lorry across Poland, by air to New Delhi and finally by Polish Jelcz vans to Kathmandu.

Our climbers were: Maciej Berbeka, Eugeniusz Chrobak, Krzysztof

Flaczynski (the expedition doctor), Miroslaw Gardzielewski, Zygmunt Andrzej
Heinrich, Jerzy Kukuczka, Maciej Pawlikowski and Andrzej Zawada (leader).
From Canada: Martin Berkman, André Frapier, Jacques Olek (deputy leader)
and Yves Tessier (also a doctor). In Nepal we were joined by Chhetrapati
Shrestha, our liaison officer, and a wonderful Base Camp team, hand-picked by
Ang Tshering from the Asian Trekking Club, whom we all took to our hearts:
Thukten Sherpa (Ang's brother and sirdar), Ang Dawa, Bal Bahadur 'Maila'
and Mohit Syangbo Lama.

En route to our mountain

By 17 December we were all in Kathmandu. Jerzy Kukuczka made a surprise
request. He asked me if he could go on two expeditions one after the other: first
the one to Dhaulagiri and then ours to Cho Oyu. It was an interesting
proposition – and the chance of a new mountaineering record: two 8000ers in
winter in the same season!

At the same time, Jerzy's departure would weaken our team very
considerably and would impose even harder work on the remaining members as
they established a route for the 'master'. I called everyone together and, after a
stormy discussion, I finally gave Kukuczka permission to attempt this feat, risky
as it was for us all. The following day, Jerzy began his race to Dhaulagiri, where
Adam Bilczewski's expedition from Gliwice in Poland had already set up Camp 2.

Our efforts to hire a charter flight to Lukla were without success. In the
end, we had to hire a Puma – a very heavy military helicopter which is always
available but at double the price (one flight cost $2000!). Fortunately Yves
Tessier, our Canadian doctor, managed to negotiate a lower price. We spent
Christmas Eve together at Lukla, in the same house and under the same
Christmas tree as we had on our Everest expedition. Only Heinrich, Chrobak
and Frapier had gone on ahead towards Base Camp with the first group of
porters.

The walk-in to the SE wall of Cho Oyu is both short and most enjoyable.
The first part was along a track familiar to us from previous expeditions to
Lhotse and Everest. In Namche Bazar there are many small hotels and little
restaurants full of climbers from all over the world. The only depressing note in
these idyllic surroundings was the sight of a stream of French mountaineers
returning from their Everest expedition with severe frostbite. When we reached
Machermia it began to snow. The whole valley, which until now had been so
green, was suddenly completely white. We suffered many heavy snowfalls
during our expedition and on several occasions we had to dig our tents out of
deep snow. The severity of the winter that year surprised us.

Our Base Camp at 5200m was in Gyazumpa Valley, on a hillock under a
moraine. Heinrich had chosen a site near water and well protected from the
wind, but unfortunately with no view at all of our wall. On 30 December we set
up our tents and by 2 January 1985 the whole team, except for Kukuczka, was
together.

The wall three kilometres high

The real mountain action started on 4 January, when Berbeka and Pawlikowski established Camp 1 on the Lungsampa Glacier. From this point, there was a breath-taking view towards Cho Oyu. The vastness and steepness of the SE wall had an almost hypnotic effect on us and we felt a surge of excitement mixed with fear as we listened to the continuous roar of avalanches and saw the overhanging barrier of seracs glittering with ice. The whole route of our ascent from Base Camp to the summit – 2800m of piled-up ice and rock – was clearly visible before us. I was beginning to understand why this precipice wall was considered impossible to climb: it was a fiendishly dangerous undertaking. Having now seen it for ourselves, we began to speak with great respect of the Yugoslav climbers who were the first to tackle the precipice. Our only chance of a safe climb of the upper parts of the face was to ascend the pillar of ice and rock which separated the S face from the E face and which was not clearly visible from where we stood. On the lower part of the wall, the main problem was a sheer rocky precipice stretching from the base to about 1200m and scarred with deep clefts and crevices. One possible way of crossing this rocky wall, with its many gullies, was up the right hand side – the same route the Yugoslavs had taken.

The approach from Camp 1 to the base of the wall required great technical climbing skill because it passed through a constantly moving glacier which stretched down from a vast plateau under the eastern wall. Every few days, some of the enormous overhanging seracs broke off and tumbled down around our fixed ropes, so that to pass under those 'ducks' and 'ships', as we called them in hushed whispers, required strong nerves.

Confronted with such difficulties, I now felt compelled to divide our team into two groups. The first group reluctantly carried equipment from Base Camp to Camp 1, while the second group, consisting of six climbers, started to climb the wall. It may surprise many people to read that we only had six people to climb a wall of this magnitude in winter. In fact, we were very lucky that nobody fell sick, otherwise we would have had no chance of victory.

We had been counting on using the fixed ropes left by the Yugoslav team, but we were disappointed. Most of their ropes had been destroyed by falling rocks and very few were left hanging. The weather conditions were also very difficult. The frequent snowstorms were creating enormous problems and we were constantly hampered by avalanches. The average temperature in Base Camp dropped to −25°C and the maximum in the shade never reached 0°C. The heaviest frost we recorded was −33°C, in Base Camp on the night of 15 February, while Heinrich and Kukuczka were bivouacking at 7700m.

On 10 January, Berbeka and Pawlikowski went up as first team. The problem was to cross a very deep crevasse skirting the base of the wall. First they abseiled down, then picked their way delicately over huge blocks of ice before reaching the wall itself. They were then able to establish our first fixed ropes on a vertical section of terrain before returning to Base Camp. As we listened to their report, it was immediately obvious that we were undertaking a climb of immense difficulty.

Camp 2 was established at 5700m by Gardzielewski and Zawada. A tent was put up on a sort of platform under an overhanging rock, well protected from avalanches and falling stones. The tent was a good old-fashioned cotton 'Turnia 2' to which we happily returned later on from higher camps, after uncomfortable bivouacs in super-light nylon tents covered in snow and ice!

The third team, Chrobak and Heinrich, pushed further on up the wall and abseiled down to Camp 2 for the night. At one point they ran out of rope and had to descend to Camp 1, returning the same day to Camp 2. Everyone was working to his utmost yet, as we looked through the binoculars at our progress, we were almost tempted to abandon the whole venture, so small was the distance we had covered in comparison with the enormity of the wall.

Our struggle to set up Camp 3

Chrobak and Heinrich had reached a cliff over which seracs, protruding from the pillar above, were suspended. We had planned to go this way on the next stage of our climb. This cliff turned out to be the most difficult part of the whole wall. Now the progress of the two climbers was halted when Heinrich was hit on the leg by a falling stone. He was very upset but, as a result of this accident, he later partnered Kukuczka on the second attack on the summit. Meanwhile, Berbeka and Pawlikowski went into action. They spent two days fixing ropes up the cliff, abseiling to Camp 2 for the night. Slowly, inch by inch, the wall of Cho Oyu was surrendering.

On top of everything else, the frequent snowstorms followed by avalanches were slowing down our climbing. At this stage, we changed the teams over. Chrobak and Gardzielewski changed places with Berbeka and Pawlikowski. They spent the next day pulling ropes out from under the snow. The following day, while carrying heavy equipment for Camp 3, they reached an icefall just above the cliff. It was getting late and we wondered if they would find a place for Camp 3 or turn back to Camp 2. Then we saw that they had put up a tent. After a while we spoke over the radio-telephone and they told us that they were in good spirits and would try to establish Camp 3 the following day. However, their attempt failed. After a whole day's climbing they reached the edge of the pillar, where steep icy gullies halted their progress. They had to spend one more bivouac in a hurriedly-erected tent, Gardzielewski had frost-bitten hands and they had run out of ropes and pitons. The next day they returned to Base Camp. Then, once again, the two Maciejs went into action. In a climb requiring great finesse, they succeeded in crossing the ice gullies, using Grivel crampons and the front teeth of their ice-axes. They finally reached the pillar but it was not until the following day that they were able to set up Camp 3 at 6700m. It had taken us almost a month to reach Camp 3 from Base Camp. We had climbed only one-third of the wall – but it had been the most difficult part. We felt a little surge of optimism!

The organ-pipes of ice

Stretching above Camp 3 was an ice-wall 500m high, with shapes like great organ-pipes formed on its surface. Somewhere in its upper reaches we had to try to establish Camp 4. The next team, Heinrich and Zawada, brought all the necessary equipment for Camp 4 to the lower part of the organ. As we made the ascent up the fixed ropes we admired the job our colleagues had done. We deposited the equipment next to the main crevasse under the organ-pipes at 7000m, after eight continuous days of action. We returned to Base Camp very tired. Over the radio we learned with relief that Czok and Kukuczka had reached the top of Dhaulagiri. We now hoped that Kukuczka would arrive in time to join our expedition before our permit expired.

In the meantime, two teams – Chrobak and Gardzielewski, Berbeka and Pawlikowski – were very active high up on the wall. Both teams had left Base Camp three days apart hoping to reach the summit. Chrobak and Gardzielewski set up a bivouac next to the crevasse under the organ and the following day they began to climb the steep ice-pipes. For the night, they abseiled down to the crevasse. In the morning they decided to abandon the bivouac and started to climb, taking the heavy equipment with them. We watched their progress very carefully through binoculars. The tension mounted. Fortunately the weather was perfect with no trace of wind. All day they climbed continuously up the wall but we could see that they would not reach the seracs, where they were to set up Camp 4, before nightfall. Everyone was on edge. But when dawn broke we looked up and saw that they had miraculously found a crevasse and had been able to put up a bivouac on a very uncomfortable and almost vertical ledge. That day their progress was slow since the terrain was very steep and difficult. They finally reached the seracs and set up Camp 4 at 7200m. It was 8 February and the day Kukuczka arrived at Base Camp.

Berbeka and Pawlikowski waited one day at Camp 3. The following morning Chrobak and Gardzielewski decided to go down. They were tired and had no ropes left. Common sense had prevailed. They returned to Camp 2, very depressed, and their place at Camp 4 was taken by Berbeka and Pawlikowski, who also took up more ropes. On the same day – 10 February – Heinrich and Kukuczka left Base Camp. Berbeka and Pawlikowski were fixing ropes on the pillar above Camp 4 all day. They spent the night at Camp 4, while Heinrich and Kukuczka were at Camp 2.

On 11 February Berbeka and Pawlikowski abandoned Camp 4. They decided to do this although they were aware what this would mean for Heinrich and Kukuczka: there was nobody to carry the equipment up to Camp 5 – but the ropes were more important. Berbeka and Pawlikowski continued slowly up the mountain and established Camp 5 at 7500m. They were in good shape and hoped to make an attempt on the summit the following day. (We informed the Ministry at Kathmandu about this.) On the same day, Heinrich and Kukuczka, after a nine-hour climb, reached Camp 3.

We reach the top – any higher is impossible!

On 12 February the weather was beautiful. We could hear the gale-force winds raging on the ridges of Cho Oyu – but otherwise the weather was perfect. After breakfast we all made our way to the moraine; everyone wanted to look through the binoculars to see what was happening. The tension was as great as in an Olympic stadium before a big race. Chrobak was filming, Jacques was rather nervously dictating into his tape-recorder, while Dawa and Maila served hot tea from thermos flasks. High up on the mountain we could see two little dots moving forward on the ice-fields. They were just below the summit. Suddenly one figure disappeared into the backdrop of the dark blue sky; then, after a few minutes, the second figure also disappeared. I looked at my watch – it was 2.20pm. Quickly I seized the radio-telephone. Surely they must say something at any moment! Then suddenly, against the deafening roar of the wind, I heard a hoarse voice shouting 'Hello, can you hear me?' 'Are you on the summit?' I screamed. 'I don't know, I don't know,' came the voice back. 'All I know is there is nowhere higher to go!' What happiness we all experienced at that moment! What a great achievement it was! To reach the top of Cho Oyu by this perilous route – and in winter! Two records had been broken and, in addition, two private ones as well. For Maciej Pawlikowski it was his first 8000m climb and a second 8000er in winter for Maciej Berbeka.

On the summit, they were unable to stand upright because of the howling gale; so, lying on their stomachs, they tied the team flags to an ice-axe, took some pictures, and then descended to Camp 5 which they reached by about 6pm.

But things were not finished yet. We were in for another great achievement and another broken record! After spending two nights at Camp 3, Heinrich and Kukuczka started to climb to Camp 4, a 900m vertical climb, on 13 February. At about midday they passed the summit team on their way down. They were very tired and climbed slowly to adjust to the altitude. At one point Heinrich fell and hung freely, suspended on a rope, until with great difficulty he jumared up the rope. Night came and they were forced to bivouac. They discovered next morning that they were only about 60m from the tents at Camp 5. After reaching Camp 5 they rested for the remainder of the day. The following morning they set off at 7.30am. Heinrich felt he was not properly acclimatized, since he had never before climbed beyond 7000m. He moved very slowly forward towards the summit. A fog began to surround them and visibility was getting worse. Finally, they reached the summit at 5.30pm and stood next to the markers left by Berbeka and Pawlikowski. It was 15 February – the day our permit expired!

Kukuczka started to film and took a few pictures and then made a quick retreat. But nightfall caught them a long way from their camp. For a few hours they continued to descend in the dark until suddenly Kukuczka slipped and fell about five metres down a serac. Heinrich abseiled down to him and they decided to wait until morning. They were at 7700m.

When they reached Camp 5 they were so exhausted that they spent the following night there. The next day they forced themselves on and, after abseiling down vertical walls of ice countless times, Heinrich was growing very weak. Only their tremendous experience, their discipline and their mutual support saw these two outstanding climbers safely through their descent down that perilous wall. They spent one more night at Camp 3 and one night at Camp 2. At last, four days after reaching the summit of Cho Oyu, they dragged themselves wearily into Base Camp late at night. Kukuczka had succeeded in climbing two different 8000m peaks in the same winter! This made him the second person to have climbed all the 8000m peaks.

One final thought. If someone were to ask me which were the most enjoyable moments to remember in the whole expedition, I would answer without hesitation: the wonderful comradeship at Base Camp and on the wall, and on Christmas Eve round our table.

Pumori – the Scottish Route

SANDY ALLAN

Surrounded by the peaceful security of the shady Alpine Club Library in South Audley Street, with its shelves upon shelves of Alpine Club reports and hundreds of aging Himalayan Journals overflowing with tales of intrepid deeds by past and present mountaineers, Mrs Johnson drops all her other work to come to my aid in finding the vital 'information'. Many of my expeditions have come to life in this manner – overnight coach to Victoria, navigate, with Highland caution, the crowded tangled streets, my goal the Alpine Club, walk down the hallway, passing under portraits of those who have gone before us, down the stairs and round the corner, the quiet welcome, the scanning of pages and pages of different texts. Then, with a bundle of photo-copies under my arm, I pay my 10 pences and return to the far north to sift through the 'information' in my humble den.

I was leader of our Pumori trip, originally coming across the permission as I cruised up the Khumbu in 1985 where I met Dave and Morris from Seattle. We shot the breeze. They told me they needed some help to climb Pumori. I said I'd be willing to have a go as long as I could take one other Brit. We drifted apart and the seed, having been sown, was left to germinate while I encountered an old buddy from a previous expedition. After a flight from Lukla, as I tripped casually through the sunny boulevards of Kathmandu, I re-encountered the Seattle pair.

Pumori was first climbed by a German/Swiss team way back – you'll find the report on the uppermost shelves of the Alpine Club (*AJ67*, 351, 1962). We pulled into Base Camp early in October 1986: Rick Allen and I and our two Sherpas. Migma Tenzing from Thame village was our Sirdar and cook, and Pasang, nursing his sore head from over-much chang, was his assistant. But the ever-reliable Pasang managed to stumble down the moraine bank to fill a kettle with water to make our first Base Camp brew. We were at 5100m on the right bank of the Pumori glacier. Our yaks had departed, the head yak driver carrying with him a letter addressed to the Ministry of Tourism in Kathmandu, requesting a change of route. We now wished to attempt an unclimbed line on the S face.

So Rick and I waited for the weather to improve and for our bodies to acclimatize. We pitched a tent on Kalipitar and spent the night there, waking up in the early morning air to fantastic views of Pumori, Changtse, Everest, a flank of Lhotse and Nuptse. Further down the valley Ama Dablam and Kantega stood tall, their distant summits scraping the azure blue sky. We gazed and descended to our Base Camp to drink mugs of steaming Sherpa tea. Then, after a full breakfast, we prepared our equipment for the climb. Down the valley somewhere Dave and Morris approached. Rick and I wished that they would soon come to Base Camp, as we were now ready to climb.

After our second night on Kalipitar, Dave and Morris arrived at Base, where we were glad to share their company and junk food. We pointed out our proposed new line which took a steep ice couloir for several hundred metres, then eased out on to lesser-angled ramps, which would probably go at Scottish Grade 3, then over several rock-steps, to take us curving up to the summit. They thought that the line was perhaps a little over the top and were not sure if they would like to attempt it with us, but were keen for us to try.

Day 1 took Rick and me to a height of 5600m at the foot of a steep buttress. We bivvied in our Goretex tent and longed for the morning. It came with perfect weather. We climbed roped-up moving together over iced-up rock. We pitched three rope-lengths of mixed buttress climbing, which led us on to a view of an overhanging rock wall, so we had no choice but to abseil into the steep couloir on our right. As I led out and began to rig up the ropes, we contemplated the dreadful consequences of snow falling higher up on the mountain, as we headed into one of the main avalanche chutes for that southern aspect of the mountain.

Once down in the couloir the emphasis was on speed to climb the steep ice and try to secure a safe bivi site on an ice arête about 300m above, which, of course, we had only seen from Base Camp. So we climbed towards this idyllic sanctuary, swinging leads of grade 4 to 5, but darkness caught us with several pitches left above. I spied a bivi to my left, which would involve a difficult traverse to the base of an overhang. It was Rick's lead, and as I hauled the sacks, the bivi tent tore loose from the side-straps and torpedoed into the oblivion below. Rick reached the ledge and belayed. We considered descending in the dark, as the prospect of four or five more nights without a tent and perhaps no snow caves was too awful to contemplate, but we decided to postpone the decision until the morning. I seconded over to Rick, carrying my rucksack, deposited it on the ledge and then reversed the pitch, leaving my ice-tools behind, front-pointing in balance to retrieve Rick's sack, which hung from a warthog.

Just as I was shouldering Rick's sack, a peg dislodged, releasing about eight metres of slack rope, which hot-footed me down the couloir. A jolt as I came to a brief halt indicated that somewhere the situation was being controlled. Then slowly I dropped several more metres as the rope cut into the snow. Rick's voice came to me in the darkness, 'Sandy, you've got to get your weight off the rope, as my hand is caught!' I tried to layback up vertical icicles and had actually managed a rise of about one and a half metres on rounded holds, when Rick unwound himself and tied the rope off. I began to sort out my prusik loops as spindrift cascades streamed down, stars shone and the moon swung round, brightening my shady place. My Chouinard 'X' tools eventually came down to me, attached to the end of our hauling line, and Rick belayed me, as I climbed out of my freezing depression. Once safely on our open ledge, we re-established pegs in blind cracks, brewed and slept.

The morning which followed was shrouded with a band of high wind clouds. Rick's pitch brought us almost to the top of the couloir. Spindrift raged at us, as we held on to our ice-tools. Chunks of ice tore at our Goretex shells. I had no helmet, but it was Rick who seemed to get struck the most. My lead –

grade 4/5 – through a stream of spindrift and biting wind, with ice-tubes frozen useless, adhering to leather-palmed gloves, made me glad of my Scottish experience, as I came to the end of the rope. Belayed to a couple of warthogs, I took in the rope as Rick came up and front-pointed on to the frozen arête. We scampered up this for a few pitches, dug a tiny narrow, cylindrical cave and were glad to be home again. It was only then that we realized that we had omitted to discuss the loss of the bivi tent. We had moved this morning thinking only of ascending. The prospect of the next few nights filled us with exhilarating trepidation.

The night passed in very deep sleep, and the climb next day gave us super, relaxed climbing, at grade 3, occasionally creeping into grade 4. We climbed like this for two days, moving together, on perfect névé and squeaky ice, leading and following as our feelings dictated, admiring the views, down to the Khumbu ice fall, across to the Geneva Spur, the S Col, Lhotse, and Nuptse. We savoured the luxury of being.

7000m and our fifth bivouac. Early morning saw my hands frozen from untangling our remaining 8mm rope. Rick led over the cornice which held our cave, then we were given a view of the rounded summit slopes. We were amazed at being so close and walked together, the wind still blowing bitterly cold. At 10am we were on the summit, and peered from our well-enveloped faces into Tibet and down to Rongbuk, where we had been only a year ago. Our eyes moved on southwards to the pinnacles of Everest's North-East Ridge and we thought of Pete and Joe, and of Brummie and his team battling there at that very moment. We gazed upwards to the high summit of Everest, and on to Lhotse and Nuptse. We were cold and, having completed our photography, we began our descent. We descended the S ridge for a few hundred metres, then unroped and began to down-climb the W face, 60 degree hard pack, front-points penetrating the smooth worn surface. We abseiled only three rope-lengths, over small rock cliffs, and continued steadily down, devising our route as we descended. As darkness came, the vast amphitheatre took on a mysterious nature. The cool breeze ruffled our hoods, occasional ice whirred by. My lithium battery gave only a tiny flicker to my head-torch bulb, so I shadowed Rick, as we climbed downwards, side by side, together into the unknown gloom, sharing the head-torch light.

One more abseil off my last remaining ice-tube, and we stumbled through thigh-deep avalanche debris, roped together till we reached the edge of the fan. 10pm saw us crawling into our Rab bags, to become instantly comatose.

The sun took ages to shine upon us on that new morning. The Changri Shar glacier groaned as we packed our sacks and meandered down and around, through its maze of crevasses and seracs, eventually tumbling out on to the moraine. Migma Tenzing's voice penetrated my tired brain: 'Namaste!'

The Altos North-East Ridge of
Everest 1987 Expedition

DOUG SCOTT

All the obvious ridges, buttresses and faces of Everest have now been climbed, except for the North-East Ridge. There have been four attempts, all British, to climb this last big challenge on the mountain.

The first was Chris Bonington's expedition in the spring of 1982. Peter Boardman and Joe Tasker reached their high point beyond the first pinnacle at approximately 8200m. How far they got beyond this point is not known, but that is where they were last seen. It is assumed that Pete and Joe, in traversing around the next pinnacle on unstable snow, fell down the north-east side of the ridge. They had been at Base Camp (5300m) and above for a total of nine weeks prior to their final summit push. It is also possible that, having lost a great deal of muscle tissue, they succumbed to exhaustion and hypothermia.

In the spring of 1985 the Pilkington expedition led by Mal Duff attempted the ridge. After one massive snow-fall (21 May) and illness amongst the team members, the attempt was called off by the leader. However, during better weather towards the end of May, Rick Allen climbed up the ridge through all the camps to bivouac solo at 7900m. Rick then went on (27 May), up the first pinnacle, to a height of 8150m. It is highly probable that, with more support, Rick would have got further.

In the autumn of 1986 Brummie Stokes and a large team came to the North-East Ridge in the post-monsoon period for the first time. The previous two expeditions had taken the ridge from the Raphu La (6510m). In the autumn the 30-degree slopes leading up from the Raphu La seemed dangerously avalanche-prone. Brummie's team climbed directly up the North buttress, meeting the ridge at 7090m. It is now known as 'Bill's Buttress', after Bill Barker who led most of the route. Harry Taylor and Trevor Pilling reached a high point of 8000m at the bottom of the first pinnacle on 16 October. Despite a very determined effort the expedition was then abandoned, because of incessant snow-falls and hurricane-force (200km/hour) winds which made any further progress physically impossible.

Despite the efforts of some of the best climbers from Britain, well organized, climbing lightweight on the first attempt, and all-out sieging with oxygen on the second and third, the North-East Ridge remained unclimbed. Once again the long ridge-climb was proving more difficult than steep face climbing. On the South-West face of Everest, for instance, the distance from Advanced Base Camp on the glacier to the summit is about 2400m and the face is often sheltered from the winds: especially as, like many faces, it is concave, protected on the sides by the containing buttresses. On the four-mile-long

North-East Ridge, lines of communication are very extended and involve a great variety of climbing.

From whichever direction the winds blow, the climber is at risk from the chill factor and the sheer impossibility of making any progress at all when the winds reach hurricane force.

Obviously the dangers of rock-fall and avalanche are less on the ridge. This is certainly so on the crest, but often the route takes the open slopes to the side, and then there is still danger from avalanche and collapsing cornices on the ridge.

All in all, the North-East Ridge can justly be dubbed the last great problem, if not *the* problem route to Everest's summit.

The Chinese Mountaineering Association knew of Rick Allen's enthusiasm for returning to the North-East Ridge and let it be known to him that an American expedition for the autumn of 1987 was unable to raise the funds. Rick was able to get confirmation of this from the Americans, who gave up their permit to him. Rick asked Sandy Allan, who had been on Everest in 1985 and with Rick on Pumori in 1986, to join him for the autumn slot. Sandy rang me on Christmas Eve 1986, asking if I was interested in going and organizing the trip, as both he and Rick were tied up at work. I accepted with alacrity, and in the next few weeks we gathered together a team of eight. Nick Kekus who had been with Rick and Sandy in 1985 was an obvious choice. I asked Stephen Sustad, an American now living in Britain and married to a British girl, who had been with me on Shivling, Broad Peak and Makalu under very difficult circumstances.

I also asked Robert Schauer, an Austrian climber from Graz, who has climbed perhaps the most difficult route in the Himalaya, the W face of Gasherbrum 4, with Wojciech Kurtyka from Poland. Robert had climbed five 8000m summits, all but Everest in lightweight style. Sandy suggested my son Michael who had climbed with me up Chamalang's eastern and central summits, Diran, and had been up to 7300m on Nanga Parbat and 7800m on Makalu. I asked Sharavati Prabhu from Bombay to join us. She had reached 7300m with the Indian women's expedition to Everest in 1984, and had climbed on half a dozen peaks in the Indian Himalaya. She was also the first Indian mountaineer to climb in Chinese Tibet. Michael brought Eva Jansson from Sweden to be our Base Camp manageress. The brothers Mangal Sing (Nima) Tamang and Sila Tamang joined the expedition as cooks. They had been with me on all my expeditions to Nepal since 1979.

Fuel and food were generously donated or given at favourable discounts by manufacturers from all over the UK, Austria and Germany. However, after many near misses, we were still very short of funds. In fact, two weeks before our departure date in July we had given up on Everest and had decided to stay in Nepal and hopefully climb Annapurna.

At the eleventh hour Rick made contact with Archie Thomas of Altos Computers who generously and wholeheartedly gave us their financial support. Rick came out to Nepal, where the rest of us were by then, with the good news.

Most of us spent 10 days in the Langtang Mountains north of Kathmandu, acclimatizing and climbing Naya Kanga (5846m). Michael and Eva were busy moving loads along the Friendship Highway towards the

Chinese border, a task made more difficult by five landslips. All the loads had to be portered round, but vehicles had been trapped between landslips, and were thus able to carry the gear to the next one, where porters were again available to carry the gear to another van, and so on until they reached Friendship Bridge. We joined them there and had porters take all our gear up to Zhangmu (Khasa) and the waiting CMA vehicles.

After two nights spent at the town of Xegar (Shekar Dzong), we arrived at Base Camp on 4 September, three days after leaving the border. After three days acclimatizing, sorting loads and waiting for the yak men to arrive, we set off for Advanced Base Camp at the head of the East Rongphu glacier. On the 7th we stopped at 'Camp 1' at 5500m, on the 8th at 'Camp 2' at 6000m, and on the 9th we finally reached Advanced Base Camp at 6400m. The yaks returned the same day and ourselves the day after to start the second yak run on the 12th and to stock Advanced Base Camp completely by 14 September.

A strong 14-man American expedition camped nearby and was already working away at the route to the North col and the North ridge of Everest.

On 15 September Robert and Sandy started to climb 'Bill's Buttress'. On the 19th Nick Kekus and I reached the top of the rib and Pt7090, where we left two tents. The rib had been climbed by all members. It was difficult because of all the snow lying on it and the high winds which blew across from the N col, so we were glad to unearth blue rope left by the Brummie Stokes expedition, and also to connect missing portions with Chinese rope found by the American lads *en route* to the N col, which they had generously given to us. Camp 1 was thus established, but tenting was abandoned after wind destruction in favour of a huge snow-cave dug out by Nick, Robert and Rick on the 22nd.

On the 25th Rick, Sandy and I attempted the easy-angled section between our first camp and the first rock-step. We had not gone far before we retreated in snow well up our thighs that seemed in danger of avalanching off. There followed severe snow-storms which lessened as the winds became stronger. It was not until 3 October that conditions improved and Steve and Robert managed to reach the first buttress. By that time Michael had decided to return home, having had constant problems with diarrhoea and sickness. He and Eva departed.

Sharavati was also having problems with her stomach, having swallowed a sharp-edged salt plum-stone which caused her to vomit blood and pass blood in her stools. Thanks to the good medication provided by Dr Tom McCullough of the American expedition, she recovered but was left somewhat emaciated and weakened.

7 October proved a more fruitful day with carries from our first camp to the first rock-step at 7500m. Sharavati carried gas cylinders, Steve carried food and Robert filmed, as Sandy and I climbed the first rock-step fixing 180m of rope, mainly because of avalanche-prone snow. At the top of the first step Rick came through and continued solo up the second rock-step to make a cave at 7900m – a very fine effort leaving us all with a haven and marker for our future attempt at the pinnacles above. Nick later made a further carry to the bottom of the first rock-step, but by now most of the team were suffering frostbite or frostnip, most particularly Robert who had spent long periods stationary

during his filming operations. Nick was also much affected by the winds and the ensuing chill factor. He had suffered severe frostbite and amputation of his big toe when winter-climbing in the Alps a few years earlier.

On 12 October, knowing that the wind and cold would from now on only increase as winter grew nearer, six of us set off from Base Camp to make our first summit push. Steve turned back at the bottom of Bill's Buttress and Sandy 300m higher, both feeling that there was no chance. Robert and Nick with numb toes retreated from the top of the first rock buttress on 13 October. Rick and I continued in high winds to reach Rick's cave at the top of the second buttress. On 14 October we set out from the cave in extremely strong winds. We climbed two-thirds of the way up the first pinnacle to a height of 8100m, at which point Rick's middle fingers had become numb and 'wooden'. It seemed prudent to descend to the cave. In any case it seemed unlikely that we could erect our bivouac tent in the hurricane-force winds that were screaming across the ridge.

On 15 October we set out again from the cave, but stopped short of our previous high point. The winds were so strong that they lifted small rocks and blew them uphill. They had us crouched over our ice axes, braced, and even so managed to blow us about and make us dance around, trying to regain position. Vast quantities of snow were blowing off the mountain in huge streamers, thousands of feet across the Kangshung Face, and we feared that the winds could blow us off as well. It was physically impossible to make any further progress, so we descended the same day all the way to Base Camp, arriving there three hours after dark on skis from the bottom of Bill's Buttress.

We talked of making a further attempt, but on the 18th the first big storm blew in, depositing about a foot of snow along the East Rongphu glacier and moraine. On the 19th a further storm, much bigger, hit Base Camp where most of us were. There was 36 hours of actual precipitation, the winds were horrendous and snow began to drift in off the hills after the actual storm.

We awaited the arrival of Sila and Nima who had remained at the half-way camp along the East Rongphu glacier. On the 20th Sila came staggering in and dropped down on to his knees, sobbing that his brother had been killed by an avalanche. Rick, Sandy and myself rushed straight off and found the avalanche on the yak trail between our Base Camp and those of American, Japanese and Irish teams on the north side of Everest and Changtse. We dug into the snow until after dark, but could not find Nima's body. On the 21st, with help from the North ridge American team, we dug again into the avalanche. Robert, using a fibreglass tent pole taped together at the joints, located the body on his fifth probe. This was the seventh such body that Robert had located over the years in the Alps and the Himalaya. That night we sadly towed Nima's body down to Base Camp. We later carried on pulling the body to the Rongphu monastery where Nima was cremated on 24 October.

Nima was a great man. All of us who knew him knew that we gained far more from him than he ever did from us. He was a man in balance who asked for nothing, was completely self-effacing, always cheerful and hard-working under the most difficult circumstances. For me this was a great personal loss, for since 1979, when he was a young cook on Kangchenjunga, he had been cooking and managing Base Camps for us whilst we climbed such peaks as Nuptse, Makalu, Chamalang and Baruntse. At Advanced Base Camp I had offered him my foam sleeping mat, as I was going down to Base Camp for a few days. Nima had said that it would be really good to have the foam, but I would come back and need it and he would then miss it, so he would rather not bother.

He was a Buddhist through and through and, if anyone knew that the body is but a garment to put on and take off, it was he. Looking back, it seemed that he was ready to pass on, but how difficult it was for us to accept that his garment was taken off so early. He was only 30, and had been married for a year to a girl from his village in Solu Khumbu.

Nima, with Sila a few paces behind, had been walking along the snowed-up track across the hillside near Base Camp when he triggered off an avalanche. He was still on the surface of the snow as Sila was going down to him, when a second avalanche from way above came down and buried him. It seemed to us that someone else wanted Nima.

Sandy, Sharavati, Sila and myself ski'd or walked on down to the village of Chadzong to bring back yaks to transport our equipment down to wherever we could get a truck. Along with every other expedition on the mountain we had problems of transport. All the trucks and jeeps at Base Camp were snowed in for the winter and had to await the spring thaw.

Rick, Steve, Nick and Robert went back up to Advanced Base Camp to bring down the more important items. Food and the larger tents just had to be abandoned. We apologize now to future climbers and trekkers who may be put out by any rubbish that could not be located under some five feet of snow and burnt. Clearly we should have disposed of our waste each day to avoid this possibility.

Finding the road from Xegar to Kathmandu blocked by huge falls of snow for some 30km, first Sandy and then Sharavati, Sila and myself went east to Lhasa. We were able to obtain Nima's death certificate from sympathetic CMA officials. Sandy flew home via Hong Kong, and the three of us returned west to meet up with Rick and the others at the hotel in Nyalam. From there we went to Kathmandu, returning home variously on 7, 8 and 9 November.

Everest and also K2 have not been climbed for 18 months, despite attempts by many expeditions consisting of some of the world's most experienced Himalayan climbers. Himalayan weather last year and the year before has been unfavourable in the extreme. The storm that put paid to our attempts and those of all the other expeditions last autumn was said to be the biggest to have hit this part of the Himalaya in living memory. There is endless speculation as to what is happening to the weather in the Himalaya and indeed all over the world at the moment. It may just be a bad point in the cycle of long-term weather systems, or it may be to do with holes in the ozone layer or the greenhouse effect from all the pollution that is being put into the atmosphere in ever-increasing quantities. Whatever it is, climbers will no doubt remain undaunted, and indeed Everest is now booked up on the South side until 1995 and on the North until 1991.

Altos, our sponsors, were pleased with our efforts and the exposure they received. On hearing of Nima's death they immediately advanced £3000 for

Nima's young widow and sufficient funds to cover the extra costs incurred because of the big storm. We could not have hoped for better sponsors. They have kept faith with us and our style of climbing and have offered to fund another expedition should we manage to get permission in the future.

Of course we hope that we will get this chance, but, if the mountain is climbed before we do, then we all hope that it will be climbed in an as adventurous a way as possible, for at the moment it remains, this North-East Ridge, a great step into the unknown, an exciting goal for the future, a symbol of all our strivings.

We know from the results of many siege-style expeditions to Everest, such as the one up the South-West face that, if enough well-led and experienced men and women are engaged on the route, if they have enough money and material and if the weather is reasonable, then the route will be climbed. So what is the point of repeating this particular exercise, since the essence of mountaineering is all about facing up to a degree of uncertainty and risk? Of course the route can be attempted after the sieged climb in lightweight style, without the oxygen and all the logistical support and fixing of ropes that taking oxygen bottles demands, but by then all the little secrets of the route will be known. It will no longer be the step into the unknown which it is at this present time, a tantalizing prospect urging climbers up to see if they have the energy and skill to negotiate the pinnacles, and if they can keep their heads on the last mile to the summit. It is not the ethics of using oxygen which puts us off, but the fact that the weight of the bottles simply does not justify the contents and that they become an unnecessary burden, particularly on steep ground such as that around the pinnacles.

The weather is crucial to any approach to this exposed route. It is unlikely that reasonable conditions will prevail after September, so the most favourable period would be pre-monsoon, or possibly during the monsoon.

The optimum size of the team on such a long and demanding route might be between six and 10 climbers, depending on their experience of very high altitude climbing and their fitness on the day. Whatever the size, the team would need to be in sympathy with each other and be able to exercise great discipline and accept precise organization, so as to make best use of the short periods of good weather. In any case, no time should be wasted at Base Camp, as higher up steady physical deterioration will set in.

It would be a fine thing if a British party, or any other, were able to complete what Chris Bonington, Dick Renshaw, Peter Boardman and Joe Tasker attempted in 1982. It would be a fitting tribute to everything Peter and Joe stood for if the North-East Ridge were to be climbed in the bold lightweight style of the pioneers.

It may be that many years will pass before everything is favourable for a successful ascent in this way. Is it not worth the wait, for by then success will be just that, in every sense of the word?

Expedition Style – A Himalayan Perspective (1976–1986)

TREVOR BRAHAM

There were 339 climbing expeditions to the Greater Himalaya during 1986. Two out of every three were large expeditions. In China, over one-half of the expeditions went to four mountains. In Pakistan 56%, 29 parties comprising 240 climbers, visited six mountains all of which are approached via the Upper Baltoro glacier, with 10 to Broad Peak, nine to K2 and six each to Gasherbrum 1 and 2. There were 52 foreign parties climbing in India, 19 of whom visited four mountains in Garhwal and two mountains in Kashmir. Nepal continues to draw the largest numbers, with the 8000m peaks providing a magnetic attraction; five of them were visited by 25 expeditions out of a total of 96 during the spring, autumn and winter. Overall there were about 45 deaths. Falls were the leading cause, accounting for over 36%, followed by avalanches (31%) and high-altitude oedema (12.5%). On K2 alone there was a disastrous death toll of 13 climbers.

Just one decade earlier, in 1976, there were 11 expeditions each in the spring and the autumn to Nepal, with one each to Everest. There were 25 to Pakistan, with one to K2. The number of expeditions in India was under 35, with one each to Nanda Devi in the spring and autumn.

It has been a decade filled with remarkable records of every description. Apart from a four-fold increase in the number of expeditions, the rise in technical standards and the sheer scale of many achievements have been quite staggering. The changes that have been most striking have not come, however, from the growth in numbers, nor from the increasing tendency to repeat much-climbed routes on the 8000m mountains. These developments after all were not unexpected with the easing of entry restrictions in the countries concerned and with the opening up of China. What does cause concern is the rapid pace of change in values, which has brought about a steady erosion of traditional mountaineering precepts and practices, accompanied by a tendency to make doubtful or unresearched claims. This appears to be symptomatic of a new type of activity in which innovation and enterprise are subservient to competitive achievement, with personal ambition providing the main driving force. We are familiar enough with the nature of these motives in our everyday lives, and it would be almost too easy to lay the blame on the all-pervading media for their introduction into the world of Himalayan climbing. Perhaps the excellence of modern equipment and the gradual dismantling of earlier physiological and psychological barriers have pushed the base-lines so far forward as to encourage too many presumptions and to allow too much to be taken for granted.

Ethical standards as related to mountain climbing, whether Himalayan or otherwise, have almost always been a matter for contention. The basic principles have generally been only broadly defined, because of the diversity of the attracting forces. Whether readily acknowledged or not, there are three main ones: spiritual, still present though less easily identifiable today; physical, the awareness of the power and skill to achieve technical excellence; moral, the discovery of unexpected personal frontiers under exposure to extreme strain. No two mountain climbers value these three forces in anything like equal proportions. Besides, the gap between the amateur and the professional continues to widen relentlessly. The latter's scale of values and commitment are based upon the need for increasingly brinkline performances and maximum media publicity. This is acceptable within the profession, where the pressure to seek ever greater challenges is essential to the preservation of a public image.

A prominent cause of many of the misadventures that seem to have become a part of the Himalayan scene has been the headlong rush into extreme ventures without the necessary physical and mental preparation.

One of the least defensible practices in high-altitude climbing, adopted originally by Japanese climbers and now increasingly widespread, is the virtual rejection of the climbing rope. It is a form of individualism, or self-interest, that illustrates how far we have departed from mountaineering tradition. In 1934, the Sherpa Gaylay, though physically able to descend alone through the storm on Nanga Parbat, died in a high bivouac rather than abandon his exhausted leader Willy Merkl. In 1937, Frank Smythe, nearing the top of Mana peak, found his companion Peter Oliver unable to continue, and was ready to forgo the summit until he was assured of Oliver's safety. In 1939 the loss of the exhausted climber Dudley Wolfe and of his three rescuing Sherpas at a high camp on K2 cast a shadow of disgrace over the expedition. On Annapurna in 1950 it is unlikely that Herzog and Lachenal would have survived without the succour of their companions. In 1953 seven climbers abandoned their high camp and their attempt on K2 in order to save the life of the seriously ill Art Gilkey. In 1975 Peter Boardman and Pertemba waited for an hour and a half on the S summit of Everest for Mick Burke, and only began their descent when a storm placed a hazard on their own lives. Routes such as the SE ridge of Dunagiri in 1975 and the W wall of Changabang in 1976 would hardly have been feasible by an unroped pair.

It is now considered unexceptional to treat an expedition as 'successful' irrespective of the climbers who never come back. It is generally accepted that the high-altitude climber no longer expects to give or receive any support from other members of his group. He is the sole judge of whether he should be there, and the responsibility for his survival is his own.

On the 'popular' 8000m peaks, it does not seem to matter if the route climbed is different from that permitted, nor if it happens to encroach upon others who are climbing their permitted route. One such case of interference in 1986 almost ended in blows, and another resulted in a three-year climbing ban.

It seems fashionable for heterogeneous groups of climbers, treading upon each other's toes, as it were, to follow trodden paths up the same mountain; achieving 'record' times; or claiming a 'solo' ascent, as on Kangchenjunga in 1984, when without help from another party on the same route, a safe descent would probably not have been achieved.

With the proliferation of 'commercial' expeditions to the 8000m mountains quality is no longer the dominating factor in the conduct of the climbs. On the biggest mountains it is exceedingly rare to achieve an alpine-style ascent in the strictest sense. Large mountains are simply not alpine in scale, nor in the physiological demands that they impose, nor in the severity of their weather. This is not to say that alpine-style climbs are not possible, such as two outstanding ascents achieved in 1985: the W face of Gasherbrum 4 and the winter ascent of the E face of Dhaulagiri. And in 1986 the N face of Everest, which was climbed in 40 hours, mostly at night, and was described technically as 'easy'. Easy, that is, for two leading professionals at peak acclimatization. Current practice tends to overlook the need for acclimatization, in the belief that technical skill and modern equipment are factors more likely to affect the outcome. The death from high-altitude oedema of Marcel Rüedi in 1986 demonstrates that nine previous 8000m climbs are no guarantee of impunity against trying to rush a tenth.

For today's supremely experienced climbers, and for those physically and mentally acclimatized to Himalayan conditions, there are unlimited new frontiers to tread: a traverse of the NE and SW ridges of Everest and K2, the Lhotse-Nuptse traverse, a traverse of the Kangchenjunga-Yalungkang-Kangbachen ridge, the unknown E side of Nanga Parbat and the Diamir-Rakhiot traverse. There are areas in Nepal immediately around the main massifs of Dhaulagiri, Annapurna, Ganesh and Gaurisankar rich in untapped opportunities. In Garhwal the NW side of Chaukhamba has not been approached for 40 years: and there is a host of unclimbed mountains surrounding the Raktvarn, Nilambar and Mana glaciers. Further west, several unclimbed 7000m mountains are to be found in the Saser, Teram, Siachen and Apsarasas regions. There are many fine climbs waiting to be done in the NW Karakoram, on the mountains rising above the Skamri and Sarpo Laggo glaciers, and on Pumari Chish, Kanjut Sar W, Kampir Dior from the east, the Pasu group, the N side of the Batura. Since certain areas will always be more popular than others, a series of positive steps will eventually have to be taken to reduce the effects of overcrowding, starting with the construction of huts in the style of the European Alpine Clubs in areas such as the Upper Baltoro glacier, using solar energy for cooking and incinerators for waste disposal.

In their enthusiasm to encourage the flow of revenue generated by tourism, there appears to be a reluctance by some of those in authority to deal adequately with the harmful effects of the tourist boom. The failure to perceive the longer-term effects of overcrowding, especially in certain areas and on certain mountains, is a breach of fundamental principles. It does not help when an avalanche of applications continues to be received for the same routes on the same mountains during the short seasons available. Herein lies the root of the problem. The compulsive urge to climb a mountain of 8000m, and then another – and yet another . . . This is the competitive approach. It also underlines the prevalence of a blinkered view of the vastness of the Himalaya. The view that it is more desirable to join the queues up much-climbed mountains of 8000m than to seek new routes, and search out unclimbed mountains and unexplored corners.

Will the meteoric rise in today's technical achievements become the commonplace standards of tomorrow? Succeeding generations will almost certainly produce a new breed of Himalayan climber with values different from those now accepted. It might seem idealistic to expect that the competitive urge and the pursuit of records will begin to diminish. It is the human factor in the end that will dictate the choice between the persistence of today's relatively narrow perspectives and the recognition of the need for a realignment of objectives, so that the Himalayan regions might retain the essence of some of those unique qualities that originally drew us there.

On Trekking

JOHN OWEN

What is it about trekking that makes sensible, seemingly normal people undertake a long and tiresome journey to outlandish parts of the world in order to endure sleepless nights on hard camp-sites, to eat indifferent food, usually sitting on the ground, not to mention dealing with the calls of nature in some barren but overpopulated place which is totally devoid of cover? There are other hazards facing the trekker: extremes of cold and heat to be coped with; sometimes unfriendly natives who look longingly at the apparently rich possessions of the foreigner, and who might be tempted to go in for a bit of tent-slashing in the night. And what about those long days when it seems that camp will never be reached, or the river crossing late in the day when the water level has risen because of snow-melt, resulting in soaking kit and clothes?

Trekking is usually undertaken in mountainous terrain, and consequently there is the miserable business of acclimatization to be endured. Today's trekker never allows sufficient time to acclimatize properly; the result is that, for the first week or two, he or she is struggling against headache, loss of appetite, insomnia and the indignity of getting out of breath after the most moderate exertion.

My wife Pat and I have been on trek together several times and, after this catalogue of misery, it is hardly surprising that I have to give thought to how to persuade her to accompany me on another such adventure. Indeed it might be appropriate to ask if I am a little crazy even to consider going again myself. Happily there are wonderful compensations to make up for the discomforts, about which I remind her from time to time.

I started to compose this essay on the penultimate afternoon of a 14-day trek through Ladakh and Kashmir. That day we had had an exhilarating walk through some breathtaking scenery to arrive at our camp-site around mid-afternoon. Tea was produced soon after we got in and, refreshed, we unpacked our kit and relaxed each in our own way. I usually take a karrimat and find some sheltered rock against which to sit; there I may read awhile or write letters, or even try my hand at sketching, from time to time breaking off to gaze at the mountains towering high above the camp-site, with only the occasional marmot cry or birdcall to interrupt the background sound of a river. That afternoon the sky was cloudless, and although the sun had gone behind the hills it was still warm enough to sit outside even though the altitude was around 3700m. Soon it got cold and I retreated to our tent to put on my after-dark clothing – longjohns, ski-trousers, a thick shirt and an extra sweater; supper was served about seven o'clock and we huddled into the snug warmth of our cook's tent. I can't remember what we had that night – probably hot soup, something faintly curried and chillied, a dessert of tinned fruit, washed down with mugs of

fragrant Kashmiri tea. Back in our tent we played a game of cribbage and then
read for a few minutes before snuggling down in our sleeping bags for the night.

The afternoon I have described is typical of any day on trek; there is an
age-old rhythm in the trekking day – 'bed-tea', wash, breakfast, walk, arrive,
tea, relax, supper and sleep. If I didn't keep a diary we would certainly lose track
of the days, for time nearly stands still. New sights are seen each day, a different
village, different people, a bird or plant not seen before is observed, an exciting
bridge is crossed or a high pass overcome; all stimulating experiences, and yet
the traveller is free from the pressures that are part of everyday life at home. The
rhythm of the journey imparts a kind of inner tranquillity that enables one to
become attuned to the feel of the mountains and heightens the sensitivity to the
wonders of nature. The contortions of the rock formations from which the
mountains are made tell of the immensity of the forces involved in their creation
and emphasize how puny are the efforts of man, an impression made even
stronger by a glimpse of a lammergeyer floating effortlessly around a peak that
would take a man days to climb.

Trekking is made up of experiences like these, and that is why I will not
have too much difficulty in persuading my wife to try it once again.

Xixabangma 1987 – Expedition Jade Venture

LUKE HUGHES

'What's that you're reading, John?'
Our Chinese interpreter had an insatiable curiosity. John House and I were huddled in the Mess Tent with him, out of the howling Tibetan winds. The rest of the climbing party had already left Nyalam for Base Camp, 25km up the valley. We'd been left to create some order out of the chaos of Chinese officialdom and their inadequate provision of yaks.

'Oh, it's some ridiculous adventure story set in Asia.'

'Much like *Jade Venture*?'

'Sort of, only at least Wilbur Smith is believable.'

It wasn't as if the expedition was exactly a fairy-tale but, as on any comparable expedition, problems with customs and transport tried even the coolest of tempers. Brushes with officialdom defied logic and reason. John, a Lance-Corporal in the Devon & Dorsets, had been the one man who always managed to be in the middle of all the fracas, and the one man who usually managed to extract solutions.

Jade Venture was the name given to an expedition promoted by the Scientific Exploration Society and authorized by the Chinese Mountaineering Association (CMA) to climb the virgin E face of Xixabangma (8027m) and to conduct scientific research *en route*. The scientific programme, directed by Dr Henry Osmaston, had been agreed with the Chinese Academy of Sciences. The climbers were led by Lt Col Henry Day, whose official report will be found in the libraries of the Alpine Club and Royal Geographic Society; it includes chronologies and references for serious visitors to the area. Col John Blashford-Snell led the scientists and support party. The climbers included Chung Kin Man, Brian Davison, myself, Stephen Venables, Lindsay Griffin, Nigel Williams, Jonny Garratt, Duncan Francis, Robert Durran, Jerry Gore, Julian Freeman-Atwood, Mark Upton, John Vlasto, Kate Phillips, Alastair Wells, John House and Jim Kimber. Eight were soldiers and, in keeping with the expedition's early association with Operation Raleigh and its aims, the 10 youngest were aged between 18 and 23. Amongst the scientists there were two Americans, an agro-chemist from Hong Kong, and two geographers from Beijing. The combination of civilian and military climbers could have created problems even before the international element was added, but none materialized. Indeed even Venables, a dedicated anarchist, was heard to remark: 'It's great, this. Soldiers do as they're told. They don't sit round arguing about the best course of action.'

In retrospect, two overwhelming successes of the expedition were the universally happy memories which it left with us, and the outstanding performance of the youngest members, especially during the most adverse conditions. Partly because of the strong presence of youth, the trip was intended to be a conventional siege of a virgin face which, while ensuring a greater chance of success than an alpine-style ascent, would also provide the widest experience for the maximum number of individuals. There are currently so few opportunities to attempt 8000m peaks, and few climbers in Britain have had any experience of them. Henry Day's vision for the future of British Himalayan climbing played a large part in devising both concept and plans. The expedition was financed principally by ICI and Mr Eric Hotung, with contributions from the Bank of Boston, Cathay Pacific, MEF, BMC, and the Army Mountaineering Association.

Time was short. Leaving England on 8 September, we had to be back by 9 November. Such a large group posed formidable logistical problems, complicated by the threat of winter. There was little time to acclimatize, and Nigel cast a superstitious spell on us all by announcing that he had been on three previous post-monsoon Himalayan trips, each of which had been abandoned after storms in the third week of October. The budget was tight, too. A great metaphoric CMA meter starts to tick as soon as you cross into China. Every cost is multiplied. A local hotel room charged at 7 yuan costs 77Y to guests of the CMA. Clothing for yak drivers attracts fees even when no clothes are actually provided. They even tried to tell us that the mileage from Nyalam to Lhasa was greater than printed on official maps or carved into the kilometre stones, because the trucks had to go round corners. Consequently, the acclimatization was planned to take place in Nepalese Langtang, close to the part of the border we had to cross.

The trek followed a pilgrim route to the Bhairab Kund, a lake sacred to both Buddhist and Hindu pilgrims. Split into groups, some of us travelled with the scientists. In the evening we would gather in the mess tent to attend seminars orchestrated by Henry Osmaston. Donnish and distinguished behind his grey beard, he would draw out from each of us what had been observed during the day's walking. Schist, gneiss, leguminosae or mill-wheels were fair game; migmatite, hypericum and orchid pollination mechanisms became part of common small-talk; and (as a cabinet maker) I found myself discoursing on joinery techniques in Nepalese buildings. It was fascinating. During the day Henry would register a rest stop with a huge triumphant grin, clutching wads of obscure foliage, and deliver an oration on the virtues of leeches. These were never fully revealed and much energy was spent keeping the blighters at bay. John Blashford-Snell suggested the application to the socks of an ammonia compound and soap – 'an old remedy, don't you know'. Every time you walked through a puddle you frothed at the lace-holes.

On 19 September we walked into Tibet. There was still something blissfully romantic about that, for all the foiled attempts to reach Lhasa, the tragic behaviour of the Chinese, the current plethora of tourists and all the hype of China's attempts to normalize relations. The prayer flags still flutter above the barren hillsides, the yak caravans bring life to the deserted valleys, and the ruins of monasteries prompt memories of the past.

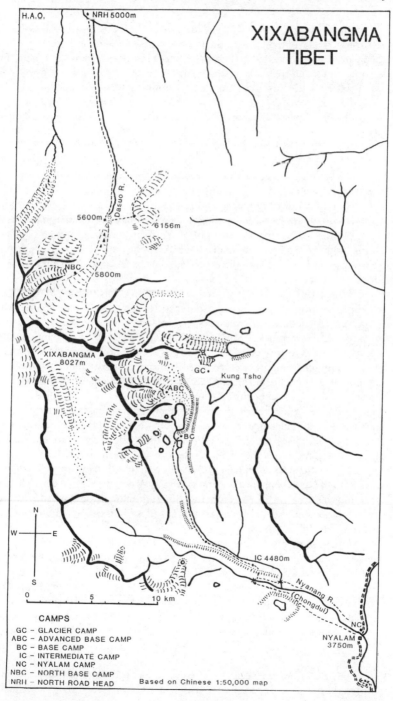

H.A.O.   NRH 5000m

XIXABANGMA
TIBET

Dasuo R.

5600m   6156m

NBC   5800m

XIXABANGMA
8027m

GC   Kung Tsho

ABC

BC

N

W   E

S

0   5   10 km

IC 4480m

Nyanang R.

(Chongdui)

NC

NYALAM
3750m

CAMPS

GC – GLACIER CAMP
ABC – ADVANCED BASE CAMP
BC – BASE CAMP
IC – INTERMEDIATE CAMP
NC – NYALAM CAMP
NBC – NORTH BASE CAMP
NRH – NORTH ROAD HEAD   Based on Chinese 1:50,000 map

184 porters helped to shift the loads over the landslips to the roadhead, 8 km inside Tibet. John Blashford-Snell stood on the steps of his hotel supervising them, and looking like that great sapper before him, Gordon of Khartoum. Two wealthy American trekkers approached.

'Hey, what's this Ikky?' they asked, pointing to an ICI logo on one of the packages.

'That's Imperial Chemical Industries – one of the largest companies in the world.'

'Uh-huh. Never heard of them, what do they make?'

'Oh, weedkiller, pesticides, fertilizer, you know the kind of thing.'

'Hey, but you got enough weedkiller for the whole of Tibet!' one exclaimed, weighing up JBS's semi-military garb.

'No, that's just expedition equipment.'

'Oh yeah . . . hey, Maisie, I heard the CIA have companies like that.'

By truck to Nyalam, where one of the advance science party had spent the evening talking to such a nice man called Reinhold something, passing through on his way back from visiting Everest. Had he climbed other mountains, asked Emma ingenuously. 'A few,' he told her.

Of the Chinese officials, our Liaison Officer was incompetent, and the interpreter was inept. Both were ill-equipped and disorganized. The failure of the CMA to provide pack animals, as arranged, caused bad feeling. That metaphorical meter ticked on. The climbers champed at the bit, and the scientists longed to get out of Nyalam to begin their investigations to the north of the mountain. Impatience seethed. Arguments arose about priorities for equipment, about who had nicked the Alpen bulk supplement, about the lack of cash; a crush on one expedition member led to sulks in other quarters. People would pick up ration boxes and move them round the camp convinced they were being useful. Heads were sore from both altitude and a Kathmandu virus. Four days later Base Camp was established, the loads began to trickle through, and no one could remember what all the fuss had been about.

The inadequacy of transport facilities remained a nagging problem, both getting up to Base Camp initially and getting down at the end. Much individual humping was necessary even before the foot of the climb was reached. This took an inevitable toll, not only on individual fitness but also on the logistics of stocking the higher camps.

Base Camp was an idyllic affair, sited above a lake in a meadow, beneath the awe-inspiring face of Nyanang Ri (7110m and unclimbed). Little stone circles where yakkers had camped in the past gave clues to centuries of use. On the sides of the moraines were those anonymous tracks that seem to appear on mountains without sight of the animals that make them. Tibetan snowcock pecked around in the morning, eagles soared above, ravens and choughs raided the BC incinerator, and marmots were pursued by JBS after dark with a night-sight. The tight geometric shape of the Phillips aerial added a hint of high technology.

The radios were excellent. The evening call became a ritual, the focal point of the day. Voice procedure was hybrid, not to say eccentric, but in its own way became quite fluent.

'Hello, Camp 1, this is Base Camp. Our noses have finally tracked down 43 fudge bars, 28 Twixes and 53 packets of Rolos . . .'

'Camp 1. Is the priority lift the food, the ropes, or for Rob to come up to acclimatize? Over.'

'Base Camp. If he left his Alpen behind he wouldn't notice the rope . . .'

Apart from logistics, the World Service was beamed across the mountain. Bombings in the Gulf, riots in Lhasa, hurricanes in the south of England were mingled with hybrid messages about Stephen's gloves, Alastair's spoon, and John House's severe attack of worms.

'Camp 2. Regards to all the family, John!'

The east side of Xixabangma presented two potential approaches. One, more direct, was heavily threatened by overhanging ice-cliffs. Had the style of the intended climb been more 'alpine' it might have been fair to attempt it. But the prospect of leaving several camps for several weeks under that threat was not attractive. The other route necessitated climbing through the southern ice-fall to a cwm between Nyanang Ri and Pungpa Ri, then up an ice headwall on to the ridge which led to the summit of Pungpa Ri (7486m), and then on, for the horrific distance of over 3½ km, all over 7000m, to the main summit. We chose the second option.

Advanced Base was established at the foot of the southern ice-fall at 5200m, thereafter known as the Ice-Fall. Stephen pioneered a route. Having joined us from the Karakoram he was thoroughly acclimatized, and he infuriated his companions by carrying huge loads faster than most, then thrusting a microphone under their noses asking how they felt (he was gathering material for a radio programme for the BBC). He then swarmed up a near-vertical 75-foot serac wall and announced that the ledge at the top would do nicely for a temporary camp. In reassuring the others he scared himself. The others slept soundly, but the serac began to creak during the night, and Stephen began an all-night vigil measuring the width of the crevasse behind it.

Camp 1 was established at 5800m and Camp 2 at the foot of the headwall (6250m). The plan was to fix the headwall, establish a third camp on the ridge (6900m) and make summit bids from there. But it was doubtful whether it was possible to cover that kind of distance without establishing a fourth camp or using oxygen. Time was so short that we would be hard-pushed to get properly acclimatized. None of us, apart from Henry Day, now laid low by pneumonia, had any experience above 6900m.

The headwall was fixed in turn by Duncan and Alastair, Brian and John Vlasto, then Stephen and me. It was finished off by Stephen and Jerry who together established Camp 3 as planned. Since yakkers had walked off with some of the ropes, we were desperately short. Only by raiding some of the rope over the fixed pitches on the ice-fall could we get enough to fix the headwall to within one metre of the ridge. We descended in turn to recuperate, leaving Nigel, Jonny, Duncan and Alastair in position at Camp 2 to make the first summit bids.

The oxygen debate continued. Stephen had decided not to use it on ethical grounds, and anyway the climbing fraternity would laugh. I had no such qualms, but each bottle was so heavy, the headwall so high, and the ridge so long that just to carry it to Camp 3 would scupper you before you even switched it on. It could only be an encumbrance. The others had no hesitation in using any means at their disposal. So the hope was that they would break the trail, using those absurd bottles, and leave a good track for Stephen and myself, oxygen-free, to sweep on through. That way we would conclude our traditional Himalayan-style assault, each according to his own ethic. The plan was set. Lindsay and John House were at Camp 1 in support, and the rest of us descended to Base Camp to recuperate.

On the night of 17 October, Base Camp evening meal was being prepared by Ajamba, our Nepalese cook. Supper was late; the stoves had been giving him trouble. With his usual ingenuity he had repaired them with spit and elastoplast. Earlier, he had made a pair of flutes out of a discarded ski-stick. The radios spluttered back to life.

'Hello, Base Camp, this is Camp 1. It's doing some serious snowing up here.'

'Camp 2. That's nothing. It's been chucking it down for three hours up here.'

'Camp 1. Low on rations too. We've got *I Claudius* and *Claudius the God*. I'm afraid Lindsay's going to eat them if we don't get out.'

'Camp 2. Hey, there's a two-foot boulder here about four foot from the tent. It wasn't there a minute ago.'

'Camp 1. Lindsay speaking – don't make a fuss. Everyone will want one.'

Thus began our experience of the worst storm in recent Himalayan history. By the morning of the 20th, when the sun eventually shone again, Camp 2 was completely buried. The climbers had dug out their tents three times with ice-axes before they finally abandoned the site, the food, and the oxygen bottles. Camp 1 was annihilated too. Advanced Base Camp was just saved by John House and Jim Kimber who watched their tent become a snow-cave as it was buried in three and a half metres of snow. Even at Base Camp, where there was a queue for every shovel, a metre and a half of snow destroyed many of the tents and buried the camp. All over the Himalaya climbers abandoned expeditions and tried to struggle out of the mountains. On the road to Lhasa, a coach-load of Westerners expelled from the city after the riots was trapped on one of the passes; one of the passengers had a wooden leg. For us the implications were serious. Apart from the loss of equipment, the abandonment of the camps meant that any further attempt was going to have to supply itself, and, worse, break its own trail all the way back to Camp 3. There were effectively nine climbing days left, if we stuck to our original timetable.

'Humph,' said Stephen, fortified by a shot of Henry's secret supply of Famous Grouse, 'I suppose it's to be alpine-style after all.'

The next morning we set off to reopen the trail. The full impact of the storm was really apparent, looking at John and Jim trying to dig out their tent at Advanced Base Camp. In the ice-fall, the fresh ascent to Camp 1 took seven hours (normal time three and a half). Every crevasse was wider, every snow-bridge smaller. It was all rather spectacular. The ascent to the new Camp 2 took four hours (normally one and a half). On the fourth day we climbed the headwall in seven hours and snuggled into the snow-cave, which was mercifully unaffected. We slit the abused copy of Robert Graves down the spine with a knife. I got 'God'. Stephen got 'I'.

On the fifth morning we moved together on to the ridge across steep ice and rock, coming out on to a sharp arête that led through various deceptively receding peaks. Concern about thin black clouds across the Nepalese horizon made us wonder about future storms. We came across a solitary rock on the ridge that was ideal for a camp and about 150m below the summit of Pungpa Ri. Resolving to get at least one summit in the bag for ourselves and our sponsors before any potential storm, we dumped the gear and trudged up the snowy ramp to the top. Alex MacIntyre, after the only previous ascent, aptly described it as an 'uncertain affair', but it offered a superb view of the remaining 2½ km to Xixabangma. Time was getting tighter, and the lack of supporting camps left us with very little food. We aimed to get away early the next morning, bypass Pungpa Ri by traversing the SW flank to the col, and get to the main summit and some of the way back in a day. That way we could risk leaving our sleeping bags and superfluous gear. It took three hours to the col, and then again it was up and down over a knife-like ridge. At one point Stephen actually sat *à cheval* and slid part of the way. Unbeknown to us, a party of four had gathered on the edge of the glacier below Advanced Base and were watching us through binoculars. To them it seemed that we had little further to go. This was reported back to Base Camp, and then to Nyalam, by telex to Beijing and back to London via Reuters for the next morning's papers before Stephen and I had got out of our snowhole – the real cause of our disappearance. Just below a rocky knoll at about 7650m, when it was clear that we were not going to make it that day, we dug in. If the weather held we would make the summit in a couple of hours the next morning. With that happy thought in our minds we settled into the armpit routine, used for fingers and toes when you haven't enough gear at high altitude.

'This is a bit like a game young lovers play: up a bit, left a bit, oooh! that's nice . . . hee! hee! . . . stop there, it tickles.'

The temperature dropped to 35C, but still morale was high when we emerged on the seventh morning, only to be hit by howling winds and spindrift driven through every weak point of our clothing. Stephen battled up the first 50m. When I caught him up I said: 'There's no way we can do 300m of this. It's desperate.'

'Well, I expected it to be cold.'

'There's cold and there's lunacy. It has to mean another night out, and we've got no food or back-up, and there's no knowing if it will go on for days like this.'

'I could go on myself . . . Good Lord, your nose is frostbitten. Quick! Back to the cave.'

With honour satisfied it was a joy to get out of the wind, now gusting at 60 miles an hour. In fact the nose was fine, but the spindrift had got around my glove inners. Hermann Buhl heroics aside, there was only one course to follow. We began our reluctant descent. We had been so close against all the odds, and yet so vulnerable when the winds really began to blow. Dragging ourselves back along the ridge and round the traverse seemed to take ages. We craved sugar. When we did get back I was aware that I had no feeling in the fingers which held my ice-axe. I banged them against the side of a saucepan in amused despair. The message of that ominous metallic ring was clear. Either by conduction, or by the restriction of the circulation, the axe had contributed to frostbite. As the fingers thawed the pain set in. I retired to my bag with a big dose of Temgesic and let Steve look after the hot chocolate. The radio crackled.

'Camp 3, this is ABC. Any news?'

'Camp 3. No news, Henry. But we're moving out tomorrow to look for them.'

It wasn't just us. The radio batteries were flat too. We could hear the other stations but could not transmit. No one had heard from us for three days. Their anxiety was matched by our frustration in being unable to reassure.

Life was more bearable after the sun was up the following morning. Soon after we had begun to move down, we met the rescue party, Nigel and John Vlasto, coming up. Relieved to find us still going under our own steam, they went on to climb Pungpa Ri themselves. Lacing boots had been bad enough, but pushing a frozen rope through a descendeur with frostbitten fingers was a little trying. That night we were all safe at Camp 2, not a breath of wind or cloud in the sky. With the camps now back in place there was not much to stop a second attempt. But officialdom had other ideas. Through the LO we were informed that the CMA had deemed that in the aftermath of the great storm (and, unstated, the riots in Lhasa) all Western expeditions were to be terminated, and their participants were to leave forthwith. Those 25km back to Nyalam in what was now thigh-deep snow took its toll, but eventually the whole expedition regrouped before dispersing – some to Nepal, others to Beijing.

By the time we reached Lhasa, my fingers were looking like bruised Norfolk sausages, and felt as though someone had hit each one with a hammer – the pain of the initial impact had died, but oh! how they throbbed.

'You must go and see Charlie Clarke as soon as you get back.' I was assured he knew more about these things than most. On return to London I rang the good doctor. He was in Tokyo, back on Sunday. His wife said: 'Yes, you must see him. And don't for goodness sake show them to anyone else; they'll cut them off. Come and have a drink on Monday.'

I turned up on the doorstep and rang the bell. Charlie answered the door, wearing a butcher's apron and wielding a carving knife.

'Jesus, it's not that bad, is it?'

'Oh, no. Sorry, I was just doing the cooking.'

Sun, Snow and Science on Xixabangma

HENRY OSMASTON

While Luke and Stephen were dawdling along their 7000m ridge and admiring the view, there were other members of the expedition who were doing a real job of work: I refer of course to the scientists.

After protracted negotiations with the Chinese Academy of Sciences and the CMA we had agreed on a programme of research on both the present glaciers and the valleys below them, where they once extended far below their present limits. Since one of my main intentions was to give Himalayan experience to young people, the core of the science group consisted of Brian Davison, a glaciologist and high-grade climber, and three of my newly-graduated geography students, Claire Roberts, Marion Evans and Jonathan Cook, all three experienced walkers and campers but not mountaineers. Besides these we had Liu Jie and Liu Changhe (generally known as Liu Two) from the Institute of Geography in Beijing, and Ivan Hui from our sponsors, ICI China, based in Hong Kong. For most of the time we worked closely with the support group consisting of John Blashford-Snell, John Davies, our doctor, and a bevy of beautiful but tough and hardworking young ladies.

Our initial acclimatization trek in Nepal up the ridges on the E side of the Balephi Khola was a painful but invaluable prelude to the generally much easier walking in Tibet. The monsoon had not yet ended, and leeches waged guerilla warfare as we toiled up emerald staircases of rice terraces to the knife-edged forest ridges. At dawn we had glimpses of Dorje Lakpa and other peaks at the head of our valley, with slender waterfalls and bank-full rivers far below us. Incision by the rivers has been so powerful and fast that most traces of former glaciers have been destroyed, but we passed one stretch of huge gneiss boulders on a ridgetop at about 2000m which must have been an old moraine, as the local rocks were all schists and phyllites. Our highest camp was by Bhairab Kund at 4400m, a little lake where local Buddhists and Hindus hold an autumn fair. All that remained were prayer-flags fluttering forlornly by the misty shore. It is one of a string of tarns and cwms near the ridge-crest which mark the positions of former little corrie glaciers and of the contemporary snowline, now 1000m higher.

We dropped 3000m to the road again and washed ourselves free of mud and blood in the hot springs of Tatopani. 180 porters took our baggage across Friendship Bridge into Tibet and up the steep hillside to beyond Zhangmu, as landslips have wiped out large sections of the road where it zigzags up a huge unstable talus slope. Our roadhead camp was 30km further up the gorge, by the river at Nyalam, where we sorted baggage and helped the climbers on their way to establish a Base Camp on the E side of the mountain.

We and the support group then went by lorry to the north of the mountain. At the Lalung Ley Pass (5050m) we stopped to admire the view. Southwards stood the ramparts of the main Himalaya, from Everest to Xixabangma. Northwards stretched the immense plains and brown rolling hills of the Tibetan plateau. Beneath our feet lay thick beds of rounded boulders and gravels, once thought to be moraines but now recognized as having been deposited by rivers in intermontane valleys, at the same time as the Siwalik beds were being deposited on the S side of the Himalaya. These beds contain fossil animals and cedar pollen which show that the range was then much lower; in a roadside cutting we found a fossil rib, probably *Hipparion*, a genus of three-toed horses which was widespread in Asia, Europe and North America, 3–10 million years ago.

We camped by Pei Ku Tsho (4580m), a slightly brackish lake, into which drain some of the sparse waters of N Xixabangma. The weather was glorious, with a warm sun blazing from a cloudless sky; we basked on the shore and Jonathan and I even had a quick swim in the sparkling blue water. A flight of former beachlines rises behind the present shore to a height of 100m, showing how much deeper and bigger the lake was in the past. It is not clear how much of this change has been due to tilting of the land, downcutting of the overflow channel or climatic changes, but the old lake sediments lap against the oldest moraines so presumably postdate them.

My three students and I then made a quick foray up the valley which leads to the long-established N Base Camp site. We hired four yaks and two delightful yak-men who had a much bigger and better tent than we had, and a splendid yak-dung brazier which gave out a tremendous heat. We soon decided to cook and eat with them. A long walk brought us to a good campsite at 5600m near the end of the Dasuo (*tag.so*) Glacier. Like other glaciers on this side of the Himalaya and a few in the Karakoram, this has a spectacular array of ice-towers along the lower four kilometres of its tongue, some of them 50m high. These features have nothing to do with the seracs of an ice-fall and indeed only develop on glaciers with a moderate slope, in a high, dry, sunny climate. They are related to *nieves penitentes*, columns of snow a metre or so high which are found on some tropical glaciers in Africa and the Andes. Though little work has been done on them, they both appear to be due to differing responses of clean ice or snow to a high intensity of incoming radiation in different situations. Any initial chance projection from the surface is surrounded by dry air, so the energy it absorbs can be dissipated by sublimation (direct conversion of ice to water-vapour) which only consumes 1/620 gram of ice per calorie. In any chance hollow, however, the absorption of radiation is increased by repeated reflections and the air is stiller and moister, so melting occurs rather than sublimation. This consumes 1/80 gram of ice per calorie, that is, eight times as much. Thus, although the whole surface is being lowered, the hollows are deepened much faster than the crests, and the relative relief increases.

Moraines of different ages lie on either side of and down-valley from the terminus, evidence of a quite recent small retreat, besides older greater extensions. 500m above the valley on both sides lie high banks of moraine-like material, previously interpreted by Chinese geologists as a moraine older than any others recorded elsewhere in Tibet. I think, however, that they may be huge accumulations of frost-shattered rock, such as form aprons to the lower slopes of most of the mountains and hills in this area. On these banks lie thin plateau glaciers, nearly stationary and probably cold-based, quite different from the active valley glaciers. We climbed up to the one on the E side of the valley, a gently rounded summit at 6176m. Though no technical difficulties were involved, we were quite pleased, as few people reach 6000m on their first mountain, and we knew that the climbing group were still slogging away well below this altitude on the east.

It was a glorious sunny day with superb views in all directions: the main peaks still high above us and the apparently infinite Tibetan plateau stretched out below. However, there was a tearing, biting wind, so the other three did not linger but made off into the valley where we had arranged to meet our yak half-a-day's walk further down. I wandered at a more leisurely pace along the crest, noticing some tracks in the snow which I thought were probably *bharal* (Blue Sheep). Presently, however, I saw a line of tracks which looked quite different, and much more like those left by a large biped. Each print was about 25cm long, and 15cm wide at one end but narrower at the other, with a step of 45cm. The snow was hard and they were only a couple of centimetres or so deep and apparently not greatly affected by sun-melt. I have an open but somewhat sceptical mind about yeti and, at the time, I assumed that the prints were those of a bear which was carefully putting its hindfeet in exactly the same places as its forefeet; many animals of course do this at certain gaits. However, I was sufficiently intrigued to photograph them and I do not now think that they closely resemble bear prints. For one thing they are only very slightly set off alternately from a straight line. Professor Michael Day, who is an authority on fossil human footprints, sees no reason why they could not have been made by a manlike biped but, being a sceptic, he prefers to attribute them to snow leopard or some other known animal. Miss Hills of the British Museum's Mammal Department is similarly sceptical. Thus my photos contribute little towards solving the yeti controversy, though they do, I think, represent the highest level (c6000m) at which 'yeti-type' tracks have been recorded, or for that matter those of any large animal.

We met the others and returned to Nyalam. Despite yak problems the climbers and their baggage were now nearly all at Base Camp or higher, whither we followed them. The whole valley is lined with huge moraine ridges which extend several kilometres below Nyalam to about 3500m. Brian had been with the climbers while we were round to the north, and was busy taking snow samples from high on the glacier up which they were climbing. These were for chemical analysis in England for traces of contaminants of natural (e.g. salt) or human (e.g. Chernobyl) origin, which are deposited even in these remote places; not enough to cause harm but enough to provide useful information for modelling the atmospheric circulation. Originally we had intended to do all our glaciological work there with substantial help from the climbers, but the dangerous access down an unstable moraine, the moraine cover on the tongue, the difficult ice-fall above, and the preoccupation of the climbers with climbing, all dictated another choice. We planned to measure the rate of flow of the glacier using stakes surveyed by theodolite, and to measure the temperature profiles in the top 20m of ice at various altitudes. For the latter we had a steam boiler, specially made for us by British Aerospace in Bristol, with a lance with which we hoped to melt a hole down which we could lower a string of thermistors. These would be allowed to freeze in and after a few days the temperature would restabilize.

Brian had reconnoitred a small and suitable alternative glacier, so we established a high camp just below it and dumped our heavy equipment up on the glacier. Now came the blizzard which was to plaster most of the Himalaya with more snow than in living memory. I was lying happily in my tent looking forward to a day spent reading *Brighton Rock* when Brian persuaded us that we should go down rather than idly consume our limited stock of food: 'No need to take any food; we'll be in Base Camp by lunchtime.' We ploughed down through deepening snow and poor visibility. Lunchtime came and went. Brian broke the trail, swearing each time he stumbled thigh-deep over some buried boulder. Jonathan and I dumped some of our loads in a dustbin bag on a boulder. Claire, only a lightweight, somehow carried on with a rucksack almost as big as herself. By dusk we were crossing a steep moraine ridge and I decided that it was time to bivouac. We dug a small ledge in the snow, partly sheltered by a big boulder, and settled down for the night. At midnight the sky cleared, and we found that we had in fact just passed the trail to Base Camp and were looking out over a part-frozen lake at the steep face of Nyanang Ri, soaring black and forbidding in the starlight. The wind, however, freshened, and the drifting snow continually threatened to bury us as we huddled together in our bags. Orion crept at a snail's pace up the eastern sky, but eventually the sun struck the top of Nyanang Ri, a memorable dawn to my 65th birthday.

We rose stiffly and repacked. Following the crests of the ridges which had been swept nearly bare of snow, we slowly made for Base Camp, and were soon cheered by the sight of Brian's fresh footprints. The previous evening, stronger and more lightly equipped than us, he had decided to press on to try to reach Base Camp and avoid a bivouac. The lake-shore was an unwelcome surprise to him, and after scrambling back up the moraine he had to hole-up between two boulders, whence he had to burrow out through several feet of snow next morning. Reaching Base Camp he sent out a rescue party to look for us, expressing doubts about our survival. They met us with a welcome flask of coffee, but then pressed on to find a group of climbers similarly benighted on their way down from Advanced Base Camp.

Those at Base Camp had spent most of the previous 24 hours digging to prevent their tents being buried and crushed, so for a few days we relaxed in the sun while the snow settled; nursed frosted toes or fingers; planned a further attempt on the summit; and debated the problems of getting ourselves and our baggage out without help from yak which could not get through the snow. JBS and Jonathan used packing cases to make sledges which went splendidly on the well-trodden paths round camp but were quite impossible off the piste.

Brian and I, with generous help from Lindsay Griffin, decided to return to our glacier. The other two each had a pair of the expedition's limited supply of snowshoes, and they dashed ahead. I slowly floundered along behind and decided to bivouac part-way at a prominent rocky bluff on the shore of Kung Tsho. There were several small caves in it and we optimistically called it Snow Leopard Rock, although the only evidence we ever found were some droppings that were clearly from a large cat and in which Miss Hills later found marmot hairs. This was a superb bivouac site on a ledge only a few feet above the clear blue lake, reflecting the snow-covered mountains.

Next day I rejoined the others who had spent the entire day trying fruitlessly to find the boiler and other gear, now completely buried beneath a smooth snow surface. We tried again the following day. Luckily we had previously surveyed the positions of two nearby stakes from a fixed rock that was still exposed. We resurveyed and dug for these in their recorded positions and eventually found them, about two metres down-glacier because of flow in the meantime. Then we probed around and soon found our boiler. Its design had been taken from one already well-tried in Canada, and we had tested ours both in the cold chamber at British Aerospace and at Base Camp. However, we found that we could not raise a sufficient head of steam to drill, even using a petrol cooking-stove to supplement the gas burner. This seemed to be due to the combination of low oxygen pressure and a tearing cold wind. Sadly we packed up and returned to Base Camp.

A final attempt on the summit by Luke and Stephen had meanwhile been driven back, and two groups had already left Base Camp for Nyalam. The first, including all the Chinese, had a hard time breaking the trail, and took three days over what could be done in one before the snow. We all followed in dribs and drabs, feeling rather like Napoleon's retreat from Moscow. At Nyalam we reorganized, faced with new landslides blocking the road to Nepal and snowdrifts blocking that to Lhasa, but by walking or by waiting patiently we finally all got out in one direction or the other. I ended up in Beijing where I had protracted and frustrating negotiations with some of the scientific authorities.

Apart from the glaciological work, we carried out various other scientific studies. Claire made a plant collection, to be divided between Kew and the Chinese Institute of Botany; Marion (who also did some filming) and Liu Two did ecological work and collected soil and water samples; and Jonathan studied the geology. The climbers had at one time planned to ferry all their stores across the lake above Base Camp, to avoid the laborious and dangerous traverse of the glacier tongue. Once there it was clear that this naval exercise would be even more hazardous, not least because the lake was partially ice-covered. However, the inflatable boat had another potential use for sounding and measuring the turbidity of the other numerous lakes near Base Camp, most of which were warmer and unfrozen as no glacier calved into them. The Support Group launched it on the Kung Tsho and took several photos and one observation. Faced with a stiffening breeze, they prudently adjourned till the morrow. That night the blizzard broke, and so far as is known the boat still rests under a blanket of snow on the lake-shore; resting too on its laurels in the *Guinness Book of Records* where John Two now holds the altitude record for rowing (4580m). We all, especially JBS who occasionally lay out at night with a 'sniperscope', took an interest in the wildlife. Blue Sheep were the commonest large animal and were often seen near Base Camp. Wolves, Tibetan antelope and wild ass (*kiang*) were rarely seen. In the India Office Library there is a beautiful old pictorial map (the 'Wise Map') of this area drawn in about 1850 showing abundant *kiang* on the plateau north of Xixabangma. There were surprisingly few colonies of marmots, possibly because of a reported campaign against them by the Chinese on the grounds of the damage done by them to the grazing. Pika (like guinea-pigs) were very abundant; after the snow, scores could be seen sitting out on the sides of the road, scampering for their holes as one drove by, or as large hawks skimmed a foot or two above the ground in close pursuit.

We owe thanks to many people and organizations for their help. Besides those mentioned by Luke Hughes, the scientists owe special thanks to British Aerospace, Avon Boats, Bristol University and the Chinese Academy of Sciences.

NOTE

The Chinese have produced a beautiful map of Xixabangma at a scale of 1:50,000 and contoured at 20m vertical intervals. It has evidently been done from air photos with close ground control, and I found it very accurate. The only errors were in the interpretation of some small lakes, probably covered with ice and snow in winter.

Amne Machin: A Closer Look

JOHN TOWN

Northern Tibet is one of the last areas on the planet still to be properly explored by the mountaineer. It holds 7000m peaks which have yet to be reached, let alone properly surveyed or climbed. By contrast, Amne Machin was known to the West in Victorian times. The reasons for its early notoriety were threefold. Firstly it is a holy mountain, the home of a God: Ma-chen, an earth lord, controls the lightning, hail and merciless elements of nature. Until the communist takeover thousands of pilgrims made the circuit of the range each year. Secondly, it is not, by Tibetan standards, a remote mountain. It lies at the NE extremity of the Tibetan Plateau, in a bend of the Yellow River, less than 300km from China. Finally, and perhaps most importantly, it is the home of the Goloks.

Until finally suppressed by the Chinese in the '6os, the Goloks were the most feared tribesmen in Tibet. They paid allegiance neither to Lhasa nor to Peking, robbing and killing with a fine lack of discrimination as to their victims. The only sins in the Golok book were cowardice on the field of battle, submission to outside authority and disloyalty to the clan. 'Golok' in Tibetan is said to mean 'head backward' or 'rebel'. The Goloks ensured that no one got near enough to Amne Machin to verify any of the strange claims which surfaced as western explorers started to nibble at the edges of their homeland.

In 1922 General George Pereira saw Amne Machin from a distance of 160km and was impressed enough to think that it might prove higher than Everest.[1] He passed this information to Joseph Rock, a prolific explorer of W China, who, in 1926, made a brave sortie towards the mountain from the Yellow River, despite death threats personally delivered by the Chief of the Butshang Goloks. From a distance of 80km he could make out the individual peaks: 'I shouted for joy as I beheld the majestic peaks of one of the grandest mountain ranges of all Asia. . . . I came to the conclusion that the Amnyi Machen towers more than 28,000 feet.'[2] By 1956, having seen the glories of Minya Konka and Everest, he had had second thoughts and 'could not help but come to the conclusion that the Am-nye Ma-Chhen is not much more than 21,000 feet'. Rather too late a vision of the truth to get in the way of a good story.[3]

In all the fuss about height, everybody overlooked Rock's clear and accurate description of the main peaks:

> '. . . the Am-nye Ma-Chhen Range has three prominent peaks; the southern pyramid (second highest) is called Spyan-ras-gzigs (Chenrezig), the Avalokitesvara, of which the Dalai Lama is believed to be an incarnation; the central lower peak, a smaller pyramid, Am-nye Ma-Chhen; and the northern, which is the

highest, a huge, round, broad dome called dGra-hdul-rlung-shog
(Dra-dul-lung-shog) "Victor of enemies wind wing". R A Stein
thinks that . . . wind wing is the name of a horse . . . The dome in
the north is the highest part, but is not so imposing as the large
pyramid at the southern end.'

There is more information for the climber in that paragraph than in any
book yet published.

The story of a peak higher than Everest was strengthened during the
Second World War, when American pilots, flying at 29,000ft 'over the hump'
between India and China, reported seeing a peak higher than themselves. In
1949 Leonard Clark, an American Intelligence Officer, penetrated the Golok
heartland with a large armed party sponsored by the warlord Ma Pu Fang. As
the result of a rough survey he calculated the height of Amne Machi to be
29,661ft. It is difficult to know when fact ends and fiction begins in his highly
readable account.[4] In 1960 the Chinese reported that they had climbed Amne
Machin and that a survey had revealed it to be 7160m (23,491ft).[5] The legend
of Amne Machin had finally been laid to rest . . . or had it?

In 1980 the Chinese opened a number of peaks in Tibet to foreign
climbers for the first time. Among these was Amne Machin, and it was revealed
that a new survey had found, as observed by Rock in 1926, that the highest
point was the northern peak (Amne Machin I), and not the southern peak
(Amne Machin II) climbed by the Peking Geological Institute in 1960.[6] The bad
news was that the height of the mountain had dropped to 6282m (20,610ft).
Mike Banks, who in 1980 was the first foreign climber to see the peaks close-up,
provided much-needed independent confirmation.[7]

From then onwards things happened very fast. In 1981 the Joetsu
Mountaineering Association were the first of three teams to attempt the first
ascent. They chose the Harlon II Glacier as their line of attack and, after having
been avalanched from below the low col at the head of the glacier, they laid over
300m of fixed rope up one of the grotty gullies leading to the crest of the spur
separating the N and S bays. They continued up a steep hanging snow arête to
the easier final slopes of Pt 5977. On 22 May, Watanabe, Yamamoto and
Miyake set off from Camp 2 at 5700m and reached the highest point of Amne
Machin I after a long climb up to and along the main ridge. The summit of
Amne Machin I itself was found to be an extensive flat snowfield.[8]

On 2 June an Austro–German team under the leadership of Sigi
Hupfauer arrived at Base Camp and started on the Japanese route, but was held
up by bad weather. Meanwhile a very fit Galen Rowell, Harold Knutson and
Kim Schmitz arrived and, with very little time available, took a much more
direct route up the sharp E ridge of the NE summit (6154m). The Americans
reached the summit on 9 June after three days of climbing, to be followed the
next day by Hupfauer, Gaschbauer, Lammerhofer, Schmatz and Vogler.[9,10,11]
Rowell implies in his accounts that the Japanese did not reach the highest point,
quoting in particular the lack of prints or other evidence on the summit.
However, the Japanese and German accounts leave no doubt that they did
succeed.

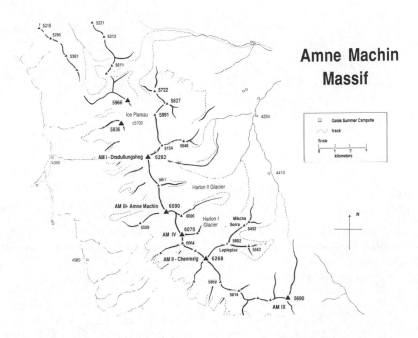

Kim Schmitz returned on 12 June to take two of his Mountain Travel party, the Canadians Judy Norman and Skip Merler, to the summit. August saw a further ascent by a Japanese party led by Yakoto Torokawa. In four months the mountain had seen four ascents by two new routes, but a further significant addition was made in September by the Australians Bartram, Macartney-Snape, Henderson, and Hall, later to be involved in a spectacularly fast ascent of Everest's N face. They climbed the impressive 1100m NE face of Amne Machin I and descended by the unclimbed 6km long NE ridge, making the first ascents of three subpeaks.[12]

Calm now descended on Amne Machin I, though a Sino-Japanese team survived being avalanched to make the second ascent of Amne Machin II (6268m) in September 1984, getting a reported 28 climbers to the summit.[13] Nobody appears to have tried Amne Machin I between 1981 and 1985 when a Canadian group of eight made ascents of Amne Machin I and IV (6070m, first ascent) in April and May. The Chinese told us that they climbed icefalls of the N bay of the Harlon II Glacier direct to the summit. An Italian team under the leadership of Arturo Bergamaschi climbed what was probably the American route in July. In 1986 an American party reached 5800m on what was also probably the American route, though, intriguingly, the Chinese told us that they tried a new route along the long curving E ridge of the main summit, which runs over Pt 5342 to abut the SE face at about half height.[14,15,16]

Amne Machin I is still something of a mystery mountain to those climbing it, and an accurately surveyed map, though it exists, is not normally available to visiting climbers. The accompanying plan should help to dispel some of the confusion. Amne Machin I sends four separate spurs eastwards from its N–S ridgeline. Thus the ridge running E from Pt 6154, the NE summit (the American route climbed by Rowell's party), has variously been described as the E, the NE and the NNE ridge. The least confusing convention seems to be to call this the E ridge of the NE summit, and the long continuation of the main ridgeline, over Pts 5991 and 5827, the NE ridge.

At the beginning of 1988, Amne Machin I, II, IV and IX have been climbed. Amne Machin III, the peak actually named after the God, remains unclimbed. The exact peaks constituting Amne Machin V to VIII remain unclear, but no one appears to have climbed on the great snow plateau or the northern part of the main ridge beyond Pts 5991 and 5827, nor on any of the peaks between Amne Machin II and IX at the southern end of the massif.

The range seemed ripe for a British visit in 1987, despite our being six years behind everybody else. After the initial surge in 1981–82 expeditions to China from this country had dried up, Everest excluded. Cost was obviously a major factor and, on the basis of initial advice, it looked as if we might be in for a tough time. In fact a number of pleasant surprises were in store, for myself and my companions Martin Hampar and Mike and Cathy Pettipher. The pound is now worth 180% of what it was in yuan terms in 1982, and the rates in Chinghai are somewhat more reasonable than in Tibet. Add to that the relative accessibility of Amne Machin (two days drive, one day walk-in) and the fact that transport is probably the most expensive element of any CMA bill, and a trip to this area is probably less expensive than to many parts of the Karakoram.

Nevertheless, we were both relieved and grateful when the Wogen Group, metals and mineral traders with a special interest in China, agreed to provide a major part of the funds required, plus the resources of their Beijing office. The latter came mainly in the guise of Ben Williams, their Beijing representative, whose caving experience seemed to qualify him at least as well as any of us for what was to come, and who was therefore quickly incorporated into the team. Ben's command of Chinese and long experience of Chinese ways ensured a trouble-free progression to Base Camp, though I sometimes missed the cut-and-thrust of East meeting West.

Lying at the NE extremity of the Tibetan Plateau, Amne Machin is most easily reached via plane to Lanzhou and steam train on to Xining. Here we were met by our friendly and efficient hosts, the Chinghai Mountaineering Association, and introduced to our Liaison Officer, Mr Gao, and the drivers of our two 4WD landcruisers, Messrs Sun and Li.

As we ventured out towards the mountains, it became apparent that the problematic inaccessibility of Amne Machin has had its back broken for ever by the Chinese. Good roads lead to within a day's walk of the heart of the massif. The journey is still an impressive one. The pagodas of the Sun-Moon Pass, the historical border between Tibet and China, lead you up on to the plateau and on through the large town of Gonghe to a great plain 80km across, with sparse pasture, sand dunes and the odd camel. Another pass leads into bandit country – rough, tough highlands with the isolated ruins of fortified compounds still beleaguered amidst a sea of black tents. Fort Ta Ho Pa, refuge to Clark and many others, seemed to have met a similar fate. By evening we had climbed to Wen Chuan where, at 4300m, the height gain for the day rose to 1800m. Without the benefit of Ben and Martin's Diamox, Mick and Cathy spent a rough night. The second day took us on to the Hua Xi Shia, with its improbable juxtaposition of satellite dish and prayer flags, and off on to the Szechuan road.

Snaking over a green rise, Amne Machin's virgin western flank came suddenly into view. As we rolled to a halt, one of the mountain's guardians strode forward and the aggressive arrogance of our first Golok was unmistakable. Mick lined up his camera only to see our friend stick out his tongue and swiftly pull a knife. The speed of Mick's withdrawal was matched only by his subject's amusement at the effect of this little joke.

Then it was turn left again, over the 4760m Majixue Pass towards Da Wu and the heart of the Golok Autonomous Region – chilly, even at the start of September. Then left yet again, on a road unmarked on the maps, which runs over into the headwaters of the stream draining the southern flank of the range, and then down a picturesque gorge to Snow Mountain Commune. Round one corner we surprised two pilgrims, boards strapped to their knees and hands, prostrating themselves full-length on the ground. In several months, body-length by body-length, they would accomplish their circuit of the mountain.

Snow Mountain Commune (Shie Shan Shang) is a surprisingly squalid community where the novelty of visiting foreigners has obviously worn off. It was nice to be off the next morning with our nine horses and two Golok drivers. The latter stayed strictly on horseback, while we and the Chinese played mule men. We followed the pilgrim route NW up the river draining the NE flank of the mountain, eventually crossing it on horseback. Where the pilgrims branched off towards the north, we continued with the main river valley as it gradually bent round to the south and the glaciers of Amne Machin I became intimidatingly visible. After 24km and 600m of ascent, there was only some perilous boulder-hopping over a side stream dropping from the NE face before we were home and dry, in a grassy hollow about a mile below the snout of the Harlon Glaciers at 4300m.

Our initial objective was the Japanese route on Amne Machin I and on 8 September we set up camp at 4800m at the top end of the N moraine of the Harlon II Glacier. We were to spend eight days at this beautiful site, reached by a delightful walk up the moraine valley which was marred only by rubbish left by the Japanese in 1981. Mick and Cathy were still suffering badly from the altitude and remained at Base Camp, where there was some compensation in the flowers and the sight of a wildcat.

The Chinese had recommended the right-hand bay of the Harlon Glacier, which they said had been climbed by the Canadians in 1986. This consisted of a series of three icefalls. It took Martin and me five exhausting hours to get through the first of these and to ascertain that it merged straight into the second. Rather than continue to bang our heads against this particular series of brick walls, we moved to the left-hand bay and the Japanese route. On a day when strong gusts were occasionally inverting our North Star dome, Martin stayed behind as ballast while Ben and I set out for the Japanese Gully up the right-hand side of the bay. To our dismay, what had seemed a simple route across a small crevassed area turned into another nightmare maze. Six hours later we emerged in a thunderstorm, and, to avoid having to find our tracks down under new snow, we took to the rocks of the spur. This was our first introduction to Amne Machin slate, where attempts to kick away loose holds result eventually in one's own personal overhang.

Things were not going too well, and the lure of unclimbed and relatively straightforward Amne Machin III was too strong to resist. On 15 September we crossed the glacier before dawn and scrambled up loose but easy ground on the side of the level lower section of the E ridge. As the sun hit us, the rock ran out and we continued up perfect 45 snow, lying to a depth of about a foot over hard ice. By late morning, we reached the crest of the ridge, at just under 5200m, where Martin elected to drop out. Ben and I continued along the ridge to the point where it takes off for the summit, preceded by a short rocky section and gap. By then I too was running out of steam, and it was obvious that we would not make the remaining 600 or 700m that day. Ben was still going strong, but it looked as if the next section would be rather more demanding technically.

We returned to pick up Martin and, rather than descend the softening snow, traversed on the tottering S side of the ridge, before running down a virgin scree gully to the Harlon I Glacier below. Our visit to this new area was spoiled by a snow-storm, but we navigated our way round the end of the ridge and off the ice on to an idyllic pasture isolated between the two Harlon Glaciers. Here lay a deep aquamarine lake, with small stone men perched on the boulders and a single blue poppy cased in ice. The weather cleared abruptly and we tramped back across Harlon II, up the moraine and home to bed.

After a day's rest we descended to Base Camp and Ben and Mick, who by now was fully fit, set off to climb Sor-ra ('Sickle', 5452m), one of the two minor peaks at the end of the long NE ridge of Amne Machin II. On their way, Amne Machin IX (5690m), the prominent southern outlier of the range, came into view. This is the peak visible from Snow Mountain Commune, and it looked attractive enough for them to change their minds and walk an extra 6km to set up a camp at 4800m on the N ridge. That night brought a fall of fresh snow, but they set out anyway, following the N Glacier towards the col to the west of the peak. A spectacular avalanche from Amne Machin II failed to deter them, but in mid-afternoon black clouds rolled in at speed and turned them back with snow and high winds. After an hour the storm departed as quickly as it had arrived, but the damage had been done.

Next morning, 20 September, our last day before the yaks arrived, Ben and Mick set out again. This time they reached the col without incident and, after some steep snow climbing, they became the first people to stand on the summit of Amne Machin IX. The day was not without incident as they left the radio aerial behind in the tent, so ensuring an interesting day for those left glued to the transmitter or the monocular.

That was it, bar the six-day journey home. We had not made much of an impression on the higher peaks, but the range had given up a number of its secrets. While the two main peaks have been climbed, there are still plenty of virgin summits to tempt the visitor. Even more interesting are the classic lines still to be attempted. Though the area will probably not yield routes of extreme difficulty, its scale and complexity should not be underestimated. The traverse of the main peaks, the NE ridge of Amne Machin II from Sor ra and the entire 30km of the W side of the range remain obvious and unanswered challenges. Amne Machin's golden age has yet to come.

REFERENCES

1 Sir F Younghusband, *Peking to Lhasa*. London (Constable), 1925.
2 J Rock, 'Seeking the Mountains of Mystery.' *National Geographic Magazine* 57(2), 131–185, 1930.
3 J Rock, *The Am-nye Ma-Chhen Range and Adjacent Regions*. Rome (IsMEO), 1956.
4 L Clark, *The Marching Wind*. London (Hutchinson), 1955.
5 *Mountaineering in China*. Peking (Foreign Languages Press), 1965.
6 *High Mountain Peaks in China*. People's Sports Publishing House/Tokyo Shimbun Publishing Bureau, 1981.
7 M Banks, 'China's Hidden Mountain.' *Climber and Rambler* 20, 70–71, 1981.
8 G Watanabe, 'Record of the Joetsu MA Amne Machin Climbing Expedition.' *Yama to Keikoku*, 1981–82 (in Japanese).
9 G Rowell, *Mountains of the Middle Kingdom*. London (Century), 1985.
10 G Rowell, 'On and Around Anyemaqen.' *AAJ* 24, 88, 1982.
11 S Hupfauer, *AAJ* 25, 292, 1983.
12 L Hall, *AAJ* 24, 285, 1982.
13 K Shimizu, *AAJ* 27, 336, 1985.
14 J Knight, *AAJ* 28, 293, 1986.
15 A Bergamaschi, *AAJ* 28, 293, 1986.
16 B A Wagstaff, *AAJ* 29, 297, 1987.

North Muztagh: Xinjiang's Forgotten Peak

MICHAEL JARDINE

The 'Pamir Knot' is a term used by geographers to describe a knot of mountain peaks in the centre of Asia rimming the uplifted plateau called Pamyi-Dunya ('Roof of the World'). Like the folds of a huge circus tent with the Pamir Knot as its centre, the great mountain ranges and deserts of Central Asia spire out in alternate extremes to the edges of the earth's largest continent, forming the natural boundaries between China's Tibet and Xinjiang, Mongolia, Siberia, Soviet Kirgiziya and Tadzhikistan, Afghanistan, Pakistan, and India.

In the centre of the Pamir Knot is a small circle of mountains, some 70km wide and 150km long, forming a contiguous ring around the Pamyi-Dunya. The huge massif of Kongur (7719m) to the north forms the most impressive side of this ring, whereas to the south the barrier is not skyward but hell-bound, dropping straight into the 'Valley of Blood', the Kunjerab. Inside the walls of the Pamir Knot are two high valleys separated by a solitary mountain that stands alone in the centre: Muztagh Ata, the Father of Ice Mountains.

The entire mountain above 6000m is a giant dangling glacier splayed out conically to the north, west, and south like a volcano, with a half-dozen glacial canyons slicing outwards from the centre like spokes, dividing the mountain into three distinct peaks with eight separate faces. Indeed, one might have concluded that Muztagh Ata is an extinct volcano, were it not for the massive and still unexplored E face, a 3000m vertical bisection of jagged rock pinnacles and cliffs plunging into a tangle of glaciers below.

At 7427m the north summit of Muztagh Ata (hereinafter dubbed 'North Muztagh') is arguably the highest unnamed peak in the world. Indeed, though it had already been climbed – albeit only once prior to 1987 – it remains virtually unknown, bypassed in favour of its two legendary neighbours, Muztagh Ata and Kongur.

Muztagh Ata, only 119m higher, is a skier's peak, still the highest to have been ascended on ski but not a technical challenge (though its sheer E face has yet to be attempted). On the other hand, Kongur is the more serious challenge to hard climbing circles; the sole successful ascent was made by Chris Bonington in 1981, after having led a full reconnaissance expedition the previous year. That there has been no successful ascent since – despite attempts every year – is a lasting tribute to the other three members of Bonington's party who made the ascent: Joe Tasker, Pete Boardman, and Al Rouse.

North Muztagh falls somewhere in between. Its main bulk is cut off from Muztagh Ata by the Yambulak Glacier which gouges a 1000m cliff-lined chasm between the two from summit to base. The only obvious non-face route to the summit is the windy N ridge, which a small Japanese party of four climbed in 1981. Our plan was to see how high we could reach on the same ridge, on ski, to acclimatize in preparation for making a quick, nonstop ski ascent/descent of Muztagh Ata.

Dick Renshaw, who had taken a season off from 'serious' climbing to join our party, referred to the N ridge of North Muztagh as 'similar to the N col route on Everest'. For him this was probably a dismissal, but for the rest of our group of office hermits and weekend mountaineers it suddenly put the N ridge into alarming perspective: questionably attainable even under ideal conditions, given our level of experience; an incalculable risk under anything less than the ideal – as we were soon to learn. Observing the ridge from the calm of the Karakol Lakes far below, one of our members, Anthony Willoughby, put it succinctly: 'I have a feeling I want to make friends with the mountain. In some funny way I find it like looking at a dog and wondering if it is about to wag its tail or bite my leg off.'

From most angles, North Muztagh appears to be the higher of the two peaks. It is much steeper and can be seen in its entirety from base to summit, a giant North Face VE-24 dome tent, with its own N face as the entrance. On the other hand, the crested main summit of adjacent Muztagh Ata flattens out at 7000m and stretches interminably towards what must be the world's highest horizon line. Like the earth before Columbus, however, this literal 'Roof of the World' drops off radically down the E side.

For this reason, North Muztagh attracted early attempts by such explorers as Sven Hedin (1894) and Sir Aurel Stein (1900). Neither of these two were accomplished climbers – we were definitely in a similar fraternity – and thus they could both be forgiven for choosing the wrong route on the wrong mountain: a low-angled ramp with even plane rising eastward out of the lower slopes at 4000m up to about 6000m, at which point it begins to yaw to the north, its S side twisting skywards whilst the north drops away into the vast amphitheatre of the Chodomak Glacier. By about 6600m it has contorted into a corniced knife-edge, its S windward side a sheer plunge nearly 2000m straight into the ice-toothed jaw of the Yambulak Glacier – a very effective barrier between North Muztagh and the main summit. Stein did not make it beyond c6000m, but his Kirghiz guides went on to report the impassable ridge which subsequently became known as 'Stein's Gap'.

Our party opted instead for the N ridge, the same as the 1981 Japanese party, but approached it from the opposite direction – the Chodomak Glacier which parallels the ridge to its south. This glacier represented the most direct access to the upper mountain: unlike the Yambulak, it is a relatively smooth freeway leading straight into a giant amphitheatre flanked by the N and NW ridges. From the NW ridge – impassable at Stein's Gap – hung huge seracs which would sometimes break off at night. During the day avalanches cascaded, catalysed by only a few hours of constant sunlight.

From our Base Camp at 4750m on the S side of the glacier, our route to Camp 1 at 5600m on the N ridge was long and varied. On ski we followed an inclined snow-gully up to the edge of the glacier, crossing on to it at a snow-bridge at 5000m. Atop the glacier we followed it straight into the amphitheatre, gradually crossing to its N side at 5300m, from where the glacier bucked skywards in a series of broken ice-falls straight to the summit dome. At this point, exchanging skis for crampons, we opted for a steeper but safer headwall leading up the flank of the N ridge. The trick was to set out from Base early enough to reach the headwall before first direct sunlight – 6.30am local time – before the frozen snow on its S face softened. Crossing the Chodomak Glacier roped to Dick was like being handcuffed to a runaway rope-tow. However, it did have its advantages: we arrived at the base of the headwall before first light, and were able to walk up its 300m face atop sparkling crisp snow in just an hour. The others, arriving less than two hours later, found crampons an impediment and took more than two hours to wade up in crusted knee-deep cement.

Our Camp 1 sat atop a protected shoulder just below the main N ridge, looking south across the amphitheatre to the hanging seracs opposite, east straight to the summit looming just above, and west to the valley of the Pamyi-Dunya and the Pamirs of Soviet Tadzhikistan, forming the W flank of the Pamir Knot just opposite.

Altitude sickness is whimsical at best. Some people can ascend Everest in 48 hours; others get sick when they step off the aeroplane in Aspen. Most of us fall somewhere in between. I felt in good hands with Dick Renshaw, who had been above 8100m without oxygen on both Everest and K2. However, on the Everest expedition in 1982 he had suffered a mild stroke after spending more than four days above 7800m, and this would be his first return to above 7000m since then. Dick was understandably very cautious in his approach to the mountain, and favoured a fast push from c6300m, with perhaps an overnight bivouac, as opposed to a more prolonged schedule which would give the climbers more time to acclimatize, but would also allow more time for their blood to thicken – which in turn causes many of the complications of high altitude, from reduced circulation (increased chance of frostbite and stroke) to pulmonary or cerebral oedema. It is generally felt that, once sufficiently acclimatized up to 6000m – an important qualifier – any time spent above 6000m is essentially unproductive, becoming 'actively counterproductive' beyond 7000m.

By the day that we occupied Camp 1 – on the third carry – we had spent 10 nights above 3800m, of which seven had been at 4750m, in excellent health. Thus Dick and I were much surprised when we both fell ill at Camp 1 with disorientation and headaches. With hindsight, this was probably more because we were in shape than out of shape; having arrived ahead of the others, we immediately set about clearing platforms and erecting two tents, whereas, in fact, we should have rested. At least, this is one explanation. Two mornings later – after one rough night and a 24-hour storm – we both felt fit, but Dick momentarily blacked out when he stepped out of his tent. This alone would have been no cause for alarm; indeed, I have experienced the same at sea-level when standing up after two hours on the floor in front of the television! However, the scare two days earlier was sufficient to persuade Dick to descend. I followed, using the excuse of my illness, together with the need to evacuate our French member Didier Gaillard who was suffering from snow blindness, to 'glaze over' the fact that I was quite frightened at the prospect of threading a

13.   Pillars of Pumari Kish.

14. Duncan Tunstall descending the right bank of the Kurdopin ice-fall.
     The ridge behind leads leftwards to Snow Lake Peak.

15. P 5979m on the upper Biafo glacier. First ascent: S (left-hand) summit
     – D. Tunstall and S. Venables, 23–25 July 1987. Main summit
     – S. Venables, 24 August 1987.

16.   *Jorkanden (6473m) in the Kinnar-Kailash range, from Kalpa.*

17.   *Manirang (6593m) right, and unnamed peak.*

18.　*Kharcha Kund N ridge and NE face.*

19.　*Base Camp on Gangotri glacier, June 1947. Kharcha Kund behind. The photo illustrates the calm and isolation experienced 40 years ago, compared with the highway that the area has become today.*

20. *Luke Hughes and Jerry Gore, leaping crevasses on way down from Camp 2 after an early morning load carry.*

21. *Stephen Venables descending Xixabangma.*

22. The E side of the Xixabangma massif. Far left: Nyanang Ri. Right of
centre: Pungpa Ri. Right: Xixabangma summit hidden behind ridge.
Route with camps is indicated. X: High point (7700m) reached by
Venables and Hughes.

23. *Unknown footprints at 6000m on edge of small plateau glacier, E of Dasuo glacier, N Xixabangma.*

24. *Ice-fall between Advanced Base and Camp 1 on Xixabangma. Climber:
Luke Hughes.*

needle – on skis – between the wind-blasted N ridge above and a smooth but unstable snow-field dropping off into the Chodomak Glacier.

Marti Kuntz, Dr Wilmer Perez, and Keiichi 'Yeti' Ozaki continued their ascent of North Muztagh, reaching 6250m on the N ridge before unstable weather and persistent high winds drove them back down. Marti, a two-time women's world-record holder for speed skiing, descended straight from the ridge down the snow-field into the Chodomak Glacier and back to Base Camp – 1500m vertical – in only 20 minutes, no mean feat even at sea level. With unstable weather and our lack of experience, the decision to forgo a second attempt on North Muztagh was relatively easy.

The conclusion to this story brings us back to the main peak of Muztagh Ata, where in 1985 we had been turned back by bizarre lightning (AJ92, 117–121, 1987). This time the static electricity was still there – Marti in particular had a tiny spot in the back of her head where she had a scar from childhood and which seemed to be the target of much electrical attention – but it was by no means as fierce and unpredictable as in 1985.

Finally, well acclimatized and with a timely break in the weather, on the day after our camel-caravan transfer to Muztagh Ata Base Camp, the nine of us set out straight for the summit. We were soon divided into three groups of three in staggered starts at two days' interval – Dick's group returning to Base at 4550m with probable food poisoning and mine returning because of equipment failure (stoves). Anthony Willoughby and his wife Victoria – on their first anniversary – together with a recovered Didier, continued straight to the summit in true alpine style, stopping overnight three times en route. The other two groups, after making necessary repairs to body and machine, then went together straight to the top, camping overnight twice at 5650m and 6200m and, on the third night, setting out from the first party's Camp 3 (6800m) at midnight under a clear sky lit by brilliant stars and a full moon. We reached the top just after sunrise, deep golden rays shooting straight into our faces across the flat white horizon of the summit. A sea of cloud had moved in at the 6000m level, bombarding Base Camp with snow, hailballs and electricity, worrying those down below who knew that this would be our summit day and who thought us to be trapped high on the mountain in such appalling conditions. On the 7546m summit, however, it was a perfect cloudless day with stunning views of the shadow of Muztagh Ata thrown across a rippled screen of billowing pink clouds towards the west and, to the north, the pyramid of mighty Kongur sparkling in the early morning sun.

All that remained was a ski lesson from Marti; 3000m nonstop to the bottom – a strange place to learn the finer techniques of above-timberline skiing!

AUTHOR'S NOTE

We learned that four Austrians, led by Bruno Baumann, achieved the second ascent of North Muztagh, reaching its summit in September. Their route followed ours up the Chodomak Glacier, apparently confirming what we felt to be the most viable route up the mountain.

Sojourn in Xinjiang

SANDY ALLAN

Located in the eastern half of the Tian Shan mountains in the north central Xinjiang province, Mt Bogda stands at 5445m. Surrounded by pine-wooded slopes where the local Kazak people dwell in their Yurts beside jade-green lakes, their flocks of sheep, goats and horses and the occasional camel grazing and recuperating on the alpine meadows between sojourns along the silk road, this area must rank alongside the most beautiful mountain landscapes of our modern world. Of course I leaped at the opportunity to lead a trekking group to this range, where we planned to explore and make ascents of several of the peaks, including Bogda Shan.

As our aircraft circled down towards Ürümqi, the capital of Xinjiang province, our mountain appeared large and enticing from above. Ürümqi lies on the edge of a massive plain. Brickwork chimney-stacks pour murk into the sky, as this is an oil and coal-producing city. On the outskirts huge prairie-like fields show evidence of grain crops. The view reminded me of early 1960 'Look and Learn' magazine photographs of modern Russian agricultural methods. The Russian influence partly remains, but Ürümqi has changed its politics and its borders many times.

During the first and second centuries AD, Huns forced their way into modern Europe from here. Then in the ninth century a Turkish people (Uygurs) established their kingdoms around Ürümqi. They held an Islamic faith, and this is strongly reflected in their architecture today. Their kingdoms became Turkestan and covered much of central Asia, but the Uygurs were later conquered by a branch of the Liao dynasty, the Kitaya. Less than a century later Genghis Khan took control of the area. The 15th century saw the Chinese taking over the Mongols, but in the 17th century Mongols from Dzungarin regained control. They were wiped out by the Manchus in the 18th century. So today one senses a most exciting blend of blood and character in this functional coal-dust-enshrouded city.

The Chinese Mountaineering Association operates from a dingy concrete building here. We were greeted warmly by our Chinese hosts, Mr Shou (liaison officer) and Mr Chi, our translator. We spent two days in the city purchasing supplies, exploring the famous Natural History Museum and dicing with death, eating chilli kebabs cooked on open charcoal braziers which lined the street.

We left Ürümqi in an air-conditioned bus and bumped along the steeply winding road to Heavenly Lake (Tian Chi) where we transferred on to a waiting boat which carried us and our cargo to the far lakeside from where we'd continue our journey on foot. We met the head Kazak farmer and the oxen and horses which would porter our loads on the two-day approach walk, and early next morning our caravan set off. The walking was easy and relaxing and only our cook experienced difficulty, as, while escorting our two sheep which were tethered together, we often saw him hauled off into dense thickets bordering the track. River crossings were a little awkward, but the wiser of us soon learned to jump on to the pack animals to save us wading.

As we approached a Yurt we saw smoke curling from a hole in the yak-skin roof and were welcomed indoors by the owner. I stooped as I entered the low door and an old wrinkled lady smiled as she poked at a wood-fire in the centre of the floor. A black soot-encrusted kettle was suspended over the flames. We were invited to sit on the carpeted side of the tent, our backs supported by neatly folded colourful blankets and animal hides which were stacked around the inner walls. We accepted the tea, freshly baked bread and dried cheese. A small argument between the Kazaks and our liaison officer arose over the small amount of money received by the locals for the use of their pack animals, compared with that retained by the CMA in Ürümqi. However, peace was regained with the production of a plastic container of the local home-brew. This and other small incidents indicated that these Kazaks were not over-enthralled with the Chinese dominance. We had to move on and continued up the valley, passing by other Yurts with the children of the families herding flocks of sheep. Every afternoon the sheep are gathered and kept in stone-walled enclosures overnight, to be set free to graze the following morning. We camped by a small stream above the tree-line, and next morning we found a covering of fresh snow. We struck camp and moved on up the valley, the sun soon burning off the early morning mist. We crossed a high col and descended on to the moraine where we established Base Camp.

I spent time with the group, leading walks and scrambles on surrounding peaks and teaching mountaineering techniques. With Glenn Rowley I climbed some difficult rock-routes on a crag immediately behind Base Camp. Our Chinese staff asked us to gather the bulbous blossom of the mountain snow-anemone which is regarded in China as a useful medicine. This we did happily in return for all the work they did around Base Camp. We were the first official Western mountaineering expedition in this area since 1948. Eric Shipton and Bill Tilman had come here with Lhakpa Tenzing in 1942 and again in 1948, when Shipton, Tilman, Tenzing and a local man, Agaska, circumnavigated the massif and reached 5200m on the E ridge before retreating because of the steep climbing and shortage of time. I was grateful for their reports and for Dr Groeber's sketch map of the area. I also had a Chinese map, but this was in Chinese and on a very small scale.

After several days of acclimatization we were ready for an attempt on the mountain, and made a small camp at 4000m. Next day we moved up through seracs and pitched tents on the col at 4600m. In the evening I led out a large coil of static line above the col, as I hoped to have as many of the party as possible reach the summit. Fixing rope was probably the only safe way to make this possible. Late in the evening I stood high on the ridge above Camp 2 and saw dark clouds approaching over the distant desert. I realized that above me the climbing was much more difficult than I had previously imagined. However, I kept this to myself as I abseiled back to Camp 2 and spent a comfortable night there. Snow fell, and a strong wind blew the following morning. Although I wanted to remain and wait for the squall to pass, my clients and Glenn (our

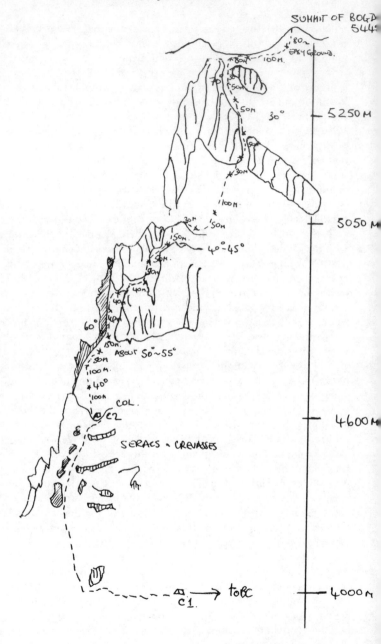

SKETCH OF OUR ROUTE ON BOGDA.

official leader) wished to descend. We returned to Base Camp and spent time climbing a small peak, awaiting an improvement in the weather.

Although the altimeter still showed a low pressure, one of the group, Evan Price from Canada, remained keen to attempt the route with me. We left Base Camp late in the afternoon of 12 August, and spent a few hours in a bivouac tent at Camp 1. We continued on that night to Camp 2, as the spell of calm weather in which we had departed from Base Camp was not going to last, and we reached Camp 2 at 2.30am on the 13th in swirling snow, to find one of our tents flattened by the wind. But the other was intact, so we had shelter to prepare our meal of haggis, oatcakes and smoked cheese, washed down with copious brews. We slept till 9am and by 10 were ready to set off.

I decided not to follow the fixed rope and took a more direct line above Camp 2. This meant more difficult climbing, but we moved quickly and saved perhaps an hour of slogging in deep snow. At about 5000m we arrived at the foot of a steep buttress which gave magnificent mixed climbing. We climbed ice-filled channels in the rock on front points and occasionally savoured technical moves, where we transferred into a new set of grooves. This led us to a rightward sloping slab with a smear of thin ice. The climbing made Evan whoop with joy. On easier ground we moved together to save time, and came across fixed rope from previous expeditions. The mountain was first climbed in 1985 by a Sino-Japanese expedition, although there had been previous attempts. Once over the buttress we traversed a slope to a second couloir which proved exciting. Easy ground then brought us to a whale-backed ridge leading to the final summit which we reached at 6pm. Evan waved his Canadian flag and we took photos before descending with many abseils to reach Camp 2 at 1am, and thence we descended to Base Camp.

Several days later Evan and I rode out from Base Camp on horseback, over the high col and down through the Tian Shan meadows and pine-scented woods to Tian Chi. My thoughts were on Mt Bogda, just climbed, on the fantastic scenery encountered and the relaxed holiday atmosphere of this trip. But they soon turned to more immediate plans and the prospect of entirely different conditions on the hostile North-East ridge of Everest, where I would be in a couple of weeks' time.

Over the Hill

EDWIN DRUMMOND

The first ascent

took nine months.
Wintry, skin-deep streams filled
harebell-blue as the two hills swelled. . .

The red slopes inched: shaken,
when a head appeared at the rim you yelled.
Then the avalanche – held
by the rope she slipped.

Now between her lips
the summit drips.

A Little Exercise

It glows
    looking up from the rocks
Stopping me

           a red hole

On Stanage
    beneath the heathery edge
a basin of shimmer   a great raindrop
living on a ledge

          rocking the sky

And I
Enough to bathe a son or daughter in
          a mirrory mortar
cupped by the tors
above the swollen   November moors

      Elbow deep
      clear as cider
      A mouth asleep in the grit

I dipped and played my hand   like a crab
clouding the sand
        waking
    breaking the waters over the lip

The wind moans and pushes
                bearing down the bone
brown buttresses

              I must make a move

Gripping   spreading my legs
I take my monstrous mother
                 earth
just in time by these last dregs of light
and quickly   clinging climb

into sight of the road.

Bête Noire at White Ghyll

Rabbitberries, black, wet,
on ledges set with juicy grass.
A nice morning to pass . . .
Blue sky, the streambed dry,
and a climb.

Then: there – and
here – grey, woollish hair
stuck to the rocks . . .

Warm as week-old underwear,
it has my climbing smell.

I tuck some at my waist
to send – from the hill and me –
post-haste to you, alone in Italy.

Until – back down –
I see the drained teabag-eye,
in that sheep that bounced
          bounced

bounced. Out of the sky.

The Climbers

(*Yosemite Valley, California*)

They smell of salami and vintage socks.
They keep food in huge, locked boxes
from the bears, though since they rarely fall
too far, they sling their long, lank hair
with sweatbands and gay bandanas,

a dash of feminity in hard rock men.
Often thin from fasts on higher things
and a lack of ready cash
– apart from an open fire – at bivouacs
they talk of hash, steaks, pancakes.
In the cracked, well-weathered hands they have
for plates, a can of tuna, and dried fruit,
for the night suffice. And sometimes ice . . .
There are no leftovers
or seconds in their world.
And very few older women.

They are the climbers, pirates
of windswept, stone seas,
blithe of the perils of society,
or who won yesterday's war in the Middle East.
Theirs is the west, and their one,
recurrent dream's to climb
out of reach of whatever long arms
would tie them down.

Slow readers of vast, hard pages,
lifers in the circle of Camp 4 boulders,
scarecrows of the white fields of light,
who would guess the poles of fear and elation
they've reached? The arpeggios of eye
-hand coordination, silently
running out on the Apron?

Puritans of straight-in cracks,
yet stretching tendons and belief
with hardware racks as keen as the Inquisition's.
Aid or clean, each move they make's a fine line:
if their holds don't break,
for days on end they take
their minds in their hands . . .
And after levitating quietly up El Capitan,
they need more cans of beer
than surgeons pints of blood in a transplant,
to cure their fear of flatness.

Solo, gamblers of eerie weightshifts dealing
with poker-faced death on the rocks
– staking all on a crystal, a smear, an expanding
flake. Reared on handshakes of golden granite,
that the sun stays up as long as they do
is their main hope. And if they cry out
– for a rope.

They hate towns, and tend to view
churches as failed spires.
Yet each would-be
engineer, erecting himself
thousands of feet above the deck, requires
the odd tool to check gravity.
With pitons, nuts and hooks they forge a way,
paying for certain sins of omission
– barely scratching the surface of the mountain.
Lean orangs of patience,
you could take one in
to clean your windows, swinging from sill to sill
for the bittersweet fruits
of years of solitary pullups.
Hairy blokes, you'll recognize one
in a city, as
he strokes the foot of a tall building.

Sometimes they hang in their hammocks for days,
trembling beneath a white sheet,
brushing off the rain.
They can take it: at worst,
in their cool eyes tears freeze.
Whose music is the silence of aloof walls,
when they're gagging with thirst a breeze;
a piton singing.

Though the best of them pause
at the bridalveil of a young spring fall,
they cannot sit still for long.
El Cap comes in . . .
gleaming granite sails a mile high.
Where they voyage deep air,
fingers sifting, juggling, weighing
how many grains of quartz,
jugs, nubbins and knife blades
will get them to port.
Where no one generally meets them.
After each safe passage
they hold only themselves,
the old block each carries
– a body of knowledge we've almost lost:
the human form, living, warm,
climbing on from the cross.

Comfortable in the clouds
these leopards – of ledges
like home – drawing no crowds

other than tourists with a telescope
seeing bright spots, believe me,
I too will not forget
my many, heavy, one night stands
with a wet sleeping bag in my hands.

What is this ocean
I seem to have been hanging around in
for thousands of years?
An old saurian
shuddering out of the granite and sandstone.
Mother Earth, Father Moon,
is this worship – reaching further than I ever have?
Can such crawling be progress,
the golden flesh
a shivering, critical mass?

The umbilicus of rope floating
below: waiting, shaking,
on the spot for hours – even days
at the same blank
I seem to have drawn myself
into a corner: the last piece or the first?
of a jigsaw, the big picture
I saw no one in before

I was held.
Spellbound – vertical dolphins
of a world full of light
half the time
on the other side of the valley
that cannot finally hold us for ever,
our rooting fingers – fins
wings   dendrites
of a nervous system called civilization;
old masters yet of the gentle art of persuasion:
that it might just go.

A chess against Death: moving
here, there,
protecting our king of joy.

It has been raining for a long time.
Now the rock is clean again: an empty page,
another day. I lift up my hands,
a kind of surrender, paean
to the way
blood climbs too, the old red and blue
rope unbroken, that lowered me down
the slippery slope when heaven opened.

Fisherman-still – one of those that get away –
on the brink of something much deeper,
hoping my luck holds,
that the wind that shook me out of bed
with the swifts swishing past,
doesn't turn cold. Steeper,

slowing down fast, over my head
a huge roof, the galaxy
– all I want to have read.
As once I climbed to reach a ledge
before night fell,
the last six feet
is out of reach.

Evening.

Grey woodsmoke,
quiet conversation. Hiss
of a stove.

Chink of carabiners in the woods.
They've been missed for a week.
Dusty, redskin-cheeked
from the sun glancing back.

'How was it?'

Cups are offered,
and placed by the fire
in a small, tribal circle of tents.

All night the wild bay laurel throws its scent.

To Be or . . .

(on Mt Sumbra)

On the butterfly-tattered ribs
I kick some rocks,
loose, jigsaw-jagged blocks

granite gasps

– Frozen: no other climbers around
the ground inching . . .
Glancing down is that blood-drop

the car?
The crash of a stream far off
– I hold my breath –

has stopped.
All a dream?
If Berkeley were here
would he shout for help
– hoping Johnson was hiking nearby?
Or fall,

silent, written on by lichen in a decade or two?
And where do
these fingers and toe-keys fit?
I climb therefore I am
so far: on the spot
where the hawk pits the mouse like a plum,
and caterpillars
crawl for the shape of wings to come?
Or back home where you are,
reading the newspaper, listening for the car?

A ring
-piton: I slip my finger in.
Time to thi –
I blink: where the sky floats,
standing at the brink, stark-white . . .
goats. Who've seen a ghost.

Pieniny – The Great Little Mountains

JERZY W. GAJEWSKI

On the map of Poland, the Pieniny Mountains are over-shadowed by other mountains situated in the south of the country, along the Czechoslovakian border. However, the Pieninys with their pointed rocky hills provide a contrast to the landscape of the surrounding Flysch Beskidy Mountains. The landscape and natural beauty of the Pieninys have brought about their great popularity with tourists, especially ramblers, resulting in the establishment of the first Polish National Park there.

In general, the Pieniny Mountains cover the area between the Białka River in the west (its source is situated above the White Water Valley on the Slovak side of the Tatra Mountains), and the Rozdziele Pass in the east, where they border on the Beskid Sadecki Mountains. The western part of the Pieninys, which culminate on Żar (879m), is called Pieniny Spiskie, because the surrounding territory – with its interesting villages, architecture, costumes and customs of the people – is joined to the Spisz region (part of this area is situated on the Slovak side, too). This is where Dębno, the village with the famous St Michael's Church, is situated. This wooden church was built in the 15th century and its interior is covered with unusual and rare wall-paintings. No wonder Dębno church is a goal for most tourists who go to the Pieniny Mountains. The eastern part of the Pieninys, although being the highest, is called Małe Pieniny (Little Pieniny). It culminates on the Wysoka (1052m), at the foot of which are four conservation areas with short but beautiful gorges (the most famous is called Homole).

But most popular is the central part of the Pieninys, situated between Czorsztyn in the west, and Szczawnica-spa in the east. This mountain range is 10km long and 4km wide. Although the main goals for ramblers are Trzy Korony (the Three Crowns; 982m), the highest point in this area, the top of Sokolica (747m), as well as the sheer 'Sokola Perć' (the 'Falcon Trail'), it is worth noting that there are other attractions in these mountains. The Dunajec River, which runs from the Tatra Mountains, cuts through the Pieninys and carves a rocky canyon there. It is 9km long, but its beginning and end are only 2.4km apart, and the difference in level between the entrance and end of the canyon is about 60m. The bottom of the Dunajec valley, which is situated 420–500m above sea-level, is dominated by several hundred metres of high rocky walls – those of Trzy Korony, Czertez, Sokolica; the scenery there is similar to that of the high mountains.

The Dunajec canyon is the result of the formation of mountains and river erosion. This process took place in the Miocene, Pliocene and glacial epochs. Above the canyon the conical hills, characteristic of the area, are covered with forests, hidden flower meadows and steep white cliffs. This unusual view can be observed and admired from the top of the hills, and from the tract of water in the canyon as well.

The beginning of tourism in the Pieniny Mountains – as remarks J Nyka, author of the best contemporary guidebook for this area – is connected with the creation of the Szczawnica-spa. J Dietl, balneologist and professor at the Jagellonian University, wrote in the middle of the 19th century that 'Szczawnica takes first place among other spas in Galicia' (at this time the part of Poland under Austrian rule). Nevertheless, the Pieniny Mountains were known earlier. The first scientists of the 18th century who wandered through the Carpathian Mountains were fascinated by the Pieninys as well. Balthasar Hacquet, a physician and naturalist born in France, explorer of the Alps and Carpathian Mountains, was one of them. He published a book entitled *Neueste physikalisch-politische Reisen in den Jahren 1788–1795 durch die Dacischen und Sarmatischen oder Nördlichen Karpaten*, which is not only a record of his geographical, geological and botanical studies, but also contains information for travellers and instructions for contemporary mountaineers. Perhaps it was this that influenced Z and W H Paryski, authors of the *Encyclopedia of the Tatra Mountains* (published in Poland in 1973), to consider this book to be the first manual of mountaineering.

At the beginning of the 19th century the first tourist trips through the Dunajec canyon were organized. L Zejszner, a Polish geologist and also professor at the Jagellonian University, became fascinated by the Pieniny (and Tatra) Mountains when he visited them in 1829 for the first time. 20 years later he wrote: 'In the morning, one starts from Sromowce, a village not far away from Czorsztyn, the flotilla consisting of 10–15 double boats. These boats have to be joined together, because they are made of hollowed-out spruce trunks and they capsize easily. The participants are preceded by a separate boat with musicians and a second boat with artillery which fires from mortars in places with an echo'.

The trips on rafts through the Dunajec canyon from Sromowce (from Kąty, to be precise) to Szczawnica have been until now the main tourist attraction of the Pieninys. To be sure, the artillery boat doesn't accompany tourists today, but they can listen to music at the time of embarkment: sometimes it is the Highlanders band, sometimes gypsy music. The rafts are guided by a specially trained rafter, born in the Pieniny villages, usually dressed in folk regional costume.

The rocky hills of the Pieninys, made of limestone from the Jurassic and Cretaceous periods (they are built over the less resistant sandstones, slates and marls), have never been of interest to mountaineers. These mountains have been visited for many years by travellers, later by ramblers with rucksacks and guests from spas in Szczawnica and Krościenko. They walk to the ruins of the Pieniny Castle and to the top of Trzy Korony; from these places the panoramic view of all the Tatra Mountains can be admired. Grim as well as romantic, the Pieninys were much more accessible than the high mountains of the Tatras, which were wild and impenetrable.

The Pieniny Mountains create a small but distinct geobotanical area. About 110 species of vascular plants occur there, several endemic plants among them. We can observe an astounding number and variety of insects, especially butterflies – about 1500 species. In the Pieniny forests beech- and fir-trees grow

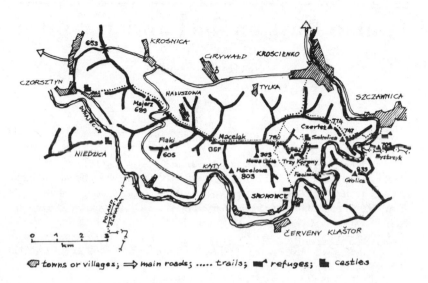

Pieniny Mountains – central part

as do yews. Pine-trees can usually be seen on the tops of hills. Hanging off the white rocks and tossed by wind, they are a very good subject for photographers.

The rich flora found on the limestone rocks, and the beautiful landscapes, influenced the decision to create a national park there. In 1921 the first reservation was founded, not far from Czorsztyn Castle. Since 1929 land in the Pieninys has been bought up from private owners, and in 1932 the Pieniny National Park was formally opened. Its area now covers 2231 hectares. On the Slovak side of the Dunajec River, near Cerveny Klastor, the Slovak Nature Reserve was also organized between the wars (the Slovak protected areas consist of about 2125 hectares today). Thus in the Pieniny Mountains – the first in Europe and the second in the world – a national park bordering on two countries was created.

The idea of building a dam on the Dunajec River in the Pieniny Mountains was first conceived between the wars. This project is now under construction. An artificial lake should stop the consequences of the dangerous floods caused by the Dunajec waters, and will be situated in the western part of the Pieninys. The dam will be constructed near Niedzica Castle and the artificial lake will stretch to Dębno village. This lake will naturally change the scenery of this part of the Pieninys, and these plans often upset ecologists and tourists. Within a few years, the reflections of the Niedzica and Czorsztyn Castles, the dark green forests and white rocks, will glance back from the sheet of water, as from a mirror. But a lot of tourists are worried that when this happens something elusive will have disappeared from the atmosphere and landscape of these mountains.

The Pieninys give the impression of high mountains, but they are not high. Nevertheless, this miniature mountain range has become known as one of the nicest places in Europe.

Damp Days on the Lalidererspitze

GEOFF HORNBY

When Hias Rebitsch finally completed both halves of the long-fancied and often-tried direct line up the Lalidererspitze North Wall, it provided Austria with one of its hardest and most striking lines. Vertical for over 750m, it looms provocatively over the Falken Hut built on the Spielissjoch. The first ascent of the route was carried out in two halves. In July 1946 Rebitsch, with Kuno Rainer, traversed in at half-height from the Auckenthaler route and then climbed direct to an exit just below the summit on the NW ridge. Rebitsch returned in September of the same year with Sepp Spiegl and climbed directly from the base of the wall to the beginning of the direct finish; he then called it a day. It was not until the following year that Hermann Buhl and Luis Vigl came to the Karwendel and seized the opportunity to make the first continuous ascent of this plum line.

I first heard mention of this route whilst discussing objectives for a summer's climbing in Europe with the late Dave Newsholme. The idea faded until I read Buhl's *Nanga Parbat Pilgrimage* and came across the account of his ascent. All I needed was a partner to go and I was set.

The first week of July found me sitting in a bar at Munich airport with Rob Neath and Steve Briggs. We had five days to kill and the plan was hatched.

Access to the Spielissjoch is via the toll-road to Eng. From there a three-hour stroll up through farmland and wooded hillsides brings you to the base of the great Laliderer Wall. This wall is 3km long and allows the prospective climber an hour or so on the trail to come to terms with its sheer enormity. The Lalidererspitze is the most westerly peak along the wall and is undoubtably the main attraction in the area.

The three of us wandered up to the Falken Hut in driving rain. Our hopes of starting up the route the next day receded as everything we were wearing gradually became sodden. However, it gave us a morning to scramble along the scree-slope beneath the wall and find the start.

Back at the hut we ran into one of Austria's top young rock athletes doing the dishes. He informed us that we had chosen a nice route but that it had a lot of E2 on it. Armed with this awesome piece of information we retired for the night.

Dawn found us stamping around and massaging cold hands at the first belay point. The plan was to take it in turns to lead three pitches each, and so Steve took over the sharp end. His leads were all airy gangways and steep traverses split by short technical walls, never very hard but then never well protected. Rob took over for the strenuous crack-line that led to the huge yellow roofs. Nasty awkward climbing, up hanging grooves and cracks, left us all feeling pumped out. Up to this point we had all felt quite pleased with our progress and, with the security of the climb, we had experienced no rock-fall danger and the belays had all been sound; but things were to change.

25. *Amne Machin I (Dradullungshog) from the E, Pt 5977 at far left, Pt 5827 at right.*

26. *The E face of Amne Machin I (Dradullungshog), NE summit.*

27. *Amne Machin II, IV and III, L to R, above the Harlon glaciers.*

28.   *Tian Shan range: Mt Bodga is the highest peak on L on the main massif.*

29.   *Looking back down the route to Evan Price as Sandy Allan nears the final summit ridge.*

My first pitch was the key to passing the overhangs. Originally a tension traverse, it now goes free with hard face-moves across a steep slab. I completed the pitch and was assembling the belay when a wheelbarrow-full of limestone bricks bounced down the slab and came whistling past my head as I hugged the wall. The whole atmosphere changed. Rob and Steve scuttled across and I was rapidly dispatched up the front-face of the adjacent White Pillar in search of a sheltered spot. The top of the pillar was devoid of any belay and a braced position was the best that I could muster. However, a hard face pitch above brought me to the security of a large flake. Time was pressing: we had climbed nine pitches and we knew we had at least another 15 to go.

Above was a two-pitch chimney system up the side of the huge Grey Tower. From the ground it appeared to be a solid pillar of limestone, but close up it was a shattered pile of blocks with a very short life-expectancy. Steve made a couple of blinding leads to another belay-less stance on top of the tower. The first lead above was a case of 'get those pegs clipped quickly, Steve' because this was getting a little bit wild.

Once over the bulge we found ourselves in the water-worn groove that is in common with the Auckenthalerweg. One pitch up this, and the groove was shut by a huge chockstone. Rob led up the left-hand wall and had just clipped a half reasonable peg when a clatter announced the arrival of rock-fall. One chunk caught Rob between the shoulder blades and we froze in fear of his falling.

This was the point where the second half of the route broke out to the right and then headed directly for the summit. A full rope-length around ribs and bulges led to a basin in the middle of the wall. From here we could see, not only the rest of the route up, but also the brewing storm-clouds away to the south: time for haste. Two easy pitches led to the base of the next feature – the Great Pillar. Now it was my turn again to make the trail. Beautiful climbing at HVS standard for two pitches up a corner system restored some of the interest but did nothing to relieve the tension. As the other two arrived on the second stance the heavens burst. We struggled into our waterproofs and looked around for shelter. Half a rope-length to the left there was a pillar with an overlap above it. Steve led quickly across and we followed, the pitch rapidly turning into a waterfall. It was now painfully obvious that we would be here for the night.

Although we had travelled light we had taken the precaution of including a double bivouac sack in the gear. This presented a problem in that three into two doesn't go, well – not very easily, anyway. The ensuing wrestling match frayed tempers, and in the end we decided that one person would just have to sit outside. The top of the pillar was the size of your average 'MFI' coffee table, so whatever the configuration we all found ourselves overhanging the edge. This didn't seem too serious until a volley of rocks, cut loose by the rain, rocketed past the outer edge like an express train. In the end I opted to be left out permanently and just sat in my harness at the back.

Dawn arrived with a break in the weather, but it was obviously not for long judging by the cloud formations in the distance. Rob pulled over the bulge and stormed up the groove above, horrendous climbing up loose limestone with water pouring down it. This was another key pitch that gave access to the easier-angled final section which eventually became a race against time. I suppose you could say that we won: we made four pitches before the rain with only three to go – some victory.

Behind the summit lies an orange fibreglass bivouac hut. We staggered in at mid-day, wet, cold and tired. The hut stove produced a brew of soup, porridge and candlewax which we consumed with relish. The enthusiasm needed to step out into the storm and start the descent took a long time coming.

The descent is back down the northern side via the Spindlerschlucht. Given Grade III with seven abseils it seemed like a tough proposition in these conditions. It was an epic in itself, two hours' wandering around the pinnacles looking for the start, and then a horrendous two hours of abseiling through waterfalls and down-climbing streams. We reached the hut just as it got dark, and out of the corner of my eye I saw the warden phone the necessary authorities announcing our safe return. Shortly after, three piping hot plates of pasta appeared and the world seemed a much mellower place again.

Next day it rained again and we trudged out, pleased with our success but with a lot of respect for the Karwendel.

NOTE

This is believed to have been the first British ascent of this route. Steve Briggs left the Alps to climb in Kishtwar and is still missing, presumed dead.

The Romansch Way

The most beautiful ski-ramble in the Engadine

WALTER LORCH

For some 150 years Brits have climbed, ski'd and charted the Alps. In 1861 members of the Alpine Club established the 'High Level Route' known today as the Haute Route – the classic crossing from Chamonix to Zermatt and Saas Fee. Early this century Arnold Lunn introduced the world to downhill racing and ski slalom, landmarks indeed.

Over the past 20 years the Nordic ski has infiltrated the Alps, Brits being notable by their absence. *Ski de randonnée* to the French, *Skiwandern* and *Langlauf* to the German-speaking people and cross-country skiing to the English-speaking world, has brought a third dimension to the world of skiing: independence from the clutter and queues of mechanical transport and access to fairy-tale lands away from the crowds. But, most important of all, ski-rambling gives a sense of physical well-being and achievement known so well to sailors and mountaineers. The choice of terrain is endless and the cost low.

After more than half a century of ski-mountaineering and downhill skiing, with an occasional excursion on Nordic skis, I decided to explore this new, yet ancient mode of snow travel over true alpine territory.

The Engadine appealed most and, finally, two factors decided my choice: firstly, the Engadine is different from the rest of Switzerland. So is the language. So are the people. So is the weather. While the sun shines in Sils and Scuol, the rest of Switzerland may be covered in mist. The route leads along the River Inn, across frozen lakes, flanked by the panorama of the Engadine giants, loved by every skier. The adjoining valleys add to the scope. These were my first criteria.

In the Upper Engadine, marked loipes and good route-maps exist. In the Lower Engadine, similar conditions apply between S-chanf and Giarsun and again between Scuol and Martina. However, I could find no marked or recognized route connecting Giarsun with Scuol – a gap of some 14km. My enquiries with local guides and ski schools resulted in one categorial statement: 'Impossible to do it on cross-country skis; take the bus'. This challenge was my second reason to explore the Engadine and put The Romansch Way on the map.

The Romansch Way starts at Maloja (1810m) and finishes at Martina (1050m) at the Austrian border, a distance of 145km. The profile and terrain are ideal for rapid progress in superb landscape, with ancient villages of real beauty and inspiring 16–17th century architecture.

THE ROUTE

Maloja-Sils

The River Inn springs from Lake Lunghin, above Maloja, runs along The Romansch Way and through Austria into the Danube, which finally decants into the Black Sea. Hence the name *ENGADIN*, Romansch for the Inn Valley. Maloja is the starting point of The Romansch Way and of the famous Engadine Marathon. We ski through woodland or on the snow-covered lakes, reminiscent of glacier skiing. Isola is an ancient alp and a good stop for refreshments, halfway to Sils.

Val Fex – Plaun Vadrett

From the Sleigh Park in beautiful Sils Maria the route climbs steeply towards Platta. Piz Chapütschin (3386m) and Piz Grialetsch (2694m) overlook the village and there is a good view of the downhill skiers from Furtschellas. The picturesque village of Crasta with Pension Crasta and Hotel Sonne offer a good overnight or refreshment stop. Val Fex is a sunny, open valley with high altitude treeland and almost vertical rock formations. Plaun Vadrett is above the tree-line: a mound encircled by a moat and one could well imagine a castle on top. The 'moat' is created by fast glacier streams.

The return route parallels the outward route. From Platta the loipe veers E in the direction of the Furtschellas cable car, coinciding in part with the downhill pistes to Sils Maria. Val Fex has a tranquillity and detached beauty rarely found outside the realm of the giants.

Sils-Pontresina

Sils consists of three parts. Sils Baselgia adjoining the church, Sils Maria, the main village, and Sils Furtschellas – near the Furtschellas cable car. Passing Silvaplana a winding track leads up steeply into the fairytale forest where the panorama of Corvatsch appears through the trees. The loipe then descends towards St Moritz. The track passes underneath the Olympiaschanze.

Climb from St Moritz Bad to a plateau and then descend in a superb langlauf schuss on to Lej da Staz. The lake restaurant makes a welcome break. The loipe winds down towards Pontresina. A major trading village on the approach to the Bernina Pass, Pontresina has imported wines from the Valtellina region in Italy since the Middle Ages. Veltliner is the wine of The Romansch Way. A stay of two or three days enables us to explore the Roseg and Morteratsch valleys and the Diavolezza region. Today's 'Wanderski' offers the flexibility vital for soft or trackless snow coupled with firm grip on ice and steep descents. Incredibly light, it offers totally new possibilities of alpine snow travel and adventure.

Pontresina – Zuoz

This part of The Romansch Way leads over the most exciting sections of the

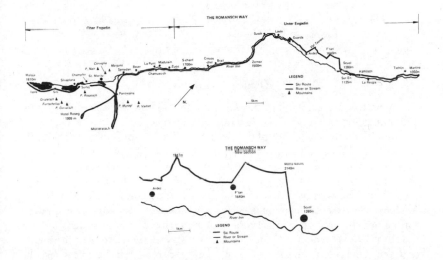

Engadine Marathon race. Passing Punt Muragl, the rack-and-pinion railway to Muottas Muragl being the oldest in Europe, the loipe then leads over wide meadowland, past Bever and La Punt, through Chamues-Ch, a charming village with Restaurant Adler as an ideal refreshment stop. Descending towards Madulain, we observe the significant landmark of Hotel Castell with Zuoz below. First mentioned in the ninth century as a place with a Royal tavern, Zuoz became the administrative centre of the Upper Engadine. The village square with its medieval tower and fountain is surrounded by patrician houses of typical Engadinia style.

Zuoz – Zernez

From Zuoz to S-chanf – some 3km – there is a wide choice of loipes: there is the actual Marathon route; a loipe through the valley close to the Inn and two tracks along the edge of the forest. Midway between Zuoz and S-chanf is the finish of the Marathon race – 42km from Maloja, with a record time of 1hr 32min, an average of almost 30km per hour. A horse couldn't do it. This point is also the division between the *Ober* and *Unter Engadin*.

In most conditions the loipe to Zernez is maintained. The route passes through scrubwood into wide open space, surrounded by sparse woodland, known locally as the golf course. We pass Val Flin, Val Torta, Val Mela and Val Verda. Crossing the Ova da Tantermozza, the route goes up more steeply with rock formations on the right-hand side. On the left the village of Cinuos-Chel appears with its significant onion-top church and railway arch of the Rhätische Railway.

From the top the loipe snakes into the valley, flattening out parallel with the railway line in an ideal schuss. On the left bank of the Inn, high up, is Sur Crusch. From this point the loipe leads again through woodland, descending all the way to the last major incline before Zernez, to a bridge over the Spöl Valley. A bendy track leads across the Inn over a covered bridge to Zernez.

The remains of an Iron Age settlement were discovered here, but sadly a fire destroyed the Engadinia houses in 1872. They were replaced with nondescript buildings leaving a dull untypical town.

Zernez – Guarda

Changing to the right bank of the River Inn through meadowland and gently undulating forest, we pass the remains of a medieval punishment centre. In common with the woodlands of the *Ober Engadin*, the forest is full of wildlife, particularly red deer. Susch comes into view where the Flüela Pass meets the Engadine. This ancient village can boast of two defence towers, one to hold a population of 140 and one with the onion top for the Lords of Susch. The fortress of Chaninas dominates the village and the highest peak in the *Unter Engadin* – Piz Linard – comes into view. After a further descent Lavin appears. The name is first recorded in a chronicle of the 12th century and is derived from the Latin *labina* (avalanche). Indeed avalanches were the scourge of the region between Lavin and Giarsun. Today they are rendered harmless by the combination of avalanche barriers and early release of massed snow by detonation.

From Giarsun a steep road leads to Guarda. The name is derived from '*guardar*' meaning lookout. Guarda is unique in being first documented in 1160. During the Thirty Year's War, 1618–1648, the village was razed to the ground by Austrian troops and rebuilt. All houses date from the 17th century, and the village was never disturbed again.

Local people and guides ruled out a crossing along the right bank of the Inn because of avalanche and rockfall danger, though there exists a summer path along this very stretch. I discussed my plan with Chasper Planta, a young ski teacher and guide and the route shown in large scale was chosen leading to Scuol via Bos-cha, Chanova, through the Tasnan valley and Ftan.

Guarda – Scuol

The loipe leads to the centre of Bos-cha, a hamlet on the same sunny shelf as Guarda, with an uninterrupted view of the Engadine's Dolomites. Cross the Valde in the direction of Chanova to an impressive, high-level path where the exciting panorama of the *Unter Engadin* unfolds with Piz Lad, Piz Lischana, Piz San Jon, Piz Pisoc and Piz Zuort (a square stone tower like a chimney). We ascend through woodland into the Tasnan valley and cross the Tasnan descending to the loipe leading to Ftan church. Ftan is situated on the old coach road between Giarsun and Scuol. The double onion-shaped church tower leans further to one side as the years go by, similar to the better known examples in Pisa and St Moritz. From here a chair-lift ascends to Prui (2058m, top of the sleigh run), or the purists and those untiring enthusiasts climbing to the same spot can continue east to Motta Naluns where the descent to Scuol begins. Scuol has nothing to offer. The old village has been overwhelmed by a concrete jungle. A marked loipe, parallel with the Inn, leads to Sur En, where Hotel Val d'Uina offers the ideal overnight stop, right on the loipe.

Sur En – Martina

The wide open terrain of the left bank is reached through a covered bridge and up on the left Ramosch appears with its square, early Gothic church tower. The loipe leads through scrubwood following a trout stream to join the Inn, now a much wider and quieter river, after its rather steep and noisy descent. For some distance we rejoin the river with its charming snow-covered rocks, looking like giant polar bears. The Inn has now become a torrent, descending noisily over the rocks. Opposite, over the steep rock-formations, a dust avalanche has descended and I note that a path has been carved through it to provide access to a small settlement – Raschvella. Once more a short and sharp descent meets our old friend the Inn. I felt like skiing along a towpath with snow-covered bollards. Gradually the rock-formations recede to less steep pasture land. Passing Strada, known as Feradastrada in former times and used by cattle dealers from as far away as the Austrian Tyrol, the village of Tschlin (1533m) comes into sight. Again and again Tschlin was destroyed by fire, enemy action or avalanches, but the tough villagers rebuilt their homes as though the danger did not exist. In front of the church stands the monument to Duonna Lupa, heroine of the 1499 Swabian War. She saved the village from the marauding Austrian troops. Everyone had taken refuge in the church except Duonna Lupa, who continued stirring a vast pot of polenta in her kitchen. When the enemy troops asked for whom she was cooking, she laughed: 'For the Swiss troops of course, who will be here any moment now'. The Austrians ran as fast as their legs would carry them.

Looking back, an impressive last view of The Romansch Way is ours and we arrive at Martina, the frontier between Switzerland and Austria.

Finale

The Romansch Way is unique. It caters for every taste. Seclusion for those who seek it. Entertainment – certainly: there is the Marathon on the second Sunday in March with almost 12,000 competitors. The nightlife of St Moritz is yours for the asking. Sils-Maria – beautiful and sophisticated for gourmet tastes. Or make your HQ in Pontresina to experience the real scope of alpine ski-rambling. But inn-to-inn touring is best: nothing to carry – the *postbus* takes your luggage to the next stop (yes, it will be there before you). Ski The Romansch Way – a day-dream of reality.

SECTIONS OF THE ROMANSCH WAY

	km	Time
Maloja – Sils	8	1hr 20min
Sils – Crasta – Plaun Vadrett	16.5	3–3½hr
Sils – Surlej – St Moritz – Pontresina	16	3hr
Pontresina – Roseg Glacier	17	2hr 40min
Pontresina – Morteratsch Glacier	17	2½hr
Diavolezza Station – Bernina Pass (Ospizio)	15	2½hr
Pontresina – Punt Muragl – Samedan – Zuoz	18	3–3½hr
Zuoz – S-chanf – Zernez	18	3½–4hr
Zernez – Susch – Lavin – Giarsun – Guarda	15.5	2¾–3hr
Guarda – Val Tasnan – Ftan	15	3½hr
Scuol – Sur En	6	50min
Sur En – Ramosch – Martina	23	3½–4hr

MAPS
Engadin Loipenkarte, parts 1 and 2.
Landeskarte Schweiz (1:50,000), 5013 and 5017.

Home From The Eiger

LUKE HUGHES

'Great things are done when men and mountains meet;
This is not done by jostling in the street'

Blake

'Six weeks in plaster, six weeks physiotherapy; I don't see you climbing again for at least another four months.' We drove away from the casualty department of St Thomas's Hospital.

'There go our chances of knocking off the Eiger this summer,' said Stephen.

'Not if I can help it.'

That Sunday afternoon at Swanage had been expensive. Never mind sliding sweaty-palmed away from an easy traverse; I'd left a crab with all Stephen's wires swinging from a distant piton above the crux. Never mind the shattered bones in my foot; but to see our trip to the Alps go for a bag of chalk was too much. Stephen was hoping to write a book about the Bernese Oberland and needed more material. I had never been there and the thought of a fortnight's dash was a dewdrop in a barren summer of hard work. 10 weeks later, fortified by a diet of calcium phosphate we set off anyway, for the kind of jaunt that keeps one high for months; the kind you read about in books. Or used to.

Mountaineering literature has recently changed so much. Where are the buckram-covered gold-tooled accounts of jolly ventures to the Playground of Europe? What has become of the *Alpine Journal*, now three-quarters full of Himalayan experiences? Coarse-cut papers and well-spaced print have given way to closely-set type and pure-coated paper. Climbers have forsaken their tweeds and sensible shoes for thermolactyl fibres and plastic boots that make your feet sweat. Who could have foreseen matching Goretex separates, psychedelic footwear, designer salopettes with stripes down the leg and the ubiquitous Sony 'Walkman'? Gone are the days when Whymper hurled rocks from the summit of the Matterhorn on to the felted heads of his Italian rivals. Gone are the days when Leslie Stephen could send down for a ladder to cross a crevasse on the Jungfraujoch.

It's not that I think it's good form to hurl rocks at other climbers; there's something about using ladders on cruxes that's not quite 'on' either, and I have to own up to Helly-Hansen underwear. But it is not just fashions that have changed; it is values, too. Some for the worse. In particular, there is a propensity amongst modern mountaineers to take themselves too seriously. We are not a bit surprised when a Frenchman describes the commitment shared by delegates at the Mont Blanc bicentennial celebrations as a common pursuit of 'La verité'. We are confirmed in our expectations when Poles brave all conditions and all weathers to battle with some fearsome route to stress an ideological point. But matters are out of hand when British mountaineers write sentences like this:

> 'We merged with and moved through this strange environment, a capsule passing over a wild uninhabited unique universe . . . We were a cohesive entity now; only the sheer professionalism and trust within the operative parts of the whole permitted the luxury of debate over the price of titanium.'

What has become of that anarchy, charm and wit that used to be such a characteristic of British climbing?

Stephen Venables is working hard to keep a few traditions alive. He indulges a little in anarchy, charm and wit, and, especially, he possesses that peculiar British characteristic of turning catastrophe into virtue and being congratulated for it. His hobby is collecting the names of other climbers who drop vital equipment from near the tops of mountains; he purchases the minimum of climbing gear on the grounds that someone else will provide. He is a delightful guest who washes up, shops, feeds babies, cats and dogs spontaneously, brings flowers and chocolates to bribe hostesses (or their mothers), and spends whole afternoons gossiping knowledgeably about horticulture (also seducing fathers). Meticulous about bread-and-butter post-cards, no one with a house near a crag (or with a word processor when he's writing a book) can resist the charm. He has developed the art of cupboard love to its zenith. He is passionately devoted to the mountains, women and music, the choice depending on the time of year. This can confuse. An able pianist himself, he was once carried away by the slow movement of Beethoven's 'Ghost' trio by his feeling for the music, and then by the cellist. I was recently concerned to see him discard his Oxfam climbing gear and squander the Boardman Tasker prize money on more streamlined outfits, but at least with his 'Walkman' he still carries an impressive collection of opera and early chamber music.

To the enervating strains of *The Marriage of Figaro* we sped off to the midnight ferry; screaming children, Sealink sandwiches, leaden eyes and snatches of sleep before the overnight romp across Europe.

Zürich greeted us with those bursts of drenching rain and lingering mists that spell doom to alpine dashes. For the next 10 days we darted about Switzerland in search of dry climbing, progressively more depressed about the weather. 'The trouble with dropping things and not reaching summits is that what you've nearly done never really counts!' moaned Stephen. It began to look as though this trip was not going to help. He was going to have to own up to being a cabinet-maker, not a climber at all. How we wandered. From the limestone needles of the Grignetta in northern Italy to the Gorge de Moutier in the Jura (where the penalty for failure was to dangle amongst the high-tension cables of the railway line), from the Sphinx at Leysin to the slabs of Handegg. We were even arrested for vagrancy in Solothurn one morning. Suffering from Oberland Fever, I made up a rhyme. It began

'I must go back to the Alps today,
    To the rock, the snow, and the ice.

And all I ask is a bomb-proof nut and a belay bolted thrice.
A tense move, a thin ledge, a knee that's shaking,
Dry mouth, cold toes, and a heart that's quaking.'

One evening the weather looked as though it might be clearing further north.
'I don't know about you, but I'd like to see more of the snow and ice and less of
the shaking knee.' Having tired of getting damp in lay-bys, Stephen hit on the
idea of placating a young lady of Meiringen (near the Oberland), to whom he
had once behaved badly. He rushed to the nearest flower shop and, balancing
blumen on his knee, urged us on to the young lady's home. She was out. We
picnicked outside, and completed memorizing the first act of *Figaro*. Her
neighbours were not appreciative and threw a bucket of water over us. It was
still raining, and there was no climbing

'I suppose there's some consolation in thinking that if all this precipit-
ation has a chance to settle, the Eiger should be getting nicely into condition.'
Then one evening the clouds cleared, the temperature dropped, and the
Oberland was clear. We sped off to Lauterbrunnen at first light.

As we wandered up to the Rottal hut Stephen poured out information
about previous pioneers, great routes and personal memories which made it
clear what an interesting book his would be were he to find a suitable publisher.
We had the hut to ourselves and woke to a perfect morning; small puffy clouds,
a view of every range in the Alps, and Stephen with a story about most of them.
We climbed the Rottal ridge to the summit of the Jungfrau, a route that my
great-grandfather Claude Schuster had pioneered a century before. I've always
admired his writing, but I'd never been convinced about his climbing prowess. I
was rather impressed that morning.

The temperature rose overnight and we retreated to Stechelberg, to the
Naturfreundehaus. At eight francs a night, these hostels are a cross between
Ruskinian ideals and the YHA. However, in winter all 'freunde' turn up with
their smocks, roll-ups and müsli, then jump into the designer ski-wear and drive
off in the Mercedes to catch the lifts to Wengen. On this occasion our
companions included three Green women from Berlin who had predictable
reactions to Mrs Thatcher, and a pair of Dutch students, one of whom used to
hover athletically in the shower area.

Undeterred, we spent one afternoon taking the little train to Mürren. It
seemed a twee thing to do, and neither of us wanted to admit that we actually
enjoyed the ride. The Swiss are to kitsch as Shakespeare is to cliché; they
invented it, and it is perpetually re-enacted. We sat in meadows taking pictures
of trains and mountains, cows and mountains, rowanberries and mountains,
old biddies carrying brand new alpenstocks and mountains, guards on trains
and mountains. In front of a memorial to Arnold Lunn we sipped kirsch at five
francs a thimble. My forebears used to go to Mürren every year with the Lunns,
and even now there are gullies around Mürren named after them. But, apart
from laying ghosts, what we really wanted to see was the condition of the Eiger
after all the bad weather. We scoured the face with our telephoto lenses whilst
Stephen took me through the 'naming of parts' on the face.

I must confess to considerable innocence about the literature and legend that has built up about the Nordwand. Tony Saunders, who made a winter ascent, has told me since that he felt as though he was carrying two rucksacks – one with all his gear, the other with all the stories that have been told. Happily I was carrying just the one sack, my innocence being such that I had hardly liked to ask Stephen why Death Bivouac was so-named when we settled down there for the night three days later. To climb the route seemed a jolly enough idea at the time, and it looked pretty as we sipped our kirsch at Mürren, gazing past the trees, cows, rowanberries and railway trains.

The next morning was glorious – just the day for the Eiger, we thought. One of our safety valves was a hotline to the Zürich weather centre. There would be a storm that night, we were assured. Looking at the cloudless sky, we could be forgiven for doubting the forecast, but we didn't and spent the day falling off a climb at Handegg. We drove to friends in Meiringen (the *blumen* had served their purpose) when the storm began. It raged and bucketed for hours. How we blessed that weather centre. How miserable, how vulnerable, how dispirited we would have been at the first bivouac.

When we did arrive at Grindelwald to catch the train there was still heavy cloud. Leaving the train at Eigergletscher Station, we could not even see the mountain, let alone the foot of the climb. There was no one to ask the reasonable question, 'Excuse me, which way is it to the Eiger?' So we just waited and waited for the cloud to lift, munching chocolate and listening to the alpenhorn serenading the tourists as they boarded the Jungfraujoch railway. Suddenly it cleared. We were off. The weather improved steadily throughout the remainder of the afternoon (we had started about 4pm) as we climbed solo to the bottom of the 'Difficult Crack'. My faith in Venables's route-finding had been sorely tested in the last 10 days, so it was with some relief that we came to the crack and the cosiest bivvy ledge a man could have desired. The sunset was classic, and we settled down to the roar of the gas stove, the trundle of the railway in the valley below and the warble of that alpenhorn. We crammed in noodles and Mars bars, cheese and salami; the lights of Grindelwald twinkled beneath us, the stars twinkled above . . . a perfect alpine bivvy. We purred, then snored.

Stephen led the first pitch of the morning. The ropes had frozen overnight and were like wire hawsers. He reached a belay at the top of the crack, and I led through. But the ropes were snarled on a projecting rock beneath his stance. He tried to pull them through, but that made it worse, and then he started swearing. Stephen has quite a vocabulary when he's cross, and what the words lacked in subtlety they made up in volume. Now the Eiger Nordwand is shaped like a huge auditorium, and the more he swore the more it echoed across the whole valley. People were startled. Suddenly there were voices: 'Ist du kommen in?', and a head popped out of the side of the face. There just below us was the gallery window of the railway, and the passengers were savouring every word. Did we want to be rescued? The appearance of a fellow wandering carefree on one of the lower ice-fields humbled Stephen and he shut up until we reached the Hinterstoisser traverse when he busied himself reminding me to take another photograph of him.

By now the world was awake, the valley was sunlit, the alpenhorn was warbling the same tune, and we settled into the climbing; up the Ice Hose (in perfect condition), across the Second Ice-field . . . we were happy and moving well. Not a rock fell from above and we had only the Mountain Rescue helicopter touting for business after lunch to disturb us. We reached Death Bivouac at about half past three just as the sun was coming round to loosen all the debris above us. The sun was warm and we were sheltered, so we resolved to settle for an early night. As we bathed in the sun, we sharpened our crampons and discussed the complexities of some of the themes in *Figaro*. Still that wretched alpenhorn warbled away – the same tune. 'A couple of bars from Mozart's horn concertos wouldn't go amiss.'

A few rocks fell as we crossed the Third Ice-field the next morning, but, once in the Ramp, we settled into a rhythm. 'I love that bit in the last Act when the Duke realizes he's been caught out and there's that reconciliation between him and his wife . . . I wish I could find lovers so understanding.' 'Have you ever noticed that the tune when the maid comes into the garden near the end is a variation in the minor of Figaro's main aria in the first Act?' 'What name are we going to give this ascent . . . how about the First Oxbridge Ascent of the Eiger . . . no one would believe some of the aesthetic bullshit we've talked over the last fortnight.'

There was a little battle up the Waterfall pitch which Stephen cleared of anything a man could get an axe into, and some extremely solid blue ice on the Brittle Ice-field. We were beginning to forget Mozart and talk of Wagner as we approached the Traverse of the Gods, when the helicopter came back to see how we were getting on.

'Don't wave. He'll come and rescue us.'

The Spider was acting like an amphitheatre to that persistent alpenhorn. 'Someone has to tell him . . . He must have something else to play. He gets enough practice throughout the day to be concert standard. Three days on the trot, and he's still pushing out the same nauseous warble.'

Eventually we picked our way across a scary, skiddy band of loose rock below the summit ice-fields. All the holds were sloping down, and the rock was perilously loose. So this was where all the junk came from that rains down on to the route below. We'd had a pretty good run really.

Grindelwald was already in the dark when we reached the summit ridge, but the light on the mountains was as magical and rewarding as one could have dreamed after such a good route. It was half past seven and we clearly had another night on the mountain.

'Well, we made it,' said Stephen, waving his axe above his head for a photograph.

'Mmmm, up,' I said, 'but not yet down,' thinking of the tedium of a night on an ice-ledge with no sleeping bag and a temperature of 17C. In the moments when sleep seemed possible, an Irishman kept waking me up throughout the night to tell me to clip into that piton that was just above my head. Three times I pulled my hood from my eyes, just to check I was really awake. There was of course no piton. The fourth time I decided to put on the stove. Stephen had been having strange dreams, too. When in doubt, brew. That's always been a good rule in the mountains.

It seemed to take ages to flex our frozen limbs in the morning, but eventually we moved up the last 200m along the Mittellegi ridge to the summit, for me the most frightening part of the climb. The wind was screaming over the ridge, and we were painfully aware how far it would be to climb back up. Down the W face to Kleine Scheidegg took two and a half hours.

'Let's save the cash, not catch the train, and buy some wine when we get down to Grindelwald. Hang on a sec . . . before we go I just want to have a word with the fellow in a frilly waistcoat and white stockings who's playing the horn.'

We left the man who was undoubtedly the prime tourist attraction in Kleine Scheidegg bemused, confused, and a little put out, and pounded our weary toes into the fronts of our boots for the sake of a couple of bottles of plonk. The supermarkets were all closed.

'Oh well, I'd rather listen to that aria in the third Act again, anyway.'

Next morning I was back at work in London, high as a kite and overwhelmed with the beauty of it all. Quite suddenly my foot started to ache again, and every morning it was an effort to put weight on it. I indulged in a few telephone calls to nearest and dearest to let them know I was back, and what we'd been up to.

'You're mad. And with your foot just out of plaster, what on earth do you think you were doing? And why the Eiger of all things? Don't give me any of that "Because it's there" nonsense.'

'Well, actually, because it's fun.'

Zinal Rothorn

TERRY GIFFORD

(for John Driskell)

Whilst Zinal slept
We moved upon the mountain,

First by torchlight on moraine
Then dawnlight on ice until

Sunlight fired first peaks,
Caught our breath in the sharp,

Thin air that distilled
My first start, first season.

It was to be your last.
Strange, that we've both lost

The photographs, as though
Memory through the whisky glass

Between us, years after
Your first illness, was stronger

Years after we moved together
Step in step upon the mountain.

Thunderstorms and Fireworks: A Bicentenary Experience

(An account of two days at Chamonix)

LEWIS J. G. PRESTON

7 August 1986: It is half past midnight, more than five hours before dawn, on the eve of the 200th anniversary of the first ascent of Mont Blanc.

I have been asleep for about three hours in a snow-hole bivvy in a cornice above the Aiguille du Goûter. At an altitude of 4000m, the previous evening had offered a spectacularly peaceful sunset above the clouds. A party each of Yugoslavs, Norwegians, Germans and ourselves came together with shared tea and conversation before the night's approaching freeze. Five hours had now passed of the morning of the eve: my three companions and I stood alone in the darkness on the highest point in Europe, awaiting the rising dawn over Italy.

Each with his own thoughts, we relished these moments in frozen silence, while the stove struggled to produce a 'brew'.

One could sense the blackness fading to a deep prussian blue, then quite suddenly a brilliant light burst over peaks and clouds below: we were witnessing dawn from the summit of Mont Blanc.

Others were now arriving to share the experience. We four descended past toiling teams while the rising sun behind cast an enormous mountain shadow in stark outline over the whole world before us.

The 'ultimate fell-walk' it had been, I considered, looking up at the big white peak that afternoon, while lounging in the sun, now overhead, back at the Chamonix camp-site. Time now to plan the bicentenary day itself (well away from the slopes of Mont Blanc). A last 'steady' rock-climb was required to wrap up the end of the holiday.

Two of us packed sacks for the *Voie des Français*, the classic 400m TDsup route up the S face of the Aiguille du Pouce.

8 August 1986: The Aiguilles Rouges lie, like the N fells of the Lake District, separated from the main massif, and the approach to the 'Pouce' is like entering 'Back o' Skiddaw' country – the isolation is all the more noticeable after leaving the crowds behind.

Despite another early start, by the time our rock-boots stepped anxiously across the threatening bergschrund it was already late morning. Just 24 hours before, we had been up and almost down the hill of that day. And so to the Pouce: I lead up a challenging first pitch away from the snow, cold in every sense: belayed, and my companion, Caval, followed. This was his third visit to the climb, after having been rained off on two previous attempts. Caval linked a couple of unspectacular pitches – were we off route already? I forced an overhanging block, traversed right and pulled round into the great central

2.   *Golden Pillar from Melangush.*

3. *Belay beneath the monstrous 'ice ear'.*

4. *Near the top of the 'slabs'.*

5.   *Summit Plateau. Ultar and Batura on the horizon.*

6. *Mick Fowler.*

7.   *Girgindil Chish (c. 6000m), from the Golden Pillar.*

8. *A temporary camp on the S Gasherbrum glacier. Gasherbrums 4, 3 and 2 in the background.*

9. *Masherbrum from the Baltoro glacier.*

SOUTH FACE
AIGUILLE DU POUCE   2,874 m.

Voie des Français

5 O = stances taken.

start

L.J.G.P.
'87

dihedral. This was it! Caval romped up another full rope-length and the climb opened out into the full vastness of the face.

I lead another double pitch and we felt certainly committed. Looking up, however, further progress seemed completely unobtainable, barred by overlaps that defied gravity in remaining attached to the mountain. Caval led up the unhopeful crack to belay 15m underneath the incredible overhangs.

I left the stance, too encompassed in the climb to notice the change in the weather. Cav shivered in the shade. Leading up to the roof I marvelled at the nerve and route-finding ability of the original ascensionists in 1960. At one point, where it seemed that wings would be required to complete the route, a finger-crack led away horizontally across an otherwise blank face. Several metres away was the first old rusty peg, followed by another. The moves were stupendous – summing up the whole reasoning for why I climb: finding a passage to an altered state of consciousness. This was active meditation in the extreme. I had left my office desk of five days a week to confront reality; to address questions of life and death, of faith and trust in oneself, in another, in mankind. The climb was itself a route, a way (up the mountain); but to climb thus is, in itself, the other 'way' – that inner experience often missing in Western (so-called) 'civilization'.

I clipped a running belay into one of the pegs and moved across to a break in the defences of the overlaps. Caval followed across, exclaiming, and led through, up, over, and out of sight. I joined him and approached the second overlap. At this point it began to rain and then immediately to hail, hard. With the crux-pitches below us we had estimated a further 150m of climbing to the end of the difficulties. Our difficulties, however, were just beginning. The face sloped back from vertical above the second overlap, and the hail-stones 'ping-ponged' down the slabs. Tiny footholds were lost and fingers began to go numb. After a few teetering pitches, Caval escaped up an awkward chimney, and above I found a passage of hail-covered grassy ledges. The storm increased, and looking up was impossible; the hail blinded, the rain soaked, sponged into one's inside. Rivulets torrented down the broken slopes up which I dragged the rope. Another lead through, and then I was in a mist-concealed 'non-place'. I dived down off the summit rocks as a thunderbolt clashed, and at the same time I was illuminated in lightning with all my ironmongery. The rocks buzzed; I had become the centre-point of nature's anniversary firework display. There was nowhere to go until Caval reached my hiding place, coiling the sodden ropes. We exchanged unspoken emotions, decided on the route, and began down.

It was very late afternoon and the storm had raged while we had been down-climbing, abseiling, re-ascending, re-routing, slipping, gripping and recovering for four hours down an invisible mile of ridge. With thankfulness at being off the Pouce, we stumbled out on to the col on which we had left my sack. It was gone, together with our spare clothing, anoraks, food and light. The situation was becoming serious. Soaked through, shivering uncontrollably, we had little mist-laden daylight left in which to re-ascend the main chain of the 'Rouges' and to descend beyond to the Chamonix valley. The storm had now ceased, leaving a strange empty silence. We hurried up to the main ridge and clattered down scree out of the mist and on to snow below in the last light.

Lewis Preston leading up under the 'Great Roof'
pitch, between belay points 7 and 8.
see route diagram.

Across the valley huts blazed anniversary lights. Then, spectacularly, the
original route up Mont Blanc became a shining trail of torches, up from
Chamonix into the mist at mid-height. We had to descend the distance we could
see illuminated, without torch, to the valley. For the next half-hour our way was

sporadically lit by 'star bursting' and 'falling lantern' fireworks kindly provided by the Chamonix townsfolk celebrating their 200 years of history.

Afterwards we were gripped by darkness and fatigue in the lower forests that cut out even the street-lights, still 1000m below. In the small hours we stumbled out on to level ground and located the car. Now, within a few flat miles of camp and bed, we were finally thwarted. Chamonix was a madhouse of motorists; thousands of them were trying to leave after the evening's festivities. We were in a jam and we could not climb out of it; we pulled off the road and fell asleep where we were.

Mont Blanc – The Girdle and the Cross

JOHN HUNT

On a day last summer my wife and I, with John Whyte and Peter Ledeboer, crossed the Col du Tricot and paused for refreshment at the Châlets de Miage, amid a crowd of tourists under the coloured umbrellas. We were half-way along the route which traces a girdle around Mont Blanc, very much in vogue nowadays among the longer alpine treks: the *Tour du Mont Blanc*. The mountain has been much in the news of late, highlighted by the 200th anniversary of its first ascent. Our journey had come into my mind while attending the celebrations in Chamonix in 1986, and I had looked forward to it, knowing that it would awake many memories: of successes and failures on Mont Blanc and the Aiguilles, and of friends with whom I had shared those climbs over a period which spanned more than one quarter of those two centuries.

As I looked up at the great head-wall to the Col de Miage, 1800m above us, one of those memories came sharply into focus; my mind flew back 32 years. David Cox, Michael Ward, Wilfrid Noyce and I had set off from these chalets on 3 August 1955 to attempt one of the great classic routes of those days: the double traverse from south-west to north-east and from south to north, known as the *Croix du Mont Blanc*. The first stage of our journey had begun at Les Contamines, which my diary records as having been 'a sweet little village, quite unspoilt and no tourists'. Now, alas! it has been transformed into a modern tourist centre.

We had started by limbering up two days beforehand with a traverse of the Aiguille de Lex Blanche and the Aiguille des Glaciers from an idyllic bivouac site where now stands the Refuge des Conscrits, but our state of fitness was severely tested as, with heavy loads, we toiled up from these chalets (no refreshments or coloured umbrellas then) towards the Durier hut. Indeed, our plans nearly foundered when, nine hours after leaving Les Contamines, we were still groping around in a thick mist, sleet and inky darkness, searching for the hut. Typically, it was Wilf who guided us to it. We were very tired and when, at 3am next morning, dense mist still persisted, I half hoped it might provide an excuse for a rest day. But our spirits rose half an hour later; the moon shone clear, near to full. So bright was it that we made quick time up the ice-clad rocks of the S buttress of the Aiguille de Bionnassay; the ice-slopes behind us on the Dômes de Miage were like polished silver.

Then, with daylight, a curtain of mist descended again, to herald a truly dreadful day. But the summit arête of the Bionnassay is too narrow to permit errors in navigation and we reached it in under three and a half hours from the hut. Likewise the snow-ridge connecting with the Dôme du Goûter guided us safely to that summit. Then our troubles began, and continued through the day. We groped our way downhill with visibility reduced to 20 yards and, even with the aid of a compass, only chanced upon the Goûter hut. Well known, even in those days, for its chronic overcrowding, we soon found the pressure of humanity wellnigh insufferable and, against all sane mountaineering judgement, decided to depart for the Vallot in a near white-out; visibility was now down to 10 yards. My diary continues the story:

> 'It was now snowing hard and there was a storm in the offing. Our uptracks were quickly filled in with fresh snow. A French guide with an American client, who had started out two hours beforehand with the same idea as ours, came running back as we left the hut. I was in the lead and persisted for one and a half hours through thick snow, peering for signs of the vanishing track but guided by compass, until opinion in the party hardened against my obstinacy. We must have been just beneath the Dôme du Goûter when we turned back.'

Within a few minutes we had lost our uptracks. Visibility was virtually at zero and at times we were uncertain whether we were going up or downhill. Then, after prolonged casting around, we suddenly found the hut close at hand and pushed our way, thankfully this time, into the pandemonium within.

We were all aroused at 3am next morning and stepped out into a peerless, moonlit arena. Forging ahead of the long trail of climbers, we reached the Vallot cabin in one and a half hours and were on the summit two hours later. I have never seen the peaks looking more clear and beautiful, and there were many familiar summits to greet us in that vast panorama. We were alone on the traverse that day and were glad that there were no signs of the tracks of Raymond Lambert, who had done it two days before us. My diary continues:

> 'On we went along this wonderful high level walk: down the Mur de la Côte to the Col de la Brenva, meeting two weary Germans who had come the old Brenva route. We made an error in trying to traverse beneath Mont Maudit and had to climb back again, along an enjoyable rock ridge. Looking back across the Brenva Face at that point, Wilf and I noted with satisfaction how nearly we had reached the summit ridge before being forced down by a storm last year.
>
> 'Then weariness set in. Mike and I both found the long plod over Mont Blanc de Tacul, down and across the Vallée Blanche, a severe trial. Wilf, as always, was a tower of strength and returned from the Torino Hut with coffee for Mike.'

Thus we completed the long arm of the *Croix du Mont Blanc*, a memorable journey in itself. We had hoped to complete the Cross – by traversing the mountain from Courmayeur to Chamonix via the Route Major – with only one overnight stop at the Torino. But I have long since learned the lesson of patience and – above all – persistence in wooing this particular snow goddess. Twice in the 1940s my companions and I had been thwarted in attempts to climb the mountain from the Grands Mulets, in weather so atrocious as to render the return journey through the *Jonction* a hazardous experience. I have been turned back, by another storm, from the Peuterey Ridge. And the previous year, as my diary has already recalled, Wilf Noyce and I had made our way up the Frontier Ridge, relatively sheltered from the tempest raging on the summit. So bad were the conditions that we had no choice but to reverse our route just below the crest. From that frustrating experience I retain one delicious memory of a moment when, facing inwards on a very steep snow slope as we made our way back to the Col de la Fourche, Wilf suggested breakfast. It was not exactly a perfect picnic spot; but we managed it, our faces pressed against the snow wall.

Now, a year later, we were back at the cabin on the Col de la Fourche in weather so thick that any thought of descending to the Col Moore for the Route Major – even another attempt on the summit via the Frontier Ridge – was quickly dismissed. Disconsolate, we steered our way by compass back to the Col du Géant and down on foot to Courmayeur via the Châlet-Refuge du Pavillon. Its *gardien* was Ubaldo Rey, fresh from the Italian triumph on K2; we were to meet again in Courmayeur in 1987, a little further along our *Tour du Mont Blanc*.

The bad weather continued to thwart us. Amid the fleshpots of the town, abetted by lavish hospitality and plagued by the importunities of attractive Italian autograph seekers, we were in danger of losing our zest and fitness for the completion of the *Croix*. We made an effort to offset these distractions by climbing the Aiguille de la Brenva by the splendid Grand Dièdre on its E face. It was a Sunday and, on returning to the Torino, we were once more besieged by starry-eyed fans. One brazen lass bared her bosom and insisted that I autograph that part of her anatomy; our morale was being rapidly undermined and stern resolve was called for. We departed once more for the Col de la Fourche.

The whole great flank of Mont Blanc, displayed in profile through the missing door of the refuge, was a spectacle sufficient in itself to restore a sense of proportion; yet in another context I was struck once again by the failure of mind and eye to appreciate contrasting scales of altitude between the biggest mountains and the lesser ones. This face is not much bigger than the W face of Lhotse; yet the Lhotse face, dwarfed by the highest and fourth-highest mountains in the world, seemed a trifling obstacle compared with the problem now confronting us.

We rested, brewed tea and invoked the lenience of the Furies, our eyes tracing those famed routes up the precipice, whose shadows were now adding emphasis to its height and sheer lines. We were waiting for the sun to slip behind the summit crest, leaving the chill shadows to harden the snow before making the crossing to the Col Moore. We looked down to the upper Brenva glacier, 120m directly below our perch. There, dug into the snow, was a sight reminiscent of the Himalaya but oddly unfamiliar in the Alps – a little group of tents. This we knew to be a camp of six Bavarian climbers; we had met them during the previous, abortive visit to the Col de la Fourche. They had already been there a fortnight and intended to remain for some 10 days longer.

Later, chatting with them over jam-jars of Ovo-Malt, we agreed that theirs was an example which might well be emulated by other mountaineers, to reduce overcrowding in the huts.

It was 6pm when we left their camp and climbed the short ice-slope to the Col Moore, at the foot of the old Brenva route. Here we had our first setback. From the col begins the long, steep traverse across a series of minor ribs and intervening couloirs in order to reach the centre of the face. In view of the poor weather forecast for the next day, we had decided to lower our sights and aim at the *Voie de la Sentinelle* rather than the Route Major, and we had intended to bivouac beneath the Sentinelle itself. But to reach it in safety and before dark the snow would have had to harden enough, after many hours of exposure to the sun. Although the shadows were now deep upon the slopes, the air was too warm and we noted that clouds were forming over the mountain. We had travelled barely a hundred yards across the steep slope, sinking into rotten, sun-saturated snow at every step, before recognizing that the task was too dangerous. We returned to the col. This was a blow, but we could still make valuable height by climbing some way up the Brenva ridge. So up we went, balancing delicately on its sharp blade.

The clouds thickened and it began to snow. It seemed that our persistence was again to be ill-rewarded. At short intervals, three avalanches broke from the ice cliffs beneath the summit and thundered down the gullies on our left: the same gullies which we would have had to cross to reach the Sentinelle. As if to underline the call to halt, there was a distant growl of thunder. About 150m above the Col Moore we stopped on a ledge on the rock buttress upon which we had been climbing, and settled down for the night. It was quite a salutary discipline, after so much *dolce vita*, to submit ourselves to a somewhat cheerless bivouac. The little petrol cooker, balanced on a slab of rock between David's knees, was spluttering comfortingly as our soup was heated.

Would it clear? Would it freeze? On the answers to these two questions rested all our hopes. No other cares in the world mattered to us at that moment. For a long while it did neither. We knew that the moon stood at three-quarters full, on the wane. If it were to shine on the face we had to cross, we could start at midnight. But a blanket of mist enshrouded everything. Then suddenly, something caught my eye. A jagged line of ridge, far above, was etched black, even against the dark sky. Stars were blinking in gaps in the clouds. Below, in the inky well of the valley, other lights were winking up at us from Courmayeur. The vision vanished; but at 3am the curtain was lifted again, this time for good. It became bitingly cold.

We stirred ourselves to action, for there was little time to waste. The cooker purred while we rolled sleeping-bags and duvets. At 3.40am we were off, stiff and clumsy, climbing to the top of the rock-buttress in clear moonlight. The sky was already paling with the new day. My diary continues:

> 'The mist still persisted, but we were off, beginning the great
> traverse upwards and across to the Sentinelle. Very steep indeed
> and I, in the dark, a trifle unsteady. Wilf led us a tremendous pace.
> We came to the deep groove referred to by Smythe: an awkward

six-foot descent into an ice runnel, tilted at a sharp angle. I came
out of the step (cut by Wilf) but managed to land on my crampon
points. (I think that we were still unroped at that time.)

'We crossed all four couloirs and passed beneath the
Sentinelle at 5 am. Continued left to the main containing wall of the
Great Couloir and on, without pause, to the lowest extremity of
the Côte Tortueuse. Here we stopped to eat, enjoying the dawn
view on a glorious clear morning. We climbed the easy rocks of the
Côte, dispensing with crampons for the next one and a half hours
before tackling the seemingly endless ice slopes, steep and exposed,
which led eventually to the summit ridge. There was no security,
for we were all moving together, with Wilf and myself as the
leading rope.

'At about 9 am there were the first indications of a change in
the weather: clouds appeared over the crest, borne by a westerly
wind. We were soon enveloped in mist which became rather denser
as we climbed. I was following Wilf, moving upwards for 30 to 40
steps before pausing for breathers as he kicked his way up.

'At last we passed the ice cliff crowning the rock rib on our
left and emerged on to the gentle slopes immediately under the
summit. The familiar wind and mist greeted us, with visibility
again reduced to 20 yards. It was snowing when we reached the top
at 11.35 am.'

At the Vallot hut a large crowd of Germans and Italians were marooned, in
conditions so uninviting that we raced on down to the Grands Mulets, passing
through a huge and recent fall of seracs on the Petit Plateau in which, we had
been told, two Swiss climbers had been buried early that morning.

And so down to Chamonix, tired but elated, to greet a number of French
and British friends: Mayor Paul Payot, Maurice Herzog, Gaston Rébuffat,
Lionel Terray and Armand Charlet among the former; Roger Chorley,
Blackshaw, Downs, Gawkroger, Fraser and Sutton among our own com-
patriots. High life in Courmayeur was as nothing compared with that being
enjoyed in Chamonix. Our arrival coincided with the *Fête des Guides*; the guest
of the Commune was no less a star than *Mademoiselle Monde* for 1955, a Swiss
beauty possessed of a charming personality. To exercise my privilege as an
honorary citizen of Chamonix, in order to dance with Miss World that night,
was an experience which I greatly enjoyed.

But already we were impatient to be away from such perils to the greater
safety of the mountains. We left next morning for the Montanvert, bound for
the *Intégrale* of the Moine by its SW and N ridges.

In the succeeding days last summer we made our way back to our
beginning at Champex, completing the Girdle of Mont Blanc. As we traversed
the high ground above Courmayeur over the Col Chécrouit and the Mont de la
Saxe, I looked across at that great southern precipice and remembered those
days so long ago. I thought of the good companions with whom I had shared the
Cross of Mont Blanc. In particular, I remembered Wilfrid Noyce, whose

effortless ease and tireless strength on a mountain were, in their day, unsurpassed and who, the most unassuming of men, was so unaware of any limits to his power and skill.

A First Look at the Dauphiné Alps

MARIAN ELMES

'C'est un paradis sauvage fait pour le bonheur des hommes, des fleurs et des bêtes.' That's what Gaston Rebuffat says about the Dauphiné Alps.

I dangled on the end of the abseil ropes and contemplated the gloomy depths of the bergschrund. It was not small, its top lip overhung and I rotated gently above it. As I swung I mused on Rebuffat's words: *'homme'* I certainly was not, *'fleurs'* were happily vegetating elsewhere, no self-respecting *'bête'* would be here.

'So where on earth do I go from here??'

'Let go and jump, you fool.'

The traverse of the Meije had been on my list for years and had proved to be a magnificent day out – then came this sting in the tail! A swing and a bounce (to stretch the ropes a bit more) and my crampons crunched into the icy lower lip, then a backwards tip-toeing movement out of the jaws of the bergschrund and we pulled the ropes down. An easy trot down to the Aigle hut for tea. The party behind was only just emerging from the Zsigmondy couloir. Hours behind. The weather broke and they finally reached the hut at 4.30am. Wonder how they enjoyed that final abseil, by torchlight, in the wind and snow.

It was my first visit to the Dauphiné area of France, and I wouldn't have gone there without the dual incentives of a club meet (the annual AC/CC/ABMSAC meet) and the need to get fit for a first venture in the Himalaya. I've always preferred higher areas of the Alps with more snow and a few 4000m peaks to bag. The Dauphiné offers more rock than snow and has only one 4000er.

I couldn't see much appeal in the area as we drove up the very industrial lower part of the Romanche valley from Grenoble to Le Bourg d'Oisans (which incidentally is the nearest place for banking facilities if you're based at La Bérarde, in the centre of the Ecrins massif.) Most of the summits keep themselves well hidden, the hillsides are barren and stony, and the side-valleys too narrow to see into.

The rough single-track road which rises in spectacular fashion from the Romanche valley into the heart of the area at La Bérarde provided several thrilling moments, because of the imaginative driving of those coming down. But there was still little hint of any interesting mountains, let alone the flowery meadows full of rare plants and wildlife such as the Tourist Office leaflets advertise. Mind you, we were in a hot dry season, and the vegetation which managed to find an insecure foothold on the crumbling roadside cliffs and bouldery banks was pretty brown and burnt. The camp-site up at La Bérarde was just as brown, and a bit rough, as were the facilities – just three very French loos and a couple of taps, but hosed clean most days, and showers were available in the village. Anyway, it was cheap!

Waking next day to a clear bright morning, after a night dreaming longingly of the Nadelgrat and Monte Rosa, I wandered off on my own across the wide, glacially-grey river and back down the other side of the valley. Immediately I found tall red martagon lilies and striking-looking white-red-and-black Apollo butterflies. Chamois were titupping across a scree just above me, and a marmot whistled its alarm from a boulder-top. This all cheered me up a bit. Exploring a tiny steep woodland trail up a hanging valley, the Vallon des Étages, I began to realize that this was really an area of secret corners and sudden surprises. Even in areas such as the Gran Paradiso National Park, I don't think I've seen such a profusion of flowers and butterflies as greeted my eyes on emerging from the woods into the level valley-meadows.

Choosing to start our real exercise on Mont Gioberney and Les Bans, we headed up next day for the Pilatte hut at 2572m, with its tame marmots (first spotted rear-end-up in the refuse bin). Mont Gioberney (3351m) offers a choice of ridges graded PD and a *Facile* glacier route, all approached most easily by a new cairned path up the rock-band immediately behind the hut. We had an enjoyable day on a direct variant of the NE ridge.

Les Bans (3669m) is a slightly more serious proposition. The route we chose (the ENE ridge, PD) gave us a longish glacier approach to the Col des Bans, followed by a nice (or nasty, depending on conditions) little ice-arête leading to some rock gendarmes at the foot of the ridge. The ridge-climbing is mostly delightful and straightforward scrambling and Grade 2 climbing, with just one little traverse of Grade 3, nearly all on good sound rock. Bright little cushions of blue *eritrichium nanum*, 'The King of the Alps', light the way.

North-west of La Bérarde, and forming the southern ramparts of the Romanche valley, are the nice rocky training peaks of Pic de la Grave and Le Râteau. The E peak of this gives fine views of La Meije dominating the one-time famous climbing centre of La Grave. We climbed the harder W peak of Le Râteau from the Selle hut. The hut is reached by a short drive or bus-ride down to St Christophe-en-Oisans, which is a typical French mountain village, plain and picturesquely ramshackle, with the original hut path meandering up between the cowsheds and the cattle-troughs.

Early next day, an awkward scramble over ice-worn slabs and bits of glacier got us up to the bottom of a steepish snow-couloir, which we climbed to the Col de la Girose. Snow-slopes then led to pleasant climbing at Grade 3 on the fine summit-pinnacles of Râteau Ouest, at a height of 3766m. On the way back down the now soggy snow-couloir, we remarked the presence of abseil-pegs up on the true left wall, quite useful for really bad conditions – if there is enough snow in the couloir to enable one to reach them. Instead of going down to the Selle hut again, we thought it would be fun for a change to traverse the Brêche de Râteau and descend the Étançons valley back to La Bérarde. This route would also give us a good look at the S face of La Meije. It did. It wasn't much fun though – you can keep your mid-afternoon descents of rapidly thawing soggy snow/collapsing crevasses/gravelly slabs/waterfalls. It reminded me of the Buachaille in spring.

The peak-baggers amongst us had the Barre des Ecrins on the list, since this tops the magic 4000m mark. We decided to follow the route by which Whymper first reached the summit in 1864. First a long hot walk from the camp-site over the Col des Ecrins (PD) and down easy glacier-slopes to the Ecrins hut. Then, next day, an early start for the glaciers on the N face, burning off those who had bivouacked outside the hut. Around various serac-bands, then a long traverse right beneath the summit cliffs (mind your head) to the Brèche Lory, a windy gap in the main ridge. We roped up to cross the awkward bergschrund just below the Brèche. We nipped up the easy snow of the Dôme de Neige, a subsidiary summit of 4015m, then back to the Brèche. To reach the main summit of the Barre des Ecrins we climbed a steep little wall leading round left, then up, to the NW arête. An hour's pleasant ridge-climbing ended us up on top, but our summit visit was a brief one – we had been watching storm clouds gathering to the south and were speeded up on the descent by icy gales blowing hail and mist across at us. We were praying it wouldn't thunder, as our descent included re-crossing the Col des Ecrins, where the fixed cables on the W side make splendid lightning conductors.

The traverse of the Meije (*difficile*) must be one of the most sought-after expeditions in the Dauphiné, with its great history of repeated attempts and repulses. Its Grand Pic remained unclimbed until 1877, when a 19-year-old youth, Emmanuel Boileau de Castelnau, together with the French guide Pierre Gaspard and his son, left La Bérarde at 11pm, and finally reached the Grand Pic via the Promontoire Arête at 3.30pm the next day. In the course of an epic descent without the benefit of abseiling (not yet invented!), they endured an uncomfortable bivouac as the weather deteriorated; but the lashing rain which accompanied their triumphant return to Le Bérarde can hardly have dampened their spirits after such an achievement. Even so, the traverse from the main peak to the Pic Central, or Doigt de Dieu, and down to La Grave, on the N side, only fell to J M Gibson in 1891.

On arriving at the Promontoire hut to attempt the traverse, we couldn't help being a bit put off by meeting a group of friends, experienced alpinists all, who had just had to bivouac twice, because of sudden storms, in order to climb the Grand Pic. Then I got a tummy bug which kept me up half the night, and despite the ministrations of a kindly doctor friend, I was sick all over the first fixed rope on the buttress behind the hut!

Things can only get better, I thought grimly, as I struggled up the first 500 feet of steep scrambling, rope-coils in one hand and stomach in the other. Only another 2500 feet to the Grand Pic, then the same again to complete the traverse . . . what a lot of rock: towers and walls, ridges and pinnacles rearing up all around. First the easy cracks and chimneys, then you leave the main arête for a long, wide, cold couloir leading up to a great platform. Then – take care. The choice is between lovely delicate climbing at Grade 3 plus, starting on the right of the mighty buttress ahead; or very much harder climbing if you miss the right line, but all on lovely sound granite. Fine positions, and romantic pitch-names: the *Dos d'Âne*, and the *Pas du Chat*. We were probably lucky in a way to get held up for a couple of hours on this section, where everyone starts pitching instead of climbing together: it gave me vital recovery time, and the weather was brilliant.

Higher up, we shot past our rivals on the Glacier Carré where it became clear that some of them had never worn crampons before. One girl, who tried to race me up the final steep ice to the shoulder below the Grand Pic itself, fell off, and only self-arrested after a fall of about 20 feet.

The 700-foot spire of the Grand Pic now loomed over us, and we took the rather loose shallow grooves just in from the left-hand edge, until the final summit wall pushed us left to the arête. Here there is a little red slab with an open corner on its right, and you go up this for a ride on the *Cheval Rouge* – a stance *à cheval* with your left boot dangling several thousand feet above La Grave. A move or two up and left, and you're on the top at 3983m, wondering if the rest of the crenellated ridge is as awkward as it looks.

No time to rest – we abseiled quickly down to some more uncomfortable *à cheval* moves on the sharp ridge crest, to the peg-belays at the start of the fixed cables. These cables lead you down and round the icy N side of the Dent Zsigmondy, and up a long and strenuous ice-couloir to rejoin the arête. I was going fine up this couloir, hauling myself up on the cable, till near the top a loose end of cable hung down just where the way tightened into a little chimney. Murphy's law prevailed as always, the loose end caught round my rucksack, and it took all the rest of my puny strength to disentangle it whilst falling out of this chimney with crampons scrabbling ineffectually on the steep glassy ice.

On we plugged over the two intermediate peaks, back in the warmth of the afternoon sun, then finally up snow and easy rocks to the Doigt de Dieu (3975m), God's finger indeed, an amazing leaning tower pointing threateningly over the hidden abysses of the S face. At last, a rest! And my first food of the day – a bourbon cream biscuit; thanks, Mike. The abseil points on the E side were easily located. Once down to the lowest part of the ridge we ignored the first lot of abseil-slings, which looked as though they would dump us inconveniently right on the steepest part of the glacier above the bergschrund. We went along, instead, to the foot of the next riser; then down to some snowy rocks from which an abseil of 45m will (just!) carry you over the bergschrund; then to the Aigle hut – a brilliant little traditional hut well run by a very friendly young couple, who lose their sleep most nights because they are watching out for torchlights along the crest of the Meije, so that they can have a brew on ready for the latecomers.

The Brèche de la Meije should have provided us with a quick way back over to the Promonteire hut, but unfortunately this was out of condition, and we were forced to spend a whole day wandering (and drinking) our way back round the valleys from La Grave, using various buses, none of which connect.

South-west of La Meije, and reached by a steep little valley cutting up north from Les Etages near La Bérarde, stands the extraordinary granite blade of the Aiguille Dibona. A real cragrat's playground, this one, with nothing 'alpine' about it except its height, at 3130m. Festooned on a fine day with multi-coloured ropes of many nationalities, it doesn't even require an early start. You can leave the Soreiller hut, already clad in your stickyboots, as late as you like.

We climbed a varied and interesting Grade 4 plus, a hybrid line which began with the Berthet route, giving us a nice logical direct start right behind the hut. We finished on the Boell route, with its splendid exposed positions out on the S and E faces. There are so many routes criss-crossing all over the place that it would be easy to get lost, but at least every route has peg-belays *in situ* on the stances, so you can tell if you are still on something. Edelweiss and little pink androsaces growing in crevices add to the interest, and give a point of focus when one's nose is jammed against the rock by eager continentals climbing all over one.

We still had enough holiday left for a quick look at the NE side of L'Olan (3560m). As the Lavey hut we started from is very low down, we thought we'd better set out extra early. This led to four members of the Alpine Club getting hopelessly lost in the dark only about 10 minutes after leaving the hut. Everyone else in the hut stayed in bed, knowing no doubt that people generally climb the Olan from a different hut on the other side of the mountain. Anyway, by the time we had regained the path and reached the Glacier des Sellettes it was too late to bother continuing very far. But it certainly looked a fine big rocky peak, and I'll be back for another go some day. We missed lots of others too: Pelvoux, Ailefroide, Les Rouies, La Grande Ruine – now there's an off-putting name!

As the variety of people on the camp-site proved, from families to botanists to rock-freaks, there's something to please everyone in the Dauphiné, and without too much hassle in the way of overcrowded huts and queueing for routes. And, while Chamonix and the Oberland are suffering in storms and rain, the Dauphiné generally basks in sunshine.

APPENDIX

MAPS

IGN (Purple) 1:25,000 Nos 241 Meije, Pelvoux; 242 Olan, Muzelle; 243 Champsaur.
New Blue series will replace these: Nos 3436, 3336, 3437 Est.
Didier & Richard 1:50,000 No 6 Ecrins.

GUIDEBOOKS

John Brailsford, ed Les Swindin, *Ecrins Massif, Selected Climbs* (Alpine Club, 1987).
Gaston Rébuffat, *Le Massif des Ecrins* (Denoel, 1974).

ACCOMMODATION

La Grave to the north (many hotels but busy valley road).
La Bérarde in centre (camping, hotel, restaurants, hut, no bank).
Ailefroide to the east (similar to above, no bank).
Many *gîtes* and huts throughout the region.

A Short Ski in the Eastern Pyrenees – March 1986

GUY SHERIDAN

The Peugeot clattered up the steep twisting road sounding more like a Norwegian fishing boat than a 305 Diesel Estate. Behind, a well-used Citroen Visa strained on its 1100cc to draw its occupants up the hill and maintain some sort of station on us ahead. There were seven of us including Molly, my wife, and François, a French friend, who were to return to Quillan with the cars once we had been dropped off. The four Norwegians had arrived a couple of days before at Toulouse, having visibly much enjoyed the Côtes du Roussillon on the Air France flight from Paris. They had come down to the Pyrenees for a short seven-day ski tour which I had pieced together over the previous 12 months.

Almost exactly a year before three of us had been in a more remote wilderness in the MacKenzie Mountains of the Yukon (*AJ91*, 120–121, 1986). But, although this part of the Pyrenees is far from remote, it is quick to transit through the scar of capitalist decadence of downtown Andorra and find oneself in wild and empty mountain country. As we clattered up the road that sunny frosty morning it wasn't difficult to notice that the snow that had been here at Christmas was nowhere to be seen.

'There's a lot more height to gain – there's sure to be some snow round the corner on the northern side,' I said without the slightest confidence.

Molly sensed my agitation. 'You must convince the Norwegians, not me, darling!' she replied candidly.

There was not a single glistening snow crystal to be seen in the sharp early morning sun as we pulled up into our planned drop-off place, 1800m up on the S side of the Sierra de Boumort, some 60km south-west of Seo d'Urgell. I feared the reaction of my Norwegian chums who had come a long way for this trip. But I had no reason to, because a five-minute soviet poring over a map spread over the bonnet of the car produced the answer.

We returned to Seo d'Urgell and drove to Arcabell, 1142m up on the Spanish side of the Andorran frontier. A short burst on foot for an hour soon found us on snow, and we were away to follow the frontier ridge over Pic Negre (2602m) and Pic Mounturall (2761m). There the steep interconnecting ridge to Pic Perafita (2756m) forced us down into the cwm to the Etangs de la Pera where we had lunch. It was an exhilarating descent; the snow had been perfect and we had made good progress. We camped high and just below Pic des Estanyons (2836m), feeling the exertions of a long day unused to the thinner air.

The fickleness of that winter's precipitation in this part of the Pyrenees revealed itself for the second time the next morning. As we topped Pic des Estanyons and ski'd down towards the Portella de Setut, the snow ran out and

there was virtually no cover over on the Pic de la Portelleta (2898m), where the frontier turned northwards. The decision was made for us; we had to descend south and walk round towards Borg Madame and get up to Porta, near the Col de Puymorens to continue the line. Our frustration was heightened when we were stopped by guntoting Spanish border police in the most unexpected place. '*Rien à déclarer. Pas de problème!*'

The next morning, after camping on the outskirts of Puymorens, we were off early to escape the hurly-burly, cacophony and litter of thousands of downhillers and were soon back in the wilderness and on our own again. A couple of hours saw us on the Col de Lanous (2468m), the bulk of Pic Carlit (2921m) looming above us, and a wonderful descent to the Etang de Lanous. The dam at its southern end stood clear and our own experience of controlled lakes in Norway told us to keep off the ice and take the longer way round its eastern shore before traversing up to the Porteille de la Grave (2420m). Descending, steep at first then easing to that angle where one is able to maintain balance and control without reducing speed, we dropped into the Val de la Grave, where we camped beside a trickle of a stream.

It snowed during the night, but the dawn was cold and clear, the fifth day of sunny weather! Our progress up the slopes to the Etang de la Llose (2238m) was watched by a couple of French Army helicopters which then buzzed off to touch-point landings on the ridge of Pic Peric far above. Otherwise we were alone all day, through terrain similar and reminiscent of parts of Sjødalen in the Jotunheim of Norway, to skirt the slopes of Pic de Terres (2540m) and drop into the top of the Val de Galbe.

The Porteille de Laurenti (2410m) was too steep on its N side to descend without ice-axes, so we traversed down into the Val and camped early in warm sunshine. A steep climb the next morning, through forest initially and then open mountain, took us straight across the top of the ski-runs of Puyvaledor with the noise and evident rubbish of the downhilling fraternity. We were glad to see them, and the scar that their sport inflicted on this beautiful place, well behind us.

That night we were in idyllic meadow under Pic de Tarbesou (2340m), with a black sky rumbling up from the west. It passed during the night, leaving behind a sharp frost, a dusting of snow and a clear dawn. The descent from the Col du Pelèheres to Camurac (1500m) went far beyond what we expected for a wonderful last day. A telephone call and two litres of wine later, Molly arrived to whisk us down to Quillan and huge eats.

180km Nordic Ski Tour 23–30 March 1986, Arcabell (Spain) to Camurac.

Members of the Party: Guy Sheridan, Erik Boehlke, Dag Dawes, Torbjorn Eggen and his son Kyrre, aged 17.

MAPS

IGN Mont Louis 1:50,000, Ax les Thermes 1:50,000, Fontargente 1:50,000, Editorial Alpina, Andorra and S Joán de L'Eran 1:40,000.

The Picos de Europa

J. G. R. HARDING

Only one range in Europe bears the continent's matronym – the Picos de Europa. Virtually unknown to the commonalty of British climbers until recently, these mountains lay claim to being the most dramatic minor range of Europe. Ptolemy knew of the range as 'Vindius' in distant *Hispania Terraconensis*. To Phoenician sailors, Spanish mariners returning from the New World and fishermen of all ages alike, their snow-whitened peaks have heralded European landfall.

Running parallel to the coast for some 40km on an EW axis, the Picos rise over 2600m to form the apex of the Cantabrian Mountains – the dominant feature of the geography of N Spain. Many are now familiar with the range in summer, but of winter ski tours I could find only one account, and that a traverse undertaken by the French Grand Raid specialists Derrieux and Parmentier. They had warned of mist, Atlantic weather and dangerous ground, yet without having seen the place for oneself it was difficult to know what to expect. Along the Costa Verde that marches with the Bay of Biscay, the rainy season is from October to January, with further unsettled weather in April. As annual precipitation in the Picos exceeds 60 inches, lack of snow was unlikely to be a problem, notwithstanding the range's modest altitude and the comparatively narrow skiable zone that lies within a 1200m band above the 1000m contour. But with the Atlantic lapping the foothills, the outcome of any short ski trip will depend on the weather and, in particular, the vagaries of the 'nodest pardo', a wind of ill repute that can persist for days.

When the choice of epoch is critical, business commitments inevitably determine start date and duration. Roger Childs, Rupert Hoare, David Seddon and I settled for a nine-day break from 7 to 16 February 1986. A week before departure, the blizzards then sweeping Europe marooned a party of school children in the Picos. Certainly, we got more snow than we bargained for, but the weather overall was kinder than expected. Two bad days out of seven is a better average than for the Pyrenees. Maybe February forms a weather window, but I would not bank on that. From our limited experience, I guess that March could be a safer though less spectacular month in which to tackle these formidable mountains.

Weather apart, a signal problem for ski tourers in the Picos is the terrain. The basic structure of the range is simple enough. Three limestone blocks – the Eastern Andara Massif, the Central Orrielos Massif and the Western Massif of Covadonga – are delineated by four rivers, the Deva, Duje, Cares and Dobra, which have carved through the rock to form some of the most spectacular gorges in Europe. Within this framework, the detailed topography is bewildering. Each massif is dissected by a chaos of transverse and converse valleys, gorges, defiles and sink holes – the 'canals', 'gargantas', 'desfiladeros', 'jous' and 'hoyos' of local nomenclature. Up above this maze rise containing walls – a complex of crenellated ridges, needles, towers, pinnacles, spires, obelisks and monoliths. There are few easy ridges or cols and a paucity of good paths, even in summer. The labyrinth of the Picos has presented travellers past and present with unusual navigational problems. Even today, the published maps of the area – save that of the Central Massif – are mostly incomprehensible or misleading. For the ski tourer, route-finding in winter is a serious undertaking with a daunting avalanche risk in anything but settled weather.

Arriving at Santander in a downpour at 11.30pm on 7 February after a train journey that had taken four hours to cover the 80km from Bilbao, Roger telephoned Robin Walker in Oviedo for a situation report. That call averted the fiasco of attempting to make our roadhead the village of Sotres which had been cut off from the outside world by snow for days. My original Grand Design had envisaged a modified traverse of both the Central and Western Massifs, emulating that of the French. Robin Collomb's *Picos* guide carried fore-warnings of what we might expect, but neither literature nor imagination are substitutes for actually seeing the ground. Having once grasped the nettle of the Picos under an unusually heavy mantle of snow, it was clear that we would have to settle for something less. A new sport plan was conceived, and with taxis supplementing ski we at least circumnavigated both the Central and Western Massifs, making slight incursions into the hard core at points of weakness.

Potes, second choice base after Sotres, was humiliatingly abandoned when Childs took flight from the Hostal Lembrana after an encounter with a dog 'bigger than a bear'. Having convinced ourselves that Potes was a touch *louche* and too low in any event, we decamped to Espinama and moved into the excellent Hostal Remona. This snow-bound hamlet whose denizens walked above the snow on six-inch high three-pronged clogs was of a genre that combined the pastoral and the picaresque. From here, on our third day out from Heathrow, we took our first steps on ski up the Rio Nevandi to the new Aliva hut through a metre of new snow and bad weather. There was never so much as a glimpse of the Pena Vieja (2613m) but several close encounters with live chamois.

With the barometer rising, next morning dawned crisp and clear. Start line was Fuente De, 'the Spring of God', which has, as its backdrop, a 3km long 800m high cirque whose ice-glazed limestone walls reflected the early sun. From here, on a magical day, we traversed 12km along the southern ramparts of the Central Massif to reach Valdeon via the col of that name in just over seven hours. Early on, ski tracks ahead revealed what must have been the only other ski party in the Picos. But the mere presence of a harmless *équipe* of Parisians, led by their Golden Age style guide, roused Hoare to paroxysms of competitive energy. First manifestation of this was an unorthodox route through beech thickets intended to secure the high ground. Thereafter there was only one team in it. The end-game was secured by our making Valdeon a night ahead of the French and bagging the best Fonda in town – the Begonia which became our base for the next three nights. Roger's Spanish and knowledge of local *mores* capitalized our initial advantage and ingratiated him with the Mistress of the Begonia, the incomparable Leandra Perez. Here, indeed, was a jewel – a

martinet with a soft heart and the best cook in the Picos. Her table d'hôte on
that first evening, Picos Bouillabaisse and 'Chorizo' with eggs piquante, served
as an entrée to what David ate next day for breakfast.

From Valdeon we made two excursions. The first an 18km exploration of
the stupendous Cares Gorge, principally on ski. The Cares is one of the wonders
of the Picos. The valley walls are easily 1000m high, but the vertical interval
from the valley floor to the highest peaks – of which little was visible that day –
is almost 2000m. Eight kilometres down valley from Valdeon in a clearing upon
which several precipitous valleys converged, just before the gorge reaches its
narrowest point barely an arm's span in breadth, lies the hamlet of Cain. This
Spanish Shangri-La, the remotest habitation of the Picos, had been cut off for
the past 15 days by snow, and we were its first visitors that year. Cain is still
renowned in these parts and in some beyond as birthplace of Gregorio Perez, 'El
Cainejo', the chamois hunter who in 1904 with the Marquis of Villaviciosa first
climbed the grandest monolith of the Picos, the Naranjo de Bulnes (2519m).
This feat became legend in the annals of Spanish mountaineering and is
commemorated in the hero's birthplace by a bronze plaque that led us
inexorably to a bar – the Pena Santa. The bar was swiftly opened by Senora who
dispensed home-cured *jamon* and *chorizo* with canned beer. The man of the
house, perched atop a stove, studied us incuriously as he whittled away at a
gnarled piece of wood that, in time, would become an artefact – perhaps a
garden rake.

Back in Valdeon that evening we made the two discoveries of the tour:
first, that Senora Leandra was the granddaughter of El Cainejo himself;
secondly, at Leandra's table over a glass or two after dinner, the real truth about
Naranjo de Bulnes surfaced. As was condescendingly explained by a local
savant, Naranjo had been climbed at least 50 times by hunters before the 1904
ascent. Many had fallen in the attempt and on hitting the ground had exploded
into small bits to have their remains carried away in sacks . . .

My original itinerary had sported a traverse of the Western Massif from
Valdeon to Covadonga via the Vega Redonda hut. But now, apparently, this
staging post no longer existed. The weather looked unsettled and, with one
member suspected of malingering by our uncompromising medic, we changed
course and settled for the Cebolleda (2050m). This peak is not of the Picos but
rises to the south in the main Cantabrian Range. Although a touch less
spectacular, this wild, off-beat country with three national nature reserves
offers scope for touring and provides sanctuary for deer, boar and other wild
beasts. Our ascent, involving nimble foot-work through dense groves of beech
and oak, at one point followed spoor that was unanimously agreed to be that of
wolf. Above the tree-line there emerged mysterious, rolling hills which
promised for the future. In descent, Childs swore that he had ski'd over a
hibernating bear.

It was difficult to break the spell of Leandra's cosseting, but three Begonia
breakfasts had sated even David's appetite. Early starts are inimical to the spirit
of these parts, but ours to Covadonga was delayed even beyond the statutory 10
o'clock by driver Miguel's discovery that two bullets had riddled his Landrover's bonnet. Throughout the dizzy descent, from the top of the snow-

blocked Puerto del Ponton to the bottom of the stupendous Los Beyos Gorge, there was speculation as to the culprit's identity. It emerged that this was not the work of some Asturian irredentist but of the Mayor of Oseja who, in the course of yesterday's boar hunt, had scored an inadvertent Inner. Down-valley we ran into the Mayor himself, sporting binoculars and directing the second day's drive. Godfather-like, he dismissed the incident but promised fulsome reparation.

Covadonga, gateway to the Western Massif, commands the entrance to the Onis Gorge leading to the heart of the mountains. Here it was that the Visigoth hero Pelayo defeated the Moors in 718 after a legendary battle waged for days through the gorges of the Picos. Pelayo's victory marks the start of the *Reconquista* that ended seven centuries later with the capture of Grenada in 1492. As the eldest sons of the Kings of England take their titles from mountainous Wales, so is the title of the heir to the Spanish throne Prince of Asturia. The Basilica of the Virgin of Battles at Covadonga, crowning a rock buttress above the Onis Gorge, recalls the historic memory and religious significance of that ancient victory. So did the Marquis of Villaviciosa, conqueror of the Naranjo de Bulnes with El Cainejo, create this area as the Picos's first national park in 1918.

Pelayo has lent his name to Covadonga's best hotel – a Parador in all but name. With a reception hall adorned with stags' horns, animal pelts and stuffed bear, the Hotel Pelayo achieves an improbable synthesis between Scottish Baronial and Spanish Ecclesiastical. The walls of the grand staircase are darkened by imaginary full-length portraits of fabled Asturian kings – Alonso, Oldovo and Ramiro – who resisted the Moors those 1200 years ago.

The Picos's one guarded winter hut is only three hours up the valley from Covadonga beside the Enol lakes. Owned by the Municipality, it was guarded by a mountain aficionado, guide and author – Juan Louis Somonao. His inscription in my copy of his *Fifty Selected Excursions in the Asturian Mountains* was a reminder that Spain was a land of mountains as well as of bullfighters and flamencos. But this we knew even before our last Picos excursion, to El Diadelliou. This belvedere gives a grandstand view of the N face of the Queen of the Range – the Pena Santa de Castilla (2596m). The mountain's outliers, so choked in snow as to resemble a gigantic mogul field, led to a fantastic summit wall surrealistically encrusted in ice, tantalizingly close yet quite inaccessible.

To essay forth on ski in the Picos in high winter was a touch presumptious. These mountains do not oblige the ski tourer. But few ranges have more drama, and each day brought some new spectacular. A pervasive sense of wonderment enhanced the senses but numbed logic. Hoare swore that the Rio Deva flowed uphill, Childs saw the dog as big as a bear and perhaps the bear itself. Certainly, all bore witness to the deer that clean jumped both Miguel's Landrover and then an eight-foot snow bank; all had been the guests of El Cainejo's granddaughter and had watched in the fading evening light the purple snows of the Cordillera Sueva merge with the Atlantic. Legend will always have a place in the Picos.

The Sierra de Gredos

J. G. R. HARDING

Enthused by the Picos, the core of the same party – Roger Childs, Rupert Hoare and myself, reinforced by Arctic Luminary Derek Fordham – determined to break further ski-touring ground in Spain the following year, 1987. Childs's choice of the Sierra de Gredos reflected the sort of local knowledge that is earned by owning a prime chunk of Spanish realty – the *Finta Prado Lobero*, or Wolf's Meadow Estate. This refuge of good things half forgotten sits high in the Gredos foothills amidst groves of olives, figs, vines and citrus trees above the little town of Candelada – the Courmayeur of the Gredos. Thus was the scene set for further induction into Spanish *montes* and *morales* over an extended weekend, 5–10 February 1987.

Although AC member John Ormsby visited the Gredos back in 1866, the range remains to travellers generally, and to the British in particular, the least-known of Spain's major sierras – *pace* the publication of Robin Collomb's 1987 guidebook which just postdated our visit, and the collective experience of those illustrious AC members who bait sly traps for any traveller unwary enough to claim priority. There is nothing here in size and scope to compare with the limestone extravaganza of the Picos. But for those who like sound granite, unusual surroundings and what, in summer at least, must be guaranteed good weather, the Gredos has much to offer. One obvious reason for the range's neglect is that its bigger rivals can offer more spectacular attractions. But the aura of inaccessibility and the unknown which still clings to these mountains, reflecting their earlier sanctity as a hunting ground of kings, gives them a special flavour. Both Carlos V and Alfonso VIII of Spain were keen sportsmen, with the latter regarded as the first conservator of the Gredos. As was the case in Britain, royal hunts preserved much of Spain's once extensive primeval forests, so ruthlessly cleared from other parts of the range. The hunting lodges of kings have become the huts and paradors of the Gredos National Park.

Some 150km long and composed wholly of granite, the Gredos is the highest of several sierras that traverse Spain's Meseta. Typically 'alpine' scenery such as arêtes, head walls and cirques – in these parts adorned by limpid tarns set deep in polished granite – will be found only in the innermost recesses of the range. Initial appearances are deceptive. Looking south to Al Manzour across the Tormes Valley, the impression is one of rolling whaleback ridges capped by the occasional tor surmounting a thick skirt of pine forest. Enthusiasts of that tiresome game Topography Snap might draw analogies with the Cairngorms, or even Dartmoor. But if you penetrate the upper reaches of the Gredos and Pinar Gorges you will find scenery of genuine grandeur. Radiating from a clutch of distinctive peaks – Al Manzour (2592m), Galana (2568m) and La Mira (2343m) – is a complex of ridges, walls and pinnacles that includes the locally famous Galayos and Los Hermanitos Towers, boasting 300m climbs on clean granite.

Unusually for ranges in the Northern Hemisphere, the southern approaches of the Gredos are the more impressive. From the plain of the Tietar, a tributary of the Tagus, the mountains rise as a 2000m wall deeply riven by wild gorges – Tejea, Blanca, Labrega and Pelayos. Here the paradox of the Spanish landscape flaunts its contrasts. Down in Candeleda, where lace makers and potato crisp merchants alike are recognized as artists, you can pick oranges off the trees that line the avenues and sit about in the main square shaded by date palms. But above the town, framed by the dark troughs of its narrow streets, a range of snow-mountains hangs as if suspended from the sky. Against this backdrop is silhouetted Candeleda's pride set high on a granite plinth – a bronze *Capra Montes Hispanica* – the ibex which is at once the symbol and talisman of the Gredos.

In February 1987, the cost of a British Airways flight to Madrid worked out about the same as a British Rail sleeper to Aviemore. Three and a half hours on from Madrid, beyond the road bounded by olive and evergreen oak where deer jumped through the headlights' beam, beyond the sump-breaking track that stopped short of the house, we celebrated our *bien venido* at Prado Lobero round a hearth of smouldering oak boughs. A vigorous Cuvée Childs was followed by a smoother Cypriot libation that claimed its lineage from the crusading Knights Hospitallers.

Breakfast next morning, 6 February, was alfresco on the terrace. The sun, which at dawn had suffused the snow-pyramid of Al Manzour pink, now warmed our backs and melted the frost that lay heavy in the fields. Floating across a shallow valley came the tinkle of goat-bells and the bark of dogs. Al Manzour, set tall in the north, rejoiced in the sun. To the south, emerging through the early morning haze, a series of receding ridges stretched away and downwards to merge in Tietar's dark plain.

In winter – and no doubt in summer too – the Central Gredos peaks are best approached from the north via the Tormes Valley. From Candeleda the mountain road winds a leisured course across the range through forests of oak, ash and pine. Where this has been cleared and abandoned a Spanish maquis of rosemary, thyme, lavender, cistus, gorse, heather and broom has taken over. Past the fairy-tale 15th century castle of Mombeltram the modern road climbs by a series of hairpin bends shadowing its near-perfectly preserved Roman model – the Calzada Romana – whose matchless engineering it strives to emulate. So to the watershed through the gates of the Puerto del Pico (1395m), framed by El Torozo's colossal granite slabs, to drop down to the Tormes Valley for a last draught and 'tapas' at the bar in Navarredonda before engaging the High Gredos.

From the roadhead at La Plataforma, the Llano hut is barely 40 minutes from your car boot. The Llano is a solid structure built of local granite, complete with guardian and rudimentary restaurant facilities in season. If the exterior is uncompromising, the interior is spartan with no concessions asked or given for either cooking or washing up. The corners of the hut were filling up with an accumulation of mouldering refuse but, as its only occupants, we were content enough. Having spread ourselves over the bare boards of the second tier, we took an evening stroll to the top of Antinuelo (2081m) to watch the sun set mauve on La Mira (2343m), objective for the following day. At peace with ourselves and seemingly detached from the world, we returned to the hut to settle down for a silent night, oblivious to the realities of the Spanish weekend.

The fun started around midnight and reached its crescendo at about 3am. From the ebb and flow of disorientated souls searching for empty spaces on the body-littered floor, one thing at least was clear: anyone with ski-touring pretensions – and many without – throughout the provinces of Avila, Salamanca, Segovia, Toledo and Madrid had forgathered at the Llano that night. The place became a disco of flashing head-torches with the discordant accompaniment of crunching boots, falling ski and untranslatable oaths which signalled the contact of cranium with seasoned chestnut beam. All this with an underlying base beat of groans from the tormented. When at last the numbing cacophony was stilled, the snores of the *compagneros* left only the sleepless to construct wild scenarios for an insomniac's revenge.

Once up and out of the hut next morning (7 February), never did the hills look more inviting. Skis coursing through virgin snow, we glided past monoliths and erratics of pink granite to make light of the climb to the crest of the skyline ridge. From this viewpoint the entire Central Gredos unfurled. South the ground fell away steeply to wild gorges that debouched into the Tietar Valley marked by a veil of haze. West the spiky peaks of Al Manzour and its satellites delineated the horizon. North-east the gendarme-studded spine of Los Campanarious led inexorably upwards towards our goal, La Mira.

With an annual precipitation often exceeding 70 inches, the Gredos does not lack for winter snow. The southerly slopes of the ridge were icy, but traversing to the north in the shade below the crest we ski'd powder and avoided the rocks. Once in the sun, snow conditions were reminiscent of a Scottish spring. It took three hours from the hut to reach La Mira whose summit is famous for its panorama. When we had stopped awhile to survey the scene and the magnificent Galayos Towers, a cold wind hastened an effortless ski descent on perfect snow to the ridge below. Following this to the Puerto de Candeleda, the eye of faith might have discerned the Prado Lobero. From this low point on the ridge a hot, laboured ascent towards Morezon (2381m) brought us to the Refugio del Rey. At this former royal hunting lodge, with the sun at its zenith, we met a genuine Saint Bernard collapsed in the snow and panting as we were. But in this hour of our need, the dog was found to lack the accoutrements of its trade. Lesser men stayed put to rest, but Hoare pressed on to bag his third Gredos 2000er – the Navasomera (2305m). If the dynamics of this feat were flawed by his unwitting descent on skins, Rupert would say that he can do it equally well with or without. The rest of us ski'd down without this handicap to take advantage of the unexceptional snow to meet up at the Llano by various routes, but at much the same time, to complete the 19km round trip.

The good news at the Llano was that the guardian and entourage had surfaced and were dishing up lomo and eggs on call; the bad was the coincidence of Saturday night. Yesterday's hut intake had vanished, but their places were fast being filled by new arrivals. Noises off that night reached a new decibel level with the advent of two Alsatian dogs. If this was hallowed Gredos tradition, it induced in us symptoms of Hut Agoraphobia and a craving to escape. The mystery of where everyone got to in the Gredos was partly unravelled next morning (8 February) when we quit the Llano for the high route across the Cuerda del Cuento to the Elola Hut. Yesterday in perfect weather the matchless viewpoint of La Mira had been deserted. Today, the trail to the Elola was like some Pennine Way. But the pilgrim's justification is simply to reach the Elola, for its setting is unrivalled in the range. The backdrop of the hut, built at the back of the Gredos Cirque just above the Laguna Grande, is an amphitheatre of granite headwalls capped by the crenellated ridges of the Ballesteros and Hermanitos which converge on Al Manzour, at 2596m the highest peak in Central Spain.

As every Alpine Fundamentalist well knows, 'Al Manzour' means 'The Victorious' in the Arabic vernacular. Manzour was the sobriquet of Mohamed ibn Ali Amir, the brilliant Moorish general who temporarily restored Islam's dominion over Iberia in the 10th century. The first recorded ascent of the peak commemorating Al Manzour's fame was as recent as 1899, only one year short of the 20th century; by this date every major peak in both the Alps and Pyrenees had long since been climbed. Childs's modest claim to have made one of the earlier British ascents was like a gauntlet to the rampageous Rupert. As Al Manzour had been the bane of medieval Spain's Christians, so did this Gredos zealot scourge the medieval mountaineers. The Elola had offered the promise of lunch in the sun. But the victor of Artinuelo, La Mira and Navasomera would have none of it. Was it not already 12.30 hours? Onwards and upwards . . .

Apart from occasional chunks of ice coming off the walls of the upper couloir that winged past, easier to hear than see, no real problems presented themselves until the Col de Crampons. This we attained within guidebook time, but then the character of the route changed. Footsteps in the snow leading round a bulge suddenly petered out in a steepening gully. This was overcoated with a thin layer of snow on underlying ice. Dripping icicles and precariously plastered accumulations of snow festooned the containing walls, but not so far above the summit was surely visible. What had started as a recce had become a bid but, with only a metre or so to go, the crux heightened that instinct for self-preservation well-developed over the years. Retreating to easier ground to reassess the situation with Derek, we were astonished to see that Rupert had already swarmed up the rocks like some frenzied Nike and was now bestriding the summit ridge. Even as we marvelled at this latest feat, an ice avalanche, as if directed from on high, descended on our unhelmeted heads. This was the last straw. Youth not only knew and could, but had harnessed Providence besides. Rupert had become Al Manzour himself: the rest were nowhere. We deliberated on the conditions and took the mature decision to head straight down. With the first British winter ascent of Al Manzour secure nothing would restrain Rupert now, although in one rare lapse he lost the lead in the inevitable race back to the hut. In trying to regain it he had to be dissuaded from the extravagance of jumping a 30m rock step which would inevitably have resulted in self-destruction. It was as good a ski descent as I remember.

The Elola's friendly guardian Ignathiou was surprised to see us back so soon. The hut was emptying fast of weekenders moving back to Plataforma over the ridge, through the chill evening shadows, in a long crocodile. Once again we had a hut virtually to ourselves, and this time undisturbed. The storm that broke that night brought an abrupt end to three days of unblemished weather and scuppered plans to penetrate the mysterious Five Lakes Basin. Return to Plataforma next morning through snow flurries, shifting cloud and breakable crust was a course of different mettle to the carefree crossing of two days back and a reminder that the Gredos are not just fun mountains. To commemorate deeds ancient and modern we indulged in that quintessence of hedonism – a double parador day. Lunch at the Parador National de Gredos was followed by dinner at the Virrey Toledo with fellow raptor spotter Julia Kemp. Whether or not we had made the first British ski tour of the Gredos, all would remember a sunlit weekend on La Mira and Al Manzour, and some the memory of a great Islamic champion from an age long forgotten when art, agriculture, science and every form of civilized refinement flourished in Moorish Spain, while the rest of Europe still languished in the Dark Ages.

The Gran Sasso d'Italia

In the Footsteps of Douglas Freshfield

JOHANNA MERZ

In May 1893 Douglas Freshfield, with his guide François Dévouassoud, climbed the Gran Sasso d'Italia. This was not a first ascent; the mountain had first been climbed nearly a century earlier by one Bernardino Delfico.[1] Nevertheless, Freshfield's ascent had a certain adventurous quality about it since he wanted to approach the mountain from the less accessible north-east side, rather than from Campo Imperatore to the south. He had no map and had to rely on advice from local people about the most favourable starting-point.

The Gran Sasso d'Italia lies in the heart of the Abruzzi and, at 2912m, is the highest mountain in the Apennine chain. Yet Freshfield was almost apologetic about bringing it to the attention of the members of the Alpine Club. 'Has not the time come,' he asked, 'when even the Alpine Club may look back to what in the natural enthusiasm of discovery it left behind for a time, and remember that its true scope is to widen, not to narrow, our love of Nature? May not its members be now and then allowed an Apennine?'[2] This enticing argument made me resolve to climb the Corno Grande, as it is familiarly called in Italy, trying so far as possible to follow the route taken by Freshfield himself. I was unable to find a climbers' guide nor even a 1:50,000 scale map; the *Blue Guide* gives, in bare outline, a few itineraries all starting from Campo Imperatore on the Aquila side of the mountain. This was not the approach chosen by Freshfield; indeed, he maintained that 'the highest Apennine seen from this side is a mean thing,' and the country generally more like 'some barren province of Asia . . . than the heart of beautiful Italy'.

Freshfield's eventual starting-point was a village called Casala San Nicola. He and his guide had undertaken 'a good deal of cross-country and up-and down-hill work' to get there, having been misdirected to neighbouring Tosiccia. At San Nicola there was no comfortable albergo to stay in; instead, they had to accept the hospitality of the village priest which, though freely given, afforded a fairly uncomfortable night. 'It was a peasant's home,' Freshfield recalled, 'and François Dévouassoud, with his large mountain experience, looked on its owner as *le plus pauvre curé* he had ever met with.'

Casala San Nicola which, in Freshfield's time, consisted of 'a few poor cottages' is still a tiny village nestling against the base of the Gran Sasso. Rambling up the hillside towards a pretty post-war church, it overlooks rich farmland – fields of golden barley and brilliant yellow sunflowers, silver olive groves and dark poplars – stretching away into the distant heat-haze over the Adriatic. Unfortunately, the village is now dominated by an enormous viaduct which carries the autostrada out of the long tunnel under the Gran Sasso and marches off with it towards Teramo. I arrived here in the early afternoon and, having booked a room at the albergo, I went to have a look at the mountain.

'A sharp-pointed precipice of yellowish-white rock, raised on a broad pedestal of beech forest, shoots up immediately overhead. The face of the cliffs is of inaccessible steepness, save perhaps in one place, where the spring avalanches, which were now lying in a broad white streak amongst the green, had tumbled over.'

Freshfield was evidently much impressed by his first sight of the mountain; my own thoughts were along the lines of 'what *have* I undertaken?'

'Immediately behind the houses the path climbs steeply into a narrow dell lying at the very base of the great horn, and keeps close to the clear copious torrent which dashes down through the beechwoods.'

I could find no 'clear copious torrent', but behind the church a path which matched Freshfield's description followed the dried-up bed of a stream. There was also another path climbing leftwards out of the village. I wanted to be sure of starting out next morning on the correct track so I thought I would try to find the village priest and see if he could give me any information. Someone pointed out to me the priest's house. It was quite modern and clearly not the same one Freshfield had stayed in all those years ago. I rang the bell and an elderly man came to the door. He did not look like a priest but I thought that, in any case, it might be helpful to show an interest in the church as a starting-point for conversation. I asked whether it would be possible to borrow the key. The priest was resting, the old man said, but I could certainly take the key; I promised to bring it back in a few minutes. After looking at the church and giving the old man a small contribution towards its upkeep, I asked him about the route up the mountain. The path behind the church was the correct one, he said. The route did not go up the difficult face visible from the village but led round to a ridge and then circled behind it to approach the mountain from the north. No technical climbing was involved but since there was still some snow on the upper slopes an ice-axe might be useful. To reach the summit would take at least six hours. I should have liked to find the actual house where Freshfield and Dévouassoud had stayed, but it was too long ago; the old man knew nothing of any former priests or where they had lived.

Later that evening I chatted with the owner of the albergo. On the previous day, he said, a *sentiero geologico* had been inaugurated by the *Club Alpino Italiano*. He produced a map of the mountain showing a new geological path, about 18km long, circumnavigating the mountain. This was a wonderful piece of luck and the small map (reproduced on page 148) was invaluable to me as it also showed, in outline, a route to the summit.

Next morning I woke very early and looked out of the window. The sky was clear and starry but there was still no vestige of light. Freshfield had started moving at half-past one after a very disturbed night but was held up by the old priest deciding to accompany him for part of the way.

'To our dismay, when we announced ourselves ready to start, he

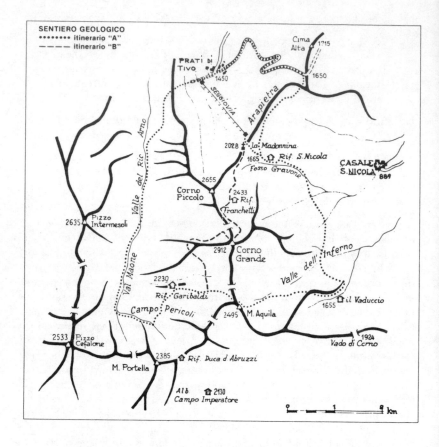

suddenly drew forth a pair of top-boots unseen before, and
commenced slowly to grease them before putting them on.' Even
so, Freshfield recalled, 'it was little more than half-past two when
we walked out into the clear moonlight'.

At five o'clock I let myself out of the albergo without disturbing anyone. The sky
was just beginning to show that faint tinge of grey which precedes the dawn. For
the first half-hour I wore my head-torch to ensure that I did not tread on any
poisonous snakes. This was no fanciful precaution as snakes do exist in that
part of Italy. Freshfield and his guide had had 'to scramble up as best we could
through the tangled thickets'. I was more fortunate for, after zig-zagging up for
some way, I found what was obviously the new geological path. High above me,
the sun-burnished twin summits of the Gran Sasso pierced the clear early-
morning sky. I followed the newly-widened path horizontally for a while until,
after crossing the bed of a stream where Freshfield's torrent had been diverted
into a pipe to provide water for the village, another path wound its way up again
through the trees, eventually emerging on a steep open meadow covered with

late spring flowers. It was now two hours since I had left San Nicola – the viaduct was a child's toy far below me. There were no signs or way-marks of any kind but a large cross on the skyline seemed to be the spot to make for. Soon I attained a wide ridge from which there was a clear view of the dramatic Corno Piccolo and the bold horn of the Gran Sasso itself. They still looked a very long way away.

> 'We were now turning the north-eastern corner of the pyramid of the Gran Sasso, and opening the long trough which runs round its northern flanks and divides it from the sharp-edged spine of the Corno Piccolo. The entrance to this was, however, still far above us, and to reach it we had a steep climb by little goat-tracks amongst rocks where the snow still occupied every hollow.'

Walking back along the ridge, I passed a ruined refuge and the top of an abandoned chair-lift. A rough path now picked its way up a boulder-slope to the Rifugio Franchetti at 2433m. It took another two hours to reach the hut; I was delighted to find that it contained a guardian – the first person I had encountered on my climb. In spite of its beauty and grandeur, the approach from San Nicola was obviously not often used, probably because of its length, steepness and relative inaccessibility. It was good to have found, through studying Freshfield's account, what I felt must indeed be the most interesting route up the mountain.

After eating and resting it was time to continue and the guardian pointed out the correct way forward: a rocky spur led to a higher ridge which doubled back towards the summit. By this time clouds were drifting up from the valley. The peaks above me were still bathed in sunshine but wisps of mist were beginning to swirl up and obscure them.

> 'We took the ridge falling northwards from the highest peak. It proved longer than expected. The limestone was loose, shattered, and tolerably steep, so that there was room for some scrambling.'

The summit was hidden from view by a mass of rough, steep limestone, but I was grateful for paint flashes which indicated a way through. Just below the final ridge, steep smooth scree, interspersed with patches of snow, fell away into a jumble of rocks below and had to be negotiated with care. Some unmistakably English voices wafted down from above and a few moments later I passed a group of young men coming down. '*Buona sera,*' they said. 'Hello,' I replied. 'Oh, you're English!' I said that indeed I was and they told me that they were theological students from Rome where they were studying for the priesthood. I wished them good luck and continued to the summit.

> 'I do not recommend any one who counts a mountain walk so much irksome expenditure of energy to climb the greatest of the Apeninnes. Those, however, who look upon the summit view as only one among the pleasures of the day will see a striking scene with a wild savage character of its own, unlooked for so far south. We repaired the stone man, which was much the worse for its wild

winter . . . Before we left the top a company of white vapours had
collected in the hollows under the mountain and was curling up its
sides, cutting off from moment to moment fragments of the view.'

As I gazed around, the mist parted for a few minutes to reveal a glimpse of red
sunbaked mountains disappearing into a hazy distance and, nearer at hand, the
sharp thrusting towers of the Corno Piccolo. Only a simple cross marked the
summit – there was no sign of Freshfield's 'stone man'. A few moments later
everything, including the rocks where I stood, was again shrouded in hazy mist.

'The ascent from San Nicolò, a matter probably of nearer 8000
than 7000 feet, had occupied six hours of steady walking (without
counting halts). The return was a very different affair. Once off the
ridge we flew down on winged heels at a pace Mercury himself
might have envied. From 9000 feet to deep in the beechwoods our
progress was a series of shoots down snow-slopes and avalanche
beds. We were actually in motion scarcely an hour and a quarter.'

To match Freshfield's speedy descent was clearly impossible, if only because the
snow on the lower slopes had long since disappeared. I thought it might be
interesting, instead, to traverse the mountain and try for myself the normal
route down to Campo Imperatore which Freshfield had carefully avoided. The
mist was not so thick as to make way-marks hard to see and on the south side of
the mountain it soon dispersed. I had obtained a more detailed map from the
guardian at the Franchetti hut which showed that the 'normale' followed a ridge
running west from the summit. Here I met a party of teenagers, about 20 of
them, following a single leader and, by mid-afternoon, still some way from the
top. They were obviously unused to this sort of work, reminiscent of Crib Goch,
and many were plainly terrified. What would the leader have done, I wondered,
if one or more of them had slipped. There was no evidence of any mountain
rescue arrangements on the mountain.

Once off the ridge, the normal route became quite boring and totally
different from the beautiful approach, over varied terrain and with lovely views,
which I had taken in the morning. A long, seemingly endless traverse across
alternate scree and snow led over a great basin and along a flattened and barren
ridge which eventually arrived at a crossroads. To the east the geological path
mentioned earlier traversed the subsidiary Mt Aquila (2495m) and led back,
after 6km or so, to the woods above San Nicola. Another path led to the Duc
d'Abruzzi hut which, at the end of June, was not yet open. The normal route
continued south to Campo Imperatore where I expected to find an albergo,
marked on the map and sign-posted. I thought of staying there overnight and
returning to San Nicola, via Mt Aquila, in the morning. However, Campo
Imperatore turned out to be the most desolate of places, with nothing but an
astronomical observatory, its silver dome glistening in the sun, and a derelict
and abandoned hotel. It would now be a long walk back to San Nicola! By a
stroke of good fortune, however, the theological students were still there,
making a last brew before returning to Rome. They generously gave me a lift to
Aquila where I was able to find transport back to San Nicola. 'It added

something to our day to be able to help you,' they said.

In a Preface to *Below the Snow Line*, Freshfield wrote:

> 'Nearly fifty years ago I published a little volume called *Italian Alps*
> which was so far successful that it still brings me from time to time
> letters of thanks from adventurers in my footsteps.'

Freshfield would no doubt be gratified to know that, 65 years on, his writings
are still a source of inspiration to followers in his footsteps.

REFERENCES

1.   D W Freshfield, *Below the Snow Line*. Constable, 1923.
2.   *et seq (loc cit)*.

Sudan Saga

TONY HOWARD

It was early January 1983 before we made our plans for that year's winter trip. Having a rather eccentric attitude to mountaineering we chose Sudan, and by the time we had made the necessary travel and medical arrangements two months had passed and the African 'winter' was already over.

We flew into Khartoum at the beginning of March, obtained our E Sudan travel permit, and three days later we had reached our first base at the oasis of Kassala, 400km to the east near the troubled Ethiopian border. We arrived on the back of a lorry in the middle of the night and, on waking the next morning and washing the sand from our eyes, were greeted with the sun rising over a miniature Yosemite! The granite towers of Kassala thrust themselves almost 600m from the desert, in domes of solid granite beckoning the climber.

We spent about two weeks in the area. During this time we went to the base of most of the walls and repeated the only climb in the area, a VS route to the highest summit first climbed by R A Hodgkin and L W Brown in December 1939, and described as 'one of the finest rock climbs in Africa' (*AJ*54, 155–161, 1943–44). A truly unforgettable experience with a bivouac at the foot of the climb overlooking the hazy hills of Eritrea and a nibble on the leaves of a tree on the summit, said to give mystical powers and everlasting life!

Our hopes of making some first ascents in the area were dashed for a number of reasons, most importantly the unbearable heat (December to February would be the best months, but even at Christmas Robin Hodgkin reported that 'the rocks were uncomfortably hot'). Another problem is the vultures which nest and roost on the peaks in their hundreds, so that almost all ledges and crack-systems are either carpeted in droppings or guarded by these huge birds, standing over three feet high with a wing-span of more than twice that size. Finally, but equally important, the main walls are virtually featureless, whilst the cracks are often mere rounded runnels rather than fissures, with no protection or belay points. The harder routes here would probably require pegs or even bolts for security.

Despite making only one ascent in the area we had a memorable stay amongst the straw-roofed villages at the base of the peaks, and further out in the desert at the camps of the various tribes – Rashaida and Haddendowah and Beni Amir (the swaggering, sword-carrying 'fuzzy-wuzzy, pore benighted 'eathen, but first class fightin' men' of Kipling). Also nearby were camps of Nigerian Moslems who had settled there whilst on the Haj (pilgrimage) to Mecca, and those of refugee Eritreans from just over the border, escaping the endless civil war and the beginnings of the great drought, at the time unknown to the outside world.

From here we returned to Khartoum where our second objective was eliminated by the refusal of permits to the Nuba Mountains where there are interesting, possibly unclimbed, peaks such as Jebel Abu Anga, as well as the fascinating and proud Nuba people with their rich tribal culture. Our third and final area to visit was the group of peaks around the long extinct crater of Jebel Marra (3000m) close to the Chad border, 1300km west of Khartoum. Permits were granted and a train journey of five days through dust, scrub and more dust ensued. In the heat of the day we squashed ourselves into the shade of compartments where 12 or 14 people occupied six seats – impossible to vacate when the train was in motion, as the corridor was a tangled mass of bodies. At each stop for a village or for prayer (or simply a breakdown), we and hundreds of others climbed out through the windows to stretch our legs. In the early and late hours we joined the multitudes travelling on the roof, rocking slowly westward through the dust-filled days. At night the choice was sleep on the roof (if you could find space) and maybe fall off – there are accidents on most trips – or squeeze back into the sardine-can below. There's little sleep or rest either way. To arrive at Nyala at the foot of the Jebels and the end of the line is a major achievement!

Not that there's anything there – just a dusty market town on the edge of the Sahara – a little bigger than most, maybe, but not a place you'd go for a holiday, and nowhere really to stay. There is one 'hotel', but it's overcrowded with no beds, so you sleep on the floor and put up with the bugs. The toilet door hangs off its hinges and the hole in the floor that indicates the possibility of a sewer was long since blocked so there's really no place even to stand for the filth and maggots even if you try (and having the 'runs' doesn't give you much choice!). There's also no running water, just some dregs in the bottom of large earthenware *zias* (or jars). Only the many regulars get the water when the jars are filled each day.

We didn't linger long (though the cafés by the market were good, with plenty of water), and we were soon moving out on top of a lorry with its load of sacks and people to the villages at the base of Jebel Marra where drivable tracks end. From there we hired a mule and its owner who were returning from the market in Niertiti to the village of Quailla higher up the W flank of the main crater. One of the Fur tribe – an Afro-Arab people – knew Jebel Marra well and offered to take us up into and through the crater. We spent a week with Abdulai who took us on an incredible journey, entering the crater by moonlight with weird silver reflections glinting from the lakes below, as we crested the rim and looked down into its depths.

The following night in the crater itself, a herd of horses galloped through our camp and wolf-like animals skulked in the bush close by. Abdulai sat up through the night tending the embers of the fire, occasionally prodding it into life, sending sparks into the gloom and emphasizing the darkness of the ring of peaks around us.

But there was nothing to climb – did we ever really think there would be? We moved out next day through a narrow gap in the E wall of the crater and left as we had entered by a tortuous maze of tracks through interweaving defiles and gorges worn into the volcanic ash by the annual rains. After a full day's walk we were little more than five miles as the vulture flies from our previous camp-site, when we stopped for the night at the village of Taratonga, 'The House of the Wolves'. It had been a fascinating if somewhat hungry journey as the famine was beginning to make its mark even here in the comparatively fertile mountains, and we had travelled for a week on a diet of dates, flour and muddy water! Another day took us to Gorlangbang and, after two days, a lurching lorry journey on the brink of more gorges, along dried-up river beds and out across the barren desert took us back to Nyala and our dream hotel.

Three days to wait for the train, and then the train was two days late, and then five days back to Khartoum – ah! the romance and luxury of travel! From Khartoum we went north down the Nile with two weeks to spare, because of our inability to enter the Nuba Mountains. (Permits for Jebel Marra were also stopped whilst we were out there.) Another train-top journey followed, first following the Nile, then out across the desert of Batn el Haggar (Belly of Rocks) to Wadi Halfa at the upper (Sudan) end of the Aswan Dam. Then down the lake in an old boat, overcrowded as always (it sank two weeks later, with a reported loss of over 300 lives) and into the ancient lands of Egypt, through which we drifted by felucca from the Temple of Karnak and the Valley of the Kings, down towards the Pyramids and Cairo, the end of our journey. Not much of a climbing trip, you may think, but mountains have more to offer than their summits!

A Pilgrim in the Atlas

KEV REYNOLDS

They say you shouldn't go back. That, if you care sufficiently about a region, it's best to remember it as it once was; that only a fool will attempt to recapture a place out of time. For nothing remains unchanged, least of all ourselves, and our perception of that place depends so much on what we once were and, even with maturity, memory plays tricks. Regret and disappointment are bound to be the price paid for misplaced nostalgia put to the test.

It was in the summer of '65 that I was in the High Atlas mountains of Morocco; a young man's first big mountains, they rose as a challenge and an enchantment. I gazed at them then with a childlike sense of wonder and took their loose pitches and crumbling gullies as part of the game. In their valleys I viewed the Berber with curiosity and distant respect; on their summits I sniffed the breezes and thrilled to huge horizons. On Atlas peaks and ridges the tentative hold that Britain's mountains had begun to clasp on me became permanently fixed. From that trip, mountains had captured me for good.

So for 21 years the Atlas retained a special place in my heart, no matter how often I visited the Alps, no matter how deep and lasting my love for the Pyrenees. As with a young man's first love affair, though not seriously tempted to infidelity, I wondered how they would be today, for I viewed them with tender affection. As the years rolled by no opportunity came to revisit Morocco, for I staggered from one financial crisis to another, cheating mountain trips abroad on less than a shoestring and at the expense of what my contemporaries considered essentials to everyday existence. There was never money to spare for a flight to Marrakech and a crafty fortnight of mountain adultery. The Atlas became a memory and a wistful dream.

Then, out of the blue, my life changed almost overnight. A fresh challenge arose, fresh fields and pastures new, fresh horizons and a vision full of enticement. The future took on a new shape, uncertain yet exciting. Then came a 'phone call; again, out of the blue and quite unexpected. It was an editor whose voice I recognised instantly. 'Could you do me a favour?' came the voice. 'Could you fly out to Morocco for me and spend a couple of weeks trekking in the Atlas Mountains? I need an article for the magazine.'

I um'd and ah'd for a full two seconds before allowing myself to be talked into it. All expenses paid; arrangements via Sherpa Expeditions.

Then came the doubts and uncertainties. How would it be after all this time? How much would the mountains and valleys have changed? I'd read a number of articles in recent years about trekking and climbing in the Atlas, whereas in '65 there had been very little to read, other than a couple of pieces in the *AJ*. With increased popularity there were bound to be changes, and almost certainly they'd not be for the better. On top of this, I'd broadened my experience in the years between, and even in my wildest moments of prejudice had to admit to myself that the Atlas could not compare in scenic grandeur with the Alps or Pyrenees; they would not display the same contrasts of colour and fragrance, the same degree of vegetation or snow cover. How then would they strike me now? Would they seem perhaps drab and lifeless? But this is nonsense, I told myself, it's about as pointless to compare one mountain range with another as it is to hold a rose against an orchid; each has its own loveliness, its own character. Go with a clear mind and absorb all the Atlas have to offer. Be as a sponge and soak it all in. So I did.

The dirt road to Imlil had a stretch of tarmac that hadn't been there 21 years before. Gone too the pool at the foot of a waterfall in which I'd bathed when the truck boiled over. But other than these small changes it was much as I remembered. Imlil, too. A few minor alterations, but otherwise little different. Overhead hung the mountains; barren, dusty, with scrub covering like freckles the northern slopes. I stood in the square at Imlil and felt the drawing power of distant valleys; felt also the presence of mountains out of memory, and knew a great sense of privilege in being here again. It was great to be back.

For two weeks we – the group I was assigned to accompany – wandered over a number of passes and visited remote yet hospitable villages. We trekked in a wide circuit of the Toubkal massif and experienced the magical qualities of these totally non-European mountains. Before, I had been here simply to climb. Now, and for the first time in my mountain career, I was trekking; wandering day after day from one valley system to another in the shadow of high mountains, carrying on my back the lightest of day-sacks containing waterproofs and cameras instead of lumbering under a huge rucksack in which all food, camping and climbing gear was kept. Now mules took the strain of rucksacks, food, drinks; everything, in fact, to make life easier for us. It took a while to get used to. About five minutes in all. And I discovered a day-sack to be a great improvement on a half-hundredweight rucksack, and, in acknowledging the ease with which I could become pampered if given the chance, I wondered how on earth I'd coped in the past.

As a sponge I soaked in all the experiences on offer without falling into the trap of comparing these with other mountains I knew well. Neither did I find that time had devalued the Atlas in any way. Or had I not yet grown out of that childlike sense of wonder with which I first saw them?

Trekking I soon discovered to be a marvellous way to explore a remote landscape. Gone were any preconceived ideas about package tours on foot; gone the fear that parties of trekkers would combine to create a locust effect on a carefully balanced environment, stretching the resources of Berber agriculture to the limit. If Sherpa Expeditions were typical of today's trekking companies, then I am confident that their effect on a delicate mountain environment will be minimal. Our leader was conscientious and caring in dealings with local people; practically all food consumed by the group had been brought from home or purchased in the *souks* of Marrakech; no wood fires were burned; all bivvy sites were chosen after consultation with nearby villagers, where there were villages in the neighbourhood. There was a constant, yet unspoken, awareness of the responsibilities we each bore in our role as guests in another land. Another world. It was another world, indeed.

On dry, sun-baked passes we peered into shafts of narrow valleys where patches of greenery betrayed the existence of simple villages. We wound down into those valleys on mule trails probably hundreds of years old, and then traversed along mountainsides, sometimes above, sometimes below, sometimes between terraces of maize, potatoes or courgettes. Around villages grew clusters of walnut trees. Irrigation channels ran in a complex maze from one terraced field to another; on rare hillsides stood gnarled and ancient juniper trees – where they'd been spared the voracious appetite of goats.

In the villages we were greeted by children, some of whom walked with us for a while, conducting us along the way, holding our hands or chatting to us in an impossible language that could best be understood by recognizing the same impish pleading that all children wear in their eyes. Women were bent double in the maize fields; dressed in bright colours they tended crops or carried water in large pots on their shoulders. They were invariably slim, graceful, shyly inquisitive with eyes that flashed and held back laughter. Their menfolk wore drab brown or cream-coloured *djellabahs* with rough sandals on their feet. They too worked among the crops or passed us by on laden mules. Now and again we would see a Berber hanging in a walnut tree, harvesting, or stripping the leaves. Village elders congregated in the shade and discussed the appalling state of the world, no doubt, and regretted the wayward youth of today. Characters all from the Old Testament; today, in the 20th century.

Sometimes we spent nights in those villages, spreading sleeping bags on the bare roof-tops under a coverlet of stars, hearing around us the life of the neighbouring houses with their hens and cows and goats, their laughing children, shrill-voiced women, wheezing mules; a distant splash of water. Dark nights lit briefly with dancing shadows as someone moved silently through an alley, a stub of candle cupped in the palm of a hand; the sound then of a door latch, the creak of a ladder step. Then silence once more. Sometimes across a village roofscape came the sound of singing; hands clapping, hollow drums beating, the shuffle of sandalled feet on bare earth. In one village I explored with one of the trekkers a water mill in operation, its base simplicity a throwback quite a thousand years. Inside the air was white with milling flour. White dusted walls, white dusted floor, white dusted ceiling. The miller, a quiet woman with long fingers and bangled wrists, was at first uncertain of us, but then, seeing we were harmless, showed her work with an obvious pride. My admiration for the industrious nature of the Berber grew.

Sometimes we were invited into Berber houses for mint tea halfway through the day's journey. Into a dark windowless room where cows and hens fed in their own dank warmth, then up a rough ladder and through a hole in the ceiling to an upper room, half open to the sky, where a heap of cinders showed where cooking was done. Sometimes we'd sit cramped in an airless room that doubled as sitting room and sleeping quarters, while on other occasions we'd move on to the roof where tea was served in the time-honoured ritualistic way; poured from a silver pot into thin glasses and drunk piping hot and extremely sweet. And overhead reared the mountains.

Our muleteers were a ragged bunch under the leadership of Mohammed. He was tall, quiet, competent. The others had their own characteristics. Most were young, in their late teens or early twenties; sometimes playful, mostly cheerful and ready to break into song. One, however, was a somewhat sallow individual who had an unfortunate habit of sitting quietly by at lunch-times studiously picking his nose. Ibrahim, at 15, was the youngest. A lad with laughter in his eyes, but with a quick temper that fired especially when he was losing at cards. When he is 18 he'll be big trouble on trek; at the moment he is controllable. Then there was Abdullah, ever-cheerful Abdullah who loved to sing and dance. Sometimes I'd walk with him and his mule, and winding up the mountainside on a dusty trail he'd begin a loud chant to catch echoes across a corrie. Encouraged, I'd join in, and he would lead me in longer and more complex rhythms, hanging on to the notes with the power of an operatic tenor that I failed to emulate, running out of breath until I jogged gasping to catch up. He would then slap me on the back and laugh, delighted at my discomfort.

When not staying overnight on a rooftop, we'd bivouac in a boulder field or in a valley by a stream, spreading out wherever a corner attracted. Sometimes it rained, then out came bivvy-bags to keep the worst of the rain off sleeping bags. One night we found that rarity in the Atlas, a grassy meadow with two streams flowing by. Earlier a storm had rumbled overhead and evening brought a steady rainfall. As darkness took the valley I slid into my bivvy-bag and lay there, 18 inches from a stream, with just my face unprotected from the rain. It was cool and refreshing and not at all unwelcome. But as I was drifting to sleep there came a 'plop' and a frog landed on my forehead. Sherpa Expeditions failed to mention this possibility in their brochure.

After some days of trekking in a devious, clockwise circuit, we came up a narrowing valley and past the uppermost village, which would be our last Berber community for some time, for we would be crossing the high ridge in the distance tomorrow, to spend a few days at the Neltner hut in order to do a little scrambling around Toubkal's neighbours. As we came past the village I suddenly recognized it from '65. Below it I had spent a truly magical evening on a patch of grass under a walnut tree while villagers brought food and sat around us in the darkness, their faces lit momentarily as they drew deeply on the cigarettes we'd passed round. Now I was back again, and it appeared not to have altered one bit. Leaving the remainder of the party and the muleteers to continue up-valley, I found myself drawn to a boulder with a view, and there sat gazing for nearly an hour at a scene from my past. In that view was encompassed a kaleidoscope of emotions tied up with a ribbon of 21 years. Floods of emotions poured over me; the memories not only of youthful days that had changed the pattern of my life, but the years between, faces and places that make us what we are. And in that I recognized the privilege that brought me back; not just to see and to do, but to feel and absorb; acknowledging the good fortune of health and strength and fitness in mind and body that has lasted long enough to make this possible, and which we tend to take for granted – until it's lost. How many friends had shared those distant times with me and have since given up for more leisurely activities – or no activity at all? Yet here was I, rejoicing not only in memory, but in the sheer vigour of reliving that memory once more. This Atlas pilgrimage was becoming a profound and moving experience.

Neltner was a busy place. Before, the night spent there had been spent alone. Now there was hardly a spare place to be had. I was glad to be active on the mountains, for there we could find space and air to breathe. It was good, too, to spend time away from the mules and to scramble for hour after hour on warm, sun-kissed rock. It may have been loose and crumbling; it may have been a case of short pitches between slopes of scree; but it was good to be again on ridges and peaks instead of passes and valleys. It made a change, and with the group split our smaller party went up on to ridges with multi-hued vistas and looked off to other valleys that started my dreams working once more. There are always fresh horizons to tease and entice. On bald summits that ought to wear snow but didn't, we lazed in contented relaxation under a Saharan sky. From those summits my eyes were led into panoramas that contained other peaks and ridges on which I'd scrambled in days of innocence. Each one held a memory; each one a personal possession. They became, for a while, my mountains.

And we had the screes; the 2000ft scree-runs that were the steepest, fastest, most exhilarating descents of any mountains I'd known, other than in winter, on ski. Now in dust and clatter and hollow gully-gulping echoes we swooped down, leaping from one shifting slide to the next, risking battered boots and broken ankles in a delight of irresponsible speed. It was so good to be utterly foolish again.

Of course it was necessary to 'do' Toubkal again. I remembered it with no great rejoicing, but others wanted to go and so I went with them. There are finer mountains with more exacting routes on them, but no one who truly loves mountains need ever be above the occasional steep walk to reach a summit with friends, and Toubkal has its rewards too; simply being there once more, gazing on cliffs and gorges and far-off hills that I had once been more than grateful to see and was now in the flush of privilege to witness with new friends under fresh circumstances. Perhaps this summit would be a symbol for them in years to come, as it had been once for me.

There was one day left. For most it would be a short downhill trek to the village of Aroumd with the muleteers, but four of us rose early and set out on a sharp haul up a band of cliffs and a deceptively steep strip of scree as day beamed over Toubkal's shoulder, and reached the little pass of Tizi n'Tadat (3730m) on the Biguinoussene ridge along which I'd had a day's excitement long ago. Over we went on the western side, crossed another col and dropped to the head of that fine valley where the huge cliffs of Tazaghârt set my fingers itching. The valley stretched long and inviting before us, a delight all the way. A goodly stream accompanied us. There were grassy meadowlands, then a gorge down which ribbon cascades poured in puffs of spray and swifts screeched to and fro. Goats somehow secured their footing on the almost vertical cliffs while their herders – a young Berber couple with their tiny baby – squatted under an overhanging rock and brewed mint tea.

We passed among juniper trees, disturbed the fragrance of mint as we brushed wild clumps growing beside streams, crossed hillsides of scrub and came to a hideously basic summer village. But the terraces fanning before it were the very essence of good husbandry and a real credit to those who worked them. We sat overlooking the fields and the village, filled with admiration for the obvious skills and hard work of the Berber people, a people I had learned increasingly to respect during the days of our trek. Every levelling of terrace was the result of intensive labour. Every channel of irrigation the product of careful thought and ingenious activity. These Berber people, I realized, lived in harmony with their environment, and I feared what might happen in the future when our Western form of civilization encroaches on their world, as it has elsewhere, to the extent of luring them from their roots with a false taste of our 'other-worldliness'. I felt then that we had more to learn from them than they from us.

Two more passes, more dry hillsides and a long uphill plod in the late afternoon, and we rejoined the main party on a roof-top with a view. It was a view of Toubkal up-valley and below to the rich greenery of Berber agriculture. In the contrasting views were symbolized the riches gained in our short sojourn in the Atlas. I had found trekking to be delightfully rewarding on so many counts. But maybe I had been additionally fortunate, for I had not only enjoyed the physical journey, the mixing with the Berbers and fraternizing daily with our muleteers, not only the friendship of the rest of our party in whose company much of the pleasure had come. I had had something special. For me it had been a pilgrimage. A gift to savour.

Agings

HAMISH M. BROWN

I remember the old man, my friend,
With his slowly slowing pace
Smoothing the gabbro of my youth
With his hill-honed grace.

I grew bitter at his failing powers,
That he, who mounted mountains high,
Should so have shrunk and shrivelled,
Be bed-bound, and die.

That was no END for a life of peaks,
For a son of sunny years;
But now, seeing my mountains slip,
I learn to hide my tears.

Pointblank

A Saga of Mal the Axebreaker

MAL DUFF

In 1262 Malcolm the Axebreaker, a Viking berserker, was unexpectedly captured at the battle of Largs. Surprised by the King of Scots, the Viking invasion was routed, with the longboats only able to escape by the sacrifice of the foremost berserkers who fought a ferocious rearguard action. Malcolm was eventually overpowered and delivered in chains to his captor, McDuff the Earl of Fife. He was spared death only because of his exceptional ability with the axe, a talent much understood in those far-off days. Over the years he was accepted into the clan, until one glorious day the Earl granted him freedom to marry. Thus started the family line traced through history. From father to son an ability with an axe was handed down until, nearly 700 years later, a boy was born who, named Malcolm in honour of his famed ancestor, became the holder of the ancient title 'Mal the Axebreaker'. As this lad grew up he became, not a tree-feller like many of his forebears, but, surprisingly, an ice-climber.

In 1983 a beautiful long-legged tow-haired woman (who will now fade from the story as she has – alas – no further part to play in it) bought, as a Christmas present for Mal, a copy of *Cold Climbs*, a book much prized at the time. Thus the scene was set.

This book was quickly recognized by British climbers to contain not only beautiful photographs, but pictures of a very revealing nature. Please turn now to page 62 of *Cold Climbs*. A wonderful shot of climbers on the crux pitch of Point Five Gully. Now let your imagination drift. Ah yes, what a fantastic groove just to the right of the gully. A line of purity and obvious difficulty. A wild, unclimbed challenge.

Mal was hooked. That line was his. All winter he pounded the Ben, guiding clients and checking conditions, until in mid-February he could wait no longer. A Saturday dawned fair, and, starting early, he left with a conscripted partner (for reference: a lad known only as Wally, easily spotted, as he was probably the only man in Britain who sported seven earrings. Of these, five were made from fox's teeth, whilst two others were removed from an unfortunate seal).

Well, they climbed a wee groove from the toe of the buttress, but the awesome slab pitch above leered blankly and scared them into a rightward scuttle. Climbing Left Edge Route (5) they departed, depressed.

Two weeks later, fired by those ancient Nordic berserker genes, Mal was once again ready to do battle. Jon Tinker, one of Mal's guides, was sworn to secrecy and shown the picture. He was in!

They were paranoid – surely every other climber in Britain would be converging on Ben Nevis, a queue would form to attempt this magic line. Rivals from the London outposts, showing great stamina and driving all night, were the most difficult to fight off. Normally they struck decisively and with total surprise. Mal and Jon resolved to wake at 4am. This plan was revised at 1am when they were evicted from the Clachaig Inn, a favoured hostelry. However, they were fired up and, although not communicating in anything more than monosyllabic grunts, were to be found cruising into the Ben car park (lights and engine muted to avoid waking any rivals) at 4.30am.

Just as dawn broke one could observe that they had reached the foot of the buttress and were roping up. To their total surprise the few climbers who had been overtaken seemed totally oblivious of the prize that was about to be snatched from under their noses.

Following the groove previously climbed was fun. They found it hard enough to get the required level of concentration going, and steady enough for confidence and nerve. Thus they assembled below the daunting slab and corners.

The next section was awful to contemplate. A thin trickle, a mere illusion of ice was the way, and up this Jon did climb. After 25m, barred by a roof, he manufactured a hanging stance. It was not the best!! Mal was encouraged to ascend and, after a bitter struggle, he did so. His task now was to make the link into the chimney crack. Tiny pockets in the underlying slab were searched out. These held reserves of ice and could be picked and hooked, allowing progress to be made. Each move was planned, calculated and the likely outcome assessed. The mental energy output was vast and unsustainable. Mal moved further from Jon and no runners appeared. With blazing crampons and monumental axework, a further 3m were overcome. He reached the chimney. It was 15 to 22cm wide! By now both partners knew that the route was too hard – above and beyond the current world of climbing.

However, mysterious happenings abound throughout our world, and on that day they were blessed with invincibility. Thor spoke, axes thudded and Mal moved on.

After 30m the powers started draining, flowing away, each loss a lightning bolt of uncertainty. A vital peg was fumbled and dropped. The previous unwavering certainty was a dream from a previous existence. This was now a fight to the death – a gladiatorial mental struggle with only one participant. Only a matter of faith, combined with abject rejection of the waiting death-fall, allowed Mal to cling, wraith-like, to the blank upper slab.

At 3pm he reached a stance. Five hours to cover 55m! Jon, cramped and cold after a belaying session beyond the call of duty, arrived eventually at the stance in a flurry of adrenalin. Of course our two berserkers are now exhausted. After a moment we can observe Mal once more climbing into the groove above. The force has returned and, although the difficulties are still great, they are overcome swiftly.

It has not been mentioned that a storm has been mounting all day, spindrift cascades from the plateau above and night is falling.

The next view, a brief one, is at the summit. Ice-encrusted grins, stiff clothes: they embrace and move into the night.

Back at the Clachaig, comrades and womenfolk drink and wonder. At

10pm the doors sway open, relief floods the company! Flagons of foaming ale are consumed and the world is a fine place to inhabit. On the first move of an easy route the next day, Mal's axe shatters!

We now move forward in time, to early January 1985. Mal is reading the *SMC Journal* and is obviously displeased. The New Routes Editor has mentioned that the traverse taken into and out of Point Five Gully, 45m up the crux pitch of Pointblank (6), spoils the purity of this route. Our Nordic adventurer, his ego pricked, memories of the awesome, overpowering nature of the climbing fading from his mind, can only agree. So the scene is set.

Part 2: Winter 1985. Mal and Jon lay their plans, but conditions are unfavourable.

Part 3: Winter 1986. Mal and Jon lay their plans, but conditions are unfavourable.

Part 4: Winter 1987. Mal and Jon lay their plans, conditions are looking favourable! Mal is climbing well, new routes flow from his glowing axes, until one fateful day he is wounded, taken to hospital and rendered out of action for the rest of the season. Jon conscripts Colin McLean, a Cairngorm specialist. One Saturday they leave, to 'straighten out Pointblank'. Mal vents his rising frustration by climbing the Pap of Glencoe on crutches.

But wait: All Is Not Going Well. Colin has climbed to the hanging stance; shaken, he brings up Jon, a peg pulls out and they fall. The original '84 peg, still clipped, twists and bends, but holds. The next view – a brief one – shows them abseiling gingerly to the toe of the buttress. Mal is secretly delighted.

Part 5: Winter 1988. Jon is climbing on K2, Mal has recovered from his knee operation and conscripts Rick Nowack from USA into the story. Rick is justly famous for the bravest act ever witnessed, that of climbing Elliots Downfall (5), a steep icicle, stark naked.

Mal resolves to lead every pitch. He has bought 75m ropes, so that the hanging stance can be eliminated. He Thors like a bird.

After four hours, by cutting nicks in the sheet of rime ice cladding the roof (the ice is too thin and delicate to accept axes) and using sticky gloves, he manages to climb through the barring roofs by a ramp and wall, thereby straightening out the pitch.

Our next view, a brief one, shows Mal in front of a word-processor. The last words on the screen are shown in slow motion and enlarged. SO POINTBLANK (6) WAS NOT AS WE THOUGHT AFTER OUR FIRST ASCENT TEN YEARS AHEAD OF ITS TIME.

Joint Universities Expedition to Northern Iceland, 1986

GORDON S. HAMILTON and H. ELIZABETH MARTIN

For six weeks in the summer of 1986 a team of 14 geographers, drawn from the Queen's University of Belfast, the universities of Aberdeen and Oxford, and Portsmouth Polytechnic, led by Elizabeth Martin, joined together to form the Joint Universities Expedition to Northern Iceland. Our goal was to continue a programme of rock glacier monitoring which began in 1977 and which was followed up by expeditions in 1985, 1986 and 1987.

Rock glaciers are found in most high mountain regions of the world and are generally located in marginally glacierized and periglacial environments. They can be defined as a mass of rock-debris which displays a surficial pattern of ridges and furrows and is delimited from surrounding slopes by distinct and often steeply-angled lateral and terminal margins. The feature often contains an ice-core or an ice-rock matrix which allows it to exhibit flow velocities of less than one metre per year.

The expedition concentrated its attention on the rock glacier in Nautadalur, a tributary corrie of Skjóldalur, some 20km south of Akureyri in the Tröllaskagi peninsula. This rock glacier was found to be a downvalley extension of a small corrie glacier.

The expedition began in mid-June when an advance party of three arrived in Akureyri to take charge of the equipment and food shipped to Iceland from England. A four-day delay in the arrival of our freight frustrated our attempts to disappear from Akureyri, a major stop on the tourist trail around Iceland; but eventually we were able to transfer ourselves and our gear to Ysta-Gerdi, the farm at the head of Skjóldalur, which was to be our Base Camp.

Skjóldalur is one of many glacially-derived valleys which debouch into Eyjafjördur. These valleys extensively dissect the Tertiary basalt plateau which reaches from 1300–1500m above sea-level, forming the highest mountain massif in Iceland and providing the characteristic landscape of Tröllaskagi. In order to transfer our equipment and supplies the 9km distance to our Nautadalur camp at 900m a.s.l., we set up a hierarchy of camps with the assistance of two pack-horses under the able control of Audur Hallsdottir.

The weather remained settled throughout the first two weeks of the expedition, and by the time the rest of the group had arrived the camps were set up, research programmes had begun and the advance party were sunburnt. During this period the majority of the spring snow-melt occurred. Consequently, by the end of the expedition, access to the high camp from the bottom of Nautadalur, by the easiest route along the snow gully, was severely restricted. In the first week we had been able to descend from 900m to 250m a.s.l. along

LOCATION OF FIELD AREA, NORTHERN ICELAND

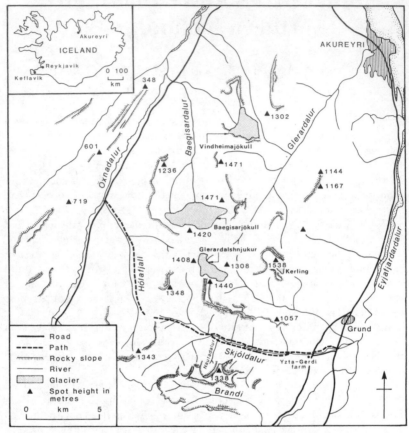

the central snow-gully in under five minutes. In general we found that climbing in this area was greatly facilitated by deep snow cover and, once this had melted to reveal an unstable rocky mantle, much more time and effort was called upon to cross the same route. The rocks in this region are particularly sharp and abrasive and were known to shred boots.

Apart from watching one's footstep, it was necessary to keep an eye on the surrounding cliffs and rock outcrops. These were extensively frost shattered and, with increasing pore-pressure in them from melt-water percolation, they were highly susceptible to rockfalls. We had a couple of very close calls when we really did see 'geomorphology in action'! The high frequency of rockfalls in this area was to form the basis of one of our research programmes and during a four-week period we recorded 52 rockfalls from the backwall of Nautadalur corrie.

Other projects included a detailed survey of the rock glacier and glacier surface, velocity profiles, lichenometry, rock-fabric analysis, and snow-pit studies. The results of these are found in the expedition report (*Expedition to Tröllaskagi Scientific Reports 1985, 1986* and *1987*, in press; *Summary of Expedition Report in Expedition Yearbook 1986*, published by the Royal Geographical Society).

Mountaineering formed an integral part of the expedition, both as a means of access to the study area and as a sport in its own right. The plateau in this area can be reached by a great number of long, steep snow gullies giving climbing at Scottish Grade 1–2. Most gullies exceed 1000m in length, and it is noted that their snow content is exceedingly diminished by early August. No technical difficulties are to be encountered, except when crossing the often considerable cornices guarding the exits. As the plateaux are entirely surrounded by steep sides with often numerous stepped rock outcrops, these gullies provide the best means of access to the summit. However, from Skjóldalur, after a steep and strenuous walk up Nautadalur, two routes to the plateau top could be taken.

The first, chosen by most members of the expedition, was no more than a short, if energy-sapping, walk up the broad E flank of the valley. In mid-June this involved struggling through thigh-deep snow, but by early July it took the form of a scramble over slippery and unstable rock. Once on the summit, one could walk over areas of stone stripes and polygons with relative ease, and spectacular views to Vatnajökull in the south were well worth the effort.

The second and more adventurous route was the ascent of the Nautadalur corrie backwall. In mid-June this route was backed-out with winter snow, concealing most of the rock outcrops. However, a month later the severity of the climb was more appreciable, with sustained ice-pitches present on the now steeper upper reaches. Snow and rock avalanches were a constant hazard and a formidable cornice was encountered at the summit. This route was only undertaken by two expedition members who had considerable mountaineering skill, a keen sense of adventure and what the rest of us thought was a streak of madness.

Two expedition members, Andy Dugmore and Gordon Hamilton, ventured from Nautadalur via the plateau top into Brandi, the extensive valley system to the south. The climb was made in late June and was aided by the snow-covered gullies. However, scrambles along narrow precipitous ridges of crumbling basalt made for heart-stopping moments. The route from Nautadalur, to the southern plateau edge of Brandi and along the valley bottom to Ysta-Gerdi took over 15 hours and made good use of the extended hours of sunshine afforded by our northerly location.

The expedition was a success, both scientifically and as an adventure. For many of its young members it provided the impetus to participate in, and even lead, expeditions in the following year. We would like to thank the sponsors who made our venture possible: The Royal Geographical Society, British Sugar plc, the Mount Everest Foundation, the Gilchrist Educational Fund, the Dudley Stamp Memorial Fund administered by the Royal Society, the Royal Scottish Geographical Society, the Gino Watkins Memorial Fund administered by the Scott Polar Institute, and Icelandair.

Wind Rivers

MALCOLM SALES

Wind Rivers? Where and what is Wind Rivers, I asked, when the place was first mentioned.

It is in fact in the USA. A wilderness area on the Great Divide in Wyoming. Roughly speaking north-east of the Grand Canyon and south of Yellowstone and the Tetons. Gannett Peak in Wind Rivers at 4207m is 10m higher than the Grand Teton and is the highest summit in Wyoming.

Wind Rivers can be quickly described as a cross between the Black Forest and the Alps. To my eyes, the area was refreshingly devoid of people. As a wilderness area it benefits by not receiving the publicity that is given to the better-known National Parks. There are none of the huts and skiing accessories that proliferate in the Playgrounds of Europe. One has to walk (or ride a horse, if that is one's fancy) and camp in order to get about.

Six of us went there in the summer of 1987: Anne and Henry Wheatcroft, who had been there before in 1984, Mike Garrett, Bob Stewardson, Chris Whitford and myself. With the American dollar so low, it was almost cheaper to go to the States than to the Alps. We flew from Gatwick to Dallas, and then on to Denver. Flying to America has the advantage that you may take as much as you wish, as long as it is kept to two items of luggage. You would be surprised at what can be crammed into a Karrimor Jaguar rucksack and an ex-services grip. The disadvantage of flying to America is the immigration control. One needs a holiday after being given the 'third degree' by that lot.

At Denver we hired a 4WD Ford Bronco, a Range-Rover-type vehicle. We also had to wait for three hours for one of our rucksacks to catch up with us. To judge by the way the airport staff took the news of our lost rucksack, it would seem that missing luggage is an every-flight occurrence which is usually corrected on the next flight. Once re-united with all our kit, we squeezed into the Ford and drove 700km through the night to a village called Pinedale, population 1000, altitude 2100m. Here we had breakfast and then purchased food in the supermarket, fuel and maps from the Outdoor Shop. The maps are not nearly as good as the British OS. The Americans, like the Europeans, rely upon well-marked trails and guidebooks to help their navigation.

Our objective, Wind Rivers, was still just a distant impression on the horizon. Before us lay a 60km drive along dirt-tracks to a trail-head and camp-site called Big Sandy Opening. From here a six-hour walk put us in the middle of some of the most magnificent mountain scenery I have ever seen. We spent five days walking and scrambling in the vicinity of a rock-climber's dream, the Cirque of Towers: a semicircular wall 300m high, with the unique Pingora at its centre. The guidebook we used, *Climbing and Hiking in the Wind River Mountains* by Joe Kelsey, gives a wealth of routes here of all grades, with plenty of scope for new discoveries.

After restocking from our car at Big Sandy Opening we went for a two-day trip to Big Sandy Lake, above which stands Big Sandy Mountain, with some spectacular sandstone towers on its SE ridge.

Once away from the Big Sandy Opening camp-site, we met very few people. Those we did meet were all American, and all expressed surprise that the British had heard of Wind Rivers. Even in the States it is not very well known.

We stopped again at Pinedale to top up, as we drove from Big Sandy in the south to Elkhart Park in the north. A one-and-a-half-day walk brought us to Indian Basin and Fremont Peak (second-highest in Wind Rivers). Another half-day's walk, and we were in Titcomb Basin, ready for Gannett Peak. We may have been ready for Gannett Peak, but the weather, which up to now had given us one day's rain and plenty of sunburn, was not. Waking up to heavy rain, Mike and I decided to wait for better weather. The others went off backpacking. Our day of waiting did indeed produce a weather change. A three-inch carpet of snow greeted us when we looked out of the tent next morning!

Time was running out. We had a plane to catch, and a long way to go to catch it. So we gave up waiting for Gannett to come into condition, brushed the snow off our tent and walked back to one of our previous camp-sites. By coincidence the others arrived at the same site, having made the same decisions.

A clear, cold night provided a magnificent morning. Bright weather with fresh snow still on the distant mountains made for a beautiful walk back to Elkhart Park.

All-in-all, it is an ideal area for those who wish to get away to the mountains, and also to get away from the crowds. Be you rock-climber, backpacker or mountaineer, this area has something to offer.

Who Identified the Highest Summit in the Eastern United States?

The Clingman-Mitchell Controversy of the 1850s

EDWARD PECK

In 1986 the mountaineering world was fascinated – or bored – by the revival of the 200-year-old controversy about who was the first to step on the highest summit in Europe: Balmat the shepherd-guide or Paccard the scholar-doctor? On this side of the Atlantic little is known of another mountaineering controversy, rather later, in the 1850s, involving not a White Mountain but a Black Mountain, believed to be the highest summit in North America east of the Mississippi River, and one in which the antagonists were a professor and his former pupil, a Senator. Doubtless many like myself have long believed Mount Washington (6288ft), in the White Mountains of New Hampshire, to qualify for the distinction of the highest point in the eastern United States. A journey along the Blue Ridge Parkway brought the discovery that this point lay not in the cold windswept north but in the sunny southern state of North Carolina, where the 2000-mile long Appalachian chain comes to its climax in thickly forested mountains of over 6000ft. Even here neither the spectacular crags and rocky summit of the better-known Grandfather Mountain (5964ft), nor the highest point of the extensive Great Smoky Mountains (6642ft), is in fact the highest summit in the east. Between these two lies the 15-mile long and unspectacular Black Mountain range, in the form of a fish-hook or the letter J, which marks the boundary between Yancey County to the north (with its centre at Burnsville) and Buncombe County to the south, centred on Asheville. The string of summits on the ridge from Celo Knob all the way round to Yeates Knob (see sketch map) vary only slightly in elevation. With the inadequate barometric equipment of the early 19th century, it was no easy task to ascertain which, among these various knobs of almost equal elevation, was the highest. In this article all heights are given in feet, as this is the unit of measurement in which they were first calculated (it is still in general use in the USA); conversion to metres would obscure some of the controversial issues. These were: which is the highest point? What is the precise height? Who first identified it? Who first ascended it?

For Europeans, the interest in the exploration of these North Carolina mountains is enhanced by the fact that the French botanist André Michaux (1746–1802) made botanical collections in the Black Mountains, his son François (1770–1855), known as the 'Father of American forestry', exuberantly sang the Marseillaise on Grandfather Mountain in 1794, while the Swiss Arnold Guyot (1807–1884) – a follower of the great Swiss geologist Louis Agassiz who himself came to the USA in 1848 – completed the most meticulous survey of the whole Appalachian chain up to modern times. Guyot is commemorated by a summit named after him in the Great Smoky Mountains.

We are more closely concerned with the assiduous local explorer of the Black Mountains – Elisha Mitchell (1793–1857) – who came to the University of Chapel Hill (North Carolina) in 1818. He first held the Chair of Natural Philosophy, which later included Chemistry and Geology, but his major work was to take charge of the geological survey of North Carolina. This led him to attempt to determine the heights of the principal mountains in the State. When in 1828 he climbed Grandfather Mountain, he expressed the view that: 'There can be no doubt that the country around the base of the Grandfather is higher than any other tract along these elevations, but I suspect the Black and Roan to be higher peaks.' The following year he went on record as saying that the Black Mountains probably contained the highest land between the Gulf of Mexico and the White Mountains of New Hampshire. It was not until 1835 that he found time to explore the mountains, spending over a week in the Black Mountains, approaching from the N or Burnsville side. For his altitude calculations he took as a base the barometric height of Morganton, reading it as 968ft above sea-level, whereas modern reckoning puts it at 1182ft. Thus all Mitchell's subsequent calculations were too low by 214ft.

At that time Celo Knob and Yeates Knob were reckoned to be the highest summits in the vicinity of Burnsville, but after ascending both, Mitchell realized that the highest point of the Black Mountains lay further south. Looking across the Cane Valley, in clear weather, he reckoned that one or other of two summits on the opposite ridge must be the highest. Deciding to go for the more northerly of the two, Mitchell set out with two guides (Wm Wilson and Allen) to follow Little Piney Ridge directly to the 'Top of the Black'.

The route led up bear trails through tangled rhododendron and dense forest to what was believed to be the highest point, though it was in thick mist. His barometer reading gave him a height of 5508ft above Morganton, a total height of 6476ft for the summit. Had his reading at Morganton been more accurate, this would have made the height of this point 6690ft, 6ft more than the modern reckoning of 6684ft (though given Mitchell's errors elsewhere, this was probably only a coincidence).

Three years later, in 1838, Professor Mitchell made two further excursions into the Black Mountains, this time approaching the range from the south, or Asheville, side, by way of the N fork of the Swannanoa River. He ascended the complex of three peaks close together – now known as Potato Knob, Clingman's Peak and Mount Gibbes. These last two are virtually equal in height. Mitchell determined one of them, probably Mt Gibbes, as being 6581ft, which is about 40ft out from the modern reckoning. Nonetheless, the middle of the three was held to be the highest, and thus the goal of tourists, becoming known for a time as 'Mount Mitchell'.

The conscientious Elisha Mitchell was still not satisfied that he had reached the highest summit in 1835. In 1844 he determined to 'try the Black once more, to which mountain I was well satisfied that the highest points are to be found, *as I was, also, that I had never yet been upon the highest*' (my italics). He was also anxious to test a new type of barometer acquired in Paris. This time he set off from the Cane Valley on the N side of the range with a guide named

THE BLACK MOUNTAINS OF NORTH CAROLINA

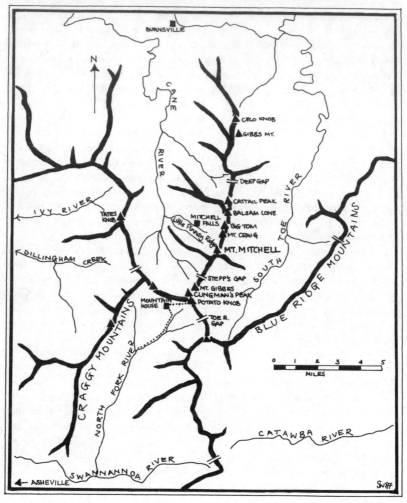

William Riddle. His route, described as 'the hardest day's work I ever performed', involved crawling through laurel and rhododendron bush and finding, prophetically, a 'shelving rock which might be a comfortable place to die'. The description of this route, both by Mitchell and later by Riddle, shows that instead of following Piney Ridge up to the highest point, as Mitchell had almost certainly done in 1835, they took a traverse which emerged three miles S of the highest peak, into the Mt Gibbes complex. Here Mitchell took a measurement with his new barometer, and calculated the height of Mt Gibbes at 6672ft, about 125ft higher than its actual elevation. He considered this to be

'Top of the Black'. He and Riddle then returned to Cane Valley after an exhausting 20 mile round trip.

American journalism, even more heady and exuberant in the early days of the Frontier than nowadays, had already accepted Mitchell's cautious claim of 1835, when the *Raleigh Register* loudly crowed that 'North Carolina now had it in its power to LOOK DOWN upon such of our arrogant sisters of the Confederacy as may insolently venture to taunt us with inferiority'. (It should be remembered that no State had by 1835 been formally constituted W of the Mississippi.) Tourism was beginning to catch on, bringing with it a made trail up the S approach from Asheville and a couple of primitive hostelries, one, known as 'Patton's Mountain House', only two miles from the S group of summits. In the early 1850s this brought a stream of tourists anxious to stand on the top of the USA, and in the early years they were content to reach what is now known as 'Clingman's Peak', virtually identical in height with neighbouring Mt Gibbes, ascended by Mitchell in 1844 and reckoned to be 'Top of the Black'. This tourist summit now became known as 'Mt Mitchell'. In due course a small observatory allowed the view to be seen without having to climb a balsam fir. Perhaps as a result the belief began to form in 1855 that this was not after all the highest point, and that the present Mt Mitchell, three miles to the N across Stepp's Gap was higher. The trail was extended over Mt Gibbes, down to the Gap and up to Mt Mitchell, meeting another trail blazed a little later up from Cane Valley to the NW.

Plenty of material here for controversy, one might say. So far no controversial personality had appeared to challenge Mitchell. It is time to introduce Thomas L Clingman (1812–1897), Senator and Congressman for North Carolina, who resigned in 1861 to become a Confederate leader in the Civil War. Clingman, 19 years Mitchell's junior, studied geology and geography under Mitchell at Chapel Hill; although a lawyer-politician, he encouraged mining in North Carolina and took a close interest in the mountain topography of his native State. For 20 years after Clingman's graduation in 1832, he and Mitchell remained on friendly terms as professor and former student. As a lawyer, however, Clingman was inclined to be controversial, while Mitchell was retiring and avoided controversy.

The seeds of controversy were there. After 20 years of visiting the mountains, Clingman had become interested in determining the highest point, since he considered Mitchell had never satisfactorily resolved this problem. On 8 September 1855 he set off with a barometer from the S side up the N Fork trail to what was then generally known as 'Mt Mitchell' (now Clingman's Peak). Having taken a barometric measurement, he continued N along the ridge to the present Mt Mitchell, there taking a further measurement which showed the pressure to be 0.19 inches lower than on the first summit, thereby indicating that the more northerly summit was higher. Clingman's rough calculations showed the S and N tops as 6732ft and 6941ft respectively, but he did not claim that his calculation of these absolute heights was accurate. Clingman did, however, write a lengthy article, submitted to the Secretary of the Smithsonian Institution and subsequently published, identifying the exact location of the highest point E of the Mississippi. The Secretary went further and introduced the paper with the statement that 'The highest point of the Black Mountain now known by the name of "Clingman's Peak" is probably the most elevated point east of the Rocky Mountains.'

So now we have the element of muddle as well as controversy. As a result of Clingman's ascent of the highest point, the present-day Mt Mitchell became (temporarily) known as 'Clingman's Peak' or 'Mt Clingman', while the present Clingman's Peak remained known as 'Mt Mitchell', at least for a couple of years. Clingman next cast doubt on Mitchell's claim to have reached the highest point, suggesting that he might have been misled because the area was then much more thickly forested. Mitchell reacted by sending the Secretary of the Smithsonian a copy of his notes of his 1835 expedition, concluding that although he had identified the highest point from Yeates Knob, his guides had misled him and he had returned 'knowing very well that I had *not* set foot upon the highest point'. But he did claim that with his 1844 ascent (of Mt Gibbes) he thought he had reached the 'Highest Peak of the Black'. Was his memory at fault? Did his guides (whose names he oddly enough could not recall) really mislead him in 1835? Were his measurements accurate? As well he might after 20 years, Mitchell began to have his own doubts. Clingman kindly suggested that controversy should cease until Mitchell could make another ascent.

In 1856 the dispute became public when rival Asheville newspapers published articles from the two antagonists, with the inevitable increase in personal animosity. Mitchell maintained that Clingman had made a 'total mistake' in suggesting that he (Mitchell) had 'failed to discover and ascend the highest peak'. If Clingman's errors in measurement are allowed to stand, Mitchell claimed, this would throw all the other heights into 'inextricable confusion' and may 'bring all the measurements made by me into discredit'.

The controversy was no longer about which was the highest peak but rather whether Mitchell had identified, ascended and measured the highest peak in the Black Mountains before Clingman's 1855 ascent. Who had measured the highest point first? This was compounded by Mitchell's confused recollections which gave Clingman plenty of material with which to pursue his side of the controversy, claiming errors of measurement by Mitchell who retorted, in August 1856, with an ill-considered attack on the Congressman. He threatened to 'expose the untruth, the weakness and the wickedness' of Clingman's pamphlet, and castigated his friendship as 'hollow and pretended'. Clingman retaliated with evidence he had obtained from Riddle, who had accompanied Mitchell as guide in 1844. Riddle described the route taken in some detail, pointing out that if they had decided to reach the present Mt Mitchell – a summit Riddle claimed to know well – they would have continued up Little Piney Ridge, which they had followed from Cane Valley. Instead they bore right-handed, southwards, to the peak since called Mt Gibbes.

The controversy then took a new turn to reach a sudden and dramatic conclusion. Mitchell, thrown on the defensive by Clingman's last devastating attack, went silent; but he made preparations for a visit to the Black Mountains in the summer of 1857, with a view to checking his earlier barometric measurements by the then new method of levelling. In mid-June he left Asheville with his son and daughter and spent a week or more levelling up to Patton's

Mountain House, the refuge not far below and to the west of the Potato Knob-Clingman's Peak-Mt Gibbes complex. On 27 June he sent his son to join his sister lower down the mountain and set off alone. He failed to return, as agreed, two days later to Mountain House. His son waited a further two days before raising the alarm. Search parties began combing the mountain from both sides. The Buncombe men abandoned the S side after three days, but the Yancey party, under the well-known guide Big Tom Wilson, persisted, picking up nailed boot tracks on the ridge leading NW from Mt Mitchell. It was consequently thought that Mitchell was attempting to retrace the route taken in 1835. The tracks led down off the N side of the ridge to a small waterfall, and in the deep pool at its foot Mitchell's body was found. It was evident that he had slipped in the dark on the evening of 27 June (his watch had stopped at 8.19), had knocked his head and then been held under water by a fallen tree. Now known as 'Mitchell's Falls', this spot is only a mile or so from the point of which he had said 13 years earlier: 'What a comfortable place it would be to die in'.

The Yancey party felt that the most appropriate spot in which to bury the body would be on the highest summit, so, taking turns, the men carried the body up 2300ft of thickly forested slope. On the top they found a group of Asheville men who wanted to bring the body down on their side. The two parties nearly came to blows, but in deference to the wishes of Mitchell's daughter, the Yancey men carried the body down to North Fork for onward transport to Asheville where it was interred on 10 July 1857.

Nevertheless, public opinion in North Carolina considered the body should rest on the highest point, and in 1858 it was taken back to the summit. The grave was first marked by a large cairn, then in 1888 by a bronze obelisk which was destroyed, partly by souvenir-hunters, and eventually by wind in 1915. The present tomb-like structure was erected in 1926, overshadowed by a stone observation tower, rebuilt and modernized in 1960.

It might be thought that Mitchell's death would provide a fitting if tragic end to the controversy, but Mitchell's supporters pursued their friend's view with even greater zeal, asserting that he had ascended and measured the highest peak in 1835 and 1844, long before Clingman's ascent in 1855. They based this claim on the testimony of William Wilson, the guide who had accompanied Mitchell in 1835, but whose name he could not remember. In 1858 and 1859 the Swiss Arnold Guyot, who mapped the whole Appalachian chain, had established with remarkable accuracy the very even heights of the various summits of the Black Mountains, but had refrained from controversy by giving the highest summit the name of 'Black Dôme' (complete with circumflex accent, doubtless in memory of his home mountains). Nonetheless, it was evident that the highest peak would acquire the name of Mount Mitchell, more as a result of the Professor's death than of any resolution of the controversy, and the name was (literally) consecrated by Bishop Otey on the re-interment in 1858. Meanwhile, Clingman had been surveying in the Great Smoky Mountains and had identified as another candidate for the highest point in the east a point of 6642ft (42ft lower than the modern estimate of Mt Mitchell) and this is now known as 'Clingman's Dome'. Ironically, the 'Mount Mitchell' of the southern complex of tops on the Black Mountains, which Clingman had demonstrated to be lower than the highest point, was, in the 1890s, given the permanent name of 'Clingman's Peak'.

To sum up, in 1835 Mitchell certainly identified the highest point of the Black Mountains as the northerly summit seen from Yeates Knob; and he probably reached it (in mist) the same year. In 1844 he climbed the southerly summit which for 11 years was considered the highest, until Clingman demonstrated otherwise in 1855. Mitchell's confused memories over 20 years led to his making an attempt to justify himself in 1857, which resulted in his tragic death. Mitchell's name is now permanently attached to the highest point in North America east of the Mississippi, while Clingman had to be satisfied with two eponymous peaks, lower by a fraction or so.

The subsequent history of the Black Mountains is rather sad. Logging companies devastated the fine stands of forest. They constructed a little puffing railway to the gap between Clingman's Peak and Mt Mitchell, later used by tourists. The balsam woolly aphid attacked the balsam fir (or Fraser's fir) which only flourishes over 6000ft in this southerly latitude. The railway was superseded by a tourist road, and finally a State Park was declared with a modern road linking the summit with the Blue Ridge Parkway. Today the highest point in the Eastern United States is effortlessly reached by thousands of tourists, but the view over the deep forested valleys and the ridges still awakens admiration for the early pioneers of this wild area.

NOTE

In writing this article I am greatly indebted to S Kent Schwarzkopf: *A History of Mt Mitchell and the Black Mountains, Exploration, Development and Preservation* (North Carolina Division of Archives and History 1985), and also to Michael Frome: *Strangers in High Places: The Story of the Great Smoky Mountains* (University of Tennessee 1980), and to *Appalachia, Vol 1, No 1*, p141, for George Dimmock's account of an ascent of Mt Mitchell in 1877.

Blue Mountain Peak

DAVID CHARITY

The road ahead looked awfully steep, and was deeply rutted. 'You've got to take it fast.' A friendly voice belonging to a native of Hagley's Gap volunteered, from over his garden fence – 'Take a good run at it, and you'll be OK.'

I considered his advice. Two Americans in an Opel had got stuck after only a few metres and were already deep in negotiation with representatives of the local youth about the cost of a push. I decided to give them 10 minutes to get well ahead, and retired for a smoke and a think.

I had left Ocho Rios at 10.15 in the morning of 27 August 1986, destination the summit of Blue Mountain Peak, at 2256m the high point of the Blue Mountain range and of all Jamaica, although only some 24km from downtown Kingston.

The road had so far taken me along the coast to Port Maria and Port Amolto, past the island homes of Noel Coward and Ian Fleming, then inland over the mountain divide to the pass at Hardwar Gap, forking left to Silverhill Gap. I had picked up a solitary pedestrian who claimed to have an aunt in Peterborough, and who claimed to have been to the top of Blue Mountain Peak many times. 'The road goes almost the whole way to the top these days', he assured me. This seemed disappointing if true, for it would deny me a decent mountain walk.

He left me at the fork where I turned left for Silverhill gap. A long descent down the hairpin bends of an atrocious track took me at last to the main road, where a left turn led through many pot-holes to Mavis Bank, and so on to the valley of the Yallah River, where the road either climbed impossibly through several large boulders to a rickety narrow bridge, or even less promisingly straight through the river.

A youth resting on a boulder assured me the correct way was through the river. I waded through first to check the depth. The water came midway up my calves; not as high as the exhaust pipe, I concluded. First gear, and through we went. No trouble at all. Then steeply and roughly up to Hagley's Gap, the settlement closest to the mountain.

The local youth appeared not to have come to terms with the Americans. A face poked itself through the car window.

'You goin' to the Peak Mistah?'

I indicated assent.

'You wanna guide?'

'No thanks, I'll just follow my nose.'

'You give us sometin' for the offer?'

I indicated dissent, and with a cry of 'stand-by' took off with racing rear wheels. The car careered up the track; not daring to slow down I raced round bends, past startled onlookers, madly dashing from rut to rut, avoiding boulders and dogs. I eventually ground to a halt behind the Americans who had stopped for a view just at the point where the road levelled out.

I manoeuvred round them with a wave. The guidebook recommended parking at Whitfield Hall, a sort of Youth Hostel where overnight lodging could be had; but the road still seemed passable, and every half-kilometre of driving would be a half-kilometre less to walk. So on I bumped; hairpins, more ruts and boulders. Thank heaven this was only a rented car. The little Toyota Starlet seemed to revel in the bumps and bends, and ground upwards slowly but surely. One particularly steep section was almost too much for its miniscule cubic capacity, about 1000 at the most. It got up at the second attempt, but only just.

The road levelled a little and came at last to a hairpin bend which was clearly the limit of its capability. I parked. It was 2.30pm. The sun stared from a fine cloudless sky, but up here with a gentle breeze the temperature was a modest 70F. The track led off rightwards, in the direction of the summit, or alternatively leftwards. The right-hand track led to a dead-end, where a pipe, remnant of some irrigation scheme, dripped forlornly. Back to the car, feeling that perhaps I was not destined to make it to the top. Oh well, may as well try the other track. It's only 3pm. I strolled casually up the other track, the sound of some mechanical agricultural contraption gradually getting louder.

It proved to be a spraying machine, manned by a Jamaican character called Joe. He introduced himself. I reciprocated.

'Where you goin'?'

'I'm going for a walk. Does this track lead anywhere?'

'It goes to the Peak. But it's a seven mile walk. You won't make it today.'

He indicated the position of the sun in the afternoon sky. 'Seven miles?' I gave a long low whistle. I suspected he was exaggerating. The guide book said it was only five miles from Whitfield Hall, and I reckoned my bumpy drive had disposed of at least two of those.

'Oh well, I'll just go a little further.'

'Come down soon, David, and then you can give me a ride back to the village in your car, when I finish work.'

I reflected on the capacity of the rural Jamaican to imagine that visitors from 5000 miles away would so easily be persuaded to rearrange their afternoons just to give them a lift back to the village. But perhaps that was unkind. I also reflected on the misinformation the locals dole out. On the one hand, the road goes almost to the top, these days. On the other, it was still seven miles on foot. Maybe it came to the same thing.

The track soon narrowed into a footpath, and led from the open scrub into the afforested peaks of the Great Ridge of the Blue Mountain Range. The path was shaded by the trees and displayed an abundance of wild flowers, particularly orchids. I passed a donkey tethered to a tree. There was no sign of its owner. After about a mile the path emerged at a prominent col, Portland Gap. The view northwards through the trees was extensive; mile upon mile of wooded peaks and ridges.

The summit was away to the east. The path led off again through the trees, level at first, then steeply rising through many zig-zags. It rose on and on, at first pleasantly, then interminably, then tediously, then both tedious and interminable. Once I felt morally convinced that, having come so far, I would get to the top today, and without risk of being benighted. Then from a subsidiary peak I saw how far away the real top still was, and I became uncertain of reaching my goal, at any rate with enough time to get back to the car before nightfall. From the subsidiary peak the path wound round to the north side of the ridge, crossed another col, and so finally up the slopes of the real peak emerging suddenly at the summit plateau, bald of trees, but graced with two rough mountain huts, for those with time to sleep on the summit, I supposed. Dawn from up there must be wonderful.

The time was 5.20pm. One hour and ten minutes until dusk. I spent five minutes working on a photographic record of the impressive surroundings, and then, mindful of the bottle of Red Stripe in the car, dashed back down the path.

After only 10 minutes I encountered the two Americans. One sportingly offered me a much-needed swig from their water bottle. I asked if they were going to the top, and reminded them that dusk fell at 6.30. The descent was easy. The many zig-zags of the ascent could all be avoided by a very steep short-cut, through trees and down an incipient gully. It went down so far that I wondered if it would not take me to the valley and bypass Portland Gap and the car as well. Fortunately it rejoined the main path, which soon emerged at Portland Gap. Down past the donkey and its absent owner. My only other encounter of the day was a strapping lad, hiking up the hill with a huge rucksack, sleeping bag, cooking equipment, the lot. 'You bin to the top?' he asked. And then in astonishment, 'Where's yo' gear?', indicating my lack of encumbrances, clad, as I was, in shorts and T-shirt and carrying only a camera and a car-key.

'Oh, it was just an afternoon walk', I replied.

'You're very brave', he volunteered. He was no doubt thinking that foolhardy would be a more appropriate epithet.

I got to the car just as darkness fell, waited 20 minutes just in case the Americans showed up, drank my Red Stripe and smoked two cigarettes. There was no sign of them. Noting the position in the evening sky of Mars to the south and Venus to the east, I bumped off down the mountain track. I noted that the car made much better progress with the hand-brake off. I only took one wrong turning on the way back to Hagley's Gap, and bumped depressingly around Hanford's Coffee Plantation for about 30 minutes, when the need to ford another stream convinced me that I was off route. More desperate first gear work, up impossibly steep inclines, with whizzing wheels and clouds of dust or smoke coming from beneath the unprotesting little car, finally returned me to the proper road.

Seeing two figures a little way ahead, I stopped for confirmation that this was the road to Hagley's Gap.

'Why sure. It's me, you remember Joe. We was comin' to rescue you, 'cos we saw you turned into the plantation. You kin easy get lost round here at night. Many foreigners git lost and spend the night in the wilds. We was comin' for you, you come and have a drink wit' us, now we found you.'

I reflected that, since they had confirmed that I was on the way to

Hagley's Gap, and was therefore not lost, there hardly seemed just cause for a celebratory drink. I excused myself on the grounds of the lateness of the hour and the many miles to Ocho Rios.

'Sure, we unnerstan' man, you no got the time fo' drink, so just give us the money instead.'

I was not sure that I followed the convoluted logic of this, but thought it politic to hand over two 20 dollar notes, in feigned gratitude for such a timely rescue.

The long drive through Mavis Bank, Gardentown, Industry, Papine, Kingston, Castleton, Port Maria and Orocabessa to Ocho Rios took until midnight, but was, apart from boulders in the road and a major tropical storm, more or less uneventful.

Alpine Club Peru Meet
(16th July–26th August 1987)

ROBERT SNEYD

Four AC members – Robert Sneyd, Rosemary and Ashley Greenwood and John Hudson – and four others – Pamela Glanville and Belinda Swift (Pinnacle Club), Stanley Thomas (Climbers Club) and Richard Weller – attended the Peru meet which was based on Huaraz. The ages of the participants ranged from 26 to 75! Meet members arrived and departed at different times, with most people staying four or five weeks. We made four trips into the Cordillera Blanca, each to a different area.

Quebrada Rajucolta

A one-hour truck ride took myself, John, Richard and Stanley to Pitec where we were joined by Juan (our *arriero*) and three donkeys. We reached the bottom of the Rajucolta valley after a four-hour walk where we found that access was blocked by a substantial wall and a locked gate. The inhabitants of a nearby village only opened the gate after prolonged negotiations and the promise of some cash upon our return. Two more hours saw us camped in the valley one mile below Laguna Tambillo. After a day's acclimatization John and I attempted Point 5377m but were driven off by rockfalls 100m from the top. We then moved up the valley and camped by Laguna Awash (4700m) before moving again to a spectacular camp-site (5100m) opposite the impressive W face of Huantsan. From there we traversed Yawarraju (5675m) before climbing Rurek (5698m). The descent from Yawarraju was notable for loose rock and constant stonefall which completely severed my brand new rope. We then returned to Huaraz to meet the rest of the party. We found the town in fiesta and the streets full of goose-stepping children engaged in endless parades.

Quebrada Ishinca

A short drive and two days' walk took the whole party to the head of Quebrada Ishinca where we found several large parties. There was also a dead donkey in an advanced state of decomposition. I was impressed by one party of Ecuadorean climbers whose baggage included two live chickens for later consumption. In the face of worsening weather, three of us decided to attempt Taklaraju (6032m) which is the major peak of the valley. We camped rather too high at about 5500m and Richard was badly affected by the altitude, so John and I pressed on, leaving Richard in the tent. In a complete white-out we plodded upwards without difficulty through impressive seracs and crevasses until the last 200m where two decent ice-pitches took us on to the summit. In thick fog and a steady snowfall we didn't linger on the top and opted for a quick descent; we had considerable difficulty finding the route, as our trail had been entirely obliterated by fresh snow.

Whilst we were on Taklaraju, Pamela and Belinda attempted Ishinca (5546m) after staying one night in an excellent hut which lies below this peak. Bad weather forced them to turn back before reaching the summit. All the peaks were now out of condition and we returned to Huaraz.

Nevada Pongos

We had considerable difficulty obtaining pack animals for this trip as the area is seldom visited except by the coach-loads of day-trippers who go to the edge of the national park to see the rare *Puya Raymondi* (a massive pineapple-like plant which grows up to 30 feet high). From Ingenio Pampa we traversed a col at 4600m to reach the lakes of Quebrada Qeshqe. The next day we moved further up the valley to the edge of Laguna Qeshqe, where we camped. The entrance to the Qeshqe valley is dominated by a substantial unnamed rock peak (5303m) with a massive S ridge. Richard and I determined to climb this and set off early the next day. We attained the ridge at sunrise and made rapid progress until we were about two-thirds of the way up where the difficulty increased to about VS. Whilst leading a steep corner Richard dislodged a rock which fell about 40ft before striking me in the back. This put an end to any further climbing, as I was completely unable to move my right arm and the rest of the day was spent lowering me off. During the 10 days we spent in this area most members of the party reached one or more of the many unnamed peaks and cols which surround the Quebrada Qeshqe.

Quebrada Llanganuco and Quebrada Yannapaccha

John and Belinda climbed Yannapaccha (5593m) from Quebrada Yanna-paccha. They were then joined by the Greenwoods and Stanley who had come up the Quebrada Santa Cruz and crossed the Punta Union. On the way out Belinda was bitten by a dog at Yanama and had to make a swift descent for rabies injections.

APPENDIX

THE ASSOCIATION OF MOUNTAIN GUIDES OF PERU

BELINDA SWIFT

In Huaraz, immediately to the east of Av Luzuriaga, on waste ground where dogs scavenge the rubbish and reinforcing rods of half-finished concrete buildings pierce the clear air, there is a surprise. A Swiss chalet stands here,

41. *Julie-Ann Clyma on the lower part of Gasherbrum 2's SW spur. Baltoro Kangri and Gasherbrum 6 in the background.*

42.   Duncan Tunstall using local transport to cross the Shimshal river.

43.   The climbing team – Xixabangma 1987. Nyanang Ri (unclimbed) in the
       background.

44. *Unclimbed Nyanang Ri (6592m) on the S ridge of Xixabangma, from the Base Camp on the east. Nigel Williams drinking.*

45. Our baggage yaks setting off from Ganji for N Xixabangma Base Camp.
     In the distance Xixabangma (right) and Phola Ganchen (left).

46. Ice towers on the Dasuo glacier, N Xixabangma.

47. *Marti Martin-Kuntz exchange skis for crampons below the headwall at 5300m on N Muztagh.*

48. A lone camel approaches Jambulak village at 4000m, beneath N Muztagh (L) and Muztagh Ata (R).

49. Crossing the Chodomak glacier at 5000m on N Muztagh, summit in background.

50. *Dick Renshaw heads up the 'freeway' of the Chodomak glacier on N Muztagh. The headwall is on L, below the ridge.*

51. *Ruwenzori: Lake Kitandara and McConnell's Prong.*

52.   *Shark's Nose (3670m), Shadow Lake.*

called the Casa de Guias. The interior, much of it wood-panelled, includes a small café, an office, a pleasant dormitory and washroom accommodation, an equipment store, and a library and lecture room still being developed.

In 1977 Camille Bournissen, the Vice-President of the Association of Swiss Guides, visited Peru and was impressed with its potential for climbing and trekking. There were no professional guides then – only a few porters with some climbing experience and limited equipment. The porter hired by two of us in 1979 had a pair of ten-point crampons and very little warm clothing. He was building up his credentials by asking us to write down in his notebook what he had helped us climb. In this year the Swiss returned to organize a training course for guides. It lasted two months. 11 people took part and they climbed 18 mountains. Eight obtained their guide certificates.

A commission was formed in 1983, presided over by Tony Lampert, and the project *Alpes-Andes*, approved by the Peruvian government, was set up. Its aims were to continue the training of mountain guides, to develop tourism in the Andes, and to build up the necessary equipment and techniques required for mountain rescue. The project is worked on by two bodies: the Swiss Mountain Guides Association and the Association of Mountain Guides of Peru – AGMP. Employment is thus provided for the young men of the valleys who act as porters, donkey-men, camp guardians or guides.

For the years 1987–88 the AGMP has produced a climbing and trekking programme covering the Cordilleras Blanca and Huayhuash from Huaraz, the Vilcabamba and Vilcanota from Cuzco, and the Cordillera Volcanica from Arequipa.

The AGMP can be contacted in Lima at: Jr Camana 780 Of 506, Lima 1. Tel 270635, Telex 25218PE CP HCRIL.

Mountaineers and Skiers in British Antarctic Territory Place-names

G. HATTERSLEY-SMITH

In the 'heroic' age of Antarctic exploration, spanning the first two decades of this century, it is strange that mountaineering and cross-country ski expertise were conspicuously deficient on British expeditions. It appears that for some reason there was no rapport in Britain between polar explorers on the one hand, and mountaineers and pioneer ski-runners on the other. So Scott, Shackleton and their men learnt an indifferent snow and ice craft the hard way – by trial and error when they reached the field.

Yet, as early as 1883, Baron A E Nordenskiöld had demonstrated the tremendous advantage of skis in polar work on his expedition to West Greenland. His example was followed by Nansen, who ski'd across Greenland in 1889, and by Conway, who ski'd across Vestspitsbergen in 1896. In the Antarctic, Scandinavians were foremost in making use of skis: first, Amundsen on the de Gerlache (Belgian) expedition to Graham Land (now part of the British Antarctic Territory (BAT)) in 1897–99, followed by Borchgrevink on his expedition to Victoria Land (now part of Ross Dependency) in 1898–1900 and O Nordenskjöld on his expedition to northern Graham Land in 1901–04. In 1912 skis were crucial to Amundsen's great triumph at the South Pole. However, the first Antarctic explorer to emphasize the importance of traditional mountaineering skills, as opposed to ski technique, was Charcot from France, who employed an Alpine guide on his expedition to the west coast of Graham Land in 1903–05. He thus ensured sound mountaineering technique among members of this expedition, a number of whom formed the nucleus of his second expedition to the same area in 1908–10. By way of example and contrast, on the British Imperial Trans-Antarctic Expedition (BITAE), Shackleton's famous crossing of South Georgia in 1916 was due entirely to the magnificent courage and endurance of his three-man party, and owed nothing to mountaineering skill which the party simply did not possess.

In the 1920s, polar exploration began to move out of the 'heroic' age, as travel by dog-sledge completely replaced man hauling and as aircraft soon became available for reconnaissance and depot laying. With improved food, clothing and equipment, expeditions were able to concentrate with enjoyment on mapping and science in new country and ceased to be survival tests of the most rigorous and extreme kind. In Britain during this transition period, important roles were played by two men, Wordie and Watkins, both experienced mountaineers who brought other mountaineers into the polar field. (Fuchs, of later Antarctic fame, was a member of Wordie's British East Greenland Expedition, 1929, and Chapman and Wager, both of later

Himalayan fame, were members of Watkins's British Arctic Air Route Expedition, 1930–31 (BAARE).) In the Antarctic, the trend of the immediate pre-Second World War period culminated in the British Graham Land Expedition, 1934–37 (BGLE), originally planned by Watkins prior to his death in a kayak accident in 1932. This expedition, one of the most cost-effective ever mounted, carried out important mapping and scientific work on the west coast of Graham Land.

British work in Graham Land, halted by the Second World War, was resumed in 1944 under the Royal Navy's Operation 'Tabarin', which in 1945 became known as the Falkland Islands Dependencies Survey (FIDS) and, from 1962, as the British Antarctic Survey (BAS). The hastily assembled members of Operation 'Tabarin' had a nucleus of men with ship-borne Antarctic experience, but none who could be called a mountaineer. But a number of mountaineers were soon attracted to the FIDS in its early days, so that there was usually at least one experienced man at each station. In the BAS today mountaineering experience is an essential requirement for a proportion of the recruits to man the present four stations in the BAT, namely, Signy (South Orkney Islands), Faraday (Graham Coast), Rothera (Adelaide Island) and Halley (Coats Land).

The wide-ranging work of the Survey over most of the BAT, on journeys for which in late years the snow tractor has replaced the dog team, has led to a steady demand for new place-names. In Coats Land new names were also needed following the work of the Trans-Antarctic Expedition, 1955–58 (TAE), and an intense demand for names arose from the first systematic air photography of Graham Land and off-lying islands by the Falkland Islands Dependencies Aerial Survey Expedition, 1955–57 (FIDASE). To resolve the problem of the need for new names outstripping the traditional sources (e.g. names of expedition members and descriptive names), the late Dr Brian Roberts, for many years Secretary of the UK Antarctic Place-names Committee, thought of naming groups of geographically related features after corresponding groups of persons or ideas. Among the groups he chose were 'Pioneers of ski-mountaineering' and 'Pioneers of polar life and travel' for the indirect contribution of such men to Antarctic exploration by reason of their expertise as skiers and/or mountaineers, and as designers of equipment. Some of those commemorated (including a few foreigners) were members of the Alpine Club; all are more or less well-known in mountain literature. Mountaineers also appear in a group of names after 'Glaciologists', and in widely scattered areas outside these main groupings. Under these categories and with reference to the map, a selection is given of those names most likely to be of interest to readers of this journal.

Place-names after pioneers of ski-mountaineering
(Graham Coast)

Pride of place must go to *Rossa Point* and *Tuorda Peak*, named after A P Rossa (1844–1917) and P L N Tuorda (1847–1911), the two Jokkmokk Lapps on Nordenskiöld's expedition to west Greenland in 1883, who were credited with

covering a total distance of 460km (*sic*) on skis in 57 hours. The first
Englishman to make a full day's journey on skis was Sir Arthur Conan Doyle
(1859–1930), in Switzerland in March 1893, so we have *Doyle Glacier*. This
journey was made only three years before the first crossing of Vestspitsbergen
by Sir Martin Conway, 1st Baron Conway of Allington (1856–1937), President
of the Alpine Club, 1902–04, and first President of the Alpine Ski Club, 1908–
11 (*Conway Island*). Pioneer British ski-runners are further represented by E C
Richardson (1872–1954), first Secretary, 1903–05, and then President of the

Ski Club of Great Britain (*Richardson Nunatak*) and by V Caulfield (1874–1958), author of *How to Ski* (London, 1910) (*Caulfield Glacier*). And German pioneer ski-runners are represented by: O Vorweg, author of *Das Schneeschuh Laufen* (Warmbrunn, 1893) (*Vorweg Point*); W Paulcke (1873–1949), who with three companions traversed the Bernese Oberland on skis in January 1897 (*Mount Paulcke*); W R Rickmers (AC) (1873–1965), explorer of the Caucasus and Pamir, and co-author with E C Richardson (see above) and C Somerville (see below) of *Ski-running* (London, 1904) (*Rickmers Glacier*); and W Hoek (1875–1951), author of *Schi und seine sportliche Benutzung* (München, 1906) (*Hoek Glacier*)

Also commemorated in the place-names are men especially noted for designing new or improved mountaineering and ski equipment, although not all were experts of technique. Their names comprise: F Huitfeldt (1851–1938), Norwegian designer of the Huitfeldt ski-binding and author of *Lehrbuch des Skilaufens* (Berlin, 1890) (*Huitfeldt Point*); M Zdarsky (d1940), Austrian inventor of the first dependable ski-binding and author of *Lilienfeld Skilauf-Technik* (Hamburg, 1896) (*Mount Zdarsky*); G Bilgeri (1873–1934), Austrian inventor of the first spring ski-binding and author of *Der Alpine Skilauf* (München, 1911, (*Bilgeri Glacier*); F Genecand (1879–1957), Swiss inventor of the Tricouni nail for climbing boots (*Mount Genecand*); V Sohm, Austrian inventor of special types of skins and waxes for skis (*Sohm Glacier*); and R Lawrie (AC) (1903–82), the well-known bootmaker and alpine equipment specialist of London, who supplied equipment for the BGLE and later Antarctic expeditions, thus helping to bridge the gap between alpinists and polar explorers (*Lawrie Glacier*).

Finally, the list includes the names of two much earlier pioneers of alpine travel: J Simler (1530–76), Italian author of *De alpibus commentarius* (Tiguri, 1574), giving the first reasonable advice on precautions for travel on glaciers (*Simler Snowfield*), and F J Hugi (1796–1855), Swiss school-teacher, called 'the father of winter mountaineering', and author of *Naturhistorische Alpenreise* (Leipzig, 1830) (*Hugi Glacier*).

Place-names after pioneers of polar life and travel
(Shackleton Range)

The two most famous British mountaineers of the 19th century, E Whymper (AC) (1840–1911) and A F Mummery (AC) (1855–95), the latter lost on Nanga Parbat, were not the best of friends in life but now rest together (as it were) in the adjacent features *Whymper Spur* and *Mummery Cliff*; both men were designers of tents that bear their names. A third tent designer, C F Meade (AC) (1881–1975), is commemorated in the nearby *Meade Nunatak*. A little further away lies *Freshfield Nunatak*, named after D W Freshfield (1845–1934), explorer of the Caucasus and Himalaya, who initiated widespread recognition of the place of mountaineering in exploration; he was Editor of this journal, 1872–80, and President of the Alpine Club, 1893–95, and of the Royal Geographical Society (RGS), 1914–17.

Place-names after glaciologists

(Adelaide Island, Loubet Coast, Fallières Coast, Foyn Coast, Bowman Coast)

Most of those commemorated in this group can be counted as mountaineers of varied expertise. A selection has been made in which pride of place must go to H B de Saussure (1740–99), Swiss physicist and geologist, who made the third ascent of Mont Blanc in 1787 (*Saussure Glacier*). Two other early alpine scientists are commemorated: J D Forbes (1809–68), Scottish physicist, who made pioneer studies of glacier flow (*Forbes Glacier*), and J Tyndall (1820–93), Irish mountaineer and author of papers on glaciers and the physical properties of ice (*Tyndall Mountains*).

British mountaineers and skiers of more modern times are represented by: G Seligman (AC) (1886–1973), Founder and first President, 1946–63, of the International Glaciological Society, and author of *Snow Structure and Ski Fields* (London, 1936) (*Seligman Inlet*); M F Perutz (b1914), crystallographer of Austrian birth, OM and Nobel Laureate, an accomplished ski-mountaineer (*Perutz Glacier*); W H Ward (AC) (b1917), a member of expeditions to Jan Mayen, 1938, and Baffin Island, 1951 and 1953, and Secretary, International Commission of Snow and Ice, 1959–71 (*Ward Glacier*); and W R B Battle (1919–53), a member of expeditions to Norway and Greenland, and to Baffin Island, where he lost his life in a glacier melt stream (*Battle Point*).

Among Americans we have: W B O Field (AC) (b1904), sometime Research Fellow of the American Geographical Society, noted for his surveys of glaciers in North America (*Field Glacier*); M H Demorest (1910–42), theoretician in the field of glacier flow, who lost his life on active service with the United States Army in a crevasse accident on the Greenland ice cap (*Demorest Glacier*); J G McCall (1923–54), an expert on cirque glaciers in Norway and Alaska, who died during a mountain rescue operation on Mount McKinley (*McCall Point*); and M F Meier (b1925), specialist on the regime and flow of North American glaciers, who was President of the International Commission of Snow and Ice, 1967–71 (*Meier Valley*). Other countries are represented by: S Finsterwalder (1862–1951) and R Finsterwalder (1899–1963), German pioneers of photogrammetric survey of glaciers, father and son (*Finsterwalder Glacier*), and F Müller (1926–80), Swiss glaciologist who carried out research in the Canadian Arctic and Greenland, and in the Himalaya as a member of the Swiss Everest Expedition, 1957 (*Müller Ice Shelf*).

Other place-names after mountaineers
(ungrouped)

The earliest first-class mountaineer to visit the BAT was P Dayné, the Italian alpine guide from Valsavaranche in the Aosta Valley, who was a member of Charcot's 1903–05 expedition (*Dayné Peak*, Wiencke Island, Danco Coast); he named the highest peak that he climbed (1415m) after Prince Luigi Amedeo di Savoia, Duke of the Abruzzi (AC) (1873–1933), Italian alpinist and Arctic, East African and Himalayan explorer (*Luigi Peak*, Anvers Island). Charcot's expeditions were well-found in ski-mountaineering equipment, thanks to

C Somerville, the ski-mountaineer and equipment specialist of Oslo (*Somerville Island*, Graham Coast).

Subsequent expeditions left widely scattered place-names after members or supporters who were mountaineers. All the 16 members of the BGLE are commemorated in place-names, but on the mountaineering side the expedition is perhaps best remembered in names after two men who did not take part – *Watkins Island* (Biscoe Islands) and *Chapman Glacier* (Rymill Coast). H G Watkins (AC) (1907–32), the originator of this expedition and the leader of expeditions to Edge Island (Svalbard), Labrador and Greenland (twice), was also a fine alpinist. F S Chapman (AC) (1907–71) brought the sledge-dogs from West Greenland to England for this expedition, having previously served on Watkins's Greenland expeditions; in 1937 he made the first ascent of Chomolhari in the Himalaya.

Following the early work of the FIDS, it was appropriate that a major feature should be named after Sir James Wordie (1889–1962), Scottish geologist and polar explorer, who was Chief of Scientific Staff, BITAE, and leader of six expeditions to Greenland and Arctic Canada between the wars; he was also Chairman of the FID Scientific Committee, 1948–56, Vice-President of the Alpine Club, 1949–51, and President of the RGS, 1951-54 (*Wordie Ice Shelf*, Fallières Coast). Others commemorated in place-names at about the same time were: L R Wager (AC) (1904–65), British geologist, who was a member of the BAARE and of the Mount Everest Expedition, 1933, and leader of later expeditions to Greenland (*Wager Glacier*, Alexander Island); F K Elliott (b1910), British rock-climber, Alpine and Himalayan mountaineer, who was FIDS Base Leader at Hope Bay, Trinity Peninsula, 1946–48, and who led a 700km sledge journey down the length of Graham Land to Stonington Island, Marguerite Bay (*Mount Elliott*, Trinity Peninsula); W R Latady (1918–79), American optical engineer and mountaineer, who was a member of the (US) Ronne Antarctic Research Expedition, 1946–48, based at Stonington Island (*Latady Island* and *Latady Mountains*, Palmer Land); and the British mountaineers E W K Walton (b1918) and A R C Butson (b1922), respectively FIDS engineer and medical officer at Stonington Island, 1946–48, both of whom were awarded the Albert Medal (later translated to George Cross) for bravery in crevasse rescues on different occasions near the FIDS base (*Walton Peak* and *Butson Ridge*). (Only one other George Cross has been awarded for Antarctic service. Some years later Walton performed another, probably more difficult, crevasse rescue in South Georgia, for which he received the Queen's Commendation.) It is worth recording that, early in 1948, with two or three Climbers' Club members by chance gathered together at Stonington Island, a meet was held during which the difficult Neny Matterhorn and other peaks were climbed.

The year 1955 saw the launching of two important expeditions (mentioned above), from which the names of four members or supporters may be selected to recall the mountaineering skills that were so much needed in the field. V E (later Sir Vivian) Fuchs (b1908), the leader of the TAE, had previously served with Wordie in Greenland and as Commander of the FIDS, 1948–50; he was Director of the FIDS/BAS, 1950–73 (*Fuchs Ice Piedmont*, Adelaide Island,

and *Fuchs Dome*, Shackleton Range). Sir Edwin Herbert (later Baron Tangley of Blackheath) (1899–1973), who had been President of the Alpine Club, 1953–55, was a member of the Committee of Management and Chairman of the Finance Committee of the TAE (*Herbert Mountains*, Shackleton Range). W G Lowe (b1924), the New Zealand mountaineer and photographer with the successful Mount Everest expedition in 1953, was a member of the trans-polar party of the TAE, 1956–58 (*Mount.Lowe*, Shackleton Range). Finally, P G Mott (b1913), of Hunting Aerosurveys Ltd, was the leader of the FIDASE; as a surveyor he had led Oxford University expeditions to Greenland in 1935, 1936 and 1938, and had been a member of the British Shaksgam Expedition, 1939 (*Mott Snowfield*, Trinity Peninsula).

Of the many young mountaineers that have served at the BAS stations over the years, space allows mention of only two. J C Cunningham (1927–80) served as Station Commander at Stonington Island, 1962–63, and Adelaide Island, 1964–65, having been a member of the privately organized South Georgia Survey, 1955–56; on 23 November 1964 he led the first ascent of Mount Jackson, Palmer Land (3180m), the highest peak in the BAT, but he is commemorated in *Mount Cunningham*, South Georgia (outside the BAT); he lost his life as the result of a climbing accident on sea-cliffs off Holyhead. J F Bishop (1950–80) worked as a glaciologist on Alexander Island, having previously been a member of expeditions to Greenland and leader of an expedition to north-eastern Afghanistan; he later took part in further expeditions to Greenland and Iceland, and in the RGS International Karakoram Project, during which he lost his life in a climbing accident near the summit of Kirkun Peak (*Bishop Glacier*, Alexander Island).

Although the Antarctic outside the BAT is not within the brief of this article, it is fitting to close by drawing attention to place-names after four most illustrious members of the Alpine Club in *Hillary Coast*, *Odell Glacier*, *Shipton Ridge* and *Tilman Ridge*, all in New Zealand's Ross Dependency.

The Mountaineer at Extreme Altitude

MICHAEL WARD

An increasing number of mountaineers now wish to climb the highest peaks in the world without supplementary oxygen, in small groups or alone, and sometimes in winter. This trend is accelerating and to prevent a high mortality several vital factors must be appreciated.

Oxygen lack and barometric pressure

The critical factor is barometric pressure. Oxygen lack at high altitude is due to the low pressure of oxygen in the atmosphere, and the pressure diminishes more the higher the climber goes. The barometric pressure determines the pressure of oxygen in the air, the lungs and finally in all the tissues and muscles, and this dictates the amount of exercise the mountaineer can take. At extreme altitude performance is exquisitely sensitive to even small changes of the pressure of the oxygen in the lungs, and oxygen pressure also determines heat production and mental performance.

Variation in atmospheric pressure

Considerable variations occur in the barometric pressure and therefore in the oxygen pressure in the body. At extreme altitude the most important is *seasonal change*. In summer the barometric pressure 'on the top of Everest' averages 255 Torr (mm Hg) (it was measured in 1981 and found to be 253 Torr), whilst in mid-winter it is 243 Torr. This means that on average the atmospheric pressure is 12 Torr (equivalent to a height loss of 300m) higher in summer. and for this reason alone Everest would then be easier to climb. In winter, because the pressure is lower, climbing at altitude will be more difficult and this will be as much a reason as low temperature and high winds for the paucity of winter ascents on peaks over 8000m without supplementary oxygen. Daily variation in pressure also occurs but the changes tend to be small.

Latitude also affects the barometric pressure. Everest lies relatively near the equator and as a result the barometric pressure for a given altitude is higher than it would be nearer the poles, as for instance on Mt McKinley in the Arctic. The reason for the high barometric pressure over the equator is that there is a large mass of cold air found in the troposphere. It seems that it is the relatively high barometric pressure on Everest, by virtue of its position near the equator, that makes it climbable without supplementary oxygen.

Oxygen pressure in the body

When air moves from the atmosphere to the depths of the lungs the oxygen pressure falls. A large fall in oxygen pressure occurs in the depths of the lungs where fresh air mixes with CO_2 which comes from cell function and which is removed when the individual breathes out. A slight fall occurs when oxygen diffuses through the walls of the lung into the blood vessels. In the tissues themselves there is a considerable fall, particularly if large quantities of oxygen are being used by working muscles.

Acclimatization to oxygen lack occurs at all levels in this chain, and its purpose is to deliver to the tissues as high a pressure of oxygen as possible. For instance, in the depths of the lung the fall in pressure is less and the actual pressure of oxygen is higher in the well-acclimatized, whilst in the unacclimatized the fall is greater and the oxygen pressure is lower. This particular adaptation takes about 20 days at 4000m.

Maximum oxygen uptake and delivery

Despite all efforts at acclimatization, the amount of oxygen delivered to the tissues is always less at altitude than at sea-level and there are other factors:

1.   There is a limit to the amount of oxygen that diffuses through the lung to the vessels, and this is one key factor determining the amount of oxygen that gets to the cells. If there is any obstruction to the passage of oxygen, because of fluid in the lungs as occurs in infection or high-altitude pulmonary oedema, the patient becomes ill very quickly. Because the brain is so sensitive to oxygen lack, the first indication may be irrational behaviour – i.e. a lung condition may be present with mental symptoms which makes for confusion in diagnosis.

2.   The heart does not function as well at extreme altitude as it does at sea-level, and when working at full stretch the amount of blood pumped each minute is less. In turn this means that less blood and therefore oxygen gets to the muscles.

3.   Some people are able to breathe more deeply and rapidly than others, and this response to oxygen lack may well be important in attempting to identify those who can go high, but it is only one factor.

4.   Oxygen that could be used for ascending may be squandered in fighting against the wind, slipping downhill on scree or soft snow, ploughing through powder snow or in many other ways. Efficiency of movement is of great importance in using available oxygen at extreme altitude.

5.   Climbers normally go uphill continuously using about 50–60% of the maximum amount of oxygen that they can take in. To move continuously at great altitude means breathing more rapidly and more deeply, until at about 7400m, in order to move continuously, they would have to breathe maximally. It is impossible to breathe really maximally for more than about one minute, and so they have to move intermittently. Near the

top of Everest it is only possible to move continuously for very short distances, i.e. up to 30–40 steps at a time, and then rest is essential. It is like running a series of 100-yard races.

6.   Whilst panting at this rate a considerable amount of both water and heat is lost from the lungs.

Cold

Whilst moving, the climber generates heat and keeps warm, but when he stops he will cool down. However, during the day radiation from the sun will keep him warm when stationary and indeed he may become so hot, even on the top of Everest, that he has to take off clothing to stop overheating. However, if the sky is overcast or after sunset, heat from radiation falls and he has to rely on heat from the muscles to keep him warm. If he is exhausted he may only be able to move slowly or not at all, heat production falls and he will cool rapidly even if fully clothed.

As he begins to cool, the blood supply to the extremities is cut off by constriction of the peripheral skin vessels. As the temperature continues to fall, shunts between the arteries and veins which are normally closed open up so that warm arterial blood is diverted to the veins without going to the skin vessels. This is a protective mechanism because it means that cold blood does not return to the brain and cool the cells in the brain concerned with regulation of the temperature for, if it did, the core temperature of the body would fall rapidly. However, because of this mechanism the skin is deprived of warm blood, cools rapidly and, if the air temperature is below freezing, it will freeze and become gangrenous (frostbite). It must be stressed that this can occur despite adequate clothing. In effect, the hands and feet are being sacrificed for the good of the whole. If the core temperature continues to fall despite this protective mechanism, hypothermia occurs.

It is likely that mountaineers who 'die from exhaustion' in fact do so from hypothermia, when all body functions, including heart rate, slow down with a low central core temperature. An individual may therefore appear dead when he is not. Attempts at resuscitation should always be made and individuals warmed up even if they appear cold and dead.

Wind is very important and even in above-freezing temperatures exposed skin can be frozen and frostbitten because of a high wind – the 'wind-chill effect'. A gale at below-zero temperatures may be so much of a hazard at extreme altitude that no movement outside the shelter of a tent or snow-hole is possible.

Dehydration

Some degree of dehydration appears inevitable at extreme altitude owing, in the main, to water loss from the lungs, the result of overbreathing. The mountaineer too may not feel that he is sweating because of the rapid evaporation of sweat in the dry air, whereas, in fact, he is losing a considerable amount of fluid.

The sensation of thirst also is blunted and, if to these factors is added the practical difficulty of melting snow, then it is not surprising that fluid replacement is inadequate.

As dehydration increases blood becomes thicker and more viscous. This is accentuated by the increase in red cells, which is an important factor in acclimatization. The tendency of the blood to clot is increased and strokes have occurred in fit young men at moderate altitude.

The extent to which dehydration occurs is still underestimated, and it may be extremely severe. Mountaineers who have been for even a few days at extreme altitude can look emaciated, but recover in a few hours after drinking a lot of water. The importance of fluid is emphasized by the fact that individuals can live for only six days without water, whereas without food they live for six weeks.

Food

Poor appetite, and difficulties in preparation which are inevitable at extreme altitude, can result in a considerable calorie deficit. Food must be easy to prepare, palatable at altitude, and of good calorie value. This combination seems from experience to be almost impossible to achieve. On pre-war Everest expeditions great trouble was taken with buying tasty food, and the food halls of Harrods and Fortnum and Mason were favourite shopping places. Now the local supermarket can provide pretty well all that is necessary. As a general rule, fresh food is always more palatable than processed food, and for the few days at extreme altitude high calorie fluids and foods should be taken, but tested at sea-level, as they can cause diarrhoea.

Brain function

Mountaineers still do not appreciate fully the effect of oxygen lack on the brain. Even at 1500m some minimal changes occur to vision. The higher centres that are concerned with reasoning and memory are the first affected, and acts that require innovation tend to be less well carried out than those that are well rehearsed. The history of high-altitude mountaineering is redolent with glaring examples of impaired judgement where wrong decisions have been fatal. Fixity of purpose is another feature of oxygen lack and, when allied to an obsessive desire to complete an ascent, may be lethal. At extreme altitude the climber is at the limits of tolerance to oxygen lack and mental function is greatly depressed. Oxygen lack not only stops the works but it wrecks the machinery, and this is as obvious in high-altitude mountaineering as it is in medicine and anaesthesia.

Drugs

Drugs are increasingly used by mountaineers, and all have some side effects; as a general rule, the fit and well-acclimatized do not need them to improve performance. In addition, the effect of drugs on an individual at sea-level may not be the same as at altitude. Antibiotics, too, can produce unpleasant side effects such as diarrhoea, kidney damage and skin complaints.

Aspirin is a mild pain-killer and decreases the liability of blood to clot, but it can also cause irritation of the mucous lining of the stomach and severe bleeding may occur with blood being vomited up.

Diamox (acetazolimide) increases the excretion of urine but it also acts mainly as a stimulus to respiration and the evidence for its preventing acute mountain sickness is good. It is a safe drug and its side effects, tingling of the fingers and toes, are not serious. It is being used more often as climbers can fly to quite high areas now before setting up camp.

Dexamethasone, a steroid, has recently been shown to decrease symptoms of severe mountain sickness and its use has enabled individuals to descend by their own efforts.

Non-steroidal anti-inflammatory agents, like Ibrufen, have also been used with success for altitude headache.

Adequate vitamins are available in fresh food and there is no evidence that deficiency occurs on an expedition of normal length.

Dilution of the blood has been advocated to counteract vascular episodes and decrease the work of the heart in pushing thick blood around the vessels, but again there is no evidence that this is beneficial and there are dangers.

At extreme altitude the relentless combination of oxygen lack, cold, dehydration, starvation and mental torpor can lead easily to exhaustion and death. The main chances of success and survival lie in thoroughly understanding the hazards to the mind and body together with the dangers of the environment, and learning how these interact. Survival depends on being fit and well acclimatized and appreciating how lethal extreme altitude can be. Here the mountaineer is on a biological knife-edge and the 'death zone' is well named.

Operation Everest II – 1985

CHARLES S. HOUSTON

Soon after the height of Everest was announced in 1864, mountaineers wondered if it could be climbed, at a time when it was generally believed that a man could not sleep higher than 6000m or climb much above this. In 1892 Clinton Dent, President of the AC and a distinguished mountaineer, surgeon and physician predicted, in a carefully worded paper, that Everest could and would be climbed. Siding with Whymper, and in opposition to Paul Bert, he believed that lack of pressure, rather than lack of oxygen, was the problem at high altitude, and he concluded that supplementary oxygen would be neither necessary nor helpful. We know today that lack of oxygen is the prime, if not the sole, cause of altitude illness and stimulates the acclimatization processes.

In Paul Bert's day the dangers of high altitude had been tragically revealed during a few balloon flights which resulted in death, although curiously a few others went equally high without difficulty. Climbers were describing unpleasant and occasionally fatal problems during the ascent of Mont Blanc and other high peaks. By the start of this century it appeared that the speed of ascent as well as the altitude reached determined the presence or absence of altitude illness. The slower the rate, the less the distress and the better the acclimatization.

Longstaff's ascent of Trisul in 1907 set an undisputed altitude record which has been steadily advanced, until today a score of men have reached the highest points on earth without supplementary oxygen. Whether they have used siege or rush tactics, success, even survival, have depended on the perfection of their acclimatization.

The earliest mention of acclimatization seems to have been in 1550 by Haidar who described illnesses in the mountains of Central Asia and pointed out that only newcomers were affected: altitude residents seemed immune. Mountaineering doctors in the late 19th century adduced several intriguing theories to explain both illness and well-being, though we know today that many were quite wrong.

In 1920 Kellas calculated the physiological adjustments which would be needed to climb to a height where there was less than a third of the amount of oxygen available at sea-level, and he concluded that Everest could and would be climbed. Four years later, Norton came close to proving Kellas right when he actually climbed to within a few hundred feet of the summit. Haldane, Barcroft and later Dill, Keyes and others outlined the framework of this adaptive protection.

Hingston, Greene and Henderson soon agreed with Kellas, but not until 1946 did men actually work at an altitude equivalent to the summit after a slow ascent in a decompression chamber. This study (called Operation Everest)

provided rich data defining the beautifully integrated changes of acclimatization which made this possible – under laboratory conditions.

The most thorough and productive study of acclimatization on a
mountain was that done by the Silver Hut Expedition of 1961, whose members
lived and worked for four months at 5800m near Makalu, measuring various
components of acclimatization.

In 1985 Operation Everest was repeated in a decompression chamber at
the US Army Research Institute for Environmental Medicine, using state-of-
the-art science to improve our understanding of acclimatization, not only to
satisfy curiosity as to how mountaineers can achieve the summit but, more
importantly, to see what lessons learned at altitude could be applied to sick men
at sea-level – a question Barcroft had asked 50 years earlier.

It took five years to perfect plans for Operation Everest II during which
eight subjects lived in a large three-roomed decompression chamber. Following
a three-day control period at sea-level pressure, the chamber was 'climbed' at a
rate similar to that used in Operation Everest I and roughly that of several
successful Everest summit parties. The subjects lived for 12 days at 7300–
7600m, and each day one or two of them made a rapid ascent to 8800m where
they remained for several hours while measurements were made on the subjects
at rest and at work.

OEII was a true team effort in which 25 scientists and 40–50 support
people shared the effort of several dozen discrete studies. Our overall goal was
to examine all stages of the oxygen transport system during acclimatization to
lack of oxygen. This includes acquisition of air by breathing, passage of oxygen
from lung to blood by diffusion, carriage of oxygen from lung to tissues by
circulating haemoglobin, passage of oxygen from blood to cells by diffusion,
and utilization of oxygen by mitochondria within the cells. We also looked at
the reverse process – the carbon dioxide transport system – but in less detail. We
studied the relationship between ventilation and circulation in the lungs and
calculated the ventilation-perfusion ratio. We matched the stages of sleep to
blood oxygen levels and electroencephalographic tracings.

Subjects were weighed underwater and CAT scans were done to
determine their percentage of body fat before and after the project. All food and
fluid ingested and the total work done were recorded to obtain the energy
balance at altitude. Retinal photographs were taken regularly. Many tests were
run on blood, and muscle biopsies were taken to learn whether muscle structure
changes during acclimatization and how muscle uses oxygen at rest, during and
after strenuous work. How much work a man could do when well acclimatized
was determined by measuring the maximal oxygen uptake (VO_2Max) while
cycling against increasing loads.

The most ambitious study required passing a small tube (Swan–Ganz
catheter) through an arm vein, into the heart, past its valves and into the lung.
This enabled us to measure blood pressure in the pulmonary artery and heart,
cardiac output, and (especially important) the amount of oxygen remaining in
venous blood returning to the heart from all parts of the body. The ease with
which oxygen passed from air to blood in the lung (diffusing capacity) was
calculated by injecting into a vein a solution of inert gases and measuring their

concentration in expired air. Together with the cardiac catheterization studies, this gave the ventilation-perfusion ratio. Other tests included psychometric, neuro-muscular and endurance studies.

To our surprise and disappointment, these men did not acclimatize as fully as we had hoped. This may have been because: (1) the close confinement made strenuous exertion difficult; (2) the rate of ascent may have been somewhat too rapid; or (3) other stresses experienced on high mountains may contribute more than we believed to acclimatization.

At 6000m headache and inability to sleep nagged most of the men to a degree which led us to 'go down' a thousand metres or so for two days; this brought great improvement, and above 6000m these symptoms were less. Appetites decreased above 3000–3700m and all lost an average of 10% of their starting weight, most of it muscle rather than fat. This was also a surprise because they were given anything they chose to eat, and because calculated energy intake was actually greater than energy output. We concluded that hypoxia, in addition to causing anorexia, contributed to weight loss.

Sore throats became a serious problem above 6700–7000m, as is the case on high mountains. But the chamber was kept at a comfortable temperature (72F) and the humidity was held above 80%. No infection was found. We concluded that not the dry cold air (as had been thought), but some element of hypoxia caused the sore throat and cough so often complained of by climbers.

In medical terms the physiological data can be summarized as follows:

Heart and Circulation

As altitude increased:
Right atrial and pulmonary wedge pressures remained normal.
Resting pulmonary artery pressure increased from 15 to 34 Torr.
Cardiac output increased with level of work but the relationship to a given oxygen uptake was maintained.
During work: the pulmonary artery pressure increased from 33 to 54 Torr.
At rest: the pulmonary vascular resistance increased from 1.2 to 4.3 Wood units.
At extreme altitude: 100% oxygen lowered cardiac output and pulmonary artery pressure but not pulmonary vascular resistance.
Left ventricular function was sustained or even enhanced despite right ventricular hypertension and reduced preload.
Heart rate for a given oxygen uptake increased with altitude and was only slightly slowed by breathing oxygen.
Systemic blood pressure did not change as altitude increased, but did increase with 100% oxygen, suggesting different control mechanisms for pulmonary and systemic blood pressures.
These observations suggest that the heart is not a limiting factor at extreme altitude.

53. *Stephen Venables and Luke Hughes.*

54. *Mont Blanc from Mont de la Saxe (1987).*

55.   *Frontier Ridge, with John Hunt (1954).*

56. *Col de la Fourche, with Wilfrid Noyce (1955).*

57. *Descent from Mont Maudit (David Cox and Michael Ward) (1955).*

Ventilation

As altitude increased:
The volume and rate of breathing at rest and during work increased progressively.

Increasing ventilation was effective in ensuring adequate tissue oxygenation during acclimatization. Respiratory muscle fatigue was not a limiting factor at the highest altitudes.

Ventilatory drive was increased rather than depressed.

A variable but increasing ventilation-perfusion mismatch was found which correlated with pulmonary artery pressure. This was consistent with increasing interstitial alveolar oedema.

These studies suggest that at extreme altitude the lung is an important factor limiting the ability to work.

Work

The relationship of oxygen uptake to workload was consistent throughout.

Maximal oxygen uptake on the summit was roughly 25% that at sea-level.

For a given level of work, anaerobic metabolism contributed more energy as altitude increased, though at exhaustion its maximum contribution was less than at sea-level.

Peak blood lactate during exercise at extreme altitude decreased.

These observations suggest that acclimatization to extreme hypoxia did not maximize oxidative function.

Oxygen Transport and Delivery

As acclimatization progressed:
The number of capillaries per muscle cross-sectional area increased, but the number of capillaries per muscle fibre did not change.

Myoglobin content of both Type I and II muscle did not change.

Oxygen transport at extreme altitude was defended principally by increased ventilation and a decrease in mixed venous oxygen.

A given oxygen uptake was achieved by lowering mixed venous oxygen in preference to increasing cardiac output.

During maximal exercise at altitude mixed venous oxygen pressure fell to between 10 and 14 Torr; at sea-level it did not drop below 20 Torr.

At sea-level more than 80% of oxygen O_2 delivered was used and at higher altitudes extraction was similar though less on the summit.

Tissue diffusion may be an important limiting factor at extreme altitude.

Nutrition

Although ample appetizing and nourishing food was provided, appetite and caloric intake declined.

All subjects lost more weight than accounted for by comparing calculated energy expenditures with measured caloric intake.

CT scans and hydrostatic weighing showed that most of the weight-loss was
   muscle mass.

Sleep

All subjects showed greater arterial desaturation during sleep than when awake
   at altitude and this was unaffected by sleep stage.

At the greater altitudes all subjects showed periodic breathing and apnoea
   during sleep; although apnoeas were abolished by breathing oxygen or
   carbon dioxide, periodicity was not.

The hypoxic ventilatory response during sleep did not increase as much with
   acclimatization as did the awake HVR.

Could these men have climbed the Hillary step near the top of Everest? Could
they have reached the summit and still have had some reserve? Only a few have
done so without extra oxygen on that mountain. How do the OEII subjects
compare with the Everest summiteer? Are they physiologically different from
you and me, or from Messner, Roskelly, and many others? Our findings agree
with others: they are not!

   It is important to remember that in 1946 and 1985 we doctors were
watching and studying these acclimatizing men with our normal sea-level eyes
and brains; no one who is unaffected by hypoxia can observe men on top of
Everest. Those who have climbed without oxygen have told us that they are
close to the limit. They hallucinate, they stagger, they gasp for breath, every step
is described as a tremendous effort, the world seems unreal. Our subjects, as we
saw them clearly, were not so badly affected.

   On the other hand they were not as well acclimatized as members of an
expedition who have spent months on a big mountain. Why, in such a
pampered state, did they not acclimatize better? Was ascent too fast, time at
altitude too short? Are the stresses of a mountain a help rather than a hindrance
in acclimatization? Perhaps the extreme work of climbing, or the bitter cold, or
the anxiety and tension all enhance acclimatization more than we anticipated.
We don't know.

Mistakes That Mountaineers Make

HARRY HILTON

'. . . I fear the painstaking, time-consuming, wide-ranging drive to
get to the bottom of a story, to search for the truth is slipping
slowly out of fashion . . .'

John Birt, BBC Deputy Director-General
in Channel 4's Opinions, 12.5.88

*Following the above comment by one of Britain's leading media
men, Harry Hilton recalls some examples in mountaineering
history where a little more time and effort might have produced a
more accurate result.*

I first became aware of inaccuracies in
mountaineering literature, at a personal level, two years after the first ascent of
Everest. The book: *Summits of Adventure* by John Scott Douglas, published by
Frederick Muller in 1955. The chapter: 'Giants of the Earth'. The page: 183.
The sentence: '. . . It (a reconnaissance of Makalu) was made by two young
British climbers, Herbert Maddock and Harry Hilton and their guides and
porters . . .' The author had got it wrong by some 240km for, in fact, we had
headed towards Himalchuli.

That same year, 1955, the Japanese mountaineer Funjiro Muraki,
writing in *The Mountain World*, stated '. . . Team B ascended the Chuling
Khola along a path untrodden by civilized man to the foot of Himalchuli . . .'
My friend, the late Bert Maddock, had, of course, in 1953 trodden that same
path one year before 'Team B' had got there, though whether Bert ever rated
that 'civilized man' tag has often nagged me!

'And there's more.' A year later (1956) the 'authoritative' and 'highly
respected' *Alpine Journal* recorded in one of its articles (p38) '. . . Hilton had
also made a solo effort on the eastern slopes (of Himalchuli) in the same year
(1954 in the article); but we gathered that none of those parties had been much
higher than about 16,000–17,000ft . . .' It was Bert Maddock, not myself, with
a local porter from the Chuling Khola (whom he refers to simply as 'G' in his
journal) who reached about 19,000ft in 1953. Our only claim to fame in those
days, and all four facts incorrect! Thus from tiny beginnings do many errors
grow; so where does truth lie?

As far as the 'investigative' journalist or scholar are concerned, truth
usually involves time, a great deal of it. At the level of newspaper, radio, and
television news reporting, with deadlines to meet, there is generally very little –
a few hours at the most – of it during which details can be checked. Even under
such pressure, some journalists, newspapers, radio networks, and television
channels are more reliable than others. Having said that I can recall catching the
Times out, and that was when it was *The Times*.

At magazine and journal level the excuse for errors of fact are less acceptable. If a 'name' or 'expert' has decided to write a piece for what is, after all, a somewhat select readership, the least he or she can do is to be thorough in his (her) research. (At this point the writer is made suddenly aware of how extremely accurately he will have to tread his way through the rest of this article!)

One camp further up this cone of credibility is the book, a little higher the television/film/radio 'documentary', and at the summit shines the reference book, for that will find its way into homes, clubs and libraries around the world, and young, not to mention old, students will tend to take its contents on trust.

Responsibility for the facts given should, in my humble opinion, be shared equally by author, editor, and publisher or TV/radio/film equivalent. Others disagree with this. The late Tim Lewis, editor of *Mountain* magazine, once wrote to me '. . . In the matter of the truth. D F O Dangar recently wrote to me correcting some facts concerning the Alps. He made the point, from his experience with the *Alpine Journal*, that the responsibility for factual correctness lies with the author. To that I would add that, if I am not the author (as effectively I am in the news columns of *Mountain*), I feel that the editor should also accept responsibility for the rest of the contents of the magazine. He doesn't have to agree with opinions, but he should, as far as is possible (the time factor again) ensure the correctness of the facts. In that context, as you know, I am always glad to be corrected and make the right version known in the columns of the magazine . . .'

Another ex-mountaineering magazine editor, Walt Unsworth, once warned me of the problems faced by the journalist/writer/editor in the quest for truth and the use of 'primary sources'. He stated '. . . I quite agree that whenever possible primary sources should be consulted, but you must not assume that the primary sources are always correct. People don't always record the truth in their journals, and they certainly don't always tell the full story. Furthermore, people when interviewed don't always speak the truth, sometimes for personal reasons and sometimes from sheer bad memory. To complicate matters: (a) they sometimes tell one story and then deny it; (b) they sometimes tell two different stories in two different publications; (c) where there are expeditions in which various members write an account of their adventures, there can be important differences of fact and emphasis between the different accounts (see the six different accounts of the Everest 1953 Expedition); and (d) stories can be slanted for political purposes . . .'

Sound advice to any potential writer. However, the late Joe Tasker accused ex-editor Unsworth of just this lack of consultation with 'primary sources' in 1977, following a piece of '. . . sensationalized misreporting . . .' in that editor's magazine on yet another yeti story. With noble courage Walter duly apologized on behalf of his reporter for letting '. . . a good story run away with him . . .', but, as Joe wrote to me at the time '. . . In this case it (the reference to the "primary sources") would have simply required a telephone call to myself or Pete Boardman, both of whom live in the Manchester area and who know Walt well and see him fairly frequently . . .'

Yet another mountaineering magazine editor, Geoff Birtles, made a somewhat sharp suggestion to me once after I had voiced my concern over a disconcerting number of errors of fact that had appeared in a mountaineering reference book. He wrote to me: '. . . Suggest you put your mouth into writing and make a comprehensive list of errors (in the book). Not an easy task . . .' Not an easy task indeed, and when I set about doing just that (in my usual distasteful manner, i.e. by actually asking questions around the climbing fraternity), editor Birtles, who had, after all, made the original suggestion to me, ended up with threatened legal action by the compiler of the book concerned. That particular tome is still to be found gracing shelves of libraries, with its 98% of correctness and its 2% of inaccuracies to be discovered by some future student of mountaineering. The threat of legal proceedings against editor Birtles was certainly enough to deter the writer of this article from declaring his further findings of errors of fact.

It is not only in Britain that such errors creep into reference books. In Italy the late Mario Fantin's *Sui ghiacciai dell'Africa* (Cappelli, Bologna, 1968) is a standard Italian reference book on Kilimanjaro, Mount Kenya, and the Ruwenzori. On page 139 concerning the early recorded ascents of Mount Kenya (the 17th in point of fact) it is stated: '. . . *Nel febbraio 1955 Adriano P Landra partecipa per la terza volta ad una spedizione dell'esercito, sul Monte Kenya. Il gruppo è guidato da H Harris e vi è presente anche Harry Hilton con una quindicina di ascari . . .*' or, roughly speaking, in English: '. . . In February 1955 Adriano P Landra took part, for the third time, in an armed expedition to Mount Kenya. The group was led by H Harris and there was also Harry Hilton with some 15 police constables . . .'

The facts of the ascent are: neither Adriano P Landra nor H Harris (whoever he was?) came with us, the leader of the expedition was 'yours truly', the '15' police constables were, in reality, two, and the climbers who reached the summit of Mount Kenya (Batian) on that particular occasion were Pat Erskine-Murray and myself. Simple errors that, once again, could have been avoided by reference to a primary and, I hope in this instance, reliable source.

Radio and television too are not immune from the occasional inaccuracy. In December 1981 (6.12.81, 11.15am, Radio 4), in the BBC's 'commercial' for the programme *Weekend* (subject: '. . . the extremes of adventure . . . mountains and caves . . .'), the announcer spoke of '. . . Chris Bonington . . . who has been to the top of Mount Everest . . .' Chris, at that stage of his mountaineering career, had not. Jim Black, Presentation Editor, Radio 4, admitted to me that the error had been 'created' because '. . . the information was not checked sufficiently within my department . . .' However, to my limited knowledge, no attempt was made by the BBC to rectify this misleading information it had 'created' and transmitted throughout Britain, but the BBC rarely admits to any errors at any time through the medium that has broadcast them, radio or television. Take, for instance, BBC1 television.

In 1978 (4.6.78, BBC1), in the programme *The Other Side of the Mountain*, Alf Gregory stated that the members of the 1953 British Everest expedition stayed at the British Embassy in Kathmandu '. . . because there were no hotels there then . . .' This was not correct. To my limited knowledge, there were at least two hotels: the Himalaya in Joodha Street and the Nepal hotel.

This latter building, where I stayed in 1953 (for a very brief period) was an amazing edifice where you could go to sleep lulled by the music of the Rendezvous Club jazz band and awake to the snarl of tigers from the small zoo that adjoined the hotel!

I wrote to *Radio Times* and *The Listener*, in this instance, to inform the BBC of the error it had transmitted. The editors of both journals found it impossible to print my letter or even the relevant part of it, and although one of them assured me that '. . . we will pass your comments, where appropriate, to the relevant BBC department . . .', no action was taken to present the truth to viewers. Which brings me to my final point – correction.

How do we set about rectifying matters, always assuming that at least a few of us still prefer 'the true facts'? The methods are varied. Through journals there is the letter and the sort of mini *cause littéraire*. I well remember the late Lucien Devies taking Lord Hunt to task in the columns of *La Montagne & Alpinisme* (No 114, 4/1978, p461) over a sentence which (through the translation – another 'true facts' trap – of Michel Schulman) had been attributed to Lucien. (It was the use of the verb 'décapiter' that upset the protester most!) The *doyen* of French mountaineering circles was not amused. As long as magazine and journal editors have the same views on the correction of errors of fact as those expressed by the late Tim Lewis earlier in this article, there is little to fear at this level of publication. However, at book level the outlook is not quite so bright.

In 1984, a significant date in many ways, I tackled Bill Birkett and his publisher Robert Hale concerning the former's statement on the possible cause of the accident which resulted in the death of the late Arthur Rhodes Dolphin (*Lakeland's Greatest Pioneers*, 1983, p148). In that statement Mr Birkett had implied that the '. . . combined weight of the rucksacks . . .' that Arthur was supposedly carrying had '. . . forced him off balance . . .' The assumed extra rucksack belonged to my friend, the late Doctor André Colard, who had just completed the S face of the Dent du Géant with Arthur ('alternate' to 'varied' leads).

The 'true facts' of the matter are, and here I quote from André's letter to me, '. . . It is true that Arthur went to get the sleeping-bags and the small amount of equipment that we left at the foot of the S face of the Géant (a reference to Dennis Gray's version of events in his *Rope Boy*, Victor Gollancz, 1970, p51). Then each of us took our own equipment and did not bother to rope up (this practice being considered unnecessary for climbers of a high standard of competency at this stage of the descent). It was towards the end of the descent of the 'rognon' . . ., in other words, after some 45 minutes of scrambling and easy rock climbing, that Arthur slipped . . .' Thus André and Arthur had been carrying their own sacks for at least three-quarters of an hour before the accident happened.

Mr Birkett was duly consulted by Mr Hale who wrote to me: '. . . We are informed that Mr Birkett's account (of the accident) was written after consultation with sources closest to the scene . . .' (24.1.84), and '. . . in the light of all the circumstances including of course the impossibility of resolving the mystery of A R Dolphin's death, the author (Bill Birkett) does not feel any change to his work is called for at this stage . . . we would like to draw your attention to the fact that no publisher can be expected to endorse all the statements and opinions of his authors . . .' (9.2.84).

I often wonder, as do André's widow and children, what Mr Birkett's idea of '. . . sources closest to the scene . . .' involved. It did not include any consultation with the late Doctor André Colard in either Belgium or Saudi Arabia.

At the other end of the scale, Macmillan London Ltd, the publisher, thanked me and assured me that the couple of errors (e.g. 'Lewis', p203) that I had spotted in John Cleare's book *Mountains* (published in 1975) had been placed in the '. . . reprint file, and this will be brought to the attention of the author (I had already respectfully informed John over dinner one evening) if and when we reprint the book . . .'

Further afield, in 1980, Professors Dieslfeld and Hecklau of the universities of Heidelberg and Trier in West Germany, through their publisher (Springer of Berlin, Heidelberg, and New York), not only thanked me for having pointed out the error of their ways (in this instance confusion over the summits of Mount Kenya), but also elevated me to the rank of 'Dr' (or could that have been a simple typing error?)

I think that it was George Orwell who wrote '. . . The first thing that we ask of a writer is that he should not tell lies . . .' (Perhaps some kind expert on Orwell will let me know if I've got it wrong?) And my plea, arising from some of the above experiences, is one that has appeared before, both in this journal and others, and is aimed at writers, editors, and publishers alike. From personal experience as a freelance journalist, writer, and lecturer I fully realize that it is frequently far from easy to discover 'the truth' about certain subjects. At home, how does a crag climber set about ascertaining that he or she is the first to ascent a Jumper or a Lothlorian? In the Alps, where should alpinists turn to make sure that they actually were the mountaineers to make the 'First British Ascent' of the S face of the Dent du Géant? (Come to think of it, what exactly constitutes a 'British' ascent?) In the final analysis, who the hell cares about the exact height of a Himalayan giant? Yet surely dates, altitudes to within 500m, correct names of members of expeditions, and correct captions to photographs (always assuming that they have been printed the correct way!) should all be within the bounds of possibility. It may take more time and effort, but, who knows, you might discover something new in the process (as I have done more than once), perhaps the greatest reward of the thorough researcher and seeker after truth.

Taken from the Librarian's Shelf

CHARLES WARREN

Many years ago I was asked to review a little book by that great climber of the thirties, Colin Kirkus, called *Let's Go Climbing*. I remember to this day how much I was impressed by this most attractively written book.

But here it is in my hands again, off the library shelf; a charming period piece which, even today, gives young people the right motives for going climbing. There is something rather beautiful about the direct simplicity of the writing here which is admirably adapted to the purpose of the book.

Let's Go Climbing is written for the novice, and it is so good because Colin never deviates from his purpose of trying to enthuse his young readers with his own thoroughly healthy emotional response to climbing. Surely this is still one of the most readable little books on mountaineering for those of us who can still think back to the magical days of our youth in the hills. It contains some useful home-truths, too: how about this? 'Climbing is not a dangerous sport if you follow the rules. People who take risks are not considered heroes in the climbing world; they are considered fools and bad climbers.' A remark to be remembered, maybe, in these days of competition for mass-media publicity in the sport, with its attendant risks.

There is even a certain nostalgia about the illustrations in this book, which in the juvenile field remains a minor classic.

Kirkus, alas, died young, in the Second World War. Perhaps, in some ways, the book is almost more precious for this, because he could not spoil it by trying to bring it up-to-date.

One Hundred Years Ago

(With extracts from the *Alpine Journal*)

C. A. RUSSELL

'The fine and settled weather which prevailed in January, and the comparatively small quantity of snow, are no doubt the reasons of the numerous and important winter ascents made this year in the Alps.'

Among those who took advantage of the favourable conditions experienced at the beginning of 1888 were Vittorio, Corradino, Erminio and Gaudenzio Sella, who on 5 January, with Battista, Daniele and Giuseppe Maquignaz, Emile Rey and two porters, completed the first winter traverse of Mont Blanc. Starting at midnight from the Italian hut on the Aiguilles Grises rocks the party, whose attempt in the previous year had been defeated by strong winds, reached the summit and descended on the French side. 'On the summit the tent in which M Vallot spent three days last year was found in perfect condition. Many steps had to be cut on the Bosses; mist, then darkness, came on; and the Grands Mulets was not reached till 10.30pm, after a very remarkable and daring enterprise.'

In the Bernese Oberland, on the same day, Mrs E P Jackson and Emil Boss, with Ulrich Almer and Johann Kaufmann, made the first winter ascent of the Gross Lauteraarhorn. 'Leaving the Schwarzegg hut at 4am, they crossed the Strahlegg Pass and made direct for some rocks running south from the peak; these were followed until a snow col at the foot of the final arête was reached. The rocks of the arête were in perfect condition, quite free from ice or snow, and warm as in summer.' On 11 January the same party, with Almer and Christian Jossi, completed the first winter ascent of the Gross Fiescherhorn, having reached the summit by way of the Bergli hut, the Ewigschneefeld and the SW ridge.

Five days later, with Peter Baumann as second guide, the party completed the first traverse of the Jungfrau in winter, reaching the summit from the Bergli hut and descending to the Wengern Alp. W A B Coolidge, whose party had made the first winter ascent of the Jungfrau 14 years earlier and who was staying at Grindelwald in January, wrote that Mrs Jackson's traverse was 'a difficult feat at any time, and in winter more so than ever from the necessity of passing a second night somewhere on the mountain. Her party spent it in a crevasse and were frost-bitten, notwithstanding which the expedition must always rank as one of the most splendid ever achieved in winter.'

The fine weather was followed by six weeks of heavy snowfalls and in many regions severe damage was caused by avalanches. 'In the North Italian valleys more than one hundred lives are known to have been lost while in the Saas Valley, in Randa and the adjoining districts, there has been loss of life, and great loss of property, especially cattle.' For much of the spring and summer conditions remained unsettled and the weather experienced throughout the Alps during the climbing season was the worst for many years, few expeditions of note being completed. In the Bernese Oberland on 22 July Coolidge, after climbing the Gross Fiescherhorn with Christian Almer junior and his brother Rudolf, made the first ascent of the heavily corniced SW ridge of Ochs or the Klein Fiescherhorn. In the Dauphiné the first ascent of the Roche Méane, to the E of the Grande Ruine, was completed on 25 July by G Merzbacher, with Pierre Gaspard junior. On 28 July in the Pennine Alps, despite a snowstorm lasting for more than two hours, R F Ball, with Ambros Supersaxo and Ludwig Zurbriggen, reached the summit of the Lenzspitze by way of the unclimbed S ridge.

The one exception to the gloomy conditions was the second week in August, when the weather was fine and settled and most parties turned their attention to the lower peaks. In the Mont Blanc range A Barbey and L Kurz, with Justin Bessard and Joseph Simond, reached the summit of the unclimbed Aiguille de l'A Neuve on 11 August and on the following day made the first ascent of the highest point of the Aiguilles Rouges du Dolent, now known as Pointe Kurz. On 14 August in the Bregaglia group T Curtius and R Wiesner, with Christian Klucker, completed the first ascent of the Sciora di Dentro, the highest peak of the Sciora chain.

One of the few mountaineers able to take advantage of the good weather was Vittorio Sella, whose party had just arrived in the Dauphiné to climb the great peaks. With perfect conditions for his camera Sella took many superb photographs, including complete panoramas from the summits of the Barre des Écrins, the Meije, Mont Pelvoux and Pic Coolidge.

The principal achievements of the season were undoubtedly those of Miss Katharine Richardson who on 13 August, with Emile Rey and Jean Baptiste Bich, made the first direct ascent of the S ridge of the Aiguille de Bionnassay. From the summit the party then completed, in descent, the first passage of the delicate E ridge and, after continuing across the Col de Bionnassay, the first traverse of the entire ridge to the Dôme du Goûter. 'It had been reserved for a lady to accomplish the traverse of an arête which had hitherto been found impracticable, and to prove that it is possible to pass over the summit of the peak straight along to the Dôme. Thus a splendid high-level route has been opened up, which has long been aimed at, though it is improbable that this will be generally adopted as a short and easy route up Mont Blanc from the western or S Gervais side.'

Miss Richardson then moved to the Dauphiné where, on 24 August with Bich and Pierre Gaspard senior, she became the first lady to ascend the Grand Pic, the western and highest peak of the Meije.

The exploits of another lady also attracted considerable interest and admiration. The Queen of Italy, who had been for some years in the habit of staying for a short time at Courmayeur, 'made several mountain excursions, such as the Mont de la Saxe and the Cramont. Her chief expedition was to the Col du Géant. Having slept at the Mont Fréty inn on the night of August 16, her Majesty started the next morning at 4am accompanied by a retinue of twenty-seven persons, including two ladies of her court, Henri Séraphin being the chief guide of the party. The caravan reached the col at 10am, but the weather became worse, and it commenced to snow, so that the party were forced to pass the night in the hut. It is stated that the Queen was much amused at this little adventure, but her ladies far less so. On the 18th the party, despite the bad weather, started downwards and returned to Courmayeur that night, the Queen displaying great courage and calmness, and being enthusiastically received on her return to her summer residence.'

In the Caucasus exploration of the range continued apace, with no less than three English parties in the field. First to arrive was A F Mummery, with Heinrich Zurfluh of Meiringen, who were accompanied by a Tartar porter. Starting from Bezingi early in July they examined Dykh Tau (5204m), the second highest peak in the range, and then spent two weeks gathering further information about the topography of the area, crossing a number of glaciers and high passes.

On 23 July a camp was established at the foot of the SW buttress of Dykh Tau and in his book *My Climbs in the Alps and Caucasus* Mummery recalled that after watching the last flicker of sunlight play round the topmost crags he and Zurfluh 'crept into the shelter of tent and sleeping-bags. The hardier Tartar refused the proffered place beside us, and, having washed his head, his feet, and hands, in due accordance with the ritual of his creed, lay down in the open beside a great rock. Zurfluh regarded these proceedings with much sad interest, feeling certain that the bitter wind would freeze him to death before morning.

'At 1am, Zurfluh, who had kept awake to bemoan the Tartar's slow and pitiable decease, crept out of the tent to investigate how this process was getting on. A few minutes later, with his teeth chattering, but none the less with real delight in face and voice, he told me that not merely was the Tartar still alive but, bare feet and all, appeared to be enjoying a refreshing sleep!'

The following day Mummery and Zurfluh overcame numerous difficulties to complete the first ascent of Dykh Tau. 'Every peak in Europe, Elbruz alone excepted, was below us, and from our watch-tower of 17,054 feet we gazed at the rolling world. Turning to the left, a few steps brought me to the culminating point, and I sat down on its shattered crest. Huge clouds were by now wrapping Shkara in an ever darkening mantle, and the long ridge of Janga was buried in dense, matted banks of vapour white and brilliant above, but dark and evil along their ever lowering under-edges. Koshtantau shone in its snowy armour, white against black billows of heaped-up storm.'

Some weeks later the second party, consisting of J G Cockin, H W Holder and Hermann Woolley, with the Grindelwald guides Ulrich Almer and Christian Roth, arrived in the area with the intention of ascending Dykh Tau, believing it to be unclimbed. At Bezingi the porter who had accompanied Mummery and Zurfluh was engaged and his account of their achievement was received with some disappointment. After camping beside the Bezingi glacier the party was compelled to abandon an attempt from the SW side due to lack of time but succeeded, on 20 August, in climbing the N ridge to the summit, where a cairn built by Zurfluh was found.

On 24 August the party, with the exception of Cockin, made the first ascent of Katuin Tau (4985m) by way of the Bezingi face and a few days later, on 3 September, Holder, Cockin and the guides reached the summit of the unclimbed Saluinan Bashi (4348m) N of the Tsanner pass. After Holder and Woolley had left for home on 4 September Cockin and the guides continued climbing in the region for a further month, making the first ascents of Shkhara (5201m) on 7 September and the E peak of Jangi Tau (5038m) five days later, in each case by a route on the Bezingi side. Finally, on 28 September, Cockin and Almer completed the first ascent of the N peak of Ushba (4695m), a fine achievement for the period.

The third party consisted of C T Dent, W F Donkin and Harry Fox, with the guides Kaspar Streich and Johann Fischer, but shortly after their arrival at the beginning of August Dent was forced to return home due to illness. On 17 August Donkin, Fox and the guides, after unsuccessful attempts on both peaks of Ushba, reached the unclimbed SE summit of Dongus Orun (4442m), at the head of the Baksan valley. This achievement was, however, marred by tragedy when, as subsequently established, all four members of the party were lost at the end of August during an attempt to climb Koshtantau. When their absence was eventually reported by an interpreter searchers were organized, but no trace of the missing party was found.

Further afield, areas of the Drakensberg range in South Africa were explored by the Rev A H Stocker and his brother, F R Stocker, who made the first recorded ascent of Champagne Castle (3377m), one of the highest peaks, on 26 April. Some months later, on 19 July, the same party completed the first recorded ascent of the Sterkhorn (2973m).

In the Canadian Rockies the Selkirk range was visited in March by the brothers H W and E H Topham. Despite deep snow they reached a height of 2750m and examined Mount Sir Donald. Later in the year the Rev W S Green, assisted by the Royal Geographical Society, carried out an exploration of the Selkirks. His party completed a number of climbs including, on 9 August, the first ascent of Mount Bonney (3050m).

Still further north the Topham brothers, George Broke and William Williams spent three weeks attempting to climb Mount St Elias. Despite a difficult approach the party explored the S and W sides of the peak and on 2 August, with the exception of Broke, reached a height of 3470m on the S ridge.

A remarkable achievement, also in the far north, was the first crossing of the Greenland ice cap by Fridtjof Nansen, the Norwegian explorer. In August and September, using snowshoes, skis and specially constructed light, flexible sledges equipped with sails, Nansen's party travelled some 440km across the ice cap from Umivik on the E coast to Godthaab, reaching a height of 2700m during the journey.

At home an important climb was completed in the Lake District on 15 July when W C Slingsby, W P Haskett Smith, Geoffrey Hastings and Edward Hopkinson made the first ascent of Slingsby's Chimney on Scafell Pinnacle. After climbing up Steep Ghyll 'to the foot of the great pitch, they turned to the right and soon reached a long narrow rock. Above this, a steep slab led the party to the foot of a nearly perpendicular chimney, which was only 18 inches wide. One of the party stood upon the shoulders of two of the others, and then wriggled up the chimney. After 110 feet of rope had been paid out to him, he found a secure place, where he sat down and drew in the rope whilst the others came up, one by one.'

In conclusion, it seems appropriate to note the following extracts from a foreword by Dent, then President of the Alpine Club, to the one hundredth number of the *Alpine Journal*, which was published in May 1888. 'Twenty-five years ago the first number was introduced in somewhat modest fashion. Little was predicted for the new venture, save that death from starvation was not an imminent probability. Such a mode of extinction is at least as unlikely now as it was then. As a matter of fact, the *Alpine Journal*, profiting by the occasional use of stimulants in the form of adverse criticism, has thriven and waxed fat; to such an extent, indeed, that an index to the volumes published up to date has become a paramount necessity. When this want has been supplied it will, we believe, be found that the *Alpine Journal*, so far as its subject matter is dealt with, constitutes the most trustworthy guide-book to the Alps and work of reference on general mountaineering exploration that exists in any language.'

It may well be, 100 years later, that many of the present readers would agree with these sentiments.

CORRESPONDENCE

Easter Torrans
Tomintoul
Ballindalloch AB3 9HJ

The Editor
Alpine Journal   30 October 1987

Mount Olympus, 1946

Sir,

John Harding's entertaining account of his 'Olympian Triad' (*AJ*92, 136–149, 1987) puts me in mind of my own adventure on the Greek Olympus in the first post-war summer of 1946.

As a young Consul in Salonica, I had naturally included in a tour of inspection of my district the summits of Mytikas and the Throne of Zeus, in case any British subjects in distress were held by the Gods. I had enlisted as muleteer and guide the excellent Costas: if not the same as Harding's Costas, then perhaps his father.

A few weeks later I received word from Sir Clifford Norton, my Ambassador in Athens, that his wife, Lady 'Peter' Norton, an enthusiastic veteran mountaineer, was anxious to make the ascent. There had already been one minor clash between Communist guerrillas and Greek military forces in the vicinity of Litochoron, but the major incident there, that was to spark the 'Third Round' of the Greek Civil War, was yet to come. I accordingly took soundings of the Greek military and police authorities in Salonica about the safety of the expedition; though non-committal, they did not expressly try to put me off. As a cross-check I asked what Costas thought. He kept in with both sides, I reckoned, in the interest of his muleteer business. Not surprisingly, he was only too ready to escort the Ambassadress and myself.

On a hot July morning we set off from Litochoron up the wooded gorge, leaving the burnt-out monastery below on our left; after toiling up the steep zigzags through the forest, it was late afternoon when we reached the Spilios Agapitos hut at 2100m. The following day Lady Peter and I enjoyed a good scramble first up Mytikas (2917m) and then up the steep ridge of Stefani, or the Throne of Zeus (2909m). My trepidation at escorting Lady Peter up the exposed section of this ridge proved unfounded. We descended, again rather late in the day, reaching the hut at about 5pm, too late to make the long descent to sea-level the same day. At the hut we found an agile Greek messenger, who had arrived with a written message from friends in Salonica. 'DANGER. DO NOT CLIMB MOUNTAIN. RETURN AT ONCE,' it cryptically read. The messenger, possibly with an eye on our food supply, did not reveal, as we later learnt, that he was under instructions to return with a reply. Instead we laughed off the mysterious message, having climbed the mountain and intending to return on the following day.

As we sat on the stone terrace outside the hut to enjoy a welcome cup of tea, I glanced down 900m to the edge of the forest below. What did I see but one, two, three, four . . . up to 30 Greek gendarmes emerging in single file from the forest? Some two hours later, as darkness fell, this force arrived at the hut. It was led by a young lieutenant who stated that he had orders to 'protect the Ambassadress'. No further details were vouchsafed. His men were a problem: the water-supply was a mere trickle some distance away; most water-bottles had been emptied on the way up; having left a torrid coast in mid-July, only a limited few had great-coats. The Ambassadorial party retreated to the upper floor, while I rashly issued instructions that men with great-coats should sleep outside, while those without might shelter on the lower floor. The entire night seemed to be spent with one group exchanging places with the other.

At last, at 4.30, the lieutenant whispered to me: 'We have done our duty. Can we go down now?' With an ill-concealed sigh of relief I said 'Yes' and we were left to sleep in peace for another couple of hours. Amid mutterings from Lady Peter of 'more zeal than judgement', we took our time to descend to Litochoron, where we were met by the major in command and a friend from Salonica. They disclosed that a message had been intercepted to the effect that the Communists planned to kidnap the Ambassadress and hold her as a political hostage. This we laughed off as rather a joke, particularly as Communist guerrillas would have had an unenviable task in dealing with a formidable and strong-minded Lady Peter. A few years later a threat of this kind would have been no laughing matter: such has been the change in diplomatic anxieties since those relaxed far-off days.

All ended happily with a lunch party in Litochoron, with presents and compliments exchanged all round. Even the gendarmes found their journey worthwhile, since in the woods near the monastery they had shot a Communist courier carrying messages from Piraeus to the north. For my part, I treasure the memory of two visits to the Gods in a couple of months, even if they were not at home, and also a beautifully bound copy of Marcel Kurz's *Le Mont Olympe*.

And in 1986 the wife of the present British Ambassador in Athens climbed Olympus.

Yours faithfully,
Edward Peck

58. *Râteau Ouest, Grade 3 pitch (climber, Mike Pinney).*

59. Top of Aiguille Dibona (climber,
    Mike Pinney).

60. Pena Santa de Castilla (Picos de Eur

61.   *The Corno Grande (2912m) and the Corno Piccolo (2655m).*

62.   *The summit ridge of the Corno Grande.*

63. *Crater Lake, Jebel Marra.*

64. *Khartoum–Nyala train journey (author, centre foreground).*

65.   *The Kassala mountains from Kassala oasis.*

66. *Leaving Crater Lake through maze of ravines in volcanic ash and debris.*

67.   *Ouaneskra – mint tea stop for thirsty travellers.*

68.   *Nautadalur rock glacier.*

2 Top Sling
Tregarth
Bangor
Gwynedd LL57 4RL

The Editor,
Alpine Journal   29 December 1987

How High? The Altimeter

Sir,

How many mountaineers with a basic scientific background really understand the intricacies of the altimeter? I certainly don't and 'learned colleagues', who have been using theirs faithfully for a great deal longer than I, are similarly in the dark.

Many discrepancies can, of course, be attributed to rapidly fluctuating weather conditions and the absence of suitable, accurately known, spot-heights. However, a sojourn in the Atlas mountains during a period of remarkable anticyclonic stability left me with the belief that I had invested a great deal of cash on an instrument which, whilst giving a fair indication of approaching weather systems and localized atmospheric instability, was singularly useless in conveying the information suggested by its appellation.

I was beginning to doubt the value of including its extra weight, when I was struck by the thought that aircraft, even in pre-radar days, were making a pretty good job of landing in poor visibility. A few well-directed questions rapidly acquainted me with the International Commission for Air Navigation.

There are a number of corrective measures that we need to consider when computing the true altitude: instrumental error, frictional drag, etc; but all these are negligible in comparison with that associated with temperature.

'Come now', you will say, 'but my Thommen is temperature-corrected' and, indeed, this is true. However, the physical interpretation, quite simply, is that, at a given altitude, fluctuations in direct localized temperatures will not

ALTITUDE (Feet)	PRESSURE (Millibars)
0	1013
2,000	942
4,000	875
6,000	812
8,000	753
10,000	697
12,000	644
14,000	595
16,000	549
18,000	506
20,000	465

alter the reading. It is the absolute value of the isotherm, at that height, which is required.

The ICAN has designated a standardized calibration for the altimeter. The ICAN law assumes a sea-level temperature and pressure of 15C and 1013mb respectively, together with a drop in temperature of approximately 1C for every 500 feet of altitude gained.

The decline in pressure with altitude is shown in the table. Note that over the first 2000ft rise the drop in pressure is 1mb for every 28 feet, whereas from 18,000–20,000ft the drop is 1mb for every 49 feet of height gained. The cooling effect predicts a still-air temperature of 24.5C at 20,000ft.

Thus an altimeter, zeroed at sea level, will correctly read 20,000ft if the isotherm is 24.5C; if it is 30C, then the true altitude is 19,500ft; if 20C, then 20,400ft; and, if 15C, then 20,800ft.

Many mountain ranges in the summer season will not cool as rapidly as ICAN suggests (freezing isotherm at 7500ft), leading to an underestimate of altitude.

There is no 'rule of thumb', and a specialized circular slide-rule is needed to compute the true altitude. Loosely speaking, in the range 20,000 to 24,000ft (c6000–7300m), by adding or subtracting approximately 80ft (c25m) for every 1C below or above ICAN, one will not be wildly amiss.

Yours faithfully,
Lindsay Griffin

Via Amola 23/1
40050 Monte San Pietro (Bologna)
Italy

The Editor
Alpine Journal   1 March 1988

K2 1986

Sir,

This letter to the *AJ* is about K2 – the tragedies of summer 1986 and just some of the writing about them (most of it without checking up with the survivors). One example '. . . back on the surface of the ice Casarotto stood up, took a few steps, then lay down on his rucksack and died' (from a Chicago mountaineering magazine); the truth is that Renato Casarotto was unconscious when we got him out of the crevasse, never stood up again and died soon afterwards. Another example: Julie Tullis in more than one report after the bivouac is 'crawling the last bit to the tent at 8000m'. This is pure invention – I pulled her, as she was just sitting and resting, when the clouds had opened up suddenly and the camp became visible just in front of us. Obviously writers love spectacular formulations. Or they keep quiet about reasons – such as in the 'spectacular' description of my getting through the ice-fall after climbing down K2, heavily frostbitten and having survived five days of storm. The writer knew pretty well that I was starving and that there was no food, that I was moving with slippery moonboots through this ice-fall, tired and with no rope-belay – as there was no rope – but he does not tell the reader this: perhaps it might have damaged the effect of the story. 'I wanted to get the feeling right – of course I may have made errors in some of the facts' was the answer of the writer when I complained. Whose feelings were respected? There seem to be new ethics coming up in mountain literature. (It all fits in perfectly with a plan, which I heard about recently: to chop up Julie's and my K2 documentary of 1984, 'The elusive summit', and make out of it a new film about the tragedy of '86; are there any limits left?)

Well, this shall be a factual letter to the *Alpine Journal*, which is known to be serious about facts, and the above should just be pointed at as samples for a terrible situation in expedition reports. If writers did really check their writing before print, it would not be possible that so many errors happen and so many inventions occur. Julie and I reached the summit of K2 at about 5.30pm on 4 August in the greyness of slowly worsening weather. How can somebody sitting at Base Camp below the clouds dare to pretend that it was as late as 7pm and end up with a negative judgement, that we should have turned around earlier – especially as the bad weather could be recognized days before? (So – why no walkie-talkie warning from Base Camp?) The facts are that, on 4 August, not only did the Abruzzi group start for the top, but so did the Americans on the N side of K2; other expeditions topped Broad Peak and Gasherbrum 2 on the same day – and I do not think they were all weather idiots. Even if Julie and I had given up the summit and had descended with Rouse or Bauer, we would have got trapped with the whole group – some hours could not have saved us, we were all one full day too late! The day which we lost on the Shoulder because of the overcrowding, it was the loss of 3 August which was fatal! If we could have stuck to our original plans, nobody would have ended storm-trapped at 8000m.

On 4 August, after the fall, Julie and I had to bivouac on top of the hanging glacier, as we were away from the route and the flash-light did not work – that night there was no storm yet up there, otherwise we would not have survived (lower down it seems to have stormed earlier . . . it's a big mountain). It is, further, not correct that the Koreans had prepared the route to beyond the Shoulder, they had in the end put new fixed ropes to 7250m (the serac-wall below Camp 3). Somewhere I read of the 'less experienced' Julie Tullis: I want to say for my good team-partner that she was very accurate, incredibly resistant and probably more experienced than a good many of the mountaineers on K2 . . . after years of being a climbing teacher and seven expeditions, in which she went four times to or above the 8000m level. Also the equipment she chose was not 'old-fashioned' (this opinion came from a person that went for rescue with no rope). Julie and I were self-sufficient in our preparations on principle and, suspecting that our Camp 4 Depot might have disappeared, had carried up everything for a new Camp 4 on the final attempt. At c7000m, after we learned about the Camp 3 disaster (that it had been destroyed too by the big avalanche several days earlier), we had offered Hannes Wieser our spare tent and gas, but he said that there was a tent arrangement with the Koreans, and he did not want to carry it up. This was the last chance to avoid the risky situation, when two big expeditions (Koreans and Austrians) relied on just one tent at 8000m for subsequent summit attacks – the Koreans certainly out of helpfulness towards the Austrians, believing they would descend to Camp 3 after their summit push of 2 August. Willi Bauer's reports of this day (he played an important part in the matter) differ strongly from mine and the Koreans', but many days at high altitude may have changed his memory partially . . . otherwise there is no explanation how it is possible that, elsewhere on the mountain, he states in one report that he 'helped Diemberger down through House's Chimney', and in another that he climbed down alone through this chimney and then waited for Diemberger in the camp below. Unfortunately, authors have also mixed up both our reports between us, while the only right way was to keep them separated. Bauer wants to have 'rescued' Julie and me, which is not true – again the authors should have checked with both of us! A detailed report by me and Dennis Kemp ('K2 – The Facts') was published in December 1986 in *Climber*, but of course I could not then foresee several justified questions, and even less could I imagine what might bloom from fantasy.

> Yours faithfully,
> Kurt Diemberger

AREA NOTES

The Alps 1987

LINDSAY GRIFFIN

These notes are intended to complement the Alpine Club Guidebooks. Lindsay Griffin would welcome further information and new route descriptions for publication in these pages and the forthcoming guidebook to the Mont Blanc Range at: 2 Top Sling, Tregarth, Bangor, Gwynedd LL57 4RL.

The 1987 summer season, typified by the tragic flooding at Annecy and elsewhere, was considered by most activists to be very disappointing. The perennial Patrick Gabarrou continues to explore the western range, discovering quality climbing of some technical difficulty on both rock and ice, in overlooked corners.

However, as in recent years, most ambitions centred on the technical and non-serious rock route (for which there is still considerable scope in the Mont Blanc massif), together with the easy to middle grade mixed climb. Most of the popular rock routes, and indeed some that are not so popular, now sport a fixed abseil descent (often two bolts for each anchor), considerably reducing the seriousness of the enterprise and the need for greater mountaineering ability.

Work is in progress on a new guidebook to the Mont Blanc range and it is thought that, in the interim, an update on the current hut situation in some areas will prove useful.

Robert Blanc Hut (275cm)

A privately owned building with room for 40, which is situated on the S side of the Aiguille des Lanchettes, at the foot of the Central Spur. Conveniently placed for routes on the S side of Mont Tondu and the Aiguille des Glaciers. It is guarded in summer and offers a meal service.

From La Ville des Glaciers (reached via Bourg-Saint-Maurice and Les Chapieux), follow the unmade road to the Lanchettes chalets (1970m; ¾–1h). Continue on a good track towards the Lanchettes Glacier and climb up right to the hut (2h).

Conscrits Hut (273cm)

An old and rather inadequate building belonging to the CAF. It is situated on the right bank of the Trélatête Glacier and, although officially only housing 40 people, normally has to contend with twice this number. It is guarded in summer and offers a meal service, remaining unlocked for the rest of the year.

From the Trélatête Hotel (1970m) follow the footpath east, taking the left branch to reach the terminal moraines of the Trélatête Glacier (45min). Continue up the central moraine until below the Tré la Grande ice-fall, where the glacier makes a prominent bend to the left. Reach the rocks on the left where conspicuous red paint-marks indicate the start of a good path. Follow this, later traversing scree and grassy slopes (cairns), to the hut (2½h).

Eccles Bivouac Huts (3850m)

In addition to the original wooden shelter with room for six (protected by an overhanging block), there is, about 30m below, a new metal hut with room for nine.

Col de la Fouche Bivouac Hut (3680m)

The old hut was replaced in 1985 by a new building, which houses 10 people.

Trident Hut (3690m)

This is always open and occasionally has a resident warden in July and August. It officially holds 25, but generally has to contend with far more. Cooking facilities are available, but one should not rely on gas being in stock.

Freboudze Bivouac Hut (2363m)

This was dismantled in 1986 and now resides in the Abruzzi Museum of Courmayeur.

Gianni Comino Bivouac Hut (2430m)

This recently-constructed building with room for nine is well placed for routes on the SE side of Mont Gruetta and the rock walls flanking the Gruetta Cirque. The property belongs to the Mondovi section of the CAI and is always open. There is no cooking equipment.

From the car park near the Arnuva restaurant (1769m) in the Val Ferret, continue along the track towards the Col Ferret for a few minutes where a left fork, signposted to the Gianni Comino Bivouac, leads to a bridge across the river. The path, though often indistinct, is well marked by cairns and red paint-flashes. Continue through a small wood (larch, rhododendrons and alpine rosemary!), then climb steeply up the crest of the moraine to reach a little valley which can often be snow-covered until late summer. Go easily left, up ledges and short walls, to reach the crest of the SE shoulder of Mont Gruetta. Bear up left over bands of rock and small grassy ledges to reach the hut (2–2½h).

Point 2802m

A short rock route has been recorded on the SE face of this small peak which lies to the south of Pic Gamba at the foot of the S ridge of the Aiguille Noire de Peuterey:

Grand Design 156m of climbing. VII/VII+.
First Ascent: P Cresswell, D Hope and A Penning, 1–2 August 1987.

Start at the right-hand side of the wall and, after an easy climb to the highest grassy ledge below a curving crackline, there are six fairly short pitches of excellent climbing on perfect granite. After following the crackline, cross the overhang and continue up vague grooves to a second overhang where an obvious ramp leads up to the right. Above the ramp climb corners on the left to the top. (The climb, with four pitches of British 5c, relates to E3 and sports bolt belays at the end of each pitch.)

Józef Nyka adds:

Grandes Jorasses – Pointe Croz

One of the most notable climbs of the last season in the Alps was the second ascent of the 'No siesta' route by the Yugoslav, Tomo Česen. He waited for suitable weather until late September. The climb was made solo on 29 and 30 September 1987, taking 14 hours. Tomo reports that it was more serious and difficult than any other ascent he has made up to now. The 1200m route (some 40 pitches) follows the left side of the Croz Spur, on ice, rock and mixed ground with continuous difficulties of UIAA VI and VI+, with some sections of A1–A2 and an overhang of VII–. Because of the predominance at this time of year of ice formations (up to 90°), crampons were used on four-fifths of the route. The crux section was in the middle of the face – vertical slabs which took him four hours to overcome. The 'No siesta' was first climbed on 21–23 July 1986 by two Slovaks, Stanislav Glejdura and Ján Porvaznik (UIAA VII–, A1–A2, 90°).

Jordan 1987: Rum Goings On

TONY HOWARD

With the publication of Tony Howard's Guide to *Treks and Climbs in the Mountains of Rum and Petra*, these recently discovered desert towers are receiving the attention of increasing numbers of climbers. Teams from Germany, Austria, France, Spain and England were in the area this spring. The Austrian team, under the leadership of Wolfgang Nairz, with the assistance of Tony Howard, Wilfried Colonna and Di Taylor, made a climbing/adventure film for Austria's TV series *World of Mountains*.

Other climbers made repeat ascents of existing routes, confirming their quality. Bernard Domenech of France took out the first guided party and included the first ascent of a previously unknown Bedouin route on Jebel Rum in his itinerary, describing it as 'amazingly beautiful'. His companion 'guide' on the trip was the incorrigible Sabbah Atieeq: a Bedu of the area who is proving himself indispensable.

The new-route bonanza continued unabated, with discoveries of two new 'mini-canyons' having perfect 100m walls on both sides. Howard, Colonna and Taylor added another half-dozen routes, including a probe on to the ubiquitous 'walls of overhangs like bracket fungi and melting candles'. The 5A/B route was named 'Where Angels Fear to Tread'. Behind the Rest House, on the E face of Rum, they added 'Mad Frogs and Englishmen', in the company of Domenech, at 5B (English grade).

Earlier in the spring, the team of Rowland and Mark Edwards climbed some excellent new routes, from 5B unprotected slab-climbing on the 300m E face of Burdah to the superb 300m and 400m 5C crack-lines of Abu Aina and South Nassrani E faces. They also added a short but desperate wall climb on the E face of Traif al Muragh, graded E6 7A – the hardest route in the area to date.

Doug Scott was also there, adding his quota of new climbs and getting benighted in the process at the top of his 350m, 5C 'Crack of Cracks' on the W face of Khazali. Finally, when we left the valley at the end of April, Miguel Gallego and partner from Spain were last seen working their way up the Jebel Rum E face, on their third day.

All the new-climbs information is being recorded in a New Routes Book, courtesy of Troll, which will be kept in the Rest House for use by future climbers, in conjunction with the guidebook.

The Hoggar mountains were visited by a Dutch expedition over Christmas 1987. Base Camp was set up on 13 December under Mount Saouinan. Hans Lanters writes:

On 14 and 15 December Hans Lanters and Erick van Heugten climbed a new line on the N face of Saouinan: 'Rêve pétrifié' (6a).

On 20 December Paul Lahaye and Philip Simons climbed another new route on the W face of this mountain: 'Via Magnetron' (6b). Erick van Heugten and Hans Lanters made the second ascent on the same day.

On 24 December Hans Lanters, Philip Simons, Paul Lahaye and Erick van Heugten climbed a new line on the superb W face of Tezoulaig-Sud (2702m): 'Les garçons du pays plat' (6a, sustained). Second ascent (not free-climbed!) by a Swiss team the day after.

Our line takes the steep, smooth and obvious pillar in the centre of the W face. This face is one of the highest and most interesting in the Hoggar mountains. 'Les garçons du pays plat' is the first route in the Atakor region which does not touch any crack or chimney. The route is probably the finest line in the whole Atakor region (and possibly in the whole Hoggar!)

To the right of our new line is the Spanish route of 1967. Hans Lanters and Philip Simons climbed this route on 19 December. The A1/A2 section went free at solid 6a. Note: Between Christmas and New Year a Spanish expedition was also active on Tezoulaig-Sud. They also made a new route to the left of our line: 'Via Queimados rute' (TD).

Finally, on 3 January 1988, Hans Lanters and Philip Simons opened a new route on the Clocher du Tezoulaig: 'Voie Iris' (TD-/TD). The line takes an obvious crack between the Edlinger–Merlin–Richard route (1981) and the Kohlmann–Roussy route (1957).

(*Editorial note*: French gradings are used in this account. Rumour has it that the new routes are 'equipped' with expansion bolts and pitons.)

East Africa 1987

ANDREW WIELOCHOWSKI

New routes

The last few years in the East African mountains have been marked by a lull in major developments. The area is very popular and most of the obvious easier lines have been climbed; there is a lack of hard climbers living in the area with time for detailed exploration. Visiting 'hard men' tend to repeat classics: for example on Mount Kenya the Diamond Couloir is still the major attraction, even in late December and January when it is basically out of condition, with the bottom pitch collapsing. Fewer visitors sample the rock-routes on Mount Kenya, many of which rival Chamonix routes.

A major achievement in recent years has been the complete ascent of the SW couloir on Batian. In August 1985 Julian Mathias and Dan Donovan ascended this couloir to the Amphitheatre and then followed Tower Ridge and finally the S ridge to the summit of Batian. The ascent took 16 hours. The couloir when in condition, which is not too often, provides a superb, hard and technical ice climb; however, there is considerable avalanche and rockfall danger once the sun hits the slopes of the Amphitheatre above. The route was graded Scottish 5+.

During a period of very poor weather an Imperial College expedition spent a week camping by Two Tarn Hut and climbed on the near-overhanging walls at the base of Point Pigott. They put up two short, very hard rock climbs, both about E3/E4 and just over 100m long. There is now little potential for finding independent new lines on the overworked main peaks, but plenty of scope for hard short routes, on excellent rock, on the minor peaks. This could well prove to be a popular alternative in the future, especially for the modern rock gymnasts.

One fairly new route which has rapidly become popular on Mount Kenya is East Gate on the E face of Nelion. It was climbed in July 1980 by Ian Howell and Peter Brettle. The climbing is of a very high quality at a reasonable grade, VS+. It finds its way up a very steep and dramatic area of rock, with all its older neighbouring routes being considerably harder.

On Kilimanjaro there has been some activity in the exploration of minor lines amongst the shattered buttresses in the vicinity of the Western Breach and the Decken Glacier. The routes generally follow ice couloirs and offer major ice climbs.

There has been more activity on lower cliffs. As popular as ever has been Hell's Gate, which has recently become a National Park. Climbers should check with the MCK whether there are any restrictions related to nesting birds – rarely a problem.

In Tsavo game park the recently developed cliffs at Kitchwa Tembo have become popular. The setting is certainly unique, with elephant roaming the lower slopes, hippo and monkeys sharing your camp-site, and vultures endlessly circling around you on the climbs. Several bolts, recently placed on the belays of Behemoth, make this fine climb much safer. Also it is now possible to abseil from the summit of Kitchwa Tembo, thus avoiding the unpleasant descent down South Gully.

In the Ndoto Mountains of Northern Kenya the great 600m walls of Poi have now one route on them. Attempts at further new ascents have hitherto failed, though there are lines to explore. The main problem encountered with these great desert cliffs is that the lack of rainfall and freeze-thaw action does not allow a good development of crack systems; instead, the great diurnal surface temperature variation results in friable, exfoliated rock.

General

For the climber, Mount Kenya is undoubtedly the most rewarding mountain in East Africa. Access to it is improving all the time. Unfortunately, at the same time the commercial exploitation of the mountain is increasing. The Chogoria Route now offers a much more pleasant, and almost as quick, approach to the mountain as the boggy Naro Moru route; very fine self-help bunkhouses have been built near the Chogoria roadhead. On the Sirimon Route two tented camps have been put up, one at roadhead and the other above Shipton's Cave. The Naro Moru Route now boasts a permanent bunkhouse in the Teleki Valley; it is run by the Naro Moru River Lodge and costs slightly more than the other commercial camps (about £7 per night), offering a bunk bed, some security, and flowing water. MCK huts are heavily used and are becoming very run-down. It is best to plan on camping. Park entry fees are reasonable.

There have been several changes on Kilimanjaro. The Arrow Glacier hut has been destroyed by rock fall; a new hut 300m lower down has been built at the Lava Tower. On the north circuit there is a new hut west of the Lent Group. Park entry fees remain high, despite recent devaluations in Tanzania; the fees for six nights for one person will not leave much change out of £100.

Access via Uganda to the Ruwenzori was very problematical in the early eighties. The situation has much improved, though the country has not yet settled down and parties approaching from Uganda must be prepared to make last-minute changes. John Matte still provides a good service on the Ugandan approach. Very little mountaineering exploration has taken place here recently. There is scope for new mountain routes, but the weather and access problems have kept activity down. The Zaire approach from Mutwanga has become much more popular; this involves a much drier route and is equally scenic, but access to Mutwanga is very difficult – about three days' driving from Kigali, which, if done by hired vehicle, could be very expensive, or a chartered flight from Goma – even more expensive.

Of interest are the major climatic changes which have made a dramatic change to the appearance of Kili and Mount Kenya. The glacial recession continues unabated. Hastenrath predicts that Mount Kenya's glaciers could disappear in the next 25 years. On the summit of Kilimanjaro the last remnants of the ice-cap are rapidly vanishing; for example, the ice cathedral in the crater has melted away. The glaciers are also receding; the Heim Glacier has been particularly badly affected.

Maps and Guidebooks

Recent additions include:

Map of Mount Kenya (1987): the main map is 1:50,000, insets include a 1:400,000 map of roads around the mountain and a 1:25,000 map of the peak area. Available from West Col Productions, Goring, Reading RG8 9AA.

East Africa International Mountain Guide (1986): this is a climbers' guide to selected routes on the major East African mountains and on smaller cliffs such as Hell's Gate and Tsavo. Available from West Col Productions.

I would be very grateful if any comments, information about recent developments or changes in East Africa could be sent to me to help update guidebook information: A Wielochowski, 32 Seamill Park Crescent, Worthing, BN11 2PN (Tel. 0903 37565).

Canadian Arctic 1987

TED WHALLEY

Ellesmere Island has, at Cape Columbia, the northern-most land in the world, at latitude about 83.1°. It is a very mountainous island, particularly on the north-west and the east sides, and its mountains almost reach the north coast – the northern-most mountains in the world.

It was from here that most of the attempts to reach the North Pole have started, including that of Peary – reputedly, but perhaps not actually, the first man to reach the Pole. Nowadays, tourist flights to the Pole by Twin Otter from Resolute Bay are common, but are somewhat expensive. The topography of Ellesmere is dominated by several large and small ice-caps which almost bury the mountains, and only the Agassiz Ice-Cap, which is immediately west of Kane Basin, has a name. On the north-west side there are two large and unnamed ice-caps, the larger of which straddles 82°N and the smaller straddles 81.5°N. There is also a large unnamed ice-cap immediately west of Smith Sound, a smaller one on the south-east tip of Ellesmere Island, and another north of the settlement of Grise Fiord on the south coast.

The north coast of Ellesmere was the home of great ice shelves, but, at about the turn of the century, the ice shelves started to break off and float away as so-called 'ice islands' that circulated for many decades around the arctic ocean, and still do. They have often been used as natural platforms for scientific expeditions. Perhaps nine-tenths of the original ice shelves have floated away.

The Independence I people lived there about four millennia ago, when the earth was warmer than it is now, and were followed by the Independence II and then the Dorset people, who disappeared about 1000 years ago. The island was rediscovered by Europeans in 1616 when the ship *Discovery*, with Robert Bylot as master and William Baffin as pilot, made her fifth journey into the region and discovered Whale Sound in latitude 77°, near the present Thule, Jones Sound, and Lancaster Sound. It was a magnificent journey, but was forgotten or disbelieved for 200 years, until James Ross verified Bylot's and Baffin's discoveries.

The east and north coasts were explored by several parties in the latter half of the 19th century. The major contributors were Otto Sverdrup and his party, who spent four years exploring much of Ellesmere and Axel Heiberg Islands, leaving behind such names as Butter Porridge Point (they ate some there). Much of the remaining geography was explored in outline by Robert Peary during his attempts to reach the North Pole for the first time. The mountains were first seen, by Europeans at least, by Adolphus W Greely from Lake Hazen in 1882. He went there because the Second International Polar Conference in 1880 planned several circumpolar stations for the years 1882–83. One of the two American contributions was to Fort Conger on Lady Franklin Bay, just west of Hall Basin, which is between Ellesmere Island and

Greenland in latitude 81.5N. In 1882 May, Greely and three men went to Lake Hazen and reported seeing for the first time the northern ice-cap of Ellesmere Island, and they named Mount Whisler. Their relief vessel did not arrive in either 1882 or 1883, and they were not rescued until 22 June 1884, when only seven of the original 25 men were still alive.

Mountain climbing in the high arctic of Canada started in 1935. Then, A W Moore of the Oxford University Ellesmere Land Expedition and Sergeant H W Stallworthy of the Royal Canadian Mounted Police travelled by dog-sled from Etah in Greenland and climbed Mount Oxford (1840m) at 82.2N, 73.1W. They saw and named the British Empire Range to the north-west. This lead was followed only 22 years later, when Geoffrey Hattersley-Smith and Keith Arnold, of the Canadian Defence Research Board, made the second ascent of Mount Oxford and determined its height by triangulation.

Between 1957 and 1967 G Hattersley-Smith and several companions explored the northern ice-cap, which has no name. They measured the heights of the highest mountains and climbed the highest, Barbeau Peak (2605m), which is also the highest point in North America west of the Rocky Mountains, jointly with a Royal Air Force party which had been climbing in the British Empire Range.

The next climbing in the northern Ellesmere was by Van Cochrane and his party from the Explorer's Club in 1982. They flew by Twin Otter from Resolute Bay and landed on the ice of the outer edge of Yelverton Inlet at latitude 82.3N. The snow on the fiord was unexpectedly deep, and so they set up Base Camp on 8 May near the snout of the unnamed glacier that flows into the inlet from the east. They ascended several peaks up to 1800m. Their return aeroplane brought Alan Errington, Steve Trafton and six others to a Base Camp north of Mount Whisler. In the next two weeks this party made 13 first ascents and the third ascents of Mount Whisler and Barbeau Peak.

The only other climbing of consequence on Ellesmere has been done near Makinson Inlet, in the south-east of the island. In 1976, Lori Dexter of Pond Inlet, Baffin Island made several climbs near the settlement of Grise Fiord on the south coast, such as the prominent 800m spire that is 6km north-west of the settlement, and several ice-filled gullies leading to the 600m plateau just north of the settlement. He, George Wallerstein and two others also climbed the 1300m unnamed ice-cap about 15km north-east of Grise Fiord. The party was then joined by Roly Reader and myself and flew to Makinson Inlet in a Twin Otter of Ken Borek Air, found a small hole in the clouds above Makinson Inlet, and landed on a gravel strip.

The prime objective was Bowman Island, in the middle of the inlet. Unfortunately the season was late that year and the ice never cleared from the inlet, so we could not reach the island. Nevertheless, about 10 mountains were climbed.

Van Cochran and Ted Whalley and their parties returned in May 1978, with Bowman Island as their prime objective. The last part was over the steep E face, which made a good climb. Van Cochran has been back to the area in both the Inglefield Mountains and the Thorndike Peaks, which are north and south respectively of the east end of Makinson Inlet. The Thorndikes were reached by

Twin Otter from Resolute Bay, and the first circuit of the Thorndike Glacier System was made. Four first ascents were made.

Lloyd Freese of Kluane National Park reports that 19 groups, comprising 90 people in all, were climbing or skiing in the Icefield Ranges in 1987, and spent 1765 person-days in the mountains. Two groups climbed the E ridge of Mount Logan, and six groups failed. One group was successful on the King Trench, and Dave Cheesmond and Catherine Freer are presumed dead on the Hummingbird Ridge. Two routes were completed on Mount Steele and one on Mount Wood, and another party failed on Mount Upton.

Tom Elliot, Chief Park Warden of Auyuittuq Park Reserve, Baffin Island, reports that nine groups totalling 39 people from five countries were in Auyuittuq for climbing or glacier skiing. Some of the climbs were of Mounts Tyr, Asgard, Thor, Bilbo, and Frodo, Breidablik and Freya Peaks. Five parties were from the US and there was one each from Spain, Germany, Canada, and the UK. The Warden Service completed two glacier ski-touring routes and climbed Gauntlet and Tuniak Peaks in order to increase its first-hand knowledge of ski touring and mountaineering routes in the Park.

Dave MacAdam continued his lone wanderings on the E coast of Baffin Island and spent several weeks in the fiords south-west of Cape Hooper. He climbed several mountains during his trip, all previously unclimbed.

I am very grateful to Van Cochrane, Lloyd Freese, Tom Elliot and Dave MacAdam for providing information.

SELECTED BIBLIOGRAPHY

A Taylor, *Geographical Discovery and Exploration in the Queen Elizabeth Islands*. Queen's Printer, Ottawa, 1964.

G Hattersley-Smith, *North of Latitude Eighty*. Defence Research Board, Ottawa, 1974.

T C Fairley, *Sverdrup's Arctic Adventures*. London (Longmans, Green), 1959.

R McGhee, *Canadian Arctic Prehistory*. Toronto (Van Nostrand Reinhold), 1978.

G van B Cochrane, *Can Alp J* 62, 22–25, 1979; 65, 40–41, 1982; 66, 28, 1983.

G Hattersley-Smith, 'Barbeau Peak.' *Can Geog J* 80, 86, 1970.

Alaska, Spring 1987

H Adams Carter contributes the following note:

The weather was very bad in Alaska, but some climbs were made. Willy Hersman, Todd Miner, Karen Cafmeyer, Larry Hartig, Jim Sayler and Blaine Smith climbed *Mount Blackburn* (4995m) from the Nabesna Glacier to the N ridge, reaching the summit on 12 May. They also made the first ascent of *P3220* on 14 May. John Bauman's party climbed *Mount Wrangell*.

In the Kichatna Mountains, Conrad Anker's group made the first ascent of the SE face of *Gurney Peak*, and Jack Tackle and Jim Donini climbed the S buttress of *P2100*. In the Alaska Range, near Mount McKinley, Scott Gill's party made a new route, the NW ridge, on *West Tripyramid*, and Thomas Bauman's and Mugs Stumps's groups both made new routes on the difficult peak, *The Broken Tooth*.

69. *Fremont Peak (4190m), Island Lake.*

70. *Bollinger Peak, Billy's Lake.*

71. *Cirque of towers, Wind Rivers.*

72. *Looking towards Nevado Kashan (5701m) from Laguna Awash (John Hudson and Rob Sneyd attempted a route up the rock-face to reach the right-hand ridge near the snow arête).*

73. *Quebrada Qeshqe with Pongos Sur (5711m) on R and Point 5303 on L. The plant is a* puya raymondi. *(The snow-peak behind the rock-peak was climbed, and the right-hand ridge of the rock-peak attempted, by Rob Sneyd and Richard Weller)*.

74. *The group. L–R: Juan* (arriero), *Stanley Thomas, Richard Weller, Rosemary Greenwood, John Hudson, Pamela Glanville, Belinda Swift, Ashley Greenwood, Rob Sneyd.*

75. *Pongos Norte (5680m) on R and Nevado Qeshqe (5463m) in the centre,*
    from Quebrada Qeshqe.

South America 1987

EVELIO ECHEVARRÍA

Through most of 1987 Andean mountaineering was marred by storms. After the end of the world drought in late 1983 a new weather pattern seems to have established itself, at least as far as the Andes are concerned. Winter and wet seasons in the last few years have been registering below-normal amounts of precipitation, but by late winter usually a greater amount occurs, lasting well into the summer or dry season in every one of the seven Andean countries. While this does not represent a serious obstacle to mountaineering, it has been somewhat different in the central districts of Chile and Argentina, where a major part of all mountaineering and skiing activities in the Andes takes place. Bad weather in the spring and early summer (November–December) means swollen and at times impassable rivers, as well as deep snow and avalanches. This in turn forces activities to be postponed until the peak of the summer (February). Nevertheless, every kind of mountain activity in the Andes is on the rise. Noteworthy is the beginning of winter mountaineering, particularly in the central areas of the two countries mentioned.

In the following notes, all activity belongs to 1987 unless otherwise stated.

Ecuador

A Venezuelan group, including a woman, Dora Ocanto, travelled to the impressive Altar chain in Eastern Ecuador. Its main objective, Monja Grande ('bigger nun') (5160m), was climbed by its exceedingly steep 'canal de hielo' (ice-gully) on its S face by J Betancourt and N Rojas (27 December 1986). The same Rojas plus C Pernalete opened a variant on the SW ridge of Obispo (5319m), highest of Altar, while Dora Ocanto and Betancourt climbed the so-called Calvario variant to the normal route on the same peak.

Peru

The Cordillera Blanca continues to be the first choice of foreign expeditions for the fashionable opening of new routes. The following deserve at least a brief mention:

Vallunaraju Sur (5630m), SE face (M Schenone, G Ghigo, E Tessera, Italians).
Torre de Parón (c5200m), S face (M Oliva, C Polanco, E de la Cal, A Madrid, Spaniards).
Huandoy Norte (6395m), dihedral left of rock wall, N face (M Freser, M Romih, Yugoslavs).
Santa Cruz (6241m), S face, with two rock bands and hard, steep ice up to 80°

(A Luznik, E Tratnik, P Poljanec, Z Tressnovec, Yugoslavs).
Palcaraju (6274m), traverse from Palcaraju Sur (E Tratnik, Yugoslav).
Palcaraju (6274m), W ridge (P Poljanec, Z Tressnovec, Yugoslavs).

An important repeat in the same district was that of the French Bernard route on
Huascarán Norte (6654m), by three Basques.

Walter Silverio, head of the Asociación de Guías (guides) de Montaña
del Perú, writing to H Adams Carter, editor of the *AAJ*, remarked that some
expeditions have been climbing very elevated peaks in the Cordillera Blanca
with incredible speed. Thus, peaks over 6000m were in the last season ascended
in a matter of hours from Base Camp, a high camp being dispensed with.

Bolivia

Two expeditions to Bolivia deserve attention. One, to the Cordillera Real, by
Yugoslavs, accomplished two difficult new routes: S face of Mururata (5868m),
and SE and SW faces of Nevado de Cotaña ('Pico Schulze') (5830m),
simultaneously, all by members of the Railway Alpine Club, Ljubljana.

The second Bolivian expedition was a massive enterprise, perhaps a
trekking, by Germans from Bayreuth, accompanied by Bolivian climbers. They
visited the northern extreme of the Cordillera Quimsa Cruz, which begins
immediately south of Illimani, and conducted there the massive ascent of rock
peaks and peaklets belonging to the Mocoya, Tarujumaña and Teacota valleys.
In all they climbed 27 summits (4700 to 5304m), nearly all first ascents. Part of
the group then moved to the SE corner of the range (San Lorenzo group) and
reclimbed some of the fine *nevados* previously ascended by Japanese and
Bolivians. First ascents of four other peaks in the San Pedro group were also
made. This was the only expedition to accomplish pioneer work in the Andes in
1987.

Chile and Argentina

Central Andes.   On the Chilean side, among very many ascents that take
place every season (December to March), the first winter ascent of the well-
known peak of San José (5880m) should be mentioned. Four women and 17
men led by Iván Vigoroux participated (15 September). In 1987 Chile had one
of its most severe winters on record.

On the Argentinian side, in order to investigate the existence of traces of
pre-Columbian ascents, university students ascended the central peaks of the
Cordillera del Tigre, which overlooks the *pampas* or plains. Results were poor,
but, among other ascents, the first of Cerro Barauca (c5400m) was carried out
by two members on 9 February.

Aconcagua, as happens yearly now, drew mountaineers who aimed at
opening new variants on its famous S face. Yugoslavs Milan Romih and Danilo
Tic examined several possible lines; bad weather and avalanches forced them to
try the right side of the French route. It took them seven days to finish it,
enduring avalanches and cold bivouacs on the way. They descended by the
normal route.

A Chilean party tried a combination of routes. C Buracchio, J Monte and C Thiele started climbing the 1982 Yugoslav variant in its lower third, combined then with the French route and finished in the upper third of the face by following the Messner variant. The Chileans had trained at home by performing winter ascents.

Andes Australes.   This is the name that Chileans and Argentinians commonly use to designate collectively the mountain regions of Patagonia and Tierra del Fuego. Early in February, Argentinians climbed Aguja (needle) Guillaumet by the Fonrouge route and the ice-peak of Gorra Blanca (2920m). But the main achievements belong to Italians. In the Paine district they reported the following activity:

Torre Sur del Paine, E face: E Orlandi, M Giarolli, E Salvaterra (20 November 1986).
Torre Norte del Paine, S spur, and Torre Sur del Paine, N spur: the last two climbs, by L Leonardi and M Manica, were the first winter ascents in the district, since they occurred in June, the first Chilean winter month. The Italians reported much wind, −25° and not much snowfall.
Torre Central del Paine, NW face: five Italians under M Ballerini (24 December 1986).

Perhaps the main event in the Andes in the mountaineering year 1987 was the first ascent of the W peak of Cerro Sarmiento (c2200m). Sarmiento, like Alpamayo, Siniolchu and Nilkanta, has been referred to as 'the most beautiful mountain in the world'. It has two great ice-cathedrals: the E or main peak (2234m), climbed by Italians in 1958, and the W peak, which had been attempted by climbers of the same nationality at least three times. Now, on 8 December 1986, four Italian climbers methodically braved the force of the wind, the cold, deep snow and overhanging ice mushrooms and reached the summit of this very fine peak. With this triumph, Italian mountaineering reaffirms its leading role in exploration and climbing in the Andes Australes.

Aconcagua Map

Jerzy Wala, Carles Capellas and Josep Paytubi: Aconcagua. Scale 1:50,000. Monochrome orographical map 40 × 50cm. The American Alpine Club, New York, 1987.

Józef Nyka writes:
The map is a beautiful example of international collaboration. Elaborated and drawn by Wala, it was prepared for printing in Sabadell by the Spanish experts from the *Servei General d'Informació de Muntanya* – Carles Capellas and Josep Paytubi, who also wrote useful appendices. The material has been supervised and revised by the South American authority, Evelio Echevarría. The production and publication was taken over by the American Alpine Club.
    The map shows the Aconcagua massif (6959m) with the surrounding mountains from Cerro La Mano (5426m) in the north to Cerro Tolosa (5432m)

in the south. The terrain features, though only in skeletal drawing, are detailed and extremely clear. The map is a continuation of the *Cuadernos de Alpinismo* (Mountaineering Notebooks), edited since 1982 by the *Servei General d'Informació de Muntanya*, where it is available: SGIM, Apartat Correus 330, 08200 Sabadell, Barcelona, Spain.

China 1987

CHRIS BONINGTON

There were 33 expeditions to China during 1987. In parallel with other areas of the Himalaya, the 8000m peaks were by far the most popular, with Everest heading the bill with eight expeditions, none of which were successful because of the weather. Second in the popularity list was Xixabangma, with seven expeditions of which four were successful – the difference of size – and then three to Muztagh Ata and two to Cho Oyu. The limited number of expeditions to the smaller peaks is partly due, no doubt, to the high cost of all climbing in China and the difficulty of getting sponsorship for small peaks.

The Chinese authorities certainly seem much more relaxed about giving permits for unclimbed peaks. In this respect we were extremely fortunate in getting permission for Menlungtse, Gaurishankar's beautiful sister peak. One thing we did discover, however, is how expensive it is if there is a long trek to Base Camp. Expeditions to mountains near a road-head are comparatively inexpensive – for instance a small expedition to Everest would probably be cheaper to run than one to Menlungtse.

The expeditions going to China were as follows. I am greatly indebted to Mr Ying Dao Shui of the Chinese Mountaineering Association for providing this useful information.

Expeditions to China in 1987

1. *The Swedish Mount Everest Expedition*
    39 members (including 8 Nepalese), from 5 March to 3 June
    (N col route of Mt Qomolangma).
    Leader, Ebbe Wahlund, MD.
    Unsuccessful

2. *The 1987 Arkansas/Mount Everest Expedition*
    15 members, from 6 March to 9 June (N face route).
    Leader, Jack Allsup
    Unsuccessful

3. *Spanish Qomolangma Expedition*
    8 members + 5 Nepalese, from 21 June to 15 September (N col route).
    Leader, Antonio Ramos Villar
    Unsuccessful

4. *China Everest 87*
    21 pax, from 4 August to 13 November (N col route).
    Leader, Steve van Meter
    Unsuccessful

5.   *Everest 87 (UK)*
            12 pax, from 31 August to 4 November (NE ridge route).
                    Leaders, Doug Scott and Rick Allen
                              Unsuccessful

6.   *87 American North Face Expedition*
            13 members, from 24 July to 11 November (N face route).
                        Leader, Scott Fisher
                              Unsuccessful

7.   *Japan National Defence Academy Alpine Club Mt Qomolangma*
                          Expedition 1987
            30 members, from 15 July to 18 November (W ridge route).
                      Leader, Takashi Kawakami
                              Unsuccessful

8.   *Tsuneo Hasegawa and U-Tan Club Qomolangma Winter Expedition*
                            1987–88
            4 members + 5-member filming crew, from October 1987 to
                      January 1988 (N col route).
                      Leader, Tsuneo Hasegawa

9.   *The 1987 Colorado Xixabangma Expedition*
            8 members, from 29 March to 2 May (Chinese route).
                      Leader, Dr Richard D Dietz
                              Unsuccessful

10.   *The New Zealand Mt Xixabangma Expedition 1987*
            6 members, from 27 April to 25 May (Chinese route).
                        Leader, Mike Perry
                               Successful

11.   *Italian Xixabangma Expedition*
            7 members, from 7 August to 4 September (Chinese route).
            Organizer, Trekking International, Mr Beppe Tenti

12.   *Italian Xixabangma Expedition*
            9 members, from 20 August to 25 September (Chinese route).
            Organizer, Trekking International, Mr Beppe Tenti
                               Successful

13.   *The Hungarian Tibet Expedition 1987*
            9 members, from 6 September to 17 October (N ridge).
                      Leader, Dr Sandor Nagy
                               Successful

14.   *Xixabangma 1987 – Expedition Jade Venture*
            29 members, from 18 September to 10 November (SE face).
                      Leader, Lt Col Henry Day
                              Unsuccessful

15.   *Polish Xixabangma Expedition*
13 members, from 17 August to 27 September (N side).
Leader, Jerzy Kukuczka
Successful

16.   *Japan Kamoshika-Dojin Cho Oyu Expedition 1987*
10 members + 11 pax of supporting group, 18 August to 7 October
(Chinese route).
Leader, Mrs Takahashi Michiko
8 members reached the summit, 20, 21 and 22 September

17.   *Australian Changtse Expedition 1987*
6 members, from 26 August to 13 October.
Leader, Louis Whitton
Successful (2 members reached the summit)

18.   *The Irish Zhangzi Tibet Expedition*
12 members, from 31 August to 2 November.
Leader, Joss Lynam
Unsuccessful

19.   *The Norwegian/British Tibet Expedition*
6 members, from 9 March to 3 May (Menlungtse).
Leader, Chris Bonington
Unsuccessful

20.   *Japan–China Friendship Joint Expedition 1987 to Mt Labuche Kang
(Xizang)*
9 Japanese + 9 Chinese, from 10 September to 9 November.
Chinese Leader, Chen Tian Liang. Japanese Leader, Kinichi Yamamori
Successful

21.   *Doshisha University Mt Siguniang Expedition 1987*
13 members, from 24 September to 29 November.
Leader, Miyazaki Takafumi
Successful

22.   *The Japanese Academic Alpine Club of Shizuoka Mt Crown Expedition*
14 members, from 1 June to 18 September (Mt Crown, 7295m, located in
Xinjiang).
Leader, Yamamoto Ryozo
Unsuccessful

23.   *Mendizaleak Kongur 87 (Spain)*
4 members, from 28 June to 13 August (SW ridge – C Bonington route).
Leader, Javier Iraola
Unsuccessful

24.   *1987 International Friendship Expedition*
9 members, from 6 July to 20 August (Muztagh Ata: N and S summits).
Leader, Michael Jardine
Successful

25.   *The Italian Expedition to Mt Muztagh Ata*
19 members, from 2 August to 2 September (Qiaodumak route).
Organizer, Trekking International, Mr Beppe Tenti

26.   *The Austrian Muztagh Ata Expedition*
5 members, from 1 September to 21 September.
Leader, Bruno Baumann
Successful

27.   *Japanese Xinqin Feng Expedition*
9 members, from 25 July to 15 August (reconnaissance).
Leader, Hideyuki Uematsu

28.   *American Expedition to Sigunian*
18 members, from 30 September to 16 October.
Organizer, Mr Peter Klika
Successful

29.   *The American Jade Dragon Expedition*
9 members, from 28 April to 16 May.
Leader, Mr Eric Salz Perlman
Successful

30.   *The British Amne Machin Expedition*
5 members, from 31 August to 26 September.
Leader, John Town
Unsuccessful

31.   *The Fukuoka Alpine Club Kunlun Expedition 1987*
9 members, from 18 July to 31 August (6699m Peak).
Leader Kyushiro Morooka
Unsuccessful

32.   *The Japanese Mt Hai Zi Expedition*
13 members, from 25 July to 23 August.
Leader, Kazuo Tobita
Successful

33.   *International Expedition to Cho Oyu*
Successful

(*Editor's Note.*   Expeditions should not necessarily be considered 'un-successful' if they fail to reach the highest point. See, for example, John Town's article on pp 77–83 of this volume. And what if 'success' is achieved at high cost in life?)

Henry Day adds:

Climbers returning from Tibet after the post-monsoon season had to contend with two hazards in addition to the usual red tape. The road between

Kathmandu and Friendship Bridge on the Nepal/China border had been blocked during the monsoon in several places, the worst being between Barabise and Lamasangu. By November the obstructions had been reduced to a single two-hour portage, with vehicles available at either side of it. The Nepalese have thrown a battalion of para-military engineers on to the job and expectations were for a serviceable motor road again to the frontier in time for the start of the spring climbing season. On the other side of the border the Chinese Mountaineering Association were less sanguine about getting vehicles to Zhangmu, the Tibet side of the border. The exceptional snowfall of late October blocked the road over the Lalung La (5020m), about 100km north of the border, as well as causing rockfalls that blocked the road 10km south of Nyalam. Snowploughs cleared the pass by 3 November, but the journey down from Nyalam to the frontier required porters for the whole distance of 25km. The CMA cannot guarantee that the situation will be improved by the spring. The other problem was political. Notices had appeared after disturbances in Lhasa on 1 October. They warned visitors not to interfere in the internal affairs of the country. Individual travellers were no longer admitted and those already in Lhasa were moved on. Only previously organized groups, including CMA-arranged expeditions, were allowed to travel through Lhasa.

There are indications that the CMA is being challenged over its monopoly on the issue of climbing permits. China International Sports Travel Corporation may be subsuming the CMA completely; similarly-titled China Tibet International Sports Travel offers a full service 'for expeditions, travels and tours' in its own region and has its own telex number. The acid test will be whether a letter or telex of invitation from the C(T)ISTC is honoured by visa-issuing authorities abroad.

The CMA continue to update their regulations and provisions governing mountaineering and trekking parties and, when negotiating with them, it is always worth bearing in mind the last rule: 'The right to interpret and revise (alter) these regulations (provisions) belongs to the CMA'. They make a high proportion of their foreign exchange from their tariff for transport and accommodation, charging well above the market rate. For example, the local charge for an overnight stay at the Chinese hotel in Nyalam is 7 yuan (about £1/US$2); the CMA charge 80 yuan even if meals are not available. For vehicles they now charge all journeys as if they started in Lhasa, even if much of the trip is notional (some trucks remain at Xegar). The distance from Lhasa to Zhangmu off the latest map and consistent with roadside marker stones is 827km but the CMA charge for 900km. The exchange rate has moved steadily in favour of those with hard currency, so much so that costs have effectively halved since the first foreign expeditions went in 1980/81. However, the charges are presently pegged at 3.7 yuan to the US dollar. Those who are climbing in China on a budget may wish to take a few precautions: read the odometer of vehicles at start and completion of journey; avoid overnight stops where possible; send a powerful negotiating team to settle the account in Beijing at the end of the expedition; note that the joining expenses of CMA's Liaison Officer and interpreter (if taken) are charged to the expedition. (They could come from Beijing and take a week on the journey.)

The published list of authorized peaks (see *Mountain* 113) lags behind those upon which attempts have been permitted. The message seems to be that, provided there are no political complications and the CMA can arrange transport, there is a chance that a permit will be issued. It is certainly worth asking.

Those wishing to hire high-altitude porters have found those provided not yet as effective as Sherpas. Permission has been given for a few Sherpas to climb in Tibet as long as they are represented as team members. There are still no rescue facilities on offer, although a helicopter is now in the Tibet region at least. It was reported to have been sent to Nyalam as part of the government's efforts to release foreign tourists trapped on their way to the Lalung La in late October. It was not seen near any expedition's camps. Casualty evacuation in Tibet remains an expedition's own responsibility.

H Adams Carter adds:

An expedition to Mount Everest, led by Jack Allsup, very nearly succeeded. They approached the Great Couloir somewhat to the east between the flanks of Changtse and the N face to 6700m. Although they established Camp 3 at 7600m at the bottom of the Great Couloir on 17 April, it was not until 14 May that they were able to set up Camp 4 at 8170m. On 21 May Eric Simonson and Ed Viesturs made a summit try. They climbed straight out of the top of the Great Couloir rather than traversing right above the Yellow Band, because of the lack of snow. Upon reaching the final summit snow-field, Simonson traversed to the W ridge, climbing ahead of Viesturs, but he turned back at 8750m below a steep rock-step. Three other summit attempts failed. On 19 June Roger Marshall, a Canadian born in England but living in Colorado, set out, hoping to make a solo ascent of the Japanese and Hornbein Couloirs. At the end of the second day, he was at the foot of the Hornbein Couloir. On the morning of 21 June he was observed to begin to descend. On the very hard ice of the Japanese Couloir he slipped and fell to his death.

Józef Nyka adds:

The First Hungarian 8000m Peak

A nine-member Hungarian team jointly led by Dr Sándor Nagy (organization) and Peter Dékány (technical leader) completed the ascent of Xixabangma (8046m) by the normal route. From Base Camp at 5000m three camps were established: 1 at 6400m, 2 at 6950m and 3 at 7400m. Peter Dékány became seriously ill. On 1 October 1987 the top was reached by Dr Sándor Nagy and Attila Ozsváth. The weather worsened. A week later the second ascent followed, made by Zoltán Balaton, László Vörös, József Csíkos and László Várkonyi. These were the 25th and 26th ascents of Xixabangma, but we are not sure if all the earlier summiteers reached the main summit of the mountain (for example, on 17 September 1987, the members of the Swiss–Austrian–German expedition stopped on the Central Summit, c8030m).

Zbigniew Kowalewski adds:

Xixabangma 1987

The lowest of the 8000m peaks, Xixabangma (8027m) rises approximately 120km north-west of Mount Everest. It received scant attention until recently, the main obstacle being political. The summit was first reached by a large Chinese expedition in 1964. The expedition followed a route up the NW face.

In 1982 a small British party climbed the SW face in alpine style. Up to 1987 no other routes had been recorded.

In September 1987, a 13-member International Expedition led by Jerzy Kukuczka put nine members on the summit via three independent routes. Hajzer and Kukuczka climbed a new route via the W ridge and the W summit (c7950m). Avila, Carsolio (Mexico), Navarette (Ecuador), Rutkiewicz and Warecki (Poland) repeated the Chinese route. These climbers reached the top on 19 September. Meanwhile, Hinks (Britain) and Untch (USA) completed a difficult new route on the NE face, reaching the top on 24 September.

The International Expedition was based on the Yebonkal Glacier. On the far side of the mountain, a British expedition was based on the Phola Glacier. Two members of the team, Venables and Hughes, climbed a new line on the SE ridge to a point about 300m below the main summit of Xixabangma. See Luke Hughes's article, pp 63–70.

(*Editor's Note* – *the height of Xixabangma*. This is variously given as 8013m, 8027m and 8046m. According to *The Shishapangma Expedition* by Doug Scott and Alex MacIntyre (1984), p26, the Survey of India gave 8013m in the last century and 8046m in 1978; a more recent Chinese recalculation gave 8027m. We have adopted 8027m in this volume.)

Nepal 1987

JOHN PORTER

Winter 86/87   Fewer expeditions were active in Nepal than in recent winters, and most expeditions were small in numbers. Those who stayed at home did not miss much. It was a winter of poor weather and high winds, even by Himalayan standards. As a result, only four of 14 expeditions were successful.

The major success of the season was on Annapurna 1 and belonged once again to the masters of winter climbing, the Poles. It was a personal triumph for Jerzy Kukuczka who led the team, Artur Hajzer, Wanda Rutkiewicz and Krysztof Wielicki, on a successful ascent of the original route from the north. After his epic ascents of K2's S face and Manaslu's NE face (with Hajzer) in 1986, Kukuczka and his team did not set up Base until 18 January. They therefore missed the usual advantage of a November start, but at the same time missed most of the mid-winter bad weather. Four camps were quickly placed, the last at 6800m on 31 January. Rutkiewicz and Wielicki descended while the remaining pair went on to place a final camp at 7400m. After a day's rest they reached the summit on 3 February at 4pm and descended to their high camp in the dark. It was Kukuczka's third first winter ascent (after Cho Oyu and Kangchenjunga) and his 13th 8000er.

A five-man Korean team led by Park Yung Bae employed nine Sherpas on an attempt on the SW face of Everest. They had reached 8300m when Sherpa Tsuttin Dorje fell to his death working between camps at 7700m and the expedition was abandoned. Another Korean team retreated from the S col at about the same time in mid-January.

All other expeditions to 8000m peaks failed, among them Spanish and Koreans on Dhaulagiri and Swiss on Annapurna. Apart from the Poles on Annapurna, the only other successes were on the outlying peaks of the Everest region. The previously unclimbed E face of Pumori received ascents in quick succession, first by the Japanese Hiroshi Aota and Yoshiki Sasahara in three days, who reached the summit on 3 December, and two days later the same route was soloed by American Todd Bibler. Lobuje West received its first reported winter ascent when three Koreans and two Sherpas reached the top on 30 January.

Pre-Monsoon   The season was notable only for its continuing poor weather and low success rate. 27 expeditions were active, but only two 8000ers were climbed. The one positive feature was that only one fatality was recorded, compared with 15–20 during the previous two pre-monsoon seasons.

The Chileans reached the highest summit yet climbed by S Americans when they succeeded on Cho Oyu, but there was a bizarre postscript to the expedition, one that fulfils the nightmare shared by all expeditions using

Nepalese permits to reach the NW side. The Chilean team repeated the normal route over the Nangpa La on to the NW face in Tibet. Shortly after placing two on top, including Sherpa Ang Rita who recorded his 10th ascent of a 8000m summit (Dhauligiri 4, Everest 3, Cho Oyu 2 and Kangchenjunga), the Chinese army commandeered Base Camp and ordered everyone off the mountain. Passports and permits were confiscated. An American team on the same route were also forced down and reluctantly retreated, with two members in position to attempt the summit. Future expeditions attempting this normal route could well face similar treatment, and only the difficult S side of Cho Oyu may be accessible from Nepal in future. Experiences reported from Tibet in 1987 indicate a general hardening of Chinese treatment of Western expeditions. Those planning the normal route on Cho Oyu are warned.

An American team to Makalu had better luck. They climbed the original route, placing leader Glenn Porzak, Chris Pizzo and Sherpa Lhakpa Nuru on top on 12 May. Four days later Gary Neptune and Sherpas Dawa Nuru and Moti Lal also reached the summit.

On Everest, an ambitious Czechoslovak expedition led by Ivan Galfy attempted two new routes on the SW face, but continuous bad weather forced them to retreat from a high point of 8300m without making significant progress on new ground. Similar conditions were experienced by a 14-strong Spanish expedition on the 1980 Polish S pillar, and their attempt was abandoned.

A Spanish team on Annapurna abandoned their attempt on the original route after Andrés Ferrer fell to his death while descending between camps. A Dutch expedition failed at 7600m on an attempt to climb the S face of Makalu, and an American team failed on the S face of Jannu. Lhotse Shar was climbed by a French army expedition via the original route, but the much-attempted SW spur of the mountain defeated a Yugoslav expedition at 7450m. The only other successes were Japanese on the SW ridge of Langtang Ri, and Americans and Greeks on the S ridge of Ama Dablam.

Post-Monsoon   A total of 55 expeditions had permission to climb during the autumn season from 1 September to 15 November. Of these, 17 were successful, although some were marred by tragedy. The weather throughout most of the season was fine and settled, the exception being a severe storm on 19–20 October which caught many teams about to make summit bids, destroying camps and sweeping away fixed ropes. Many teams abandoned their attempts in the face of the havoc and the dangerous snow conditions which ensued, despite the fact that thereafter the weather was near perfect. Continuous high winds also played a role in the failures on many 8000m peaks.

For the second year running, Everest was not climbed from Nepal (but see *Winter 1987/88*, below). A 26-member international team employing 20 Sherpas failed at 8400m on the S col route, reaching their high point on 2 October. Peter Hillary's four-man Austro–NZ team was blasted off the 1981 American S pillar at the end of September by winds which Hillary estimated to have reached 200mph. Kim Logan and Michael Rheinberger were both frostbitten, and the wind prevented further attempts.

A strong 16-member international team to Lhotse's S face succeeded in putting two members on the summit ridge, but, as in the case of the Yugoslavs in 1981, the summit was not reached. Led by Krysztof Wielicki, the team included 10 Poles, two Brits, two Italians and two Mexicans. They followed much the same line as the Polish attempt in 1985, but tragedy struck early on the climb when an avalanche on 15 September swept Doctor Czeslaw Jakeil to his death and badly injured Walenty Fuit. The team regrouped, and by 14 October had reached 7800m. Then came the big storm and avalanches seriously threatened Base Camp. Improved conditions at the end of October allowed Wielicki and Artur Hajzer to complete the difficulties above 8000m, and the summit ridge was reached on 29 October, 200m from the top. Strong winds stopped further progress. This was the eighth expedition to this massive face, and it came nearest to success.

On Lhotse Shar, four well-known Spanish climbers died in an attempt on the SE ridge on 27 September. Toni Sors, Sergio Escalera, Francesc Porras and Antonio Quinones were moving up to establish Camp 5 at 7850m when they were caught in a slab avalanche. An Anglo–American team also failed on the route. Two attempts on the S spur of Nuptse, the route first attempted and given high praise by Jeff Lowe, also failed. The Italian pair of Enrico Rosso and Fabrizio Manoni managed to reach 6700m.

There was a good deal of activity on nearby Pumori. A 10-strong Japanese team fixed the entire SW ridge, assuring success for eight Japanese and one Nepali on three successive days, 12–14 October. Permission for the route belonged, however, to a four-man German–Italian team who reported that the Japanese had already occupied the ridge when they arrived and, although they left most of their 3000m of fixed ropes, small sections had been cut. All four reached the summit. On the E face, a French party guided by Marc Batard found the going too hard, so Batard proceeded without clients but with three Sherpas, completing the ascent on 25 October.

A number of successful and impressive ascents were made in the Kangchenjunga region. Two Australians, Michael Groom and John Coulton, made a semi-alpine-style ascent of the SW face, without oxygen or the aid of Sherpas. From a high camp at 7900m, they completed the first Australian ascent of the mountain of 10 October, but, when they were descending in twilight, their vision became blurred and their minds disorientated. Groom fell into a crevasse, but what might have been a disaster proved a godsend, since Groom was unhurt and they now had shelter for the night. Although badly frostbitten in both hands and feet after their bivi at 8000m, they completed their descent next day. Two other Australians, James van Gelder and Terry Tremble, were meanwhile attempting a lightweight repeat of the British route on the NW face. They had reached 7500m when the big storm struck and, on returning to their Camp 2, they discovered that much of their equipment had been lost or destroyed by avalanches, so further attempts were impossible. An American attempt on the S face of Yalung Kang was forced to retreat from 8100m. Jim Farkas fell about 300m and, although he was not badly hurt, he and his Nepali partner Narayan Shrestha decided to descend. Farkas was frostbitten by the time they reached Base Camp, where the shortage of supplies brought a halt to further attempts.

There was success and disaster for a six-man Dutch team who repeated the Japanese N face route on Jannu. Base Camp was established on 17 September, and by 3 October the team had reached Camp 2 at 6100m above the difficult 'Wall of Shadows'. A week later leader Gerard van Sprang and Edmond Ofner set off for the top, but at the second bivouac, at 7250m, van Sprang discovered that both his feet were frostbitten, so he waited while Ofner continued alone to the summit on 11 October. As they descended, Ger Friele and Rudolf de Koning passed them on the way up and reached the summit on 13 October. The next day the second pair were seen descending the 'Wall of Shadows', but they never arrived at Camp 1. Falling ice killed them 60m above Camp 1, where they were buried two days later. Thus this milestone in Dutch mountaineering was sadly marred by the loss of two of its members.

There were two other successful ascents of Jannu. Pierre Beghin and Erik Decamp made a fine alpine-style ascent of the N face; they followed the NZ line and reached the summit on 25 October. A variation of the 1962 French route on the S ridge was climbed by another French team. Michel Vincent and Frederic Valet reached the summit at dusk on 6 November and managed to regain their high camp safely in the dark.

Further up the range, Manaslu was climbed by an Austrian expedition via the normal NE face; two members and a Sherpa were placed on the summit on 7 October. A Japanese attempt on the E ridge of the mountain was called off when the team had reached the beginning of the difficult pinnacles at 6500m. After descending to Base Camp, one member collapsed and died after an apoplectic fit.

Two Spanish expeditions reached the summit of Annapurna I within three days of each other. On 8 October two members from a Tarragona expedition reached the top; from a high camp on the 1980 German line on the central peak they traversed new ground to join the original French route. On 11 October two members and a Sherpa from a Valencian expedition reached the summit by the same route, although severe winds resulted in varying degrees of frostbite for all three. A Japanese attempt on the S face of Annapurna II retreated from 7500m as a result of the winds and the threat of ice-fall. An American, Tim Schinhofen, with Sherpa Pemba Norbu reached the summit of Annapurna IV via the previously unclimbed rib on the N face.

Dhaulagiri I's E and S faces were both scrutinized, but the warm weather made both faces extremely dangerous. The Japanese on the unclimbed S face went home without making a serious attempt. Hiroshi Aota, the leader, suggested that the winter might be the only safe season. Americans likewise abandoned the E face, but Catherine Colhoun, John Culberson and Colin Grissom reached the summit via the normal NE ridge on 16 October. A small Spanish team was stopped at 8000m on the same route when one member was hit by falling ice.

Failures on 8000ers included American, Swiss and German expeditions to Cho Oyu, all of which stuck to their permits on the S side, and Austrian, French and Swiss expeditions to Makalu.

Success on smaller peaks included a Yugoslav ascent of Ngojumba Kang 2 by a new line on the S face, Koreans on a new route on the W face and W ridge of Longpo Gang, Poles on the SE ridge of Langshisha Ri (but only as far as the SW summit), and the first Liechtenstein success on a Nepal peak, when one climber from the little principality, supported by 13 Swiss, made an ascent of the NE ridge of Khatang. Ganesh 5 was climbed by two Japanese and two Sherpas, by the previously unclimbed S ridge. The Spanish Ski Tukuche 87 expedition managed to use skis between Camps 1 and 2, and crampons for the rest of the way, three members reaching the summit by the NW ridge on 4 October. Clients on the guided British Taweche Expedition found the going on the SE face too difficult, so Mal Duff and Andy Black attempted it alone, reaching 6350m before Duff's illness forced them to retreat.

Winter 1987/88   There were 12 expeditions in Nepal during this season, but, at the time of going to press, news of only four has been received. Everest had its first ascent from the Nepal side since October 1985 when S Korean Huh Yong-Ho and a Sherpa reached the summit from the S col on 22 December.

Dhaulagiri had two ascents early in December, both teams apparently taking advantage of the good weather that often occurs at the end of November and in early December. On 2 December, Frenchman Marc Batard and Sherpa Sundare reached the summit by the normal route. It is not known whether they started prior to the official opening of the season on 1 December, but it seems almost certain that they did. Two Yugoslavs, Iztok Tomazin and Marjan Kregar, made a fine four-day ascent of the Kurtyka-MacIntyre route on the E face. Starting on 1 December, they climbed alpine-style, apparently bivouacking three times on the way up, and returned to Base Camp on 7 December. Both expeditions were planning further attempts. It is also understood that two Japanese climbers reached the summit of Annapurna from the S side on 20 December, but both died during the descent. The full report will be given in AJ94 (1989/90).

A Polish expedition led by Wojciech Maslowski made the first winter ascent of the difficult Langtang Lirung (7234m). They followed the normal route via the SE ridge. Base Camp was established on 10 December, and on 3 January Kazimierz Kiska, Mikolaj Czyewski and Adam Potoczek reached the summit. Three camps and 2000m of fixed rope were used.

There were one or two interesting postscripts to the year in Nepal. The most important event at the beginning of the year was a review of the environmental impact of expeditions and trekking groups on sensitive high-mountain areas. The current Minister for Tourism, Mr Ramesh Nath Pandey, threatened to close the worst-affected areas unless greater care was shown by groups visiting these areas. The problems are twofold: pollution by garbage and simple overuse because of numbers. The former is the easier to tackle by visiting groups, but control of numbers will be the responsibility of Mr Pandey's Ministry. At year end it seems unlikely that a decision to close areas completely will be made in the immediate future. The smaller numbers of groups, and the greater care they took during 1987, seem to have prevented this, although there will undoubtedly be a continuous assessment of the situation, and it seems inevitable that more exclusive use of some areas, and additional expedition expense to support a clean-up programme, are not too many years away.

Expeditions to peaks in Tibet increasingly come through Nepal, and a good workable system exists between the Nepal and CMA officials. Nepalese staff, especially cooks, are also accepted by the CMA, as long as they are listed as full members on the permit.

Finally, Trekking Peaks have been renamed Alpine Peaks, a welcome change which removes the implication that all the peaks on the list could be walked up. Many provide a very considerable challenge and are an excellent low-cost and short-time alternative to the highest peaks.

Józef Nyka adds:

A 13-member Japanese expedition led by Kuniaki Yagihara attacked Annapurna (8091m) via the S face, following the 1970 British route. On 20 December 1987 the summit was reached by Noboru Yamada (his seventh 8000er), Teruo Saegusa, Yasuhira Saito and Toshiyuki Kobayashi. During the descent the last two fell at 7900 and 7300m and lost their lives.

India 1987

HARISH KAPADIA

As I climbed up the Malathuni ridge on the way to the Nanda Devi Sanctuary in 1974, a porter from Lata came within earshot and whispered, 'Don't tell anyone, but last few years "they" have been carrying things up and down Nanda Devi secretly.' This 'don't tell anyone' activity of 'they' was known to many – climbers and politicians alike – but it was an open secret for many years. In 1978, with a change of government, it was leaked from knowledgeable sources in all newspapers that there had been four Indo–American expeditions, two each to Nanda Devi and Nanda Kot in the 1960s, to put nuclear isotopes on summits of these peaks to detect any nuclear testing by China in Tibet. These peaks were in a straight line with the Tibetan plateau. The first expedition (with many famous American Everesters included) could not reach the top and left their cargo (no one knows exactly what it was) two-thirds way up, highly secured. Next year when they returned, it was missing! Despite many speculations, no one knows what exactly happened to it. Then another expedition in another year put the device atop Nanda Kot, which is relatively easier. After a year or two, when the satellite technology was fully developed, it was removed by another joint expedition. These four major expeditions were not recorded at that time and this remained a major lacuna in the record of mountaineering history. In 1978 the Indian government announced that our Ganga was polluted by Americans – the missing device was supposed to have fallen in Rishi Ganga!

All these oropolitics were brought alive once again this year with the Indo–Japanese expedition which climbed Nanda Kot on 6 October 1987. Three Japanese and four Sherpas reached the summit, while an inexperienced Indian team sat around Base Camp. This peak was officially climbed by the Japanese in 1936 and the Indians in 1959. This year the route was the same. The year had also begun with a flourish. An Indian and British army joint team battled with Saser Kangri I (7672m) by the unclimbed W ridge, and 10 Indians summitted on 25 June. Earlier, first ascent of Saser Kangri IV (7410m), also known as 'Cloud Peak', was achieved by four Indian and British soldiers on 6 and 7 June. In the east, another army expedition achieved ascents of Kabru Dome (6600m), Forked Peak (6108m) and Rathong (6679m). In this religiously sensitive area they had a permit to climb Rathong only, but the other two peaks were climbed as a 'recce' on the way to it. Ultimately they crossed Rathong La to Yalung glacier (and in Nepal) and climbed it by the route of the first ascent of 1964.

At the same time, the army was in the news nearby – on the E face of Kangchenjunga. This dream route of Paul Bauer's was first climbed by the army in 1977. Now another 62-member team (claimed as a record!) assaulted it under Major-General P L Kukrety. On 25 May, Phu Dorje (of Everest, Saser Kangri II and many other peaks fame) and two others were reported missing.

The second team of four reached the summit on 31 May and found their flags 8m below the summit; it was concluded that they had reached the summit and were perhaps blown off on return (one has to remain a little below this holy summit).

One member of the second team slipped soon thereafter and fell to his death. News in press and other interviews were the only thing available, as in its usual style the army blocked out all the details whenever there was trouble. This did not stop the leader from claiming another record: to have reached 21,000ft – the highest any General has ever climbed! Any researchers willing to work on this? This team, as preparation for Kangchenjunga, had climbed 'virgin' Chomo Yummo (6829m) in the area, in September 1986. This peak had been climbed by Dr A M Kellas in 1910 and T H Tilly in 1945, but pointing this out made no difference to their boasts. A 38-member team of Indo–Tibet Border Police climbed Chaukhamba (7138m) near Badrinath-Gangotri watershed. This difficult peak thwarted their first attempt on 29 May, when two members fell in a crevasse 100m below summit. Ultimately six members and two Bhotia dogs (sic) reached the summit. Five summiteers ski'd down from the summit to Bhagirath Kharak glacier and Base Camp (4724m), covering 11km in 12 minutes. The other summiteer and the dogs took three days to reach Base Camp! A little to the south, Yugoslavs (led by Vlado Vidmar) achieved a very difficult ascent of W face of Trisul I (7120m). Many teams had been defeated by this in past years. Two summiteers made a para-jump, while others climbed down to Trisul II (6690m) and Trisul III (c6100m) to the south by the connecting ridge. Trisul II and III were first climbed by the Yugoslavs in 1960 under Ales Kunaver. On this expedition Kunaver's daughter, Ms Vlasta Kunaver, climbed Trisul I and was one of the para-jumpers.

Two joint expeditions were also operating in Garhwal/Kumaon. The Indo–British team attempted Changuch (6322m) above Kafni glacier in September. They failed on this, but three first ascents were achieved nearby: Nandakhani (6029m), Nadabhanar (6236m) and Laspa Dhura (5913m). This was a really worthwhile effort on this difficult glacier. An Indo–French team on Sri Kailas (6932m) in Gangotri ran into difficulties. The French group withdrew from Camp 1 on 30 July (plane bookings, or different planes of thinking?), and two Indians climbed the peak on 8 August.

Amongst other noteworthy climbs in this area were: second ascent of Swagarohini II (6247m), attempt on Purbi Dunagiri (6489m) on the rim of the Nanda Devi Sanctuary, attempt on Nandakhat (6611m) by Indians, ascent of Bamba Dhura (6334m), attempts on unknown Kuchela (6294m), and Durpata (6468m). A British team climbed P6721m on the Gangotri glacier, while many battled with Shivling, Vasuki Parbat and Thalay Sagar, Bharte Khunta, Kharcha Kund (see note at end) and Satopanth. Gangotri area was the most popular with foreign teams, while Indians were mostly on Kamet and Abi Gamin. Ryszard Kolakowski and his Polish team made an excellent new route via the 1800m W pillar on Brigupanth (6772m) on 17–20 September. Difficulties were encountered on rock up to UIAA VI, A1 and ice up to 45. It was descended by normal route, S face and climbed again by the S face. Two climbers of the same team climbed 800m high E face of nearby Thalay Sagar

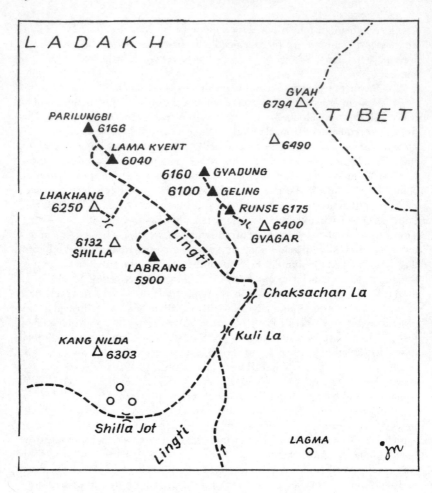

▲ *peaks climbed in 1987*
O "   "   *in 1983*

(6904m) but did not proceed to the summit, 150m higher, over an ice-face. This was the best climbing team in terms of new achievements.

Very early in the season a professionally organized trek of 90 young students (ages from 8 years) ran into difficulties in the Bhilangana valley. In a spate of bad weather two students were reported missing and ultimately declared dead when helicopter and army search failed to locate them. This incident aroused strong discussions and thoughts about adventure for the young in India. Without proper, methodical and legal outward-bound traditions like those in Britain, nothing could be done. Such deaths should cause a better system to be evolved.

In the W Himalaya many teams were active. Phabrang (6172m) is a shapely and difficult peak, particularly by its S face. It was climbed by a British team from the east; after traversing the summit they descended by the SW face. A team from Bombay reversed this route – a notable achievement. Nearby, in Lahul, army engineers climbed Shigri Parbat (6526m). Two officers made the second ascent of the peak on 2 June, little aware that on the same day two other officers fell into the turbulent Chandra river in a freak accident and were drowned. Kulti valley, which is very easy of access, was visited by three teams: Japanese climbed Akela Killa (6003m), while Indians climbed Jori (5790m) and Sara Pahar (5620m). For anyone with a shortage of time and serious climbing ambitions this valley will offer a lot.

For a large area like Spiti, there was plenty of exploration and climbing left. In fact the large 60km-long Lingti valley remained unvisited. A team from Bombay returned this year to explore this valley fully. Penetrating over high passes, unknown terrain and making difficult river crossings, it reached the head of the valley. A high pass, Yangzi Diwan (5890m) led them across to Ladakh where Parilungbi (6166m) was climbed. Their attempt on the N and E ridges of the legendary peak Shilla (6132m) failed, but they climbed Runse (6175m) and three other peaks. One of their major achievements was to locate and photograph Gya (6794m) and the approaches to it. It is the highest peak in Himachal: an imposing rock-monolith which defies imagination and strength. This three-member team returned by another high route to complete their inquiry.

Jorkanden (6473m), the highest peak of Kinnar Kailash range in Kinnaur, was also reported climbed by a team of local police, but no further details are available. Chau Chau Kang Nilda (6303m), CB 54 (6096m) were other Indian climbs, while Japanese climbed KR IV (6340m), British RAF climbed Hanuman Tibba (5928m) and many teams were busy on Nun Kun and Pinnacle peaks in Ladakh.

During the year, Dr Salim Ali passed away at the age of 94. He was a leading ornithologist and Honorary Member of the Himalayan Club and the Bombay Natural History Society. In fact, almost until the last decade he travelled extensively in inaccessible areas of the Himalaya in search of Himalayan birds. He was instrumental in locating the rare black-neck cranes around Pangong lake in Ladakh, one of his many firsts. He wrote many books on Himalayan birds.

Józef Nyka adds:

In September a British team composed of Robin Beadle, Bobby Gilbert, Rob Tresidder and Pete Scott completed the first ascent of the N ridge of Kharcha Kund (6612m). The 5½-day route goes via a series of pinnacles and towers, giving climbing of UIAA VI, A1 on rock and on ice up to Scottish 5. (See article on pp 35–40 of this volume.)

A Japanese party led by Yoshiki Yamanaka climbed the E face of Bhagirathi II (6512m). The summit was reached on 16 October.

An important decision was taken by the Indian authorities: they called into life for the Gangotri area the first Indian voluntary mountain-rescue service. Three members of this 'Himalayan Evacuation and Life-Saving Project' (HELP) were trained in rescue techniques in Europe. During summer 1988, a light-weight mountain-rescue refuge (12 6m) will be constructed on Tapovan (4400m). The programme will be sponsored by the Inlaks Foundation of London.

Karakoram 1987

PAUL NUNN

Poor weather afflicted the area between May and early August. Subsequently there was some good weather, but it seems that only a few parties were in the field to take advantage of it. Thick snow lay to quite low altitudes until well into July.

Early success was achieved by a Swiss party on Broad Peak (8087m). Norbert Joos reached the top on 29 May and Ernst Muller and Bruno Honegger on 7 June. Their approach march had been made in particularly snowy conditions from Urdukas. A number of other parties were less fortunate. Yugoslavs, who reached 7500m, Mexicans, two French parties led by Louis Adoubert, the climbing Abbé, and by Pierre Mazeaud failed, as did Norwegians led by Hans Christian Doseth's sister Ragnild Amardsen and a British party involving Richard Falley, Norman Croucher, John Watt and leader Mark Hallum. On 29 August Josep Estruch and Luis Vandellós reached the fore-summit (8030m) when their six-member Catalan party decided that the snow was too dangerous to continue on the ascent of the main top.

Even in the better weather of mid-August, K2 defeated all comers. A note from Doug Scott on the British–American expedition to K2's E side appears at the end of this section. A French party led by Martine Rolland, the first woman guide in Chamonix, withdrew after her hand was smashed by a falling stone on the Abruzzi, and a Japanese group withdrew from 6900m on the same route. A bold line on the W face attracted Voytek Kurtyka and Jean Troillet. They waited 45 days for suitable weather and eventually made their attempt in early August. Bad weather on 9 August forced them down. Earlier, Erhard Loretan, Troillet's companion on the fast alpine-style ascent of the Hornbein Couloir of Everest in 1986, had been prevented from joining this venture by a winter accident. Subsequently two parties remained. A Japanese–Pakistani expedition tried the Abruzzi in mid-August, reaching the Shoulder, and a group of Basques climbed the SSE spur to the same point. A total of eight climbers then reached 'The Bottleneck' at 8300m before worsening weather forced them down. Sadly, Akira Suzuki fell to his death during the retreat.

In the Gasherbrums, the same poor weather and hostilities with the Indians proved hazardous. A New Zealand party was unable to climb on Baltoro Kangri because of the Indian military threat. Four Pakistani army climbers died in an avalanche on Gasherbrum 1 and their attempt, with those (seemingly) by Japanese and New Zealand parties, failed on the same mountain, as did that by a Spanish party.

On Gasherbrum 2 there was more success. On 25 June three Americans, Phil Powers, Michael Collins and Malachy Miller, reached the top, followed on the same day by Jean-Pierre Hefti, a Swiss member of the British–New Zealand expedition, and by Germans Sigi and Gabi Hupfauer. Hefti lost his life attempting a ski descent from 7500m, slipping on ice during the diagonal section on the route to the S face ski-descended by Michel Metzger and Thierry Renard in 1985. On 9 July Guy Halliburton, Iain Peter and Donald Stewart reached the top. Peter then ski'd from 7500m to 7000m that day and completed the descent on skis next day to 6000m on the S Gasherbrum Glacier. In the same period Michel Dacher (54) reached the top, apparently with Ulrich Schmidt. It was the German guide's tenth 8000m peak, all without oxygen.

In the August improvement New Zealanders Carol McDermott and Lydia Bradley, after abandoning attempts on Gasherbrum 1, made a successful ascent of Gasherbrum 2 with Basques Juan Oyarzabel and Aixo Apellaniz. This is the first ascent of an 8000m peak by New Zealand women. Another success involved Eugene Berger of Luxembourg and Italians Sergio Martini, Fausto de Stefani and Mauricia Giordana. In a first attempt Berger's companion Pascale Noël (Belgian) withdrew on 30 July from 6600m. The second alpine-style push began on 5 August and succeeded on the 8th. Berger narrowly failed on Nanga Parbat (by 30m) in 1986, and Martini and de Stefani have now climbed five 8000m peaks.

Fortunes were similarly mixed elsewhere in the 8000m league. The Italian Quota 8000 Expedition succeeded on the Kinshofer route on the Diamir face of Nanga Parbaf. Tullio Vidoni and Soro Dorotei reached the top in three days' alpine-style on 5 July. Benoit Chamoux then soloed the route in 23 hours, as he had done on K2 and Broad Peak in 1986. A Spanish expedition also succeeded. Pedro Exposito, Domingo Hernandez, Juan Martinez and Fernando Alvarez reached the top. A Japanese expedition succeeded in mid-August. Their countrymen were less favoured on Rakaposhi. Munchiko Yamamoto led a party of three via the N flank to the N peak (7010m), but bad weather prevented them from continuing towards the main summit.

In general, British parties were more numerous in the fields of exploration of smaller peaks and new routes, as were some other parties operating under trekking regulations. In the 7000m category was the magnificent ascent of the NW pillar of Spantik. This 'Golden Pillar' has attracted travellers crossing the Barpu Glacier above Nagar for years. The expedition comprised Liz Allen, Phil Butler, Bruce Craig (NZ), Dr John English, Mick Fowler and Victor Saunders. After initial build-up and acclimatization the latter pair climbed the route, which was over 2000m long and very steep throughout the upper reaches. The top was attained during a nine-day push on 11 August, from whence they came back via a snow-ice spur two kilometres to the west of the route of ascent. Their success is the more impressive for its completion within a six-week leave from the UK – a second winner in succession for the Nick Estcourt Award.

In the same Hunza–Nagar region other parties were active. John Sylvester and Mark Charlton tried the steep face of the granite spire of Biblimotin. This is an 1100m rock wall on a spire of around 5700m. The summit has been climbed by a line of least resistance, but the face remains a major challenge, defeating this party as it has done British explorations in 1986. Further to the north Richard Haszko's group succeeded on the fine snow peak of Tupopdam (6061m). John Stevenson and Andy Cave reached the top in early July. The Shimshal Valley also saw traffic. The Plymouth Polytechnic Group reached the Kurdopin Glacier and climbed a 5000m-plus peak on the right bank. In the Yazghil Glacier area Clair and Peter Foster climbed Yazghil Sar North (5820m), and Jack Brindle, Earnie McGlashan and John O'Reilly climbed Yazghil Sar South (5920m).

The Thames Valley MC expedition to the Koro Valley was in similar vein. Setting up Base Camp in June they waited long for good weather. At last Dai Bowman, Martin Hignell and Dave Wright repeated Cavalry Peak and made the first ascent of Mongouo (c5900m) via the S ridge.

Further east, Stephen Venables, Duncan Tunstall and Phil Bartlett trekked up the Biafo Glacier in mid-July, and Venables and Tunstall climbed P5979's S peak between 23 and 25 July. Venables returned later and climbed the Central Peak on 24 August. This peak is on the Biafo–Solu watershed. In late July a crossing was made from there to Shimshal.

In the same period the Cambridge–St Andrews Expedition climbed west of Hobluk. They climbed Ghur, Hobluk and the Goblin, and did work on the sexing of the ablation valley willows. As so often, changeable weather favoured the flexible and lightweight, and disadvantaged those tied to higher and more technical objectives.

This was well illustrated in the Latok range, where the bigger peaks exceed 7000m. Ted Howard led a powerful siege of the unclimbed NW ridge of Latok 1. At 7145m this is the highest Latok, and second only to The Ogre (Baintha Brakk) within the group. It has been climbed once from the south via a long and difficult route from the Baintha Lukpar Glacier. On that Italian ascent in August 1977 there was a large number of climbers and much fixed rope was used, as was the case on the Ogre. The NW ridge has now been attempted in 1976 (Japanese), 1977 (UK), 1978 (UK), 1985 (Japanese), and again in 1987.

The party consisted of Ted Howard, Bill Barker, Mo Anthoine, Joe Brown, Dr John Hancock, Paul de Mengel, Brian Mullan, Paul Nunn and Captain Farooq Azan. The advance party in late May was much hampered by heavy snow, and the traditional Base Camp site was never occupied for that reason. Advanced Base was set up below the great col and the slope to the Latok Col was fixed, with a camp set up at 6000m in early July. Despite poor weather all the British members except Dr Hancock, who had to return early, climbed on the ridge above 6000m to a camp set up below rock barriers around 6600m, and steep technical sections were fixed to allow continued efforts in poor weather and dangerous snow conditions. With Brown, Anthoine and de Mengel in the top camp, and Barker, Nunn, Mullan and Howard supplying it, all boded well for the attempt on the technically hard upper section of the ridge which no party has yet broached. This came to nought when the heavy snowfall of 10–15 July caused an avalanche which swept away the fixed ropes above Camp 3, and made all the lower sections very hazardous. Without a very long sojourn at Base Camp to allow conditions to settle, success remained remote and the expedition was abandoned. Interestingly, a two-man Swiss party likewise trying technically hard climbs on the Ogre's Thumb and elsewhere made little progress. A French attempt on the N ridge of Latok 2 from the Choktoi appears to have fared no better.

The lesson appears to be that technical climbs, on higher peaks especially but also on lower rock spires, are unlikely to succeed in bad weather. Success is most assured where high mobility can be achieved, a decreasing likelihood when the climbing is genuinely hard.

Elsewhere in the technical vein, Michel Piola, Stephane Schaffter, Michel Facquet and Patrick Delale completed an impressive new route on the Trango Tower. Over 1100m long, it was graded 6c (French) and A4, and Facquet made a Parapent descent from summit to Base Camp.

More British 'trekking' groups were active in the Hushe Valley. Simon Yates's group did some good routes in the August good weather, and, though Pat Littlejohn and Steve Jones missed that, they climbed Crested Peak and Raven's Pyramid, virgin mountains on the Buesten Glacier, a tributary of the South Chogolisa Glacier. The Pyramid had 23 pitches of fine granite climbing, with some of 5c (UK, about French 6c), and none easier than 4b (French 5b).

It is evident that Karakoram climbing has hived off into several quite distinct schools. The most conformist activity is the repetition of well-known 'ordinary routes' on the great peaks, in most cases within the Messner 'League Table' of 8000ers. Linked to that is speed ascent, where athletic achievement substitutes for other forms of novelty.

Apart from that, there continues the search for novelty in the form of new routes on peaks already climbed, especially high ones, and exploration involving first ascents of smaller mountains, or the climbing of technical, difficult routes on them. This is reviving – and a very good thing too!

Please note that this account was compiled without the usual 'official' information from Tourism Division of the Government of Pakistan, as that had not arrived by late December. Thanks are therefore due to *Mountain Magazine* and its correspondents, and in particular to John Porter.

Expedition plans for 1988 indicate a continuing interest in Britain in both the largest peaks and a large number of innovatory 'new-routing' ventures.

H Adams Carter adds:

An (American) expedition including Phil Peabody made a new route on Lupkilla Brakk and the first ascent of Uzum Brakk. [For the British attempt on Uzum Brakk (Conway's Ogre), see *AJ86*, 191–197, 1981.]

Doug Scott adds:

On 16 June, Tim McCartney-Snape (Australia), Greg Child (Australia), Steve Swenson (USA), Phil Ershler (USA), Michael Scott and myself (from Britain) arrived in Islamabad to begin the journey north, to the E side of K2. The American lads brought with them Carolyn Gunn, who was to be our head cook with Rassoul and Fidor, two Balti expedition men from the Hushe Valley.

We were accompanied by a support trek of 10 trekkers organized by Karakoram Experience who would be contributing towards the finances of the expedition as would a film unit, also walking in with us to Base Camp. They were using our permit to K2 to film this part of the Karakoram mountain range for a Hollywood production of a film entitled 'K2'. By regulation we had to have two liaison officers, one the excellent Captain Asim Nafumi, and for the film team the first woman liaison officer to be fielded in Pakistan, Shad Meena, who added to our enjoyment of the walk-in.

On 20 June we set off walking from Dassu. 11 days later we arrived at Base Camp (5000m). On 1 and 2 July some of our trekking friends went with us along the upper Godwin Austen glacier, through the ice-fall past the Abruzzi Spur route, to 5500m, and then returned to Base Camp with the film crew. Shad Meena accompanied them.

On 4 July Mike and Stephen ski'd up to a point opposite the E face of K2 and established our Advanced Base Camp. During the following days we all ferried loads up to this camp in between snow-storms. The E face did not look inviting with all the avalanches streaming down it, and huge slabs of snow poised to break off above the prominent buttress we hoped to climb. Still, it was early days and we hoped that the winds and the hot sun between storms would improve the situation whilst we acclimatized.

On 8 July we ski'd up to Windy Gap and back to Advanced Base Camp. On 9 July we climbed some 900m up the side of Peak 6812. It was not possible to climb again until 17 July, because of deep falls of snow. On the 17th and 18th we went up on to Skiang Kangri and then decided that the E face of K2 would remain too dangerous for us to climb this year, so we retired to Base Camp, taking down in one carry all the gear, food and fuel we had brought up to our Advanced Base Camp.

We acclimatized some more on Broad Peak as far as we could go in the deep snow (to c7000m). The snow continued falling off and on until the end of the month, at which point Tim, Michael and myself walked out, arriving in Islamabad on 7 August. Steve, Phil and Greg stayed on for three more weeks attempting the Polish South Pillar Route, reaching 7000m, then the South Pillar route which Jean Afanassieff, Roger Baxter-Jones, Andy Parkin and I had climbed to the Shoulder in 1983. They eventually abandoned that route at 7000m and the mountain towards the end of August, because of more snow-storms and high winds above.

The Eight-Thousanders

JÓSEF NYKA AND ZBIGNIEW KOWALEWSKI

Olympic Medals for Mountaineering?

Reinhold Messner and Jerzy Kukuczka were honoured by the International Olympic Committee in Calgary. The first men to climb all 14 8000m peaks received the Silver Medal of the Olympic Order. This is not the first time the medal has been awarded for mountaineering achievements. In Paris 1924, Charles G Bruce was awarded the Gold Medal, in Los Angeles 1932 the Schmid brothers were awarded Gold Medals, and in 1936 Oskar and Hettie Dyhrenfurth were also awarded Gold Medals.

Jerzy Kukuczka's 8000m Peaks

1.	Lhotse	8516m	04.10.1979	Normal Route
2.	Everest	8848m	19.05.1980	New Route, N Pillar
3.	Makalu	8463m	15.10.1981	Solo, New Route, NW Ridge
4.	Broad Peak	8047m	30.07.1982	Normal Route
			17.07.1984	New Route, Traverse of the Massif
5.	Gasherbrum 2	8035m	01.07.1983	New Route, NE Flank
6.	Gasherbrum 1	8068m	23.07.1983	New Route, NW Wall
7.	Dhaulagiri	8167m	21.01.1985	1st Winter Ascent
8.	Cho Oyu	8201m	15.02.1985	2nd Winter Ascent, SW Pillar
9.	Nanga Parbat	8125m	13.07.1983	New Route, W Pillar
10.	Kangchenjunga	8586m	11.01.1986	1st Winter Ascent
11.	K2	8611m	08.07.1986	S Face
12.	Manaslu	8163m	10.11.1986	New Route, NE Wall
13.	Annapurna	8091m	03.02.1987	1st Winter Ascent
14.	Xixabangma	8027m	18.09.1987	New Route, W Ridge

List of climbers with five or more 8000m peaks. (Main summits only.)

Collated by Zbigniew Kowalewski, 1 January 1988.

1.	Reinhold Messner	Italy	14	1970–1986
2.	Jerzy Kukuczka	Poland	14	1979–1987
3.	Marcel Rüedi (d Makalu, 25.09.1986)	Switzerland	10	1980–1986
4.	Erhard Loretan	Switzerland	9	1982–1986

5.	Michael Dacher	Germany	9	1977–1987
6.	Hans Kammerlander	Austria	7	1983–1986
7.	Noburo Yamada	Japan	7	1978–1987
8.	Takashi Ozaki	Japan	6	1977–1986
9.	Kurt Diemberger	Austria	6	1957–1986
10.	Siegfried Hupfauer	Germany	6	1973–1987
11.	Norbert Joos	Switzerland	5	1982–1987
12.	Hans von Kanel	Switzerland	5	1977–1981
13.	Robert Schauer	Austria	5	1975–1984
14.	Krysztof Wielicki	Poland	5	1980–1986
15.	Fredi Graf	Switzerland	5	1980–1987
16.	Peter Worgotter	Austria	5	1977–1987
17.	Benoît Chamoux	France	5	1985–1987
18.	Tullio Vidoni	Italy	5	1984–1987
19.	Giovanni Calcagno	Italy	5	1984–1987
20.	Sergio Martiny	Italy	5	1983–1987
21.	Fausto De Stefani	Italy	5	1983–1987

Pamir 1987

JÓZEF NYKA

The Soviet International Climbing Camps in the Pamir, which have been running since 1974, are an excellent school of high-altitude climbing for people from different countries. The main camp is on the Achik Tash meadow and has two sub-camps on the Moskwin and Fortambek glaciers. The popularity of the camps is increasing: in the last season more than 450 mountaineers from 18 countries (including Australia and New Zealand) participated, most of them from Bulgaria (116). Americans climbed in four or five different groups. Unfortunately, they met with very bad weather: low temperature, winds, only few days without rain or snowfall.

During the rare spells of better weather ascents of all three 7000ers were completed: Pik Lenina (7134m), Pik Korzhenevskoy (7105m) and Pik Kommunizma (7483m). Pavel Bogdanov, 17 years old, became the youngest boy to climb a Soviet 7000er. Several female ascents were also made. A Bulgarian party climbed a virgin 5000er (5684m), north-east from Pik Korzhenevskoy, and gave it the name of their national hero, Vasil Levsky. A French team ski'd down from Pik Lenina via the Lipkin Cliffs. A Czechoslovak completed an acrobatic ski descent of Pik Kommunizma. Aside from the international camps, numerous Soviet teams climbed in the Pamir. A very strong party, including three women, trained for the 1989 Kangchenjunga traverse. Unhappily, because of severe conditions, there were numerous accidents. Todor Batkov from Bulgaria writes, 'only during our stay there were 13 deaths in the area'. The greatest tragedies occurred on Pik Kommunizma, where five Soviet climbers were killed in an avalanche, and on Pik Klary Zetkin, where four Soviet mountaineers died in the same way, among them the member of the 1982 Everest expedition, Vladimir Moskalcov.

Other international climbing camps are running in the Caucasus, the Altai (at the foot of Bielukha), and near Alma Ata. During 1987 (winter and summer) more than 1000 foreign mountaineers participated. The 'Sovalptur' which is organizing the camps is considering the possibility of starting a new centre, in the Tien Shan at the foot of Khan Tengri (6995m) and Pik Pobedy (7439m).

New Zealand 1987

BILL KING

Highlights of 1987 include the continued activity by solo climbers, new winter ascents, a successful international climbing meeting, the continued widespread interest in rock climbing, and New Zealand mountaineering successes overseas.

Throughout the summer season the weather thwarted many plans. However, John Fantini continued his innovative and fast solo ascents of Mt Cook, completing 10 ascents in one season, including one new route and the first solo of 'White Dreams' on the S face. Fantini now has the most recorded ascents of Mt Cook, numbering 22.

Other important ascents included Carol McDermott's solo ascent of the Caroline face of Mt Cook in 7½ hours; Steve Elder's first ascent of the N face of Mt Sefton; Nick Cradock's second solo ascent of the Balfour face of Mt Tasman, and an ascent of the Caroline face of Mt Cook by Maryann Waters and Mike Roberts. This was the first ascent of this notorious face by a woman since it was first climbed nearly 20 years ago.

In late summer (March) New Zealand held its first international climbing meeting which was attended by over 70 people from 12 different countries. Europe was well represented with teams from France, Britain, Germany, Russia and Spain. Although the weather was bad for most of the 14-day period, over 30 climbers managed ascents of Mt Cook by a variety of different routes.

There was the normal amount of climbing carried out elsewhere in the Southern Alps, but no exceptional routes were claimed. In the Darrens region Murray Judge and friends have managed to climb some very impressive free routes on the Fiordland granite.

Although winter climbing is still very much for the minority, some good ascents were recorded. Bill McLeod continued to show his experience and very careful planning with the first winter solo of the Balfour face of Mt Tasman, and the Yankee/Kiwi couloir of Mt Hicks. This last route is an 800m grade 6 ribbon of vertical ice and rock, graded harder than the Balfour face. Joined by Steve Elder he also completed the first winter ascent of Logan's Run on the S face of Mt Hicks. Steve comments, 'the climb was superb, steep and sustained. 11 pitches in total. The top ice-fields were climbed unroped by torchlight. I received mild frostbite in both big toes on the descent, with a windchill temperature down to −30°C.'

New Zealand rock-climbing standards continue to improve. Many of the top climbers have now been around for some time, and most have considerable overseas experience gained from such places as Arapiles in Australia, Yosemite, and the Verdon Gorge in France. The influx of visiting top overseas climbers including Kim Carrigan helps to push local standards continually higher.

The increased standard of climbing in New Zealand has also helped to contribute to the success of New Zealand mountaineers overseas. In the

Himalaya, New Zealand mountaineers made two ascents of 8000m mountains. These were important ascents because, although NZ mountaineers had previously climbed 8000m mountains, they were always part of an overseas-organized expedition. The ascents of Xixabangma and Gasherbrum 2 were made solely by NZ-organized expeditions.

Further afield, in Patagonia, Nick Cradock and Russell Braddock made very impressive ascents, within a few days of each other, of both Cerro Torre and Fitzroy. Elsewhere, NZ mountaineers enjoyed successes in Peru, Bolivia, USSR (Pamir), India (Gangotri) and in Africa (Ruwenzori).

Mount Everest Foundation Notes 1986–87

EDWARD PECK

The following notes summarize reports from expeditions which have received the approval of the Mount Everest Foundation, and this is in most cases accompanied by a grant. MEF approval is generally an essential first step to seeking assistance, financial or otherwise, from other organizations. It should be noted that the MEF only 'sponsors' expeditions in exceptional circumstances, e.g. the 1981 Mount Kongur Expedition.

Copies of the full reports of these expeditions are lodged, when available, with the Alpine Club Library and the Archives Section of the Royal Geographical Society, and may be consulted in these places. Some expeditions will already have been described in the *Alpine Journal* and other mountaineering periodicals.

The expeditions summarized in the following notes, with one exception, took place between April 1986 and August 1987. These notes are based on reports received up to 1 December 1987.

North America, including Arctic

84/29 *Cambridge British Columbia Expedition* (June–August 1984)

This two-man two-woman team of geologists studied the internal hydrology of the SW Bridge Glacier, and the relative dating of the late Quaternary glacial deposits in the vicinity (Lillooet area, near Vancouver). The climbing team made first ascents of Bridge Peak and another unnamed peak, also Stanley Peak and Mt Fugora, using skis over the Lillooet Ice Cap.

86/7 *Sunderland East Greenland Expedition* (July–September 1986)

After a four-day storm in the first week out, this four-man team abandoned their objective of the SW face of Laupersbjerg in favour of Rodbjerg, an attractive red-rock peak, on 16th September Glacier. Two attempts by different routes failed to reach the summit.

86/14 *British Universities East Greenland Expedition* (July–September 1986)

After making first British ascent of Mt Forel by the S ridge (used by Roche in 1938), this four-man team continued into the largely unexplored country of Schweizerland by the Franche Comté Glacier. On their return to the coast a lichenometry study in the Tasilaq Valley was carried out.

87/7 Greenland 'Two Summits' Expedition (July–August 1987)

All four members made the third ascent of Greenland's highest mountain, Gunnbjornsfjeld, from the previously unvisited N side of the Watkins Mountains. In the course of the 180-mile trek, stores from the 1935 expedition were found in good order.

87/35 British Tasilaq East Greenland Expedition (June–August 1987)

Skiing out for two weeks from the head of Tasilaq Fjord, three members of this party attempted the NE face of Laupersbjerg, but the climb was abandoned when two climbers were swept down the face by an avalanche (only minor injuries), a short distance below the summit. Some geological work (lithological and structural data) was carried out S of the mouth of Tasilaq Fjord and some glaciology 30km N on Ningerte Fjord.

South America, including Andes

86/30 British West face Salcantay (6271m) Expedition (July–August 1986)

Altering their objective from the W face, this five-man team made the first ascent of the technically difficult and avalanche-risky SW ridge, reaching the lower summit (6030m) on the fourth day, descending by the E ridge in 1½ days. This objectively dangerous route is well illustrated with topos drawn soon after the climb.

86/37 Cambridge High Andes Expedition (August–September 1986)

Three glaciologists and two geologists carried out research in the areas of Cotopaxi (which was climbed), of Sangay, a highly active volcano, and in Loja Province of Ecuador. Specialist studies included 'cross-sectional studies of glacial margins' and 'transition of cryoconites to dirt-cones'. A short film was made of Sangay, on which a safer route than that taken in 1976 (when two were killed by the eruption) was reconnoitred.

86/38 'Janka Raju' 1986 (June–July 1986)

Climbing teams from this six-man group achieved first ascents of the NW face of Nevado Cayesh and of P5420 to S of Nevado Cayesh; also attempted the unclimbed E ridge of Nevado Caras II.

86/46 Anglo-Scottish Women's Andean Expedition

This party retreated at 5500m on Cololo in Bolivia. On the descent one member became very ill. Their camp was looted and one member was threatened.

86/47 *Venezuelan Lost World Forest Resources Expedition*

This team of seven British and three Venezuelans succeeded in their objective of making the ascent of an unclimbed *tepui* (a sheer-sided table-top), Padapue Tepui, also carrying out surveying, ornithological, geomorphological and zoological work in this area of SW Venezuela. A TV film was also made.

87/30 *Glasgow University Andean Expedition* (July–September 1987)

This four-man team climbed the NE ridge of Vallunaraju (5868m) and made the first traverse of the SW-NW ridges of Nevado Huandoy Este (probably first British ascent).

87/33 *Laguna Paron (Cordillera Blanca)* (July–August 1987)

This four-man team spent five weeks at 4000m, studying the bathymetry of this glacial lake, and the glaciology of the ice-filled moraine (Hatunraju) at its foot. Findings will be made available to Electroperu. Some mountaineering was attempted on the SW face of Artesanraju (6025m) and the N face of Pisco Este.

◆ Himalaya

86/5 *Lhotse Shar, South Face* (April 1986)

Mal Duff and Sandy Allan, the climbing pair of a five-man team, attempted the S face of Lhotse Shar in alpine style, reaching 7100m when Duff was hit on the head by a falling block of ice, suffering a fractured skull. They descended successfully.

86/13 *British Seligman Harris Mt Everest NE Ridge Expedition* (July–October 1986)

This large and strong team under Brummie Stokes established Advanced Base at 6400m on 18 August. Making a new approach to the NE ridge, they placed a snowhole camp below the first buttress; two weeks later ropes were fixed to 7770m and the foot of the pinnacles at 7900m was reached on 15 October. Violent winds prevented the high-level team of two from crossing the pinnacles and, after four heavy snowstorms, the expedition retreated on 19 October.

86/15 *British Bhutan Expedition* (September–November 1986)

This team of six aimed to make the first ascent of Gangkar Punsum, highest mountain in Bhutan (7550m) by the S ridge. They turned back at 6700m in view of strong winds on the heavily corniced ridge. Beyond this point there are two near-vertical rock-steps before the summit.

86/33 *Sickle Moon* (August–September 1986)

Persistent bad weather in the first half of September prevented this team from getting much beyond their Base Camp at Sattarchin at 3440m.

86/34 *Paldor – Ganesh Himal* (October–November 1986)

This team succeeded in first ascents of the W ridge of Paldor (5928m) and of the satellite peak, the Fang (5894m). One member suffered from cerebral oedema; the party was robbed on its way out.

86/40 *British Kishtwar Expedition* (August–September 1986)

This light-weight alpine-style party succeeded in their objective of the first ascent of Peak 6230m, tentatively named 'Kishtwar Weisshorn', by the SW face direct. The peak's substantive name is Dandago Purum.

86/43 *British/Indian Police Himalayan Expedition* (August–September 1986)

Parties from this team of 18 British police and, as it turned out, one Indian policeman succeeded in the first British ascents of Jogin I (6465m) and Jogin III (6342m) in the Gangotri area. Bad weather forced retreat from the N ridge of Peak 6529m.

86/49 *American-British Pumori (7145m) Expedition* (October 1986)

The two-man British team operating independently under Sandy Allan climbed the S face of Pumori by a steep ice couloir, gaining the crest of the SW ridge just below the summit. Six bivouacs (14–19 October). A new and technically difficult route, alpine-style.

87/11 *Kharcha Kund N Ridge Expedition* (August–September 1987)

Four members of the Oread Club made the first alpine-style (and first British) ascent of the N ridge of Kharcha Kund (6612m) in the Gangotri area, descending by the normal W ridge. Useful topos of the pinnacled N ridge.

87/12 *Menlungtse Norwegian-British Tibet Expedition* (February–May 1987)

Bonington and Fotheringham and their four Norwegian partners approached Menlungtse (7182m), designated in Chinese as Qiao Ge Ru, from Tingri and the north. After inspecting the N side of this magnificent mountain, they moved to the S and tackled a buttress, reaching 6100m before being forced off by abnormal weather and thunderstorms. Tracks of a 'chuti' or small yeti were seen.

87/13 *Anglo-French Garhwal Geological Expedition* (March–May 1987)

Eleven British and four French geologist/climbers visited the Bhagirathi and Shivling area of Gangotri, collecting granite samples. The climbers made three unsuccessful attempts on the NW ridge (up to 6250m) of Shivling (6543m) and one, also unsuccessful, on the NW face.

Karakoram

86/21 *British Fullers K2 Expedition 1986* (May–August 1986)

In a year when nine expeditions were given permits and 13 climbers perished on the mountain, this strong team of prominent British climbers, led by Al Rouse and John Barry, were forced by prolonged and violent storms to abandon attempts at a first British ascent of K2, first by the NW ridge, then by the Abruzzi Spur. Al Rouse made a further attempt with members of other expeditions and, after achieving his ambition of reaching the summit, tragically died, storm-bound, on the descent.

86/45 *St Mary's Hospital Expedition to Lobsang Spire* (July– September 1986)
(Second Dr Peter Thexton Expedition)

Eleven members went to the Baltoro area with the scientific objective of ascertaining, using specially designed equipment, whether small blood-vessels are affected by altitude; and with the mountaineering objective of a new route on the W ridge of Lobsang Spire. The latter was successfully accomplished in (mostly) good conditions, using some fixed ropes.

87/2 *Latok 2 Karakoram Expedition* (May–July 1987)

This strong team, after climbing to over 7000m on their objective – the W ridge of Latok 2 (7145m) – were forced to retreat after three days stormbound at the highest camp.

87/3 *Plymouth Polytechnic Kurdopin Expedition* (July–September 1987)

From a Base Camp near the snout of the Kurdopin Glacier, an unnamed peak of 5800m was climbed, believed to be a first ascent. Exploration of the Virjerab Glacier area revealed other peaks believed unclimbed.

87/6 *British/New Zealand Gasherbrum Expedition* (May–July 1987)
(Nationwide Estate Agency Karakoram 8000)

Following the Austrian 1956 route on Gasherbrum II (8035m), two members reached the summit on 28 June, but on skiing down J P Hefti skidded on ice and suffered fatal injuries from a fall. A further three members reached the summit on 9 July; one completed a ski descent for a film.

87/8 North London Mountaineering Club Spantik Expedition 1987
(July–August 1987)

Fowler and Saunders succeeded in climbing the formidable NW Pillar of
Spantik (7027m), a monolithic feature rising in a continuous sweep of 1800m,
approaching it by the Barpu Glacier from Nagar.

87/9 Markhun Karakoram Expedition (June–July 1987)

This five-man team succeeded in the first ascent of Tupopdan (6106m) in the
Karun Koh area.

87/10 Leeds Bublimotin Expedition (July–August 1987)

After establishing Base Camp at the foot of the Bublimotin Spire, this party was
forced by severe food-poisoning to abandon their attempt on the SW face.

87/15 Cambridge & St Andrews Karakoram 1987 (July 1987)

This four-man team made first ascents of Hobluk (5360m) by the NE/N ridge,
of 'The Goblin' (5670m) – their name – and Ghur (5790m) by the N face – all in
the Biafo Glacier area.

87/16 Karakoram Hushe Valley 1987 (September–October 1987)

This two-man team made successful first ascents of 'Crested Peak' (5560m)
from the Buesten Glacier (tributary of the Chogolisa Glacier) and of the SE ridge
of 'Raven's Pyramid' (5300m). This involved 1000m of technical climbing,
much of it on perfect granite.

87/19 Bublimotin 'Hopefuls' 1987 (July–August 1987)

Although failing to make much impact on the 1100m SE face of this remarkable
spire (c6000m), the Hopefuls produced a useful profile of the spire and analysed
possible routes to other peaks in the Ultar Group.

87/27 Indo-British Mt Changuch Expedition (August–September 1987)

Six Indian and four British members found their objective, Changuch,
unapproachable from the Pindar Valley and instead made the first ascent of the
N ridge of Laspa Dhura at the head of the Kafni Glacier, descending by the W
ridge.

87/28 British Expedition to Broad Peak (8047m) (May–August 1987)

This four-man team included Norman Croucher, the remarkable double-leg
amputee. The party, including Croucher, reached 6900m, but avalanche risk
and weather conditions put a stop to further progress.

Elsewhere

(Norway, East Africa, China)

86/17 Oksfjordjokulen Sheffield University Expedition (July–August 1986)

Eight graduates and four students undertook an extensive survey of the
Oksfjordjokulen ice-caps and of the 'Fall-Jokul' (detached glacier cones), in
particular their geomorphological impact. The head of the Jokul Fjord in the
Troms District of N Norway was described by Kennedy in *Peaks, Passes and
Glaciers* (1862) as 'one of the strangest glaciers in the world'.

86/41 Manchester University Expedition to Shira Plateau (June–August 1986)

This party conducted botanical fieldwork (distribution of giant groundsel –
Dendrosenecio Johnstonii – and regeneration of *Phillipia Trinera* after
burning), collected small mammals and made a census of birds on the Shira
Plateau, on the W slopes of Kilimanjaro, which was climbed by way of the (now
destroyed) Arrow Glacier Hut.

*87/5 Royal Navy/Royal Marines Mountaineering Club Joint East Africa
Expedition* (January–February 1987)

Most of this large group of 22 succeeded in climbing Nelion of Mt Kenya by the
normal route. Some teams did more difficult routes, including the Diamond
Couloir and the Ice Window. Others climbed glacier routes on Kilimanjaro. A
medical research team of three, including Dr Milledge, studied various aspects
of acute mountain sickness, including hypoxic ventilating response, capillary
fragility and fluid balance.

87/29 British Amne Machin Expedition (August–September 1987)

This party succeeded in the first ascent of Amne Machin IX (5690m), the
prominent S outlier of this range in NW Central China. A thorough exploration
of the E side of the 30km-long massif was carried out. They failed in a first
British ascent of Amne Machin I (6282m), owing to deterioration of the ice-falls
since the Japanese ascent; and in a first ascent of Amne Machin III, turning back
600m below the summit.

BOOK REVIEWS 1987

COMPILED BY GEOFFREY TEMPLEMAN

The Mystery of Mallory and Irvine
Tom Holzel and Audrey Salkeld
Jonathan Cape, 1986, pp xii + 322, £12.50

This is an unusual book where there is scope for some difference of opinion. It originates in the interest which the American Tom Holzel developed in 1970 in the question whether Mallory and Irvine in fact reached the summit of Everest before they perished in 1924. He found it amazing that Mallory's two biographers do not speculate about how he died and largely ignore the question whether his great ambition to climb the mountain had been crowned with success. He not only read up all the available literature on the subject, he corresponded with Mallory's contemporaries and, since the northern side of Everest was still out of bounds, planned and got permission for an expedition to Makalu, intending to make a clandestine foray into Tibet 'only 12 miles away' to look on his own for traces of the two climbers. Nothing came of this plan, but it shows the extent of his enthusiasm for the project. In parallel with this activity, appreciating the limitations of existing oxygen equipment he developed a new type of chemical closed-circuit set. This, however, is only briefly referred to in the book.

His interest was further excited in 1980 when the Japanese Alpine Club reported to him, in reply to his enquiries, that one of their Chinese porters, on the day before he was killed by an avalanche on the N Col, had told a member of the expedition how in 1974 the Chinese had found two bodies of Englishmen, one evidently Maurice Wilson, the other 'at 8100m on the NE ridge route', presumed to be Irvine.

Holzel's next move was the sensible one of enlisting the help of Audrey Salkeld. He also, as the Tibetan side of the mountain became legitimately accessible, renewed his plans for an expedition there to search for fresh evidence and obtained permission for this after the monsoon in 1986. Surprisingly, the present book was written before the expedition took place, and it was intended to follow it with a second, to be entitled *The Search for Mallory and Irvine*. Bad weather and heavy snowfall made the expedition abortive, and the second book is presumed to have been abandoned. There is certainly no room for another on the subject, but a film has been made this year (1987) which further examines the evidence about the events of June 1924.

The book divides, it seems to me, into two quite distinct parts. The first part, consisting of the first and penultimate chapters, is an exposition of Tom Holzel's ideas which are that, contrary to the consensus reached in the twenties and thirties (see for instance the 1924 and 1933 Everest books), the likelihood is that, with insufficient oxygen to get both climbers to the top, they separated; Irvine went down alone and fell where the axe was found in 1933, while Mallory went on alone, very possibly reaching the summit but perishing on the descent. The evidence on which he draws is that of rates of ascent achieved with oxygen on later climbs, but this part of the argument is not presented in detail. More emphasis is laid on recent knowledge, from the Chinese, Japanese and Catalan ascents of the NE ridge, of the nature of the last 300m of the mountain, including the second step itself. The Chinese climbed this with the help of a ladder and the most detailed description, by the Catalan party, records that it has one pitch of grade IV/IV sup or v diff/mild severe.

Holzel's preferred scenario is briefly as follows. It is not the first but the second step where Odell sees the two climbers. The ridge brings them to within 5m of the top of the step which they successfully climb. But it is now 1pm and their oxygen supply is running low. Realizing that they cannot both make the top they decide to separate. In the continuing fine weather Irvine should be able to manage without oxygen the descent over the slabs as far as Camp 6. Having seen Irvine down the second step on the rope Mallory transfers Irvine's partly filled bottle to his own frame and, with about three hours' oxygen supply left, starts for the top. There is still a vertical height of 230m to climb and, at the speed they achieved from Camp 6 to the second step, it is touch and go if he can make it. 'The Chinese in 1960 got down on hands and knees and crawled the final stretch to the summit. Would Mallory have done less?' Despite various objections and doubts over this reconstruction of events, it is not inconceivable.

This same penultimate chapter reports in part the vigorous rebuttal which an earlier statement of Holzel's ideas (*Mountain* 17, 30–35, 1971) drew from Sir Percy Wyn Harris (*Mountain* 21, 32–36, 1972). Both are worth reading in full in the original source. Wyn Harris castigates Holzel for two things, first the suggestion that Mallory's contemporaries (e.g. Norton and Ruttledge in their comments on the events of 1924) were motivated by jealousy, second for the contention that Mallory could possibly have so far ignored the ethos of the time as to abandon Irvine, high on the mountain, to make his own way down while he, Mallory, sets off alone for the summit 'in one great effort of self-glorification'.

The remainder of the book, by far the greater part of it, is a retelling of the Everest story from the beginning up to the 1924 expedition and its aftermath. Inevitably it covers the same ground as Unsworth's book *Everest*, published in 1981. Sometimes the story and the speculations and the disputes with the Everest committee are spun out too long. 'Because it's there' rates a whole chapter, nor are we spared the fatuous idea quoted by Unsworth that Mallory chose Irvine as his companion for aesthetic reasons. 'It would have been characteristic of Mallory with his own superb proportions to choose of two objects the more beautiful.' But, though familiar, the story is presented with a new slant, for it is told to a considerable extent through quotations from the letters and writings of Mallory and his friends. There are some fascinating contemporary comments on Mallory from people as diverse as Robert Graves, Karl Blodig, Tom Longstaff, General Bruce and A R Hinks. There is a great deal of new material here, and these middle chapters constitute a new and very worthwhile biography, well written and carefully documented, presenting an excellent picture of Mallory the mountaineer. One thing that remains unexplained is the contrast, to which Unsworth drew attention, between Mallory's central position in the mountaineering world of his time, with his interesting and distinguished circle of friends, and his undistinguished professional career. Another puzzle to me is the fact that, while most prewar Everesters with wide interests found Tibet a fascinating place, Mallory dismissed it as hateful. The whole of the book is eminently readable but this 'biographical' part seems to me by far the most valuable, a genuine addition to Everest history.

In the end one must ask oneself the question: to what extent does Holzel's vision of the events of 8 June 1924 carry conviction? One crucial factor is the nature of the second step which is now confirmed as a pitch of genuine climbing difficulty which, at 8500m and with the encumbrance of oxygen cylinders, would hardly have been quickly overcome in the short interval during which Odell had them in view. The second is, naturally, the point on which Wyn Harris seized so emphatically, i.e. the break with the traditions of the time in sending an inexperienced second down alone over treacherous ground to allow the leader to go ahead solo. (For Norton and Smythe to go on a short distance on the open ground of the N face, when each had very nearly shot his bolt, was quite another matter.) No member of my generation will easily accept this, but contemporary climbers may well see it differently. For my part I am happy to have the mystery unsolved and let Mallory and Irvine rest in peace in the fame they won.

Peter Lloyd

K2. Triumph and Tragedy
Jim Curran
Hodder & Stoughton, 1987, pp219, £12.95.

K2. Savage Mountain, Savage Summer
John Barry
Oxford Illustrated Press, 1987, pp187, £9.95

These two very different books, both written by members of the 1986 British K2 Expedition, make compulsive reading. Both are well illustrated. John Barry is in the heat of the action, involved, emotional, and partial, but thankfully retaining his very considerable Irish sense of humour. His narrative is, in general, limited to the story of the British expedition.

Jim Curran, film-maker, stood a little apart from events to record the now well-known carnage on K2 with a compassion which did not blur his sharp and experienced perception of events. He had the advantage of spending a good deal of time in the quite extraordinary tented township of Base Camps set up at the foot of the Abruzzi Ridge by an unprecedented number of expeditions from all over the world. He was therefore a witness at first hand of many of the tragic events which were to leave 13 dead on the mountain.

Jim Curran imparts a feeling of impending Greek tragedy in the way he unfolds the story of the British expedition. K2 was billed as 'The World's Hardest Mountain', which it probably is not. The members described themselves as the strongest team of climbers ever to set off on a British expedition, which they possibly were. But, with so many stars in the party, competition and summit-hunger soon surfaced. Internal dissent was exacerbated by Al Rouse's uneven leadership which Curran deals with sympathetically but honestly. We see Al Rouse, the apostle of the ultra-lightweight alpine ascent, reluctantly committed to siege tactics on the unclimbed NW ridge. He also made the elementary mistake of dividing the party into two teams, with the totally predictable result that two rival cliques were created. While being fulsome in his respect for Rouse's formidable talent and climbing record, Curran has to admit that 'I found Al intensely irritating at times . . . but he, more than anyone else on the expedition, had an awesome determination to climb K2. . .'

Their strength eroded by deep snow and foul weather, rather than by technical difficulties, the British assault petered out at about 7400m. The strong men to emerge were the powerful Burgess twins who pronounced the route unclimbable that year and opted for a quick, unauthorized dash up the Abruzzi Ridge. The expedition disintegrated, with the mercurial Rouse ditching Dave Wilkinson and opting to climb K2 with the Polish woman climber Mrufka Wolf. And this is where Curran's book really gains momentum.

From here on Curran describes the unfolding tragedy of that summer with consummate skill and sensitivity. He was present during the harrowing radio exchange when Michel Parmentier, near the end of his tether and lost in cloud at 8000m, was directed towards the fixed rope below a vital gap in some seracs. He was present when the Frenchman Benoît Chamoux returned from his incredible 23-hour ascent of K2. He went up to help with the rescue of Renato Casarotto who, on his descent from a fine but unsuccessful attempt on the SSW ridge, fell to his death in a crevasse within sight of Base Camp and his waiting wife. He was a witness of the last terrible act when the British climbers Al Rouse and Julie Tullis were to die after their successful ascents. When all hope had been given up, he saw Willi Bauer stagger into Base Camp and had the presence of mind instantly to climb to Advanced Base just in the nick of time to help down a frostbitten, exhausted Kurt Diemberger. Curran concludes with an analysis of events which seems broadly fair to me but on which everyone will have their own opinion. This book must have a strong claim to be the definitive account of the summer of 1986 on K2.

If Curran paints on a broad canvas, John Barry fills in the absorbing detail of the ill-starred British expedition. He has his strong points as a burgeoning writer which we now begin to identify. He is a master of the self-deprecatory anecdote and this is nowhere better displayed than in the opening chapters dealing with the preparations and approach march. It is his sharp eye for the quirks and incongruities of people and events which makes his writing so attractive. He may also, I fear, be gaining a reputation for misprints. At the very opening we are told that Mallory and Irvine attained a ceiling of 7535m (24,715ft) on Everest in 1924!

The bulk of Barry's book is in the form, which I never like, of diary extracts. A certain immediacy is achieved, at the expense of the story being jerkily told. As fillers-in he quotes cold, long extracts from expedition circulars, official biographical details (which Barry, with his wry wit, could surely have improved upon) and reprints from *Mountain* magazine.

We do, however, get an inside view of the day-to-day goings-on. This brings everything out into the open. It early becomes clear that John Barry and Al Rouse are oil and water. Rouse's perceived shortcomings as a leader are thoroughly catalogued. Eventually Barry is in some danger of hammering the nail out of sight. This is, I suppose, the inevitable result of publishing honest, unedited thoughts recorded in one's diary.

Clearly, the last word has not yet been written on K2. These two books, but Curran's in particular, tell the story well and bring out the rewards and the harsh penalties of every technique possible on the world's biggest mountains, from the Koreans' cautious success using siege tactics and oxygen at one extreme to *Le Sportif* dash by Benoît Chamoux on the other. One dread message is clear: don't hang around at 8000m.

Mike Banks

Living on the Edge
Cherie Bremer-Kamp
David & Charles, 1987, pp214, £12.95

In December 1985 Cherie Bremer-Kamp and Chris Chandler made an alpine-style attempt to climb Kangchenjunga, the third highest peak in the world, at 8586m. They reached a high point of 7800m when Chandler contracted oedema. He died on the descent and Bremer-Kamp had to leave him on the mountain and continue down without him. They had been accompanied by their sirdar, Mongol. *Living on the Edge* gives an account of the 1978 American Expedition to K2, the occasion where the couple first met, goes on to describe their own expedition to Yalung Kang in 1981, and ends with the harrowing story of the ill-fated winter expedition to Kangchenjunga.

The opening chapter of the book is a gripping account of how the couple were caught in a storm in their yacht, Laylah, off the west coast of America, while sailing to Alaska for some Himalayan training. During the storm Bremer-Kamp was nearly drowned twice, and she recalls that, the second time, 'As the ship rolled, I was plucked free. This was the very edge of life. There was nothing left to cling to.' On that trip fate had spared them both, but the following year, on Kangchenjunga, she is faced with choosing between life and death. In the final chapter, when she is coming to terms with Chris's death, she writes, 'As I lay there looking into a bottomless pit, I was drawn closer and closer to the edge. I was suspended in space. I wanted to go with Chris, to seek out where he had gone. A subtle presence became more strongly felt. I recognized it as my two children standing there beside me, looking solemnly at the scene without pleading, grief or tears. . . . Although they never asked for help I turned towards them, and Chris went on alone.'

The writer herself admits that it was in many ways tragic that she and Chris met, since they were both already committed when they did so. It is the intensity of the new relationship that dominates the book and very much influences the character of the climbs, probably to adverse effect: Cherie's desire that they should be together, and 'alone', coupled with Chris's violent temper, could not have helped when making climbing decisions. It certainly leads her to make some fairly ungracious remarks about Mongol's presence on the mountain.

Bremer-Kamp is very critical of the way in which the American K2 Expedition was carried out. As the only female in an all-male climbing team (the photographer and Base Camp manager were the only other women), she was dismayed at the resentment she felt directed towards her. This obviously raises the thorny old question: is this her own inferiority complex or are they a bunch of Sexist Nasties? Well, we can go on debating this *ad infinitum*. She further takes issue with the style of the large expedition. Having previously only climbed alpine-style, she was apprehensive of the organization and tactics of the Big Expedition. Four of the 12-strong team, chosen by the leader, went to the summit. Everyone else carried loads. There was no team-spirit and no discussion of strategy. Orders came from above and had to be obeyed. One of the summiteers was abandoned on the top to make his own way down – nearly losing his life in the process. The myth, therefore, that there is safety in numbers was blown, and Bremer-Kamp concluded that there was nothing to recommend the large-scale expedition. For Bremer-Kamp climbing is a metaphor for life and a tool of moral development. Neither of these views was shared, in her opinion, by anyone else on the K2 expedition.

Three years later, in 1981, she returned to the Himalaya with Chris Chandler to attempt the previously unclimbed N side of Yalung Kang (8505m), the W peak of Kangchenjunga. This was also to 'purge' themselves of all the 'garbage' they carried from K2. This way, they felt, they would be able to make their own decisions, take their own risks, and rely on their own expertise. On consulting the Oracle, they were given fair warning of the dangers, but, rejecting ancient Chinese wisdom in favour of Christian piety, they chose to believe that humility would bring them success. Their experience on K2 should have taught them that the brazen have as much chance of success as the humble, if not more so (whether in terms of summits or survival). And, as if to prove the point, Yalung Kang remained elusive, despite their honourable intentions.

On Yalung Kang Cherie and Chris having rejected the easier option of following the Czech route, reached the same high point as on Kangchenjunga four years later. Here, as throughout their time together, they chose to go it alone, to take the option closest to the edge: accepting permission to climb Kangchenjunga in winter and K2 less than six months later indicates the force of such obsessiveness, for which they paid a heavy price. Their courage was admirable: their foolhardiness was greater.

There are many enjoyable passages in the book describing aspects of local life, from Hindu myths to lavatorial practices. Unfortunately there is no index and no list of illustrations: a lack that I always find infuriating. All measurements have, irritatingly, been given twice, in metres and feet.

Kangchenjunga – which means Five Treasure Houses in the Snow – is inadequately illustrated with only one picture, showing Yalung Kang in the foreground. The maps, however, are excellent.

Margaret Urmston

Extreme Rock
Compiled by Ken Wilson and Bernard Newman
Diadem Books, 1987, pp296, £27.95.

It is the same well-tried and trusted formula. Spectacular pictures galore and articles by the enthusiasts.

Its appeal may be limited by the number of climbers able to aspire to the dizzy grades glossed across the pages, but it must rate high on the birthday/ Christmas present list for aspiring stars. A smattering of E6s, E7s and inclusion of an E9,6C on Cloggy's 'Great Wall' mean that the hobby, amongst some, of ticking off all the routes could prove more problematical than with previous books in this mould. Queues on 'Indian Face' seem unlikely.

One only has to glance through the book to see the huge amount of effort that has gone into putting together a vast series of superb photographs. They are the most striking feature of the book and, with many of them being Bernard Newman's own work, his efforts must have demanded immense dedication, not to mention enviable powers of persuasion to get the performers in the right place at the right time.

My only criticism, if any, is that too much is crammed into the book. Personally, with the possible exception of some outcrop areas, I would prefer the one-route/one-author syndrome. I certainly question the wisdom of having four or five routes covered by one article, as is the case on the main cliff of Gogarth. My sympathies are with Pat Littlejohn as he struggles to write a flowing piece of text about five routes which share many characteristics and are squeezed on to a 50-metre section of crag. The aim throughout the book does seem to have been to pack 'em in as tight as possible; the result is coverage of far more routes than *Hard Rock*, but with some unusual combinations where routes on completely different crags share the same article: 'Unicorn/Kingpin' and 'Freak Out/The Clearances', for example.

Nevertheless, these criticisms are minor. The true strength of the book lies in the way that it captures the atmosphere of modern climbing via both the dynamic photos and the often revealing literary pieces. Andy Pollitt's writing on 'Disillusioned Screw Machine' sums up the tremendous effort which climbers are now prepared to make, and their equally tremendous determination. Gone are the days when it was possible to shuffle up to the foot of the crag and, throwing off vegetation and loose rock, make truly on-sight first ascents ranking with the hardest of the day. I must admit that it is with a sense of harsh nostalgia that I see the old values recede into the distance and the vibrant new scene of athleticism take over from the rugged, scruffy, death-defying days of Brown and Whillans. But the changes are happening fast, and it is great to see them documented.

The book concentrates on the new, but the odd truly exploratory mountain route of the 1960s such as 'Thor' (Skye) makes an appearance, contrasting sharply with modern challenges ranging from the serious 'The Bells, The Bells' at Gogarth to the strenuous and technical 'Revelations' at Ravenstor. For me, though, it is the photos which really capture the 1980s sensation. Whilst the question of who out of Andy Pollitt and Martin Atkinson will become male model of the era is left open, the book is liberally sprinkled with the stars of the day engrossed in various horrific-looking positions. Glenn Robbins's photo of Martin Atkinson on the final overhang of the 'Prow' (Peak) epitomizes the levels of strength and fitness required to succeed on the harder routes, whilst Chris Gore's writing admirably captures the willpower and ability necessary to stand a chance of success.

It has taken eight years to compile the book. One can sympathize with the delays caused by the stars directing enthusiasm at the rock rather than the pen, but it is an eye-opener to realize that, when the idea was born, many of the routes finally included had not even been climbed. Deciding when to call it a day and ignore the ceaseless tide of superb new lines must have been difficult.

Needless to say, climbing standards continue to rise as do levels of seriousness. 'The Scoop' (Harris) has been free-climbed since publication and pushes hard towards new heights, ensuring that the scope for *Harder Still Extreme Rock* will be there. Doubtless, the preparation work will start soon!

For the time being, though, you won't find a better selection of illustration narratives covering the state-of-the-art up to 1987. At £27.95 it is not cheap – but then the best in any field rarely is.

Mick Fowler

A Dream of White Horses
Edwin Drummond
Diadem Books, 1987, pp224, £10.95

Ed Drummond's collection of autobiographical essays and poems (many of them published before) makes compelling reading. He is, of course, the notorious *enfant terrible* of the climbing world, and his 'iconoclastic spasms' (his words) cover his famous big-wall climbs, his 'protest-climbs' of public buildings and the problems of personal relationships. He has been accused of publicity-seeking, but for me his insights are genuine, his appraisal of the climbing and human scene critical and, on the whole, just. His social analysis is not profound, but it appeals to me: 'The history of civilisation is the story of the determination of small numbers of people to remain sane in the most difficult of circumstances.' A climber's credo? It is from 'JimLove Menwords', Drummond's review of Jim Perrin's *Menlove*, which is included in this volume and which, it is suggested, was rejected by the *Alpine Journal* for prudish reasons. In this thoughtful discourse on the nature of free will, determinism and responsibility, Drummond presents a powerful case against Perrin's position without convincing me of his own. However, one doesn't have to share Drummond's philosophy to be impressed, stirred – and perhaps troubled – by the imagery and power of his prose and poetry.

But the book's theme is climbing; it is addressed to climbers and it makes

76. *Aiguille de Bionnassay.*

77. *Lenzspitze with (R) S ridge.*

78. *Dykh Tau from S, 1886.*

79. *Champagne Castle, Drakensberg.*

80. Dutch Hoggar Expedition '87–'88. Saouinan (2650m), N face, Rêve
Pétrifié *(6a).*

81. *Dutch Hoggar Expedition '87–'88. Tezoulaig-Sud (2702m), W face,*
Les Garçons du Pays Plat *(6a).*

82. *Ruwenzori: the Stanley Plateau from near the Scott Elliot Pass.*

83. *Ruwenzori: Alexandra (5091m) and Margherita (5109m) from the Stanley Plateau.*

84. *Bowman Island, Makinson Inlet, Ellesmere Island, from the S.*

85.   *The summit tower of Bowman Island, from the E. It was climbed up the ridge, the snow-ramp to the L, and the crack to the R from the top of the ramp.*

86.   *The NE face of (Gangotri) Shivling, climbed by Italians (1986) and Yugoslavs (1987).*

few concessions to its readers: they are supposed to command the jargon. Within this context Drummond has an exuberant way with words – he experiments without inhibition and his style is full of quotable, arresting phrases, metaphors and neologisms. Here is an extract from 'Frankenstein and Linda', describing his nine-day solo ascent of The Nose of El Capitan: 'There is no more public stage than this titanic auditorium, these one night stands on Dolt Tower or El Cap ledge, aloof pantomimes whose only audience is those flowers in the meadow who throw no bouquets at the end of your tremendous, silent soliloquies. Only your heart applauds wildly the laggardly madrigals you make up the blunt prows and shields of this bastion of eternity, and probably no more than a haul bag spinning in the wind will ever thump you on the back, when you climb El Cap alone. As for music . . . True, you have been known to whistle when all's well, jingling your tools like a cap-o-bells as you skip up a tricky crack, or hum a hymn while you're fixing dinner on a ledge with plenty of light – but, let there be the merest rumble on the drums beyond Half Dome, a cymbal flash of lightning, or the wind rise, booming bassoon behind some hollow flake, or flaring the slack from the trailing haul line like a vast, trembling clef as you pound on the jams, and you don't want to hear.' Obviously such a rich diet can become a bit indigestible, but in general Drummond's way with the English language is remarkably successful. 'Stone' contains a wonderful description of incipient hypothermia (again on El Capitan). 'A Grace Period' is the tale of the failure of an expedition (to Makalu) and a marriage. Dreams and nightmares play an important part in the narrative. There is a splendid account, by a seven-year-old, of climbing on Half Dome, in a place called Yesummertee.

Drummond's famous recitals, on his 'portable 7000mm mountain', should provide proof enough of the symbiosis of poetry and climbing ('words are holds'). Peter Ackroyd's remark that prose may be the more difficult art, but poetry is the higher, applies to climbing literature too (and I hope that one day soon a volume of poetry will win the Boardman-Tasker Award). Drummond's merits seem to me particularly well brought out in the poetry. There is high art in the deceptive simplicity of the style. Amidst so much that is mediocre in mountain literature, Drummond's writing stands out – long may he continue to topple the idols that we worship in our complacency.

Ernst Sondheimer

Native Stones – *A Book About Climbing*
David Craig
Secker & Warburg, 1987, pp10 + 214, £10.95

By the time a reviewer gets round to reading, and writing about, a book for the *AJ*, it has usually been published for several months and will already have been reviewed in all the climbing magazines and, if it is an interesting book, in the quality papers as well. Such reviews are normally remarkably similar in tone. *Native Stones* is rather different. It received rather muted praise in some quarters, a distinctly hostile review in one magazine, and yet, in the heavy weight-Sundays, two eminent literary critics each listed it as one of their chosen books for 1987. As they only chose two books each in total this was high praise, one describing David Craig's book as '. . . a classic . . . unforgettable', whilst the other said that it ought to be 'put on the same shelf as Burton's *Anatomy of Melancholy*'. So, opinions differ. The dust-jacket tells us that the author teaches Creative Writing at the University of Lancaster, which probably explains why the book finds such favour with literary critics. Personally, I found some of the poems rather uninspiring, but for the greater part of the book I have nothing but praise.

The author's aim is to put on paper exactly what climbing means to him, the smell of the rock, the sensation of fear, the enjoyment of the environment and of the literature that the sport has spawned, and to link all this with his own personal climbing experiences. There is nothing new in this. Smythe, among others, was very successful at this in his day, although he is somewhat out of fashion at the moment. This is not an autobiography but it has a logical climbing sequence, starting with the author's boyhood days on the hills and leading on to the introduction of his own sons to climbing. Eventually, of course, son overtakes father. The book ends with the author trying to coax other 'old timers' to come out and reclimb some of their early ascents – with varying success. The descriptions of all these climbs are superbly done, but it is the thoughts arising from the climbs that are the real meat of the book. Occasionally lapsing into long-windedness, they are nevertheless continually thought-provoking and a delight to read. This is a new classic in climbing literature and, whilst I probably won't read *Anatomy of Melancholy*, I will read this again more than once, I'm sure.

Geoffrey Templeman

Norman Collie. *A Life in Two Worlds. Mountain Explorer and Scientist 1859–1942*
Christine Mill
Aberdeen University Press, 1987, ppxiii 197, npq

This appears to be the second biography of Norman Collie, a previous one entitled *The Snows of Yesteryear* by Professor William Taylor (whose help is acknowledged by the present author) having been published in Canada in 1973. However, Taylor's work has the character of an illustrated sketch rather than a life-portrait, and the present book is both more compact and more complete.

Such a study is overdue and my only criticism is that one would have liked more imaginative comment about this very interesting and complex personality, perhaps at the expense of some of the *curriculum vitae*.

Of Collie's two worlds, mountains clearly took precedence, so that he was sometimes dubbed a 'part-time chemist'. On the day when, with Mummery and Hastings, he made – *à cheval* – the first guideless traverse of the Brenva ice ridge, back at University College his senior colleague, Professor Ramsay, discovered Argon! Collie got his own back to some extent later by designing the first neon lamp, and also taking the first X-ray photo, showing metal in the human body. His scientific papers, 77 in all, are listed at the end of the book, in addition to his 75 first ascents and his many contributions to mountain literature.

The long saga of climbs includes well-written chapters on Scotland, the Lake District, the Alps, the Himalaya, the Rockies, the Lofoten Islands (a land 'worn down to the bone' as Collie called them) and of course Skye, his greatest love, to which he returned as to a magnet.

To whet the reader's appetite, here are a few highlights: Collie's Step on Moss Ghyll which he cut with Hastings's ice-axe, after which he cried *peccavi* and then completed the pitch; the great shadow on the face of Sron na Ciche by which he first discovered the Cioch; the three seasons of the 'Three Musketeers' – Collie, Mummery and Hastings – ending sadly in the disappearance of Mummery with two porters on Nanga Parbat in 1895; the first traverse of the Grépon; and a host of others.

His character was paradoxical. He was a life-long bachelor but no misogynist; a connoisseur of wines, antiques and much else; an experimental scientist who hated fools and small-talk; but also a man greatly beloved by his chosen friends, an artist and mystic with a deeply-rooted belief in another world, unseen and inaccessible to science. The latter he attempted to explore not merely through the medium of mountain beauty, to which he showed exceptional sensitivity, but also in the occult – even proposing for membership of the Alpine Club a black magician later known as the 'Great Beast 666', but, luckily for the Club, without success.

Appropriately, the book closes with the last years in Skye, where Norman Collie, after John Mackenzie's death, became more and more a recluse; so that, when war came in 1939 and found him already there, he simply stayed on, living out the remaining three years of his life almost in silence in the inn at Sligachan. Many climbers of those days, myself amongst them, cherish an unforgettable memory of a tall, unstooping figure, upright in his chair, looking out to the hills. He was distant with strangers, even when they came to climb, and it may be that increasing preoccupation with the dark, mystical gods which held so much fascination for him, together with the loss of all his close friends, contributed to the sadness of his demeanour in those final days. However that may be, his stature as mountaineer and scientist is beyond question, and the author has given us all a thoroughly readable and well-researched account of his life.

There are excellent illustrations, taken almost entirely from Collie's own slide collection, now in the possession of the Alpine Club.

Edward Smyth

Treks and Climbs in the Mountains of Rum and Petra, Jordan
Tony Howard
Cicerone Press, 1987, pp8 + 144, pb

The outside cover answers the usual first question 'Jordan is *flat desert land brown and hazy*?' No, it definitely is not . . . Tony has tried to portray the vivid colours, the beautiful scenery, the amazing people who have remained changeless for well over two centuries. He has managed to write an overall guide to Jordan whatever your tastes and pleasures are. It is a wonderful eye-opener for anyone considering a trip to this country. Not only has it got the many climbing areas covered, it also gives you an insight into the way people live, the cost of living, the political way of life and their many customs which date back to the Nabatians over 3000 years ago. He has covered in detail all the interesting sites, buildings and cultures of those long-past tribes and kinsmen.

The climbs are well described, the areas marked, with suggestions of when and how to use the local Bedouin transport – such as four-wheel drive or camels. These can be easily arranged (at a price) from the local Bedouin. Situated by the rest-house at Wadi Rum, where there is a large Bedouin village or settlement, if you make yourself known and behave in a friendly manner you will be rewarded tenfold. They are a very proud, fit, large, extended family.

When you establish yourself at Wadi Rum and compare the gigantic walls all around you to the routes Tony has entered and described, you will then fully understand the amount of virgin rock awaiting first ascents – so you can either do the classic routes already established or go for completely new ground. One thing you learn very quickly is that shade is a pleasure to climb in where direct sun is far too hot. Bivouacs are fun, light sacks are great and also essential.

Tony quotes Lawrence of Arabia's *Seven Pillars of Wisdom* as saying of Wadi Rum: 'Rumm the magnificent . . . vast echoing and GODLIKE . . . a processional way greater than imagination . . . the crimson sunset turned on its stupendous cliffs and slanted ladders of hazy fire down its walled avenue.'

A must for all people visiting Jordan is a trip to Petra, 'the rose-red city half as old as time'. Climbing in and around Petra would seem sacrilegious but there are many walks, scrambles and great trekking areas – a visit to Aaron's Tomb on one of the nearby summits is a must.

As I said at the beginning, Tony's book is a complete guide covering all areas, whatever your leisure and pleasure – it makes excellent reading and is great value.

Brede Arkless

With O'Leary in the Grave
Kevin Fitzgerald
Michael Russell, 1986 (Oxford University Press paperback, 1987) pp176,
£9.95

'My father was usually a rich man.' From its splendid opening sentence, Kevin's book is brilliant. His father, maddeningly, unpredictably embarrassing, teetotal and verbose, stalks around these stories of youth and childhood and gives the book its thread. There is only a premonitory flake or two of mountaineering in it. Nevertheless, it is even better stuff than Kevin's extremely funny and surrealist mountain writing.

The book has the same luminous quality as Sassoon's early memoirs – *The Old Century* etc – but is funnier. It raises a question which touches on all travel writing and which is connected with the boringness of so much autobiography: why do the anecdotes and detail in popular travel writing and radio features sound so false? Yet quite a number of Kevin's marvellous stories can't have been literally true either; and yet they have the ring of truth and of

hilarious or painful reality. Another great Irish writer (possibly Wilde) said
something like this: 'a good story is not only superior to an established fact; it
has a positive duty to expel it.' But what is it that makes these stories good? I can
think of two tentative answers. One is to do with Kevin's loss of his self-
indulgence. The other is the many vivid layers of memory: family, faith,
holidays (with sand in the shoes still), farming (a marvellous bit on ploughing),
hills and disasters. They are all gathered and stitched with loving irony by a wise
old man whose failing sight and shining memory have served him, and his
friends, well.

Robin Hodgkin

Chronicles of John R Jenkins, Mountaineer, Miner and Quaker
Edited and privately published by Dulcibel Jenkins, pp330, £6.95 + £1 p&p

John Jenkins was such a rich and ebullient personality that anyone, mountaineer or other friend, who enjoyed his companionship in the thirties and forties
would have been hard pressed to convey an adequately distilled account of what
he was and did. He fell to his death, with Nully Kretschmer, when descending
the Old Brenva route under fine but treacherous conditions just over 40 years
ago. 50 years ago last year he and Michael Taylor did their splendid new N face
route on Tetnuld in the Caucasus. This was on an expedition which was, for all
its members, a wonderful pre-war high spot, with fine new climbs. These and
many other mountaineering exploits are recorded, through diaries, letters,
snapshots and sketches, in this book which his widow has compiled. It has not
been heavily edited and it is in effect a printed archive of Jenkins material.
Anyone who knew John or who is interested in that effervescent mountain
epoch will find here an unpolished yet highly characteristic and, in some ways, a
moving collection. Not the least interesting are John's papers on economics,
socialism, Quakerism and mining. They may sound a little naive today, but they
were true to him and to his generation. At the beginning of the war he resigned
from a comfortable family engineering business because of its 'defence'
contracts and settled for an uncomfortable but challenging mining job in
Northumberland.

Robin Hodgkin

Porophyllum Saxifrages
Radvan Horný, Mirko Webr and John Byam-Grounds, with illustrations by
Eva Zoulová
Byam-Grounds Publications, Stamford, 1986, pp372, £25

The saxifrages are an extensive and very varied race, having evolved over the
past two million years to survive the advance and retreat of the north-polar ice
and occupy specialized niches from the arctic to high mountains and temperate
lowlands. Many species are truly alpine and some are found as far apart as our
British hills, the Alps, the Canadian Rockies and Asia. Botanists have
recognized some 15 Sections of the genus, one of which comprises the nearly
100 species of the *Porophylla* (including those formerly known as Kabschias,

and distinguished by their secretion of lime near the margins of their leaves), which prefer a high intensity of radiation and reasonable warmth and so are not found north of the Alps, the Caucasus and the Tien Shan of Central Asia. Many saxifrages have proved very garden-worthy and they have received much attention from hybridizers during the past century, leaving much confusion about origins and nomenclature. Nearly 80 years ago, Reginald Farrer wrote, 'In no great family is there more fearful confusion as to names; some Oedipus is sadly needed to take the race in hand and unravel its riddles.'

The book under review derives from studies of the *Porophylla* over many years by the two Czech authors and by our member John Byam-Grounds who, on retirement, created an outstanding alpine garden near Llanrwst where he grew most of the *Porophylla* species in current cultivation and almost all known surviving cultivars. It differs in some respects from the Czech version published by the Alpine Garden Club of Prague to take note of British conditions and availability of works of reference. To my unprofessional eye it is a comprehensive and unique treatise on both species and cultivated *Porophyllum* saxifrages. Who will now take on the other 14 Sections of the genus?

Frank Solari

A Little Walk on Skis

Peter and Beryl Wilberforce-Smith

Dickerson, 1987, pp12 + 258, £12.95

This book is a gem. Alpine traverses have been described before and the distinguished lineage includes Martin Conway and Frank Smythe – the latter the only author to do much of the traverse on ski. The present work is in the best standard of a great tradition.

It is an entertaining and thoroughly informative work – well written and illustrated, and with a wealth of meteorological, glaciological and topographical detail. Its subject, however, is an account of a journey made over several seasons from the Col de Tende to Austria.

The very special thing about it is that it represents a very personal record of years of endeavour by the authors and their friends – some of them distinguished members of the Alpine Ski Club and the AC. The indefatigable partnership of the Wilberforce-Smiths is reflected in the text – most of the earlier part written by Peter and the later chapters by Beryl. Their happy team was broken by Peter's death in 1976, and the final years of 1977 and 1978 were undertaken by Beryl with friends, amongst whom were our members Fred Jenkins and Richard Brooke. The reader cannot but sense that Peter Wilberforce-Smith remained an integral part of the expedition and his physical loss must have been eased by his spiritual presence.

No ski-mountaineer should miss this book. It is one to keep, enjoy and re-read. The mountaineers and skiers who have not yet tasted the delights of ski-touring will learn hugely from it and may well be tempted to broaden their horizon of enjoyment.

It is, at the least, a first-class account of an alpine expedition with an infinity of valuable information. At its best, it is a record of a great physical and emotional progress.

P S Boulter

William Wordsworth and the Age of English Romanticism
Jonathan Wordsworth, Michael C Jaye and Robert Woof
Rutgers University Press/Wordsworth Trust, 1987, ppxviii + 262, npq

This volume is much more than just the catalogue of what must have been one of the finest exhibitions ever to have been mounted in the world. It is a series of essays by eminent writers on the whole history of the Romantic Movement in English literature and art at the close of the 18th century which ended with Talleyrand's cry for the old regime, 'They who did not live before 1789 know not the sweetness of life' and then Wordsworth's welcome for the new with his 'Bliss was it in that dawn to be alive'.

But romance has to do with the imagination, and never before have I read a better explanation of what 'romanticism' really is than in the glorious essays in this catalogue.

It must be the fourth essay on 'The Discovery of Nature' which will be of most interest to our readers in the Alpine Club. But I defy anyone who has once picked up the book not to go on reading and looking at it. It is quite fascinating reading and the illustrations are superb. Where on earth will you see collected together such lovely reproductions of the finest pictures, borrowed from at home and abroad, as in this sumptious production?

Readers, do not miss a glance at this book. It is far more than just a catalogue, good and scholarly though the latter part is; it is a great literary exposition of the meaning of English Romanticism as centred upon the life and writings of William Wordsworth. And how important it is.

Charles Warren

Garet el Djenoun. *Escalades*
Josep Paytubí and Servicio General de Información de Montaña
Edición del Servicio General, Barcelona, 1987, pp53, npq

The 'Servicio General' at Barcelona had previously published two successful monographs on Aconcagua and Chaltén (FitzRoy). Each one of these monographs is practically a guidebook. This third one now treats Garet el Djenoun (2330m) in Algeria, the most remarkable mountain in the Hoggar massif. Although written in Catalonian, this book will now become the basic source for anybody planning to visit the Hoggar and the peak of Garet el Djenoun itself. Its information can be easily followed. It covers history of exploration, climbing, access, routes, grading of routes and variants, useful data, maps and bibliography. Its 12 black-and-white photos and 27 sketch-maps and line-drawings make reading very easy. All in all, it is a good guidebook for this area, recommended not only to rock-climbers eager to visit the Hoggar, but also to trekkers and tourists.

Evelio Echevarría

Climbing
Ron Fawcett, Jeff Lowe, Paul Nunn, Alan Rouse. Ed Audrey Salkeld
Bell & Hyman, 1986, pp256, £15.00

This is one of those books which is a cross between an instruction manual, a descriptive volume on mountains in general, and a set of personal reminiscences. No one would dispute, at any rate in Britain, that the four authors are supremely well qualified to deal with their particular specializations, but the subject-matter itself means that the results are uneven.

Fawcett and Lowe, dealing with rock and ice-climbing respectively, are the least interesting, since much of the content is taken up with descriptions of technique, equipment, etc, which can be found in many instructional manuals. With Paul Nunn on alpine climbing we are in a wider field, and the interest grows. Nunn gives a broad historical introduction, and then recommends a number of climbs by which a hill-walker or rock-climber might start alpine climbing, going on to more difficult and grander courses. Each example is described in some depth and laced with personal reminiscence. This method works well.

In the final section, Alan Rouse deals with expeditions, and this will prove the most interesting to many people. In some 50 pages, he packs into a small space an incredible amount of information on arranging an expedition; everything from likely costs, weather conditions in various parts of the world and handling of porters, to fund-raising and dealing with bureaucracy. There is very little personal reminiscence here, but a wealth of experience is made available to all; it is only sad that it turned out to be Al Rouse's last book.

This book is therefore rather uneven, but it is very good in parts and is well illustrated.

Mattia Zurbriggen. *Guida Alpina*
Felice Benuzzi
CAL, 1987, pp108, pb, npq

This 52nd publication of the *Museo Nationale della Montagna 'Duca degli Abruzzi'* is a monograph on the famous alpine guide Mattia Zurbriggen from Macugnaga. Zurbriggen had a particularly far-flung career for, in addition to his exploits in the Alps with Rey, Whymper, Kugy and others, he was with Conway in the Karakoram, Fitzgerald in New Zealand and on Aconcagua, Borghese in the Tien Shan and the Workmans in the Karakoram. The museum does a great service to mountaineering in general by publishing such excellently-produced books, and it is a pity that an English edition cannot be produced. The ever-growing band of amateur alpine historians and book-lovers would surely welcome such a step.

The Guiding Spirit
Andrew Kauffman and William Putnam
Footprint, 1986, pp256, $21.95 Canadian

When the Duke of the Abruzzi climbed Mount St Elias in 1896 he had with him several Italian guides. These were the first professional mountain guides to be employed in North America. The next year, Prof Dixon employed Peter Sarbach from St Niklaus for several weeks' climbing in the 'Canadian Alps', and then, the year after that, it was suggested to the Canadian Pacific Railway that they should engage some Swiss guides to be available for their patrons in the mountain regions the company was seeking to exploit.

One of the young men who came was Edward Feuz Jnr, and it is through his life that this story of the Swiss guides in Canada is told. 'Uncle Ed', as he was always known, died in 1981 at the age of 96, but the authors had had numerous interviews with him in previous years to get the full story. Many well-known mountaineers, such as Don and Phyl Munday, Leo Amery ('a gentleman') and Whymper ('not such a gentleman') are featured in this well-illustrated, continuously interesting book.

Moments of Doubt *and other Mountaineering Writings of . . .*
David Roberts
The Mountaineers, 1986, ppxvi + 238, pb, $8.95

When David Roberts's first book, *The Mountain of My Fear*, about his second ascent of Mt Huntington in 1965, was published, it was realized at once that another member of that rare breed, the good mountain writer, had been born.

This book is a collection of 20 essays and articles on mountaineering and adventure, culled from magazines and journals such as *Outside*, *Ascent* and others over the past 20 years. The articles are very mixed in content, but each one is a joy to read.

White Limbo. *The First Australian Climb of Mount Everest*
Lincoln Hall
Weldons, 1987, pp262, £17.95

In 1984, Tim Macartney-Snape and Greg Mortimer, of the first all-Australian expedition to Everest, reached the summit via a new route on the N face. This magnificent book by Lincoln Hall is a record of the expedition and, to a lesser extent, the expeditions to Annapurna and Ama Dablam that preceded it. The author tells this story of a great achievement well, but the book's main attraction is in its photographs; surely one of the best collections ever assembled for an expedition book. Very good value for the British reprint.

Scotland's Mountains
W H Murray
Scottish Mountaineering Trust, 1987, ppxi + 305, £15.95

In 1976 Bill Murray's book *The Scottish Highlands* was published; it gave an excellent general description of Scotland's mountains. This has now been enlarged, updated and given a new title, in the now standard SMC format. Sections on topography, geology, plant and animal life, and man in the Highlands, are followed by guides to each area, rounded off by histories of mountaineering and skiing and various appendices. The book forms a first-class general introduction to the SMC's detailed area guides.

De Saussure et le Mont-Blanc
Région Autonome Vallée d'Aoste, 1987, pp84

Publication by the local Tourist Board celebrating the 200th anniversary of de Saussure's ascent of Mont Blanc, including the catalogue of an exhibition.

Holding the Heights: *a rock-climbing diary*
John Bassindale, Richard Sale, Annette Jones and Kevin Bassindale
Constable, 1987, pp192, £12.95

The authors of this book split down as follows: John and Annette did the climbs, John (mostly) writes about them, Richard and Kevin took the photos. It is a diary of rock-climbs done in England and Wales in one year between May and October, with descriptions, thoughts, etc, and with copious photos. One is tempted to ask: who is really interested in one couple's efforts in one year? – and certainly some of the photos showing sequence after sequence of holds are rather tedious – but perhaps that is a little unfair and sales of the book may prove me wrong!

H. W. Tilman. *The Eight Sailing/Mountain-Exploration Books*
Diadem, 1987, pp 966, £16.95

Diadem have now completed the service they have already done the mountaineering fraternity, in publishing the omnibus editions of the Tilman and Shipton mountain travel books, by producing all eight of the sailing books. I suspect that many climbers started off by reading the first, *Mischief Among the Penguins*, when it was first published, and then read one or two more, but tailed off after that in the belief that they were purely for sailing *aficionados*. The present collection shows that this is a fallacy, as mountains and wild places were always the ultimate goal of every voyage. Best of all, though, Tilman's marvellous writing makes the reading of every volume a joy, and I think it is the first time that colour photos of HWT's voyages have been published as well. A marvellous compilation.

The Mountains of Central Asia. *1:3,000,000 Map and Gazetteer*
RGS/MEF, 1987, ppxxviii + 98, £14.95

The RGS and MEF have produced this small-scale map of Central Asia, spanning a region from the southern Nepalese border up to Urumqi and the Bogda range in the north, and from Tashkent in the west to Chengdu in the east. Following a general introduction by Michael Ward, there is a 98-page gazetteer of place-names, mountains, etc. From the mountaineer's point of view, it is a pity that, whilst the names of many, many mountains are included in the gazetteer, so few are shown on the map itself, but it is most useful to have this vast area shown on a single sheet at last.

Ski Mountaineering
Peter Cliff
Unwin Hyman, 1987, pp160, pb, £12.95

Fawcett on Rock
Ron Fawcett and John Beatty with Mike Harrison
Unwin Hyman, 1987, pp158, £14.95

The publishers Unwin Hyman have brought out two excellent instructional books in these two volumes which are hard to fault.

Peter Cliff's book covers all aspects of ski-mountaineering, with very clear diagrams, particularly good in the chapter dealing with crevasse rescue, and ends with a selection of tours suggested both by himself and other experts.

Ron Fawcett puts his expertise on rock into words (always a difficult task), aided by John Beatty's action shots, and covers training, equipment and technique with equal thoroughness. Both books contain sections of colour photos.

In the Footsteps of Scott
Roger Mear & Robert Swan
Jonathan Cape, 1987, ppxiv + 306, £14.95

In 1985, Robert Swan and Roger Mear, with Gareth Wood, followed Scott's route to the South Pole, pulling their sledges in total isolation, without radio links or back-up supply depots. This excellent book tells the story of their 883-mile journey from Cape Evans to the Pole, and includes details not only of their preparations, which included the first solo winter ascent of Mt Erebus, but of the official hostility they faced from the American Antarctic authorities. Their enforced evacuation makes sober reading.

The Ice. A Journey to Antarctica
Stephen J Pyne
Arlington Books, 1987, pp8 + 428, £12.95

The author is an American professor of history who spent three months in Antarctica as the recipient of an 'Antarctic Fellowship'. This book is the end product, and it really is a monumental work. From the title, one could well imagine purely a travel book, but it is far from that. Amongst subjects treated are the history of exploration, the literature and art of the continent, its geopolitics and, above all, the scientific reasons for its being the way it is.

On High Lakeland Fells. *The 100 Best Walks and Scrambles*
Bob Allen
Pic Publications, 1987, pp190, £9.95

The number of walking guides to the Lakeland hills produced from the time of
Wordsworth onwards must be almost beyond count. Many have been
pedestrian in the worst sense of the word, until, a few years ago, came
Wainwright, with a series of guides which, for their lovingly-prepared detail, hit
a new high. Now comes another such success. Bob Allen has written and
illustrated a first-class book on the walks and scrambles of the Lakeland fells.
The descriptions provide just the right amount of detail spiced with anecdote,
the maps give adequate indication of routes, the scrambles are shown on
charming pencil sketches, but the real joy of the book are the whole-page colour
photos, many of which are taken in wintry conditions. They form one of the
best collections of Lakeland photos seen for some time. This is Pic Publications'
second venture and it forms a worthy successor to *Welsh Rock*.

Mountaineering Literature. *A Bibliography of Material Published in English*
Jill Neate
Cicerone Press/Mountain Books, 1986, pp296, pb, £14.95

In 1978, the author produced *Mountaineering and its Literature*, the first
serious attempt to give the English-speaking mountaineering world a bibliography of its literature. That book contained, not only an author-index of 949
entries, plus selections of guide books, fiction, etc, but also a subject-index and
an index of all major mountains in the world. Ms Neate has now produced a
vastly-expanded version of the bibliography section which, at my count,
contains over 3600 items. This represents an incredible amount of research, and
will ensure that it remains the mountain book collector's bible for years to
come.

Alan Rouse. *A Mountaineer's Life*
Compiled by Geoff Birtles
Unwin Hyman, 1987, pp224, £12.95

When Al Rouse died on K2 in August 1986, the British climbing community lost
not only one of its stars, but one of its best-loved members. Everybody seemed
to know him and to have a story about him, and Geoff Birtles has collected
reminiscences from a number of his friends in this book. They range from the
escapades of wild early days to the more factual accounts of later Himalayan
expeditions, and include a few articles by Rouse himself from magazines and
journals. Whilst there is a certain amount of unavoidable repetition in some of
the earlier accounts, they all add up to a fascinating picture of a rather complex
character. The compiler did a great job in getting so many contributions from a
diverse bunch of climbers (not best-known for buckling-down to writing when
pressed!) and into print in such a short time. It only shows in what regard Alan
Rouse was held.

From Kinder Scout to Kathmandu. *A Rucksack Club Anthology 1907–1986*
Ed by Peter Benson, Mike Cudahy & Ian Grant
Rucksack Club, 1987, pp240, £10.00

There cannot be all that many people around who have complete sets of the *Rucksack Club Journal* on their shelves, and it is therefore good to see the appearance of this anthology – a sort of *Peaks, Passes and Glaciers* of the Rucksack Club. One or two obvious classics by Doughty, Holland, etc, are here, and it certainly seems as if the earlier journals contained the best writing. There are 10 articles pre-1930, six in the 30s and eight in the 50s, but only one each in the 60s and 70s, and two in the 80s. Having said that, 'The Crossing of Greenland' in '82 and 'The Pennine Way in Three Days and Five Years' in '83 are as good as any.

There is something here for everyone interested in climbing history. Copies can be obtained from: 'R C Anthology', 4 Raynham Avenue, Didsbury, Manchester M20 0BW. Price £10.00 inc p&p, less 10% for AC members.

The Magic of the Highlands
W A Poucher
Constable, 1987, pp200, £14.95

Walter Poucher has returned to the Highlands for a second selection of colour photographs in his series of large-format colour-plate books. There are more full double-page spreads in this volume but, as in the previous selection, this leads to problems of distortion in the middle of the plates, anything right in the middle being lost.

Mont Blanc. *Jardin Féerique*
Gaston Rébuffat
Denoël, 1987, pp240, npq

This fourth edition of Gaston Rébuffat's history of Mont Blanc has the addition of a list of historic ascents in the Mont Blanc range by Alex Lucchesi, and a number of new illustrations. It remains an excellent illustrated account of the mountain.

The Price of Adventure. *Mountain Rescue Stories from Four Continents*
Hamish MacInnes
Hodder & Stoughton, 1987, pp192, £10.95

Hamish MacInnes's volumes of rescue stories seem to become almost an annual event, but this particular batch ranges even wider afield than usual. Scotland is, of course, well represented, but we also travel to the Alps (the Dru), the Andes, Mount Kenya, Mount Washington, the Tatra and Mount Cook. The author always writes well, and includes here a piece on himself as victim on the Dru with Bonington and Whillans in 1958. The stories range from 1925 to 1985 and, although there may well be morals to be learned from them, most readers will just enjoy them for the good adventure tales they are.

Reinhold Messner. *Ier Vainqueur des 14 huit mille*
Tr. Noëlle Amy
Denoël, 1987, pp248, npq

This is the French edition of *Überlebt – Alle 14 Achttausender* by Messner, telling the story of his ascent of all the 8000ers between 1970 and 1986. The book splits naturally into the 14 sections, each of which contain a brief history of ascents of that particular mountain, a selection of superb colour photographs of Messner's expedition(s), the story of the expedition, and a brief article by another eminent mountaineer on an aspect of the mountain. Some parts, such as the 14 portraits of Messner forming the frontispiece, are a little 'over the top', but the book is an excellent production, with splendid photos, and it provides a first-class summary of all Messner's Himalayan exploits.

Wo Europa den Himmel Berührt. *Die Entdeckung der Alpen*
Gabriele Seitz
Artemis Verlag, 1987, pp238, DM98

Where Europe touches Heaven is an extremely attractive coffee-table book on the lines of Lukan's *Alps and Alpinism* of several years ago. Chapters deal with the early history of the alpine regions, the coming of mountaineers and tourists, the start of skiing and so on, each chapter ending with quotations from contemporary authors and including a marvellous selection of illustrations, none of which are later than the 1920s.

The Swiss and the British
John Wraight
Michael Russell, 1987, ppxiv 474, £17.95

Sir John Wraight has written a fascinating history of the relationship between the Swiss and the British from all aspects. In a lengthy introduction he covers the historical perspective and then proceeds to discuss, in general terms, travellers and visitors, cultural relations, education, science and economic relations. The main body of the book, however, is a chronology of Anglo-Swiss relations, commencing in medieval times and progressing to 1984. From the 1690s onwards, events are noted for each year. The detail to be found here is fascinating and all mountaineering events of note are recorded. The book is copiously illustrated and has a number of detailed appendices, the bibliography alone running to 62 pages. As British Ambassador to the Swiss Confederation from 1973 to 1976, Sir John's knowledge of Switzerland and the Swiss is unrivalled, and it is our gain that he has made such a large part of his studies available.

Polskie Wyprawy Karakorum Alpinistyczne
Zbigniew Kowalewski and Andrzej Paczkowski
Wydawnictwo 'Sport i Turystyka', 1986, pp240, npq

This book is a mainly pictorial summary of Polish expeditions to the

Karakoram between 1969 and 1984. Each expedition is given a maximum of half-a-dozen pages of brief summary, map and selection of black-and-white photos. Then follow three sections: 'Karawana', mostly pictures of approach marches; 'Panorama' which, as the name suggests, are general mountain photos; and a final selection of colour shots. Whilst the minimal text will not be intelligible to most *AJ* readers, the photos, although not too well produced, will be of great interest to those contemplating a visit to the Karakoram.

XII Apostoli – *un rifugio, una chiesetta*
Annetta Stenico and Roberto Bombarda
Grafiche Artigianelli, 1987, pp50, npq

A little memoir of the Rifugio XII Apostoli and nearby chapel-in-the-rock in the Brenta Dolomites.

Going Higher. *The Story of Man and Altitude*
Charles S Houston
Little Brown & Co, 1987, ppxii 324, npq

Charles Houston has now brought out a revised edition of *Going Higher*, his comprehensive book on the effects of altitude on man. It brings current medical thinking up-to-date, and in addition there is a greatly enlarged bibliography for those who wish to carry their studies further. Although the book is technically very comprehensive, it is written in such a way as to provide a fascinating story for the lay reader.

The Great Backpacking Adventure
Chris Townsend
Oxford Illustrated Press, 1987, pp6 226, npq

The 'Great Adventure' series continues with Backpacking. Chris Townsend is well known in this field, being the editor of *Odyssey* magazine, and here describes his major expeditions: the Pennine Way, Lands End to John O'Groats, and Corrour to Ullapool in Britain; along the Pyrenees; around the Markarfljot in Iceland; and the Pacific Crest Trail and Continental Divide in the United States.

Island in the Sky. *Pioneering Accounts of Mt Rainier, 1833–1894*
Ed Paul Schullery
The Mountaineers, 1987, ppxiv 202, $10.95, pb

14 accounts of pioneer ascents and explorations of Mt Rainier which the author found when he was researching literature for a project on elks in the Mt Rainier National Park.

Classic Rock Climbs in Great Britain
Bill Birkett
Oxford Illustrated Press, 1986, pp172, £14.95

In this book, the author takes five major climbing areas of Britain from south to north – South-West England, Wales, Northern England, the Lakes and Scotland – and describes a number of climbs in each which, in his opinion, are 'classic'. Many are of proven status, that of others is arguable, but each gets guidebook treatment, plus a short historical-cum-personal experience chapter, and is illustrated by the author's own photographs.

The market at which this book is aimed is uncertain, but the photos are good and the text is interesting, and it is worth a look-through by any climber.

A Wilderness Original. *The Life of Bob Marshall*
James M Glover
The Mountaineers, 1986, ppx + 326, $17.95

The autobiography of Bob Marshall, one of the leading lights of the American conservation movement in the Twenties and Thirties, after whom the Bob Marshall Wilderness in Montana is named. He was particularly known for the years he spent in Alaska and the books he wrote on his life there.

Denali Diary. *Letters from McKinley*
Frances Randall
Cloudcap, 1987, ppxxiv + 136, pb, $9.95

In the busy summer months the park authority hires an organizer to run the Base Camp on the Kahiltna Glacier on Mt McKinley, to keep track of climbing parties, transmit weather reports, communicate with pilots, co-ordinate rescue operations, and so on. From 1976 to 1983, Frances Randall had this job and became quite a legend among climbers. A symphony violinist by profession, she often entertained her visitors to an impromptu concert in the snow, and herself climbed McKinley. She died from cancer in 1984.

She wrote numerous letters whilst at Base Camp which give an excellent picture of life on the glacier. These have been gathered together here, with a number of tributes and recollections.

Moving Mountains. *Coping with Change in Mountain Communities*
Sara Neustadtl
Appalachian Mountain Club, 1987, ppxiv + 210, pb, $14.95

The mountain ranges of the world are facing ever-increasing challenges from mining, forestry, tourism and other potential disasters. The author takes seven examples, from the Rockies, Alps and Himalaya, of individuals who have moved mountain communities to act against impending environmental disasters.

87. *Saser Kangri IV on L, Saser Kangri I (W face) in centre and 'Plateau Peak' on R.*

88. *Parilungbi (6166m), S face.*

89. *Phabrang (6172m), SW face.*

2·25

2·24

90. *The S face of Mt Hicks. (2.27, Yankee—
ice and rock'; 2.32, Logan's Run: '. . .
pitches in total'.)*

2·32

2·31

2·33 2·34

2·30

2·29

2·27 SHEILA GLACIER

2·26

...oir: 'an 800m ribbon of
...teep and sustained. 11

91. *Una May Cameron (1904–1987), at her villa in Courmayeur in 1953, when she was at the height of her powers.*

92. *Conrad O'Brien ffrench (1893–1986).*

93. *Henry Snow Hall, Jr (1895–1987).*

Mount Everest
Z. Kowalewski and A. Paczkowski
Wydawnictwo, 1986, pp193, in Polish, ZL. 2000

This is considerably more than the 'coffee-table' book it at first appears to be. It includes an historical list of Everest ascents, a bibliography and detailed photo-diagrams of all current routes on the mountain. The main part of the book consists of colour photographs of the ascent of the mountain, taken from the three Polish ascents, by Wanda Rutkiewicz in '78 and the expeditions of Winter '79/80 and Spring '80, but presented as one continuous sequence. It is definitely a book worth looking at, even if you can't read Polish.

Les Alpes Valaisannes à Skis. *Les 100 Plus Belles Descentes et Randonnées*
Denis Bertholet
Denoël, 1987, pp240, FF 228

The 20th volume in the series 'Les 100 Plus Belles . . .', created by the late Gaston Rébuffat, deals with ski routes in the Valais. It has the usual high standard of production, with excellent illustrations – every alternate page being in colour – and covers every grade of difficulty.

Grande Traverse and the Mont Blanc Tour
Malcolm and Nicole Parker
Diadem Books, 1986, pp64, £6.95

A 'book-size' guide to the 400km traverse of the Alps from the Mediterranean to Lake Geneva, covering the route in both summer conditions and as a winter ski tour. The maps are clear, the descriptions on a day-by-day basis, and the colour photographs excellent. The tour of Mont Blanc is added on, and appendices give details of accommodation, transport, maps and a short bibliography.

Ohmi Kangri Himal 85
Club Alpin Suisse, nd, pp48, npq

The report on the joint Swiss-Nepalese expedition to the Janak Himal in 1985, which reached the summit of Ohmi Kangri (7045m).

Himalaya Conference '83
Deutscher Alpenverein, nd, pp176, npq

The report on the results of the Himalaya Conference held in Munich in March '83. Papers on tourism, ecology, porters and guides, etc, in English.

Climbing
Thomas Hrovat
H. Weishaupt Verlag, Graz, 1987, pp160, npq

A large-format colour photo book of modern rock climbing at Yosemite, Joshua Tree, Frankenjura, Buoux, etc, including a few pictures of Malham, Kilnsey, Tremadoc and other local crags. Well produced, with text in both German and English.

Le Huitième Degré. *Dix Ans d'escalade libre en France*
Jean-Baptiste Tribout and David Chambre
Denoël, 1987, pp186, pb, FF 98

The story of modern free climbing in France, including competitions, climbing walls, etc. In French.

L'Escalade
David Belden
Denoël, Paris, 1987, pp260, FF 240

The latest French manual on the '*connaissance et technique*' of climbing, or, rather, rock-climbing, as there is another volume on *L'Alpinisme* in the same series. This is a large-format, glossy production, with many colour photos and hundreds of diagrams and black-and-white pictures covering every aspect.

The Stone Spiral
Terry Gifford
Giant Steps, 1987, pp42, pb, £2.50

This is Terry Gifford's first collection of poetry, 26 poems in all. The majority are about wild life, climbing or mountain landscapes, and they make pleasant reading. Al Alvarez describes it on the blurb as 'an impressive collection'.

Mountaineering in the Andes. *A Source Book for Climbers*
Jill Neate
Expedition Advisory Centre, 1987, ppvii + 279, £9.95

This source book is in three roughly equal sections. Firstly, topographical descriptions and climbing history of all the ranges that make up the Andes; secondly, a peak gazetteer listed by country, range and group; and thirdly, a bibliography plus appendices on a few general matters. It is obvious from looking through this book that a vast amount of research has been carried out by the author – there are over 2300 references in the bibliography alone! It will prove an indispensable aid for many years to anyone researching Andean mountains.

Degrees of Difficulty
Vladimir Shatayev
Mountaineers, 1987, ppxii + 196, pb, $10.95

In 1974, six Russian women died on Peak Lenin. One of them was Elvira Shatayeva, leader of the women's team and wife of the author. In 1977, Vladimir Shatayev published this book in Russia, giving his climbing experiences and culminating in his detailed account of the 1974 tragedy. It has taken 10 years of effort for the work to be translated and published in America. It makes very interesting reading, showing how people become climbers in the USSR, and how that structured, orderly system works. It also gives graphic accounts of some climbs in the world's greater ranges, as well as a very moving account of the events on Peak Lenin.

Ski Powder
Martin Epp
Fernhurst, 1987, pp64, pb, £5.95

One of Switzerland's leading guides has written this instructional book for those who wish to leave the crowded piste slopes for untrodden powder snow.

Neubranljivi Izziv. *(The Irresistible Challenge)*
Dudley Stevens
Državna založba Slovenije, Ljubljana, 1987, pp232, npq

This book covers the author's climbing experiences in Snowdonia, the Highlands and the Alps, from 1946 to 1960, and in the Julian Alps from 1960 to 1972. The introduction and many of the photographs are by Walter Poucher. The author's story is full of wisdom and interest. The book is a translation into Slovene of the author's English typescript version which has been deposited in the Club Library, where it can be seen on application to the Librarian by anyone researching the Julian Alps.

Abode of Snow
Kenneth Mason
Diadem/The Mountaineers, 1987, ppxviii + 366, £12.95

Abode of Snow, originally published in 1955, has become the standard history of Himalayan exploration up to 1953 and is increasingly hard to find in second-hand bookshops. This new photo-reprint edition by Diadem has the benefit of 82 excellent photographs, many of great historical interest, a forward by Doug Scott, and a list of amendments suggested by Trevor Braham. In his review of the original book *(AJ60, 416–7, 1955)*, Hugh Ruttledge said, 'All British lovers of mountains will welcome this book; and I hope it will be translated into many languages'. The translation hasn't happened, but this modern reprint must indeed be welcomed by all mountain-lovers today.

Land of the Snow Lion. *An adventure in Tibet*
Elaine Brook
Jonathan Cape, 1987, pp238, £10.95

The author joined Doug Scott's expedition to Xixabangma in 1982 with the intention, not of climbing high, but of leaving the party after a while to go trekking on her own through Tibet. We have already had Scott's version of the personality clashes that occurred, in the book *The Shishapangma Expedition* (*AJ91*, 243–4, 1986), and now we have Ms Brook's. It makes interesting reading and readers can make up their own minds as to whose 'side' they are on. After these 90-odd pages Ms Brook is on her own and on her way to Lhasa, without permission and chased on her way by the Chinese authorities. Her experiences ranged from very pleasant periods with Tibetan families, to very much less pleasant experiences with the authorities; all are recounted in a very readable manner.

Catherine Destivelle. *Danseuse de roc*
Catherine Destivelle
Denoël, 1987, pp188, pb, npq

The French rock-climbing star Catherine Destivelle has written a book in two parts, the major part describing her climbing activities to date, the second illustrating the exercises she does to prepare for her climbs. The first part is illustrated by numerous excellent colour photos which will appeal especially to young male rock-climbers.

Ski Mountaineering in Scotland
Donald Bennet and Bill Wallace (eds)
Scottish Mountaineering Trust, 1987, pp122, £12.95

The SMC have followed their excellent volume on hill-walking on the Munros with this equally good volume on ski mountaineering. The presentation is similar, with maps and colour photos for each mountain group, and is uniform with recent SMC publications. As the authors say, 'This publication is a significant step, for it is the first SMC guidebook to recognise the present status of ski mountaineering in Scotland'.

Climbers' Guide to Central and Southern Scotland
Jerry Handren
Scottish Mountaineering Trust, 1986, pp302

The SMC has drawn together the small guides previously issued for the lowland Scottish crags and has published one huge all-encompassing volume to Central and Southern Scotland. It makes interesting reading, from the early days on the Whangie to the latest epics at Dumbarton, and is complete with modern gradings and starred routes.

Rock Climbing Guide to the Burren
Ed Calvin Torrans
Federation of Mountaineering Clubs of Ireland, 1986, pp114, npq

The first detailed rock climbing guide to Ailladie sea cliff and the inland crags of the Burren.

Alpi Lepontine. *Sempione-Formazza-Vigezzo*
Renato Armelloni
Club Alpino Italiano/Touring Club Italiano, 1986, pp480, npq

The latest Italian climbing guide, detailing routes on 588 summits in the Lepontine Alps north-west of Locarno. It is in Italian, but the clear maps and diagrams make for easy reference.

Cascade Alpine Guide - Climbing and High Routes *I. Columbia River to Stevens Pass*
Fred Beckey
The Mountaineers, 1987, pp328, $16.95

The completely revised and updated second edition of Fred Beckey's mammoth guide to the southern area of the Cascades. An incredible amount of work has gone into the production of this volume. It is the bible for anyone wishing to visit the area, which includes Mt Rainier.

The High Mountains Companion
Irvine Butterfield
Diadem, 1987, pp112, pb, £4.95

The text of *The High Mountains of Britain and Ireland* in condensed form for practical use, with a log-book at the end to record one's exploits.

The Hills of Cork and Kerry
Richard Mersey
Alan Sutton, Gill & Macmillan, 1982, ppix + 160, pb, £5.95

A comprehensive guide to walking in the hills of south-west Ireland.

Llanberis
Paul Williams
Climber's Club, 1987, pp306, £9.95

The guide to the Llanberis area has come of age – 306 pages, including some of the best action colour photos seen in a pocket guide, with a large section devoted to the recent wonders (horrors?) taking place in the quarries. A good historical introduction, interesting first ascent list, and a generally humorous approach make it a good read, even if you can't do half the routes in it!

Trek the Sahyadris
Harish Kapadia
The Mountaineers, Bombay, 1987, ppx + 160, pb, npq

This third edition of the guide to the Sahyadris, or Western Ghats, along the western coast of India, will cover the needs of anyone trekking or climbing in the area.

Klettersteig. *Scrambles in the Northern Limestone Alps*
Paul Werner, tr. Dieter Pevsner
Cicerone Press, 1987, pp176, £7.95

Originally published in Munich in 1983, this selected translation covers the best of the *via ferrata* in the northern limestone Alps, from the Allgäu in the west to Berchtesgaden in the east.

Classic Climbs in the Dolomites
Lele Dinoia and Valerio Casari. Tr. Al Churcher
Cicerone Press, 1987, pp176, £7.95

93 selected/recommended routes taken from the Italian edition of '84.

Malta. New Climbs. *1986 Supplement*
Roger Brookes and Simon Alden
Fylde MC, 1987, pp78, £2.99

An update on the 1971 RNMC Malta guide, giving new climbs since that date.

Wye Valley
John Willson, David Hope, Tony Penning and Matt Ward
Cordée, 1987, pp288, £7.95

A much-enlarged second edition, covering Wintor's Leap, Symonds Yat, Wyndcliffe and Shorn Cliff.

Walking Switzerland. *The Swiss Way*
Marcia and Philip Lieberman
The Mountaineers, 1987, pp272, $10.95

A guide to walks in the Swiss Alps, using vacation apartments, hotels, mountain inns and huts, both from selected centres and on longer tours.

Rock Climbing in the Lake District
Bill Birkett, Geoff Cram, Chris Eilbeck and Ian Roper
Constable, 1987, pp14 + 298, £7.95

The third edition, revised and extended, in a new 'guidebook type' plastic cover.

Rock Climbing in the Peak District
Paul Nunn
Constable, 1987, ppxxiv 316, £8.95

Fourth revised edition, in series with the above.

The Corsican High Level Route. *Walking the GR 20*
Alan Castle
Cicerone Press, 1987, pp80, £4.50

North Wales Limestone
Andy Pollitt
Climbers Club, 1987, pp224, £5.95

The latest guide to Craig y Forwyn and the Great and Little Ormes. The size of this guide shows the expansion that has taken place since the first guide, published as recently as 1976.

Peak Limestone – Stoney. *pp284*

Peak Limestone – South. *pp304*

Peak Limestone – Chee Dale. *pp344*
BMC, 1987, £7.50 each

The limestone cliffs of the Peak District now need three volumes, a total of 932 pages, with simply masses of climbs and with excellent illustrations, both from diagrams and photographs.

Idaho Rock. *A Climber's Guide to the Sandpoint Area and Selkirk Crest*
Randall Green
The Mountaineers, 1987, pp120, pb, $8.95

This climbing guide to North Idaho covers the practice rocks in the Sandpoint area and then the whole of the Selkirk Crest. The illustrations show what a fascinating area it is.

Buttermere and Eastern Crags
D Craig and R Graham/J Earl, A Griffiths and R Smith
F&RCC, 1987, pp288

The latest edition of the combined Buttermere/Eastern Crags guide, which kicks off the Fell and Rock's seventh series of guidebooks. A good production.

The Mount Cook Guidebook
Hugh Logan
New Zealand Alpine Club, 1987, pp144, $NZ 25

This second edition of the Mount Cook guide has been revised and up-dated from that issued in 1982, and gives a very comprehensive list of ascents in the whole area, from the Mueller Glacier region in the south to Mt Elie de Beaumont in the north, with numerous photo topos.

Les Dolomites Occidentales
Gino Buscaini and Silvia Melzeltin
Denoël, 1987, pp240, npq

The 21st volume in the '100 Best . . .' series created by Gaston Rébuffat covers the western Dolomites. All of the really classic climbs on the Marmolada, Sella, Brenta, Pordoi, etc, are covered, plus many lesser-known climbs and walking routes. The excellent standard of previous volumes is maintained.

Walking on Dartmoor
John Earle
Cicerone, 1987, pp 224, £4.95

A selection of 43 walking routes on Dartmoor, plus four longer routes, with a detailed introduction to the moor, by one of the 'local experts'.

East Africa. *International Mountain Guide*
Andrew Wielochowski
West Col, 1986, pp152, npq

This guide covers not only Mt Kenya, Kilimanjaro and the Ruwenzori, but the numerous rock-faces, towers and pinnacles that exist in Kenya, Tanzania, Uganda and Zaire. The author includes a selection of the best routes in these areas, plus notes on trekking and caving.

The following are new guides from Édisud, to their usual high standard, complete with maps, topo diagrams and photos:

Randonnées et Ascensions en Haute-Maurienne. *La Vanoise*
Roger Féasson

Randonnées et Ascensions en Haute-Maurienne. *Les Alpes Grées*
Roger Féasson

Escalades dans le Massif des Dolomites
Bruno Brenier and Marlène Dossetto
Selected climbs over the whole Dolomite area.

Escalades dans le Luberon. *Buoux*
D Gorgeon, S Jaulin and A Lucchesi

Randonnées Pédestres dans les Monts Auréliens
Alexis Lucchesi
'Between Sainte-Baume and Sainte Victoire.'

Randonnées au Ventoux et dans les Dentelles
Isabelle and Henri Agresti

The following, in Italian, are new from Edizioni Mediterranee:

Abruzzo con Lo Zaino. *Le più belle escursioni sopra i 2000*
Adriano Barnes
Walks and ascents in the Abruzzi region.

Corsica. GR 20. *180km di trekking da Conca a Calenzana*
Luca Pennisi

Grandi Trekking Italiani. *200 giorni di cammino su Alpi e Appennini*
Riccardo e Cristina Carnovalini

Verdon. *Incontri scelti con il calcare più bello del mondo*
Marco Bernardi
Selected climbs.

Marmolada. *Parete Sud. La Parete d'argento*
Maurizio Giordano
A detailed rock-climbing guide to the Marmolada.

The *Museo Nazionale della Montagna* '*Duca degli Abruzzi*' publish regular monographs on mountain themes as the official catalogues for exhibitions held in Italy. The most recent are:

No 52. Mattia Zurbriggen Guida Alpina
(Reviewed above.)

No 53. Nuova Zelanda. *Alpi e Vulcani nel Sud Pacifico. 1987. pp152.*
In Italian.
Mountaineering and mountain tourism in New Zealand.

No 54. Aimé Gorret. *L'Ours de la Montagne. 1987. pp56.*
In French.
The life story of Abbé Gorret of Valtournanche.

IN MEMORIAM

COMPILED BY GEOFFREY TEMPLEMAN

The Alpine Club Obituary	*Year of Election*
Noel Ewart Odell	1916 Hon 1973
Henry Snow Hall	1924 Hon 1962
Albert Jenkins Taylor	1958
Ian Kerr	ACG 1984
David Woolridge	1986
John Poole	1931
George Herbert Webb	1950
Ronald William Clark	1974
John Risdon Amphlett	1939
Count Alain de Chatellus	1976
Andrew Dykes Scott Bankes	1979
Herbert Horatio Mills	1964
Brian David Chase	ACG 1967
Miss Una Cameron	LAC 1929
The Right Rev Thomas Bernard Pearson	1966
Oliver Eaton Cromwell	1925
Joseph Sanseverino	1948

The following two tributes are from last year:

Alfred Maurice Binnie 1901–1986

Maurice Binnie, who died on 31 December 1986, was born on 6 February 1901. He was educated at Weymouth College and Queens College Cambridge. He worked for two years for the Bridge Stress Committee, before being appointed to a University Demonstratorship at Oxford in 1925. He joined Balliol and moved to New College as a lecturer in 1933. In 1944 he returned to Cambridge as a university lecturer in engineering, in charge of the hydraulic laboratory, and was appointed to a fellowship at Trinity where he lived until his death.

As an undergraduate, visits with relations in the Lake District aroused his interest in climbing, and the first climb he recorded was in Wales in 1923. His first visit to the Alps was in 1924, and for the next 60 years he seldom missed an opportunity, and for a don there were many, to visit the hills or the mountains. He was elected to the Club in 1929 and served on the Committee in 1936. There are few valleys or mountains in the Alps which he did not visit, and he was just as happy in the little mountains as on the 4000m peaks. One of his best years was 1927, when he was qualifying for the Club and climbed, among others, the Bernina, Roseg, Disgrazia and traversed the Matterhorn, up the Zmutt and down the Hornli ridges. On this last, he was accompanied by Eric Shipton and Bill Younger.

He took a keen interest in the OUMC and the CUMC; he was Senior Treasurer of the latter, and many meetings took place in his rooms. At Oxford he met Harold Herbert, then an undergraduate at St John's, who became his most regular climbing companion until Herbert died in 1981. He spent many Easter holidays at Wasdale in parties made up mainly of the Herbert family (four brothers) and their friends.

In 1932 he was awarded a Rhodes Travelling Fellowship, and from November 1932 until September 1933 he was abroad, visiting Australia, New Zealand and Canada, where he was able to combine climbing with his scientific duties. In New Zealand he did several mountain walks and climbs and was involved in one event which should be recorded here as he was always extremely reticent about it himself.

He and Miss Katie Gardiner (later President of the Ladies Alpine Club (LAC), 1941–45) and the guides Vic Williams and Jack Pope set out on 8 February to climb Mt Tasman. The following account of what happened appeared in an obituary notice of Miss Gardiner, who died in 1974.

'The party consisted of Katie, her friend Mr A M Binnie, Vic Williams and Jack Pope. The weather seemed perfect. An advance camp was set up on a ledge at the head of the Fox glacier in preparation for the climb, but in the middle of the night the weather suddenly changed and a violent storm burst. With his usual foresight, Vic Williams had noted a nearby crevasse as a likely refuge in such an emergency and while the others clung onto a tent fly, Jack Pope got down into the crevasse and cut out a platform. With a meagre supply of salvaged supplies and their sleeping bags, the four huddled in the crevasse for the rest of the night, hoping for the storm to pass. But dawn brought no respite. Thunder and lightning continued and there was little daylight. The blizzard continued for over a week, during which the party existed on a food supply that had been intended to last for only a couple of days and which was almost exhausted after six. On the sixth day Katie wrote a will to the effect that, should they not survive, Jack's and Vic's wives were to be cared for. Conditions outside the crevasse were so bad that Vic Williams doubted that anyone in the open could have survived for more than half an hour. Jack Pope made a vow never to climb again. Finally, on the ninth day, the storm abated. The party was weak from lack of food, but four eggs had been held in reserve and, after eating these, they decided to get down the glacier. As they started to descend they were met by a rescue party led by the Maori guide Joe Fluerty who, while surrounded by sceptics, had remained convinced that they were alive. A few hours after the descent to the Chancellor Hut the weather once again closed in, but by then they were safe.'

Others occasionally referred to the time 'he spent a week in a crevasse with a woman', but this would be received with only a grunt.

In July he was in Canada and spent some time in the mountains, which he described in 'Western Canada in 1933' (AJ46, 81–88, 1934). Here he again met and climbed with Miss Gardiner, also with Mr and Mrs I A Richards. One comment he made in that article is worth quoting. They were on the summit of Pinnacle. 'From the summit we were able to discuss the North Tower of Eiffel. It appears inaccessible except by those detestable engineering methods with which we are now so familiar.' This would have meant using a few pitons, and was a typically forthright opinion which was shared by many members of the club 50 years ago.

He was in Corsica in 1928 and returned to Canada in 1935.

Other expeditions included one to Norway in 1932, where he climbed in the Horungtinder, crossed the Jostedalsbrae and went up to Romsdal. In 1938 he went to the Lofoten Islands which he described in his humorous way in 'A Month in Lofoten' (AJ51, 43–53, 1939).

After the war he went several times to the Pyrenees with H W R Wade, who also accompanied him to the Dolomites and in Scotland.

When not elsewhere, he visited the Alps almost every summer and was sometimes able to spend two months there. In addition he spent very many short holidays in the hills and mountains of Britain.

His scientific achievements have been recorded elsewhere. He was very distinguished in the study of hydraulics and was elected to the Royal Society in 1960. His inquisitiveness must have led him to many new ideas and discoveries, and nothing in the least unusual missed his attention.

He was a splendid companion and as Wade has written: 'He was always excellent company, with his keen sense of humour and sly comments on people and things. He had a marvellous repertoire of stories with which he used to regale me on summits and elsewhere.' And to quote from his notice in *The Times*: 'He was above all generous and entirely devoid of malice. He loved climbing and nearly all his holidays were spent in the Alps or the British hills. Those fortunate enough to have his company on these expeditions could appreciate him at his best.'

Alec Malcolm

Conrad O'Brien ffrench 1893–1986

Conrad (Tim) ffrench, who died last year at the age of 93, was elected to the Club in 1933, recommended by Colonel Strutt on qualifications which included both Alpine and Himalayan climbs.

His early life was adventurous. Born in Montpelier Square and raised in Italy, where his father held the rank of a papal Marquis, he decided at the age of 17 to emigrate to Canada and join the Mounted Police. This experience taught him skills of handling both men and horses which were to prove of great value throughout the rest of his life. Returning to England at the beginning of the First World War he was gazetted as a subaltern in the Royal Irish Regiment, only to be wounded and taken prisoner a few weeks later in the Battle of Mons.

During his captivity he learnt to speak fluently in Russian as well as German and French, and on release became a secret agent for British Intelligence in the guise of a military attaché in Stockholm and elsewhere in Europe. This period, lasting two decades, forms the main subject of his delightful, personally illustrated autobiography *Delicate Mission*, a copy of which can be found in the Library. It ended on the eve of war in 1939 with a dramatic dash across the German frontier into Switzerland with the Gestapo at his heels.

Conrad returned to Canada in the latter part of the Second World War and lived in North America for the remainder of his life, at first in Vancouver and then in Banff where he built Fairholm Ranch, a beautifully designed log-house in the heart of the mountains with unlimited opportunities for climbing, skiing and horsemanship, in all of which he excelled. In 1958 the house was leased by the Canadian government to accommodate Princess Margaret and her party during her three-day visit to Banff.

I first came to know him when we lived in Calgary shortly after the war and thereafter our friendship never flagged despite our being for the most part on opposite sides of the Atlantic. On a steep bank at Fairholm, Conrad taught me the principles of the Christie turn and together we climbed and ski'd in the Lake and Fairholm ranges, where I soon came to appreciate his steadiness and confidence as a rock-climber and his qualities of companionship in the mountains and in life generally. Happy days to remember with our two families in close, friendly contact.

Conrad was an artist by profession, and a highly gifted one who had studied extensively in Paris and at the Slade School in London under Professor Henry Tonks where he became an outstanding draughtsman. Later in life he taught and lectured on Art and Philosophy at the University of British Columbia and also at the Community in Loveland, Colorado, where he lived.

Lastly, but to him of first importance was his religious faith. Brought up as a member of the Catholic hierarchy in Rome inheriting the dual titles of Marquis of Castel Thomond and Senior Knight of Malta of the Irish Langue, Tim came in middle life to reject the Roman dogma, and gave himself to a search for God within the framework of a revealed, created natural order whose origins inevitably pointed to a Supreme Designer, to whom all men might become attuned by hearing his voice within themselves. In his latter years Conrad became a much-loved resident elder-statesman of the 'Community of Divine Light' at Sunshine Ranch, Colorado. Although this group does not hold orthodox Christian beliefs, Conrad's own approach to faith could be well summed up in Ronald Knox's rhetorical and epigrammatic enquiry: 'How can anything matter unless there is Someone who minds?'

He was twice married and leaves a daughter, Christina, who lives in Sweden; and a son, John, in Revelstoke, British Columbia.

Edward Smyth

Noel Ewart Odell 1890–1987

Noel Odell joined the Club in 1916, was elected Vice-President in 1945 and honorary member in 1973. He was also a founder member of the Himalayan Club and honorary member of a number of other mountaineering clubs including the American Alpine Club, the Canadian Alpine Club, the New Zealand Alpine Club and the Norsk Tinder Klub to which he was particularly attached. His wife Mona was also a member of long standing, having joined the LAC in 1921 and remaining a member till her death in 1977 (see *AJ83*, 270–1, 1978).

Odell qualified for the Club in the golden years of alpine climbing before the First World War and was a near contemporary of such great figures as Geoffrey Young, George Finch and Alfred Zurcher. His proposal form was seconded by Haskett-Smith. But we remember him most of all as our last survivor of the dramatic 1924 Everest expedition in which he played such a memorable part, spending many days above the N col, going twice up to Camp VI in support of Mallory and Irvine's attempt on the summit and being the last man to see them alive. His performance that year is all the more remarkable when it is remembered that this was his first Himalayan expedition and his first experience of high altitude, his selection for Everest having been based on his Alpine record combined with the strength and endurance he showed on sledging journeys in Spitsbergen. He had to withdraw for personal reasons from the 1933 expedition but came to the Himalaya in 1936 with the Anglo-American expedition to Nanda Devi, and this was his second *annus mirabilis* when at the age of 46 he with Bill Tilman made the first ascent of this noble mountain, then and for some years the highest to have been climbed.

He was back on Everest in 1938 with Tilman's expedition but, as events turned out, did not go very high that year. After the war he continued to climb and explore actively in the Canadian Rockies with Frank Smythe, in Yukon and Alaska with an American expedition, and especially in New Zealand during his time at Otago University. On his return from New Zealand he was 66, but he remained active and vigorous right to the end of his life. Even at the age of 93 he attended the 75th anniversary celebrations of the ABMSAC and made his way, with some mechanical assistance, up to the Britannia hut.

As an expedition member Noel was a genial and easy-going companion. On Nanda Devi he was, apart from Graham Brown, the oldest of our party and, being a somewhat patriarchal figure, earned the nickname, which he rather relished, of Noah.

On Everest in 1938 he was teased unmercifully about his rather ponderous glaciological researches and took it all in good part. He was an impressive man in his prime, and Charles Warren reminds me that when the

Dzongpen at Shekar entertained us that year the chang girls characterized him as a godlike figure. I remember him most clearly of all on a little side-journey we took together, crossing back into Sikkim over the Lonak La, an excursion we both greatly enjoyed and one about which he often reminisced in later years. The only thing one found to criticize about him was his extreme slowness in dealing with his kit and in doing camp chores. Such things have a dispro-portionate importance at high altitude, and I have long suspected that it was this quality which made Mallory reject him and prefer Irvine for the final assault in 1924.

Odell was a geologist, trained at the Royal School of Mines where, after the interruption caused by the First World War in which he served in the Royal Engineers and was three times wounded, he qualified as ARSM. In the early twenties he joined the geological staff of the Anglo-Persian Oil Company, working first in London and then in Persia; he next moved to Canada, working for a mining company and later as a consulting geologist. From 1928 to 1930 he was at Harvard as lecturer in geology, and from there he came to Cambridge, first as PhD student then lecturer in geomorphology, and was supervisor of studies in geology and geography at Clare College. He remained at Cambridge till the war started, and despite various interruptions Cambridge was to be his main base for the rest of his days.

The first of these interruptions was the Second World War which saw him, aged 50, recommissioned in the Royal Engineers, serving initially in this country but later transferring to the Indian Army in the Bengal Sappers and Miners.

Odell never was, and probably never aspired to be, in the front rank of geological research. His career was the result of perseverance and endurance, for he was not awarded his PhD till the age of 49, nor did he get his first professorship till he was 60, this being at the University of Otago in New Zealand, which must have been a very congenial post. A part of his rather splendid inaugural address at Otago in praise of mountains was read out at his memorial service in Cambridge. It is now in the University Library. After a spell back at Cambridge he did a further two years abroad, starting in his 70th year at the University of Peshawar. Geology had provided him with an extraordinarily varied life, giving opportunities for field work in many continents and for making a host of friends with whom he kept regularly in touch. He was a great letter writer. Clare College finally made him an honorary fellow in 1983, and he was a most loyal and devoted member of both College and University.

Loyalty is also the word that comes to mind in thinking of Odell as a member of the AC, for he was intensely proud of the Club and, even in his eighties and nineties, was an unusually regular attender at Club meetings and indeed at other mountaineering gatherings. Members for whom the events of 1924 and 1936 are ancient history will remember him as an upright and distinguished figure, still possessed of all his faculties and contributing, sometimes at great length, to discussions at Club meetings. Even in the week of his death he was at the memorial meeting organised for Don Whillans at the Royal Geographical Society. His sudden death that weekend was surely the perfect end to a long and active life.

The Noel Odell evening organized by the Club in his memory was a unique and fitting tribute to a distinguished and popular member.

Peter Lloyd

H Adams Carter writes:

Noel Odell had a long and important connection with American mountaineering, extending over at least 51 years. He was the guest of honour at the American Alpine Club's Annual Meeting and Dinner on 29 December 1926. He became a member of the American Alpine Club in 1928 and was made an honorary member in 1936.

Noel, or Noah as many of us affectionately called him, was a lecturer in geology at Harvard University from 1928 to 1930. While there, he was a great inspiration to the members of the recently formed Harvard Mountaineering Club. On weekends he helped hone our climbing skills. A still well-remembered new ice route pioneered in the bitter cold of Huntington Ravine in the White Mountains bears his name, Odell Gully. Before this time, the students had restricted themselves mostly to rock: he introduced them to steep ice. He inspired these Harvard climbers to organize expeditions to the great mountains of the world. It was his legacy that for the next 30 years all American mountain expeditions that were worth their salt were well represented by Harvard. In the summer of 1930 he was the senior member of the Harvard Mountaineering Club's summer camp in the Selkirk Mountains of Canada. He was with Americans in Labrador's Torngat Mountains in 1931 and in north-east Greenland in 1933.

When four of us naïve Harvard boys decided to tackle the Himalaya in 1936, of course we invited Noah to join us and to suggest which three other British climbers should make up the party. We all know how he and Bill Tilman reached the summit of Nanda Devi, which held the record as the highest summit reached for the next 14 years. I was lucky enough to be teamed up with Noah for much of the expedition, an education and a privilege I shall never forget.

After the Second World War, Noah returned a number of times to America. In 1947 he climbed in the Lloyd George Range with Henry Hall, an American Honorary Member of the Alpine Club, who died at the age of 91 a couple of weeks after Odell. In 1949 he was in the summit team of an American expedition that climbed Mount Vancouver in Alaska, at that time the highest yet unclimbed peak in North America.

Noah never forgot his American friends in his later years. We welcomed him on our shores and were also warmly received by him in Cambridge and elsewhere. We would never make a trip to England without making an effort to see him. We are greatly in his debt, not only for what he did for American expeditionary mountaineering, but more especially for the inspiration and friendship he gave so freely to many of us American climbers.

Martyn Berry writes:

In about 1960 Noel Odell came to Oxford to lecture to the OUMC. Afterwards I mentioned to him that in a nearby room in the Geology Department (where I think Wager was still at that time Professor) a friend of mine was doing some important research in geochronology. The good Professor asked if he could have a look at the project. There was, of course, no one else about at that time of night, so I showed him round my friend's lab, trying desperately to remember what I could about mass spectrometers and talking glibly about isotopic ratios. Looking back, I am amazed at the kindly forbearance with which Odell treated a bumbling but enthusiastic undergraduate.

For some years I have been attending lectures at the AC as a guest of my colleague John Temple. I have often seen Odell, and a couple of times I have seen him in the Library being consulted by young Himalayan expeditioners, his head and theirs bowed over maps and books covering the table.

John and I arrived very early for the September 1986 meeting. I was reading in the Library when there was a loud thud from the stairs. A few moments later John came in and told Pat Johnson that a doctor was needed. She rushed out, came back immediately saying, 'O God, it's Professor Odell', and phoned up to the Committee Room. I wandered unhappily towards the door, doubting whether I could be of any use.

Odell was standing in the washroom, his profusely-bleeding head being cleaned up with loo paper by John. He was embarrassed but cheerful. Someone nearby said that Odell had fallen the full flight and hit his head on the wall. Hamish Nicol appeared, brisk and professional, had a good look and said there was no serious damage. As soon as the bleeding stopped Odell said he had to go back up to meet the Bradford Washburns, and firmly resisted attempts to get him to sit down. So up the stairs he went, with John following close behind. 'D'you know', said Odell to no one in particular, 'I've never fallen any distance on a mountain yet.' 'Plenty of time for that,' said John.

Odell stood by the bar with a glass in his hand and talked animatedly for the best part of the next hour. When we moved in for the lecture he at last sat down, but was shortly on his feet again to deliver a brief and eloquent tribute to his old friend Jumbo Wakefield. He listened intently to Bill Brooker for the next 80 minutes, and contributed twice to the discussion. When we left he was standing, glass in hand, still talking.

Next morning I asked John whether the old boy might have woken up with a headache. 'Only a hangover,' said John.

Henry Snow Hall, Jr 1895–1987

Bradford Washburn, an Hon. Member of the AC and a lifelong friend of the Hall family, was asked by Lydia Hall to speak at Henry Hall's funeral service on behalf of all his friends. This is what Dr Washburn said:

Barely two weeks ago, I had a heartwarming experience. Late in the afternoon I was starting homeward from my office at the Museum of Science, and I decided at the last moment to make a tiny detour through the beautiful Atrium of the new Omnimax Theatre building – just to take a peek at the many new exhibits being installed there.

Right in the midst of a milling sea of visitors were Henry and Lydia Hall and their guide and neighbour, Sam Leland! Henry and Lydia were just standing there with Sam, marvelling at the beauty of the new hall and the happiness, indeed joy, on all the faces around them.

Something was clearly going on, deep inside them. Something that they shared with only a tiny handful of New Englanders: the thrill of knowing that nothing that was going on around them could possibly be taking place, had it not been for their own courage and faith and generosity.

We drove home together on our last trip to 154 Coolidge Hill. It was a beautiful early-spring afternoon and I will always cherish the memory of those last happy minutes of a 61-year friendship.

Henry Hall meant different things to many different people. To some he was one of a small group of men who convinced General Marshall that the United States should train Mountain Troops. They did – and the 87th Mountain Infantry was deeply involved in the attacks that broke the back of the Axis in the Aleutians and in Italy.

To others he was always present at the meetings of the Harvard Traveller's Club – a member of the Explorers' Club, the Appalachian Mountain Club, a 30-year Trustee of Boston's Museum of Science – a constant and generous enthusiast of our great Symphony Orchestra.

But, to the largest group of all, Henry was a *mountaineer*. I choose this word carefully because he was not at all just a mountain *climber* – someone who hurries directly to the top, cuts a notch in his ice-axe and then rushes elsewhere to add a new summit to his growing list.

Henry simply loved to be *in the presence* of great mountains, preferably unexplored ones. He didn't have to get to the top to be happy! He loved the forests and the wilderness – and he loved to be there in the company of others who shared this love. And, most of all, he loved *young* mountain people.

Like many of us here this morning, his climbing started with hikes and snowshoe-trips in our own White Mountains; often with Bob and Miriam Underhill and Carl and Dorothy Fuller. He'd climbed the Matterhorn before he was 16 and joined the American Alpine Club and the AMC in his early twenties. Over a span of nearly 70 years he attended virtually every AAC meeting, no matter where it was held – and served on its Board of Directors as Member, Secretary, President and finally as its first Honorary President.

Without Henry Hall's faith and generosity, his close and ever-admired friend, Adams Carter, could never have led the *American Alpine Journal* to the point where today it is universally considered to be the most distinguished mountaineering publication in the world.

Over the years, Henry didn't confine his activities to the mountains of New England and the Alps. He climbed Africa's Kilimanjaro, Elbruz in the Caucasus, and ventured to South America to make the first ascent of

Colombia's Sierra Nevada de Santa Marta – the highest coastal peak in the world – with his lifelong friends, Tom Cabot and Walter Wood. In the early thirties, he and Lydia and their friends, the Croziers, flew across central Alaska to get a closer look at Mt McKinley – and he was a member of the team that was first atop Mt Logan (Canada's highest peak) and, similarly, later, went to Mt Hayes in the Alaska Range. But Henry's very special love was the exploration of the great peaks of the Canadian Rockies and British Columbia – to which he returned year after year, always accompanied by old and trusted friends and guides.

One might easily think from all this that Henry Hall was miserable when he was not on, or at least *near to*, mountains. That was indeed true for a while, but as early as 1924, when he was one of the founders of the Harvard Mountaineering Club, his greatest joy developed out of chatting, planning and dreaming with *young* climbers and explorers. He loved to share information. His Cambridge home was a veritable mecca for everyone who loved the wilderness – and particularly the high wilderness.

It was barely possible to squeeze with him into his tiny study – jammed, piled and cluttered with an unrivalled wealth of books, journals and maps from every nook and cranny of the world! This was the spot where hundreds, possibly thousands, of us youngsters always found a listening ear, an infinitude of facts, thoughtful advice and boundless enthusiasm – for what *we* wanted to try to do.

Henry Hall was never a leader, but he was a source of information and a catalyst of the first order – and, because of this, he was held in the highest esteem by the mountaineering fraternity throughout the world.

When Barbara and I visited the Royal Geographical Society in London last fall for meetings related to our map of Mount Everest, we spent a stimulating evening with Noel Odell – the last man to see Mallory and Irvine alive when they disappeared into the mists of Everest's final pyramid on that fateful June afternoon in 1924. Odell, well over 90 years of age, discussed with us the tiniest details of the upper reaches of Everest as if he'd been there the day before – but the very first question he asked us was: 'How are Henry and Lydia Hall?'

Why did Henry Hall love the wilderness and the heights so much, and why did this enthusiasm leave us so many vivid memories and shape the lives of so very many of his friends? I think that it was because those of us who love the same things realize that, in these high and distant places, we are all deeply moved by the magnificence and wonder and glory of nature when we see them in never-to-be-forgotten terms.

Hudson Stuck, the Archdeacon of the Yukon, once declared that standing on the summit of Mount McKinley meant more to him than owning the richest goldmine in Alaska. And his young partner, Robert Tatum, exclaimed that the view from McKinley's summit was to him like 'looking out the windows of Heaven!'

May I close these reflections about our dear friend, Henry Hall, by reading a sonnet by John Magee, a young RCAF fighter pilot who lost his life in the Second World War. Although it's not about climbing, it marvellously conveys the sense of wonder and beauty that tempts us to the heights.

HIGH FLIGHT
by John Magee

Oh! I have slipped the surly bonds of Earth
    and danced the skies on laughter-silvered wings.
Sunward I've climbed, and joined the tumbling mirth
    Of sun-split clouds – and done a hundred things
You have not dreamed of – wheeled and soared and swung
    High in the sunlit silence. Hov'ring there,
I've chased the shouting wind along, and flung
    My eager craft through footless halls of air . . .

Up, up the long, delirious, burning blue
    I've topped the wind-swept heights with easy grace,
Where never lark, or even eagle flew –
    And, while with silent, lifting mind I've trod
The high untrespassed sanctity of space
    Put out my hand and touched the face of God.

God bless you, Henry – for your sharing – your caring – your generosity; but, above all, for opening doors and broadening horizons for a host of youngsters – for over half a century.

John Poole 1899–1987

John Poole was 87 when he died last year. One of four brothers who were all interested in climbing, he was proposed for the Alpine Club by M G Bradley in 1931 with the most impressive list of supporters ever seen – eight in all, including Haskett Smith, Claude Wilson, Edwin Herbert, Geoffrey Bartrum and S B Donkin.

His whole life was active, until illness prevented first climbing and then mountain walking. He recounted much of his activity in his article 'Senior Member' in the CC Journal for 1979/80, part of which was reproduced in Milburn's Helyg.

John was a meticulous man. I knew him first as a meticulous town clerk when we were both of that persuasion. He was a meticulous climber, as I learnt when I joined him for the first time on Tryfan, a mountain on which he seemed to know intimately every hold on every route. Of course, he had the occasion to know Welsh rock intimately, spending so much of his time there from 1918 onwards, and later alternating long summer holidays there with equally active holidays in the Alps. No wonder that he retired from being town clerk of Uxbridge to Anglesey, within sight of his beloved mountains, at the earliest possible moment. The advantage of Anglesey, and of retirement, was that he could see what the weather was like on the hills and choose when to climb.

When he started climbing, having acquired nailed boots, a 60-foot Beale's rope, with that famous red strand in the middle, and a copy of Abraham's *Rock Climbing in North Wales*, he set about climbing all the routes in the book, staying with brother Harry for weekends at Ogwen. Apart from his brothers, his early climbing companions included I A Richards, Dorothy Pilley, Will McNaught, M G Bradley, W J Williams and his son Gwyn, Herbert Carr and Herbert's father! With the last two he opened his alpine book when he climbed Mont Blanc, and then had a long alpine record.

He had five seasons there prior to joining the Club – Chamonix, Fionnay, Bel Alp and Stein – climbing mainly guideless with his wife and others, including traverses of the Grépon and Grands Charmoz. In 1935 he wrote in *AJ47*, 263, how, when ascending the Matterhorn in 1931, he had photographed the Schmids on the first ascent of the N Face (a print is in *AJ44*, opposite p70).

But his real love was Wales, to which he returned constantly and in which he lived for the last 28 years: a 'retirement' which many of us would envy, except for the last few years of illness which John bore with fortitude, however much he disliked his disabilities. In Wales he became an active member and, for a period, President of the Mountain Club of North Wales.

His wife, Irene, survives him. Under his inevitable influence she became an active climber and, via the Ladies Alpine Club, a fellow member with him of the Alpine Club.

John's influence will live on, through the many friends to whom he introduced the mountains.

Harry Sales

Douglas Milner writes:

When I went to the Dolomites in 1947, under Allied Military Permit, I climbed the Adang Kamin from the Gardena Hut, where a special book was kept for that climb. During the war years the only signatories were Graf von X or Oberst Y, and a very large one: 'Luis Trenker', the well-known Austrian film star. The last English signature before the war was that of John Poole, whose name I knew, though I had not then met him.

Three years later we were both members of a party of 7: 4 ACs, 2 LACs and A N Other. Only two still are around, Mrs Poole and myself.

We climbed the Torre Inglese (for the sake of the name), traversed the Zwölferkofel, Einserkofel, and the Kleine Zinne (by the Innerkofler route). A most enjoyable holiday.

Although I was in the CC from 1955, I never met John in North Wales.

Ronald William Clark 1916–1987

Ronald Clark died after a short illness on 9 March 1987, collapsing in his study at Camden Street, London, still working. He was proposed for membership of the Alpine Club in 1974 by Sir Arnold Lunn, primarily on the basis of his contributions to mountain literature. He was in fact an experienced mountaineer, but preferred the mountains of Scotland to the higher ranges, although he climbed the Ecrins in 1947 and the Schreckhorn in 1948. I first met Ronald at Idwal Cottage Youth Hostel in 1940; we were taking our first steps at rock-climbing with our Lawrie boots and newly-acquired Jones Golden Seal Hemp Rope. He was tall and slim, but then so were my brother Arthur and I in those austere war years. We were devotees of Owen Glynne Jones and the Abraham brothers. Ronald was several years older than us. I was very impressed that he was a journalist and worked in Fleet Street, one of the 'Gods of modern Grub Street'. I was still at school!

Born in 1916, he had a conventional upbringing, educated at Kings College School, Wimbledon, leaving school to enter a journalistic career in magazine writing. He later progressed to the British United Press where, early in the Second World War, he was a night editor. He was appointed a War Correspondent and followed the First Canadian and Second British Armies through Europe to the war's end; he then stayed to report on the Nuremberg War Trials. After the war he wrote on a variety of topics, including the problems of postwar Europe. He was very fond of cats; I remember visiting him around 1951 at Camden Street when he was asked for 600 words on cats to fill a space in a magazine: these he gave by reply, with barely a pause, over the telephone.

His main interest, then, was writing about mountains, and in the late 1940s and early 1950s, he wrote a series of books, *The Splendid Hills*, *The Early Alpine Guides* and then, in 1953, *The Victorian Mountaineers*. He made accessible to a wider and younger range of readers the lives and writings of many of those who have enriched the history of climbing. With the late Edward Pyatt he wrote *Mountaineering in Britain* which became a reference book in its day. In his early days he would first make a mock-up of the book he wished agents to consider, with photographs and chapter headings in the appropriate order and with chapter summaries, in an old book turned upside-down and most of the pages stuck together. In *An Eccentric in the Alps* he wrote of the climbs of W A B Coolidge and his pioneering assaults on the Meije. His quotation of Coolidge's description of his descent from the Glacier Carré in 1878 as 'the most arduous and terrible piece of climbing' reminded me of our retreat from the top of the South Face Direct across the unforgiving ice of the Glacier Carré, in growing darkness and threatening weather, unroped, as we gambled for mutual survival. I think my companions would have agreed with his description of the descent off the great wall as 'ten times worse' than the ascent.

Ronald Clark wrote many books for young people which found a wide audience. *Great Moments in Mountaineering* was a modest volume which a top newspaper reviewed, saying how pleasant it was to read a book with so few long words. He thought this was meant to be a compliment. It sold worldwide and I have a copy, with the Japanese edition alongside it. In all, he wrote more than 60 books, as well as innumerable magazine articles. A series on stations of the now, alas, defunct Department of Scientific and Industrial Research led him into writing on scientific matters and personalities. He was asked to write a history of British contributions to the making of the atomic bomb, *The Birth of the Bomb*. Despite a lack of 'higher' education he had developed a formidable talent for writing readable books. They were the product of intense research and concentration on the job in hand. He wrote a shrewd life of Sir Henry Tizard, the wartime scientific adviser. He spent several months in India researching the life of J B S Haldane, the Communist scientist, who did so much to advance the art of deep-sea diving by his work on high pressures during the war, and who sought refuge in India afterwards. His *Life of Einstein* might have deterred a lesser man, but he knew where to go for the information and the scientific magazine *Nature* could find neither typographical errors nor errors of fact. Some of his more literary critics were less kind. His major biographies ranged from Bertrand Russell, Sigmund Freud, Thomas Edison, Benjamin Franklin and Ernest Chain to his last book, *Lenin*, which is shortly to be published.

Although we kept in touch from time to time through the years, I only once walked again with him, on the North Downs after our meeting in Wales. He once unsuccessfully tried to persuade BOAC, who were carrying out route-trials with the Comet airliner to Nairobi, to give us a free flight so that we could try to climb Kilimanjaro in a long weekend! Despite his serious approach to his work he had a whimsical side which revealed itself in his few fiction books. His *Queen Victoria's Bomb* revealed that one man developed a destructive device during her reign and tested it in the foothills of the Himalaya. The blast was so great that accompanying army observers thought it could only have been caused by a terrible natural event, so the Queen insisted on secrecy, and the discovery lapsed after the death of the inventor.

Ronald illustrated many of his books with photographs, taken with his faithful Rolliecord; he made many enlargements which he systematically indexed and bound into albums. He also kept a collection of Victorian alpine photographs. Although he planned his books like a military operation, he was a private person with a reluctance to step outside his chosen profession. He could have excelled in academic historical research and might well have succeeded as a barrister or television presenter! – but he stuck to his 'last'. He contributed a thoughtful article to *AJ81*, 1976 on alpine pollution in its broadest sense.

He was married three times, but had no children. His wives Pearl, and later Elizabeth, writers in their own right, supported him professionally throughout his career, unselfishly relieving him of many of the tedious tasks of writing, like indexing, for – true to his Fleet Street background – he never adopted the word-processor. He is sadly missed by his wife and friends.

Dave Thomas

Alain de Chatellus 1907–1987

I first met Alain de Chatellus after he had written a very flattering review of one of my books. He was of the old nobility and very scathing about 'newcomers' who added a 'de somewhere' after their names; usually choosing some remote village in Réunion, Madagascar or Mauritius (there are many such 'newcomers' in prominent positions in French politics today). On learning that my wife and I had recently been involved in a nasty road accident, he quite typically picked us up at our hotel on leaving his Paris office and drove us to his house at St Cloud for dinner with his wife, and back again to our hotel.

He was a very successful business man, but it was his mountaineering record that led me to propose him for membership of the AC. His friend Lucien Devies was more than happy to second him.

Alain climbed much in Chamonix, often with Georges Charlet, the younger brother of our late Hon Member Armand Charlet. They did many of the standard Aiguilles and included the Peuterey Ridge of Mont Blanc. His other claim to fame was his climbing in and exploration of the remoter mountains of N Africa, in the Tibesti and Hoggar mountains, where he made a number of first ascents, as described in his book which is available in the AC library.

Alain was only once able to attend the AGM and dinner of the AC. We were able to make up a 'French' party for the latter and arrange transport for him and others, to repay belatedly the debt we owed him.

Douglas Busk

Andrew Dykes Scott Bankes 1955–1987

It was with great sorrow that we learnt of Andrew's death in June 1987, following a cancer illness which had lasted for over a year. Andrew had fought the illness for many months, and at times during the early part of the year it was encouraging to see his temporary recovery.

Andrew was born and lived in London, but his family home near Mold in North Wales instilled in him a fondness for the mountains at an early age. He started mountain-walking as a child, and his interest in climbing was developed at Eton College and encouraged by his housemaster, John Vesey.

When Andrew left school he went to Durham University and continued his climbing whilst close to the more mountainous regions of the United Kingdom. He then moved back to London to start his career in the legal profession. He studied successfully for the Bar and practised from chambers in the Temple for a number of years. During this period he became a very active climber and joined both the North London Mountaineering Club and the Alpine Club, where he became a member of the Committee with responsibility for arranging informal meetings. Although he spent virtually all his weekends climbing, he nevertheless found time to meet and marry his wife, Ariane.

In addition to climbing together, Andrew and I used to run regularly in London, over Hampstead Heath. Although we used this primarily as a means to get fit for the mountains, he successfully completed the London Marathon in 1984. He led me to believe that he found this more gruelling than any climb! We always seemed to be in a race rather than just going for a friendly run; this reflected his competitive nature which was so apparent when one was climbing with him.

Andrew was a very keen and enthusiastic climber. He won many friends within the climbing world, not only because of his enthusiasm for getting out into the hills as often as he could – which is not easy from a London base – but also because, once there, regardless of the weather, he would spend from dawn to dusk (and sometimes into the dark) walking and climbing over the mountains. Whatever the climb, he viewed it as the most important thing to him at that moment and we always had a feeling of great accomplishment when we succeeded on any route, no matter how tame. During the long car rides to the mountains from London, his amusing conversation and wit were always highly valued. Many a journey was shortened by stories of his encounters in court during the previous week!

Andrew was primarily interested in the larger and more challenging mountains, although he was also a keen rock-climber during the summer months. He was active in Scotland on ice for a number of winters, and he also climbed in the Alps. His most notable ascents were the traverse of the Matterhorn and the Mönch. Andrew also visited the Himalaya twice, and it was in 1984 that he made a successful ascent of a 6200m peak in the Mulkila group in Lahul and Spiti.

Andrew was a good friend of mine and of many other climbers from both the North London and the Alpine Clubs. We missed him during his illness and his absence will be felt more deeply now.

Anthony Wheaton

Herbert Horatio Mills MC, MA, PhD 1917–1987

I first met Bertie Mills when he joined the staff of Sedbergh School in 1963, where I was Chaplain for many years. We soon realized that we had in him a personality of distinction. But he was a shy and humble man, so reserved about his accomplishments that probably few realized how distinguished his career had been.

Born in Gloucestershire, the youngest of five, he was educated at Marling School, Stroud, where he excelled academically: he was head of school, captain of cricket, and in the football XI. In 1936 he entered King's College London to read modern languages. He interrupted the degree course to spend a year at Grenoble University, but then war prevented his final year at King's College, and he joined the Somerset Light Infantry, transferring later to the Parachute Regiment.

On the eve of D-Day he was dropped over Normandy, and for his part in taking the Pegasus bridge at Rainville he was awarded the MC. Subsequently he became Brigade Major and took part in the Rhine crossing, where he was mentioned in despatches.

After demobilization he went to St Catharine's College, Cambridge, where he took two 'firsts' in modern languages, gained a rugby 'blue' in 1947 and 1948, and was a reserve for the England XV.

It was a restless time for many: what to do with life? A spell in journalism, a year's Research Fellowship at Pennsylvania University, and back to Cambridge for a doctorate, with 'one of the best and most original theses' his tutor had ever seen. Unsatisfied, he wanted, as he wrote at the time to 'give, give, give to young people'. Part of a term teaching at a school in Folkestone set him on that road.

The life of a schoolmaster in a boarding school is demanding, and Bertie gave in full measure: the teaching of languages, organizing the school's football, coaching the 1st XV as well as humbler players, were exhausting activities, not to mention routine duties. A series of successful teams showed how successful he was as a coach – yet after work in the small hours he would read a chapter or so of a book of substance.

Sedbergh is well placed for fostering a love of the hills. In the spring of 1956 he joined my small party on the cliffs of Snowdonia, and in the summer I introduced him to the High Alps. For a number of years he was in my alpine parties, until I had to bring those halcyon days to an end. He was elected to the Alpine Club in 1964. In later years he used to say that of all alpine memories those that lingered most happily were his ascent of the Dent Blanche and the serene evening view from the Hörnli hut, the evening before he climbed the Matterhorn.

In 1962 he was appointed Rector of the Edinburgh Academy. Now he had to spend much time with the plans and problems of a headmaster, but he had by no means 'lost the magic of long days'. The Alps still drew him, but the Scottish hills were nearer: and for the rest of his days he made good use of them as opportunity offered, with occasional revisits to Lakeland. He was keen to get the young into the mountains, accompanying parties and, an idea near to his heart, he managed to persuade the school to buy and equip Blair House in Glen Clova as a base for field work and walking. In a way it is his unofficial memorial.

He retired in 1977, and found life at first depressingly empty. But he became Scottish secretary for ISCO, and, though ignorant of gardening, set to work to learn and was soon producing flowers, fruit and vegetables that outdid his neighbours. Over the years he ascended all the Munros and was a strong goer and a delightful and caring companion. He joined the SMC in 1973.

On 29 July 1987 he married Miss Rosalind Henn, and all seemed set for a blissfully happy life together. But less than a month later, on a Cornish beach, he had a heart attack which brought to a close a life of integrity, singleness of purpose and devotion to the young.

Austin Boggis

John Risdon Amphlett 1900–1987

J R Amphlett who died recently at the age of 87 was elected to the Club in 1938. He was a very likeable person. He started climbing in the Pyrenees in 1932 and did a number of traverses across the main chain. He also climbed the Aneto. In 1937 he started his alpine career and did the Fletschhorn, Lagginhorn and traverses of the Rimpfischhorn, Allalin and Alphübel. Then he did the Südlenzspitze, Nadelhorn and Stecknadelhorn from the Dom hut. He moved to Zermatt to do the Matterhorn by the Hörnli route and then back to Saas for the Jägigrat from the Weissmies hut. Then back again to Zermatt to climb the Wellenkuppe, Obergabelhorn, with descent of the Arbengrat and the traverse of Monte Rosa from the Betemps to the Margherita with, next day, the traverse of the Liskamm, Castor and Pollux, with descent to Zermatt via the Breithorn; all this in three weeks. In 1938, which was a bad summer, he started in the Dauphiné with Pic Coolidge and a day or two later climbed the Ecrins. Then he moved to Chamonix and traversed Mont Blanc before returning to Saas to do the Weissmies and traverse the Täschhorn and Dom from a bivouac on the Mischabeljoch. Lastly he traversed the Zinalrothorn from the Triftjoch to the Mountet, returning next day via the Point de Zinal. All his climbs were guided, except some in the Pyrenees.

There is unfortunately no record of any ascents after 1938.

T A H Peacocke

Brian David Chase 1943–1987

Brian's range of friends in the climbing world never ceased to amaze me. On meeting another climber for the first time, one always searches for common experiences and common friends. More often than not, among contemporaries, Chase would be a memorable figure. Typically, stories would be told about a long lean figure, with a dry sense of humour and a loud and infectious laugh, lounging on the Chamonix camp-site, or in a bar, passing time with and entertaining whoever happened to be there. He could give an air of contented indolence which only disappeared when an opportunity to climb presented itself; then he would shamble off, still seemingly unconcerned, but provide a drive and determination which usually took his team safely over the mountain.

He started climbing young, as one of a number of pupils from Derby School whom Bob Pettigrew introduced to climbing. From early beginnings on gritstone he developed into other areas, and in 1961, together with a group of other novices, organized and executed a first alpine season in Arolla and Saas Fee. By the time he went to read Natural Sciences at Cambridge in 1963 he was a highly competent mountaineer, as was demonstrated by his tally of 16 routes in Chamonix the following summer, notable amongst which was an early British ascent of the NW ridge of the Grands Charmoz. The next year he joined a Keele University expedition to the Cordillera Carabaya, which made 11 first ascents on various peaks. A couple of notable alpine seasons followed, culminating in ascents of the Route Major and N face of the Triolet in 1967, on the basis of which he was elected to the Alpine Climbing Group.

At Cambridge he was an active member of the Mountaineering Club, playing a leading part in both its climbing and its more notorious gastronomic/ alcoholic activities.

Despite being President of the Club he managed to take a good degree, and moved on to Imperial College, London, where he did research in applied physics and became involved in the London climbing scene. He also took part in the Innominate Mountaineering Club Swat Kohistan expedition in 1968, making what at the time was believed to be the first ascent of Miangul Sar.

In 1970 he moved to Hampshire to work as a research engineer for IBM. Thereafter, a new career, and a happy marriage, took him away from serious climbing for a number of years. When he re-emerged at an Alpine Club meet in 1979 he brought old habits and skills to enliven the more traditional side of mountaineering, leading parties up routes such as the Frontier Ridge of Mont Blanc du Tacul, the Whymper Couloir on the Aiguille Verte and the Täschhorn–Dom traverse.

The cancer which was finally to kill him first appeared in 1983, stopping a much-planned trip to the Karakoram. However, it did nothing to dampen his zest for life and new experiences, and he managed to find time to add caving and diving to his mountaineering and to his busy home and professional lives. He joined the Club's Garhwal meet in 1986, and was in the first party up Thelu (6002m) and Saife (6166m).

The pleasure of being on the mountains with him was that you could certainly reckon to have an enjoyable day, and generally a successful one. While slightly larger than life in many ways, he retained a low-key and modest approach (I only became aware of many of his achievements in writing this note). His self-professed and seemingly genuine air of indolence concealed a sense of determination which when harnessed made him unstoppable; when you climbed with him, it was usually with success. We did an unpleasant route on the Alphubel (the NW ridge) as an approach to the Täschhorn. It started badly when I fell off leading and was held only by the accidental jamming of a knot (Chase: 'I'm glad about that; I didn't have a belay'). Next he got off route and caused a stonefall which cut both ropes in the middle (Chase: 'Well, we'll have to climb on four ropes now'). Thereafter a stonefall just missed breaking my kneecap (Chase: 'It didn't do any real damage, did it?'). The idea of retreating never really occurred to us, and we went on to do the Täsch–Dom traverse the next day.

We all miss him, remembering some very entertaining and exhilarating times. Our sympathy goes to his wife Elaine and daughter Lisa.

Stephen Town

Una May Cameron 1904–1987

In the summer of 1914 Una Cameron, with her mother and twin sister Bertha, were caught in Switzerland by the outbreak of war. They stayed on for two years in Montreux, where the girls went to school; and during holidays in the mountains (as her uninfected twin recalls) 'the climbing bug got Una! and it never left her.'

Una was born at West Linton in Peebles-shire in 1904; she was Scottish in family, Scottish in speech, and firmly Scottish in drink – the family fortune was based on whisky, as she liked to tell her friends. From school in Switzerland she went to Cheltenham Ladies' College, then on to the Central School of Arts and Crafts in London. There she specialized in woodcuts, and she pursued this line further at art school in Rome, where she met Hazel Jackson, an American sculptor whose enthusiasm for climbing matched her own. Una had climbed a bit in her school and college days, but with this congenial spirit it became a real dedication. With Hazel she joined CAI expeditions to the Julian Alps and the Dolomites, and spent several seasons in the Western Alps. Her application to join the Ladies' Alpine Club in 1929 had a strong list of classic climbs, which included the Dent Blanche by the Viereselgrat, the traverse of the Matterhorn by the Zmutt and Italian ridges, the Via Miriam on the Torre Grande, the Via Dimai on the Punta Fiammes, the Guglia de Amicis.

In the Dolomites she climbed with local guides; from about 1930 she climbed almost exclusively with the Courmayeur guides Edouard Bareux and Elisée Croux (affectionately referred to as The Monster) – always regarded as friends and partners rather than employees. Courmayeur became her mountain headquarters, and the south side of Mont Blanc her climbing-ground. I don't think her record on the mountain has been equalled by any Briton. Between 1933 and 1939 she had traversed it in most of the possible ways: from the Col du Géant over Mont Maudit and down to the Dôme hut; from the Brenva Ridge and down to the Grands Mulets; from the Peuterey Ridge (two bivouacs) down to the Dôme hut – then up to the top again via the Quintino Sella hut; up the Innominata and down by the Aiguilles Grises; up the Brouillard and down by Tête Rousse; up the Rochers and down to the Col du Géant. She climbed two of the routes pioneered by Graham Brown and F S Smythe – the Red Sentinel in 1935, the Route Major in 1938 with descent by the Bionnassay Ridge! On the S face, too, there were ascents of the Dames Anglaises, and a traverse of the Aiguille Noire de Peuterey, with a first descent to the Brenva glacier in storm when they had to bivouac twice, and Una popped her drawing-book inside her trousers to make a seat at night. These separate ascents culminated in the climb of the whole Peuterey Ridge of 1935, when Una, Edouard and Elisée were accompanied by Dora de Beer and her guides. Dora, whose experience had been mainly in New Zealand, had been led by Una to believe that 'it was just one of the usual routes', and till it was over had no idea that they were the first women to go up it.

With Edouard and Elisée, Una went far afield. In 1932 it was the Caucasus, with Hazel Jackson joining them: in spite of rotten rock – 'a sinister mixture of stone books and suitcases that rattle down just as you are about to put a finger on it' – they climbed seven peaks in the Kasbek area ('as far as can be ascertained all first ascents') in the six fine days they snatched from a rainy season. In spring 1933 it was ski-touring in the Canadian Rockies round the Yoho Valley and Lake Louise. In 1938 it was East Africa, with ascents of Mt Speke and Mt Baker in the Ruwenzori, Kilimanjaro ('dull') and, not at all dull, Mt Kenya. From Nelion they traversed to Batian, where Una was the first woman, and where Edouard and Elisée were following those earlier Courmayeur guides, Brocherel and Ollier, who had made the first ascent with Halford Mackinder in 1899.

Once Courmayeur had become Una's alpine base she decided to build her own home there, above La Palud, near the old mule-track to the Mont Fréty; later, the téléférique to the Col du Géant passed right above it. It was a solid stone house with marvellous views that exactly suited the character of its owner; she created an alpine garden, bringing back plants from as far as the Ruwenzori; the garage at the foot of the steep path housed her succession of fast Italian cars.

During the war Una served first in the Fire Service in London, then with the FANYs, mainly in Scotland with Polish troops, and for some months in 1945 in liberated Singapore. In 1946 she returned to Courmayeur and a heart-warming welcome from the friends who had made it their business to keep German soldiers away from the Villa Cameron. The garage had gone – but in an avalanche! – and 'my home with its red-leather chairs and books, even clothes and some bottles of fiery liquor, were all as I had left them and the house a great deal cleaner than if the owner had been in residence for seven years'.

After the war Una would speak cheerfully of 'getting into training for the Pear', the climb which would have completed Graham Brown's triptych on the Brenva Face – but the days of her great exploits were over; she had put on weight, she didn't want to be a liability to others. This was to the advantage of her friends, who were more likely now to find her in when they passed by the Villa Cameron. She would regale them with Italian food and Scotch drink ('fire-water'), invite them to camp in her basement, bathe in her swimming-pool. She would help with their plans, calling in Edouard (who became something of a majordomo to her establishment) to advise on a route or a guide, or where a large party with teenagers could be most cheaply accommodated at La Palud.

When the LAC was coming up to its Jubilee in 1957, there was no question who should be President. Una had the presence, and a climbing record known far beyond the Club; she had edited the Journal and cheered it up no end with her woodcuts, which also adorned the menus at Club dinners. The LAC meant a lot to her, and she never felt quite at home after the merger with the Alpine Club, and seldom came to meetings. She now travelled rather than climbed; she walked in Nepal and Borneo (though there she did go up Mt Kinabalu), she visited Mexico, the Galapagos Islands, China, Angkor Wat. Her horizons narrowed as her health declined; her last years in a nursing home were cheered by a smuggled kitten – cats had always played a large part in her life. She died on 15 October 1987.

Una Cameron was a great character, though not always an easy one, for she had strong prejudices which she didn't bother to hide. She had a large body – 'I felt it handy to be heavy' she wrote, after a storm had nearly blown her party off the Brouillard Ridge – and great stamina. She stood out in any company – *elle porte le pantalon et elle fume la pipe*, a Courmayeur man described her to me in 1934, when trousers on women were not so common off the mountain, and before her pipe gave way to villainous-smelling cigars. She belonged to Courmayeur in the way passing climbers couldn't. She was fluent in French and Italian, the two languages of the Val d'Aosta; she supported the local Waldensian church (as she supported St Columba's Kirk in London); she knew everybody and everybody knew her. But that was in the days before the new roads, new hotels, the Mont Blanc tunnel and the huge extension of skiing – and before the death of Edouard. When she had to give up the Villa Cameron, it was no longer the wrench it would once have been.

Una was able to climb in a style that must amaze today's young climber, with limited means and limited holidays – able to transport her guides overseas, to build her Alpine home. She was privileged, and she knew it – but what matters is the enterprising use she made of her money and leisure, and the way she shared with others the pleasures they made possible. She made many first ascents, and many more firsts by a woman. But though she was pleased by such successes, they were not what she chiefly climbed for. After the 1935 season she wrote in her diary: 'First the Aiguille Noire de Peuterey and then Mont Blanc several times, in fact employment that I would not swop for entertainment by archangels, with the Heavenly choir in the offing.'

Janet Adam Smith (Janet Carleton)

The following two tributes to non-members are included as being of unusual interest:

Lady Tangley 1909–1987

Lady Tangley, Gwen to her friends, was the wife of one of our most distinguished Presidents – Sir Edwin Herbert, later Lord Tangley. She will be remembered with affection by many older members whom she and her husband entertained during and after his years of office from 1953–1956. Those were years which saw, amongst other changes, the transfer of leadership on Everest from Shipton to Hunt, to be followed soon after by the replacement of Graham Brown by Keenlyside as Editor of the *AJ* – both situations being handled by Herbert with outstanding aplomb and the minimum of ill-feeling.

Lady Tangley was also a well-known figure in her own right. As a musician at the Royal Academy of Music she had unearthed a previously unknown work by Bach, and later she became a talented concert pianist. She was born and spent the greater part of her life in the Guildford area, where the Herberts made their home and where she undertook many duties and responsibilities, musical and otherwise, at county and local level, including governorships of Cranleigh and its sister school, St Catherine's.

The warmth of her personality, along with all her faculties, continued to glow brightly to the very end of her life, and those of us who were privileged to enjoy her friendship will always treasure her memory. To her son and three daughters who inherit her musical skills we offer our affectionate sympathy; and it is good to remind ourselves that her nephew, Paul Herbert, continues to maintain an unbroken family tradition, now over 60 years old, of membership of the Alpine Club. Her grandson, James, now a cadet at Sandhurst, is also an enthusiastic climber.

Edward Smyth

Edwin Garnett Hone Kempson 1902–1987

After becoming a Wrangler in the Mathematical Tripos and taking up mountaineering whilst at Cambridge, G, as he was known to all at Marlborough College, returned to serve the College which he loved so much, and remained there for the rest of his life. He became an Assistant Master, then House-master and in the interregnum, in 1961, between Masters Garnett and Dancy (Garnett was a distant relation), he was Acting Master. In addition, he was involved in the affairs of the town both as a Borough Councillor and Mayor in 1946, and he was also an extremely active member and officer in the Wiltshire Archaeological and Natural History Society, lecturing often about the history of the town. During his period as Mayor he discovered an important collection of 17th century books which became known as the Vicar's Library. This was housed in the College for many years where he researched and catalogued it with loving care, until finally the collection was handed over to the Bodleian. Later he was Archivist of the College, a post that he relinquished in 1986.

For many years after returning to Marlborough from Cambridge he took boys climbing during the holidays in North Wales, the Lake District, Skye and the Scottish Highlands. In the summer he often visited the Alps with small groups, going to the Dauphiné, Chamonix, Val d'Isère and other regions, whilst in winter he did a great deal of ski-touring. The first issue, in 1934, of the Mountaineering Club Journal of which he was Editor had a suitable introduction by Geoffrey Winthrop Young, himself an old Marlburian, who used to play host at dinner for parties of schoolboys led by G at Pen-y-Pass.

G went to Everest on the 1935 Reconnaissance, when with Tilman and Warren he surveyed part of the southern portion of the Nyonno Ri Range. Whilst attempting to reach the North Col his party came across the body of Maurice Wilson on its lower slopes, and later with Warren and Shipton he reached the Col itself. The reconnaissance party then split up and with Warren and Spender, the surveyor, G surveyed the country between the E Rongbuk glacier and Doya La. Whilst doing so they climbed 'Kellas' peak, followed by one peak of 6880m and two over 6400m, from which photographs were taken to supplement the survey. Returning to Rongbuk, Warren and G took a theodolite to the summit of two further peaks over 6700m, and then climbed Kharta Changri, 7030m. G then had to return home for the autumn term. However, he had acclimatized well and, had the weather been reasonable in 1936, he would have been a strong contender for the summit party. But this expedition was storm-wracked and snow-bound, and little was achieved. However in the book of these two expeditions, *Everest, the Unfinished Adventure*, he contributed a characteristic and unusual appendix on the Tibetan name for Everest, which gave scope to his wide interests and meticulous scholarship. Luckily, too, and characteristically, he found time and energy on this expedition to visit the Lho La to look into Nepal, and he was able to photograph the Western Cwm and the Everest Ice-fall. Many years later, in 1951, whilst searching for suitable photographs to convince the sceptics that there was a possible route up Everest from Nepal, I remembered reading about this, wrote to him and back came the photograph, a vital link in the chain of evidence.

He was a pleasant and stimulating companion, and with quick bird-like movements he seemed to flit easily from rock to rock and from tussock to tussock, and his mind moved as phenomenally fast as did his feet. He was still going and interested when those around him almost ceased to move or think from sheer exhaustion. A gentle man with many and diverse interests, music, bird-watching, natural history, he was slow to anger and always cheerful with a puckish humour.

G will be remembered as an outstanding and kind schoolmaster who never put himself forward when he could foster another. He was a man with an unassuming manner and penetrating mind that thought quickly, lucidly and thoroughly around all problems, and a strong character greatly respected by all at the College as one who expected good behaviour and therefore discipline to come from respect for the individual.

For mountaineers he will be remembered as the 'Father' of a group of Marlborough mountaineers (Kempson 1935, 1936, Wigram 1935, 1936, Ward 1951, 1953, Hunt 1953, Wylie 1953) who were much concerned with the fight for and the first ascent of Everest. I consider myself very fortunate to have had the benefit of his knowledge and enthusiasm for mountaineering in those impressionable schooldays.

He is survived by his wife and three children, two daughters and a son.

Michael Ward

ALPINE CLUB NOTES

OFFICE BEARERS AND COMMITTEE FOR 1988

PRESIDENT..	G C Band
VICE PRESIDENTS.....................................	Lt Col M W H Day
	Sir Alan Pullinger
HONORARY SECRETARY	S W Town
HONORARY TREASURER............................	R A Coatsworth
COMMITTEE: ELECTIVE MEMBERS	Miss M Agrawal
	M E B Banks
	Mrs R Greenwood
	R J S Hoare
	A H Jones
	Mrs H Larsen
	Major D V Nicholls
	G W Templeman
	S M W Venables
ACG CO-OPTED MEMBERS........................	A V Saunders
	C Watts
HONORARY LIBRARIAN..............................	R Lawford
HONORARY ARCHIVIST..............................	E H J Smyth FRCS
ASSISTANT ARCHIVIST	V S Risoe MBE
HONORARY KEEPER OF THE CLUB'S	
PICTURES...	Dr C B M Warren FRCP
HONORARY EDITOR OF THE CLUB'S	
JOURNAL	Professor E H Sondheimer
ASSISTANT EDITORS..................................	Mrs J Merz
	A V Saunders
	G W Templeman
HONORARY GUIDEBOOKS EDITOR.............	G L Swindin
CHAIRMAN OF THE HOUSE COMMITTEE.....	G W Templeman
CHAIRMAN OF THE LIBRARY COUNCIL.......	M H Westmacott
ASSISTANT HONORARY SECRETARIES	
ANNUAL WINTER DINNER	Mrs J Merz
CANDIDATES.............................	A N Husbands
LECTURES	S M W Venables
MEETS	M Pinney
TRUSTEES	M Bennett
	A Blackshaw
	J G R Harding

HONORARY SOLICITOR.............................   S N Beare
AUDITORS ....   A M Dowler
                                                  Davey & Co.

GENERAL MEETINGS OF THE ALPINE CLUB 1987

13 January	Tony Howard, *Climbs and Travels in the Sudan*
10 February	Pat Littlejohn, *Adventures on Rock from West Penwith to Norway*
2 March	Joint AC/RGS: Nick Clinch, *Great Ice Mountain*
10 March	John Brailsford, *Delectable Dauphiné*
14 April	Douglas Milner, *Mountain Travels in the Antipodes*
12 May	Lindsay Griffin, *Out of the Way Ice – Climbs in Greece and Venezuela*
15 September	Jim Fotheringham, *Menlungtse*
13 October	John Harding, *Turkey*
10 November	Andrzej Zawada, *8000 metres in Winter*
24 November	Prof John West, *The Life and Work of Alexander Kellas* (extra meeting)
30 November	Annual General Meeting: *Mont Blanc* (see below)

CLIMBING MEETINGS 1987

24–25 January	Lake District. FRCC Hut, Brackenclose, Wasdale.
14–15 February	ACG Winter Meet. Glencoe.
14–15 March	North Wales. Informal dinner with lectures by Graham Elson and Peter Stokes on the two most recent Alpine Club Himalayan Meets in Chogolungma and Gangotri.
16–17 May	Derbyshire. University of London hut, Fallcliffe Cottage, Grindleford.
18 July–1 August	Argentière. Joint Meet with Climbers' Club and ABMSAC based at Les Frasserands.
23 July–7 August	Cornwall. CC hut, Bosigran. Family meet held jointly with Climbers' Club.
July–August	Greater Ranges Meet: Cordillera Blanca.
26–27 September	Lake District. Informal dinner with lecture by Mick Fowler, *Spantik*.

CLUB REPRESENTATION AT OTHER FUNCTIONS

Peter Ledeboer was present at the opening, on 27 August 1987, of the exhibition *Les premiers photographes des Alpes* at the Musée de l'Elysée, Lausanne. The display consisted of historic early photographs of the Alps, lent by the Alpine Club.

The President, Roger Chorley, John Hunt and Hamish MacInnes attended a conference on 'Mountain Wilderness', at Biella (Piedmont), on 31 October and 1 November 1987. This was sponsored by the Sella Foundation, and Vittorio Sella's magnificent panoramas of the Alps, Caucasus and Himalaya were on display.

Stephen Venables gave four lectures in Bombay at the Diamond Jubilee celebrations of the Himalayan Club (February 1988).

The Club was represented at Annual Dinners of Kindred Clubs as follows: the Fell and Rock Climbing Club (14 November 1987), George Lowe; the Yorkshire Ramblers' Club (21 November 1987), Tony Husbands; the Scottish Mountaineering Club (5 December 1987), the Honorary Editor. The last of these, with two ladies present, was a truly historic occasion.

THE DON WHILLANS MEMORIAL LECTURE

This meeting, one of a set of three, was organized by the Alpine Club on behalf of the Don Whillans Memorial Fund and was held at the Royal Geographical Society on 18 February 1987. It had the purpose of both commemorating a remarkable life and also raising funds for a memorial to Don Whillans. The proposed memorial is a camp-site for British climbers in Chamonix, ideally with toilet and washing facilities. This is particularly appropriate since Don spent many summer seasons camping at Chamonix.

There were four speakers who covered different periods and aspects of Don's climbing life. Nat Allen gave a fascinating portrayal of Don's early days with a mass of early pictures from the 1950s when Don Whillans and Joe Brown were pioneering a series of routes enormously harder than anything that had been done before. Chris Bonington took up the story from the first British ascent of the SW pillar of the Petit Dru in 1958, to Don's attempts on the N wall of the Eiger and the first ascent of the Central Pillar of Frêney, and on to the first ascent of the Central Tower of Paine in Patagonia and the S face of Annapurna with Dougal Haston in 1970. Completing the lecture, Doug Scott told the story of some of Don's more recent Himalayan expeditions – SW face of Everest in 1972, Shivling in 1981 and Broad Peak in 1983. Joe Brown acted as Master of Ceremonies and linkman with a host of amusing and, at times, poignant stories.

Chris Bonington

MONT BLANC 1787–1987: A BRITISH BICENTENARY

Following the bicentenary celebrations of the *first* ascent of Mont Blanc in 1786, the Club felt it appropriate to mark the occasion of the *fourth* ascent of Mont Blanc on 9 August 1787, since this was the first British ascent in the person of Col Mark Beaufoy.

Accordingly, a small exhibition was organized on the Club premises by Jerry Lovatt and Bob Lawford. It was opened at the AGM by the President in the presence of Mrs Guild, great-great-granddaughter of Col Beaufoy. Short accounts of the role played by British climbers were given by the President, Jerry Lovatt, Mike Banks and Roger Payne. Exhibits included a number of historic documents, notably Col Beaufoy's narrative of the ascent, a letter by his guide, Cachat *le Géant*, a certificate of the ascent of Mont Blanc issued by the *Compagnie des Guides* of Chamonix, as well as a memorial urn of Col Beaufoy's scientific achievement presented to him by the Royal Society. In addition, there was the usual excellent photographic display, illustrating British ascents in the area over the 200 years.

Col Beaufoy was Colonel of the Tower Hamlets Militia, a scientist by profession and a philosopher of considerable eminence. He made the first British ascent of Mont Blanc purely for the pleasure of doing so while on an extensive tour of Europe. An account of his ascent is illuminating as described in extracts from a letter from his son written in 1837, following a visit to his guide:

'Scarcely had [de Saussure] quitted Chamouni, when an English gentleman named Beaufoy, his wife, a nurse maid and infant daughter arrived; and as usual with the guides, Cachat and others waited on the Colonel at the Inn . . .

On descending the rough and difficult mountain to the source of the Aveiron, which must have been a most fatiguing trial to our mother as in those days no footpath existed, Cachat was surprised by the lady who was leaning on his arm telling him "my husband has a strong inclination to ascend Mont Blanc and I would wish you to spare neither money nor precautions in order that the excursion may be accomplished safely and successfully". That same evening the Col spoke himself to Cachat, who having consulted with a comrade and written down every article which was requisite, then fixed up 10 guides as sufficient; each to carry between 25lbs and 30lbs of provisions, and ladders, ropes, etc. And the preparations being all made, the party started at seven o'clock the next morning and returned in three days to Chamouni, having been favoured with weather without a cloud.

Cachat told me that the Colonel walked as boldly and actively as any of the men with him, that his only anxiety was to arrive on the summit before twelve o'clock in order to measure the height of the sun with his Quadrant; and that they did reach the highest point at eleven of the second day, having slept in the rock of the Grand Mulet, where they also passed the second night on their return. They remained about one hour and a half on the summit, and what Cachat told me was unusual, the whole number of ten guides were also able to reach the top of the mountain. When I asked him if the Colonel's lady was not afraid at the dangers her husband might experience, he said "how could she be fearful when she encouraged the Colonel to make the attempt, for she was as eager as himself".'

Peter Ledeboer

ALPINE CLUB SYMPOSIUM 1987: CHINA

Around 100 people congregated on Saturday 28 November 1987 at the National Mountaineering Centre, Plas y Brenin, at this meeting entitled 'Climbing in China'. This followed the very successful meetings of previous years – 'Lightweight Expeditions to the Greater Ranges' (1984), 'Climbing in South America' (1985) and 'The Karakoram' (1986).

The President of the Alpine Club, Mr George Band, chaired the meeting. The speakers were: Chris Bonington, Mike Banks, Bill Ruthven, Doug Scott, John Town, Michael Ward, Dickon Bevington, Nick Clinch and Henry Day.

Very considerable experience and expertise were assembled, with speakers who had visited all the mountain regions of China since these began to be opened in 1980. Two themes recurred throughout the Symposium – financial difficulties caused by the high price of Chinese mountaineering, and the cultural differences between ourselves and the many different ethnic groups within the Peoples' Republic.

Climbing in China is expensive, but speakers from smaller expeditions (John Town) indicated ways in which money could be saved and pointed out that they had been able to run small expeditions to 6000m peaks for around £2000 a head from Britain.

The cultural differences, together with the high cost, have led to discord with the Chinese authorities on several trips. Other speakers indicated how helpful and efficient the Chinese had been, and it would appear that an acceptance and an understanding of our differences by visiting mountaineers would ease these problems.

Even after the recent troubles in Tibet there is no indication that the Chinese authorities are 'clamping down' on expeditions, though the single traveller may find it more difficult to visit remote areas.

C R A Clarke

THE ALPINE CLUB LIBRARY

1987 was a year of steady progress. Renovation of the older volumes continued, with the valued help of the National Association of Decorative and Fine Art

Societies. Faster progress was made with the cataloguing of the 'tracts' – bound volumes of miscellaneous printed documents dating from the 1870s onwards – with the help of Mrs Sonia Jacobs, a visitor from Boulder, Colorado. The work done on the photographs in recent years by Bob Lawford has paid dividends, with loans for important exhibitions in Canada and Switzerland bringing both favourable publicity for the collection and a financial contribution.

The first steps towards computerization have been taken, in initiating design of a cataloguing system. Implementation of such a system, leading to publication of a catalogue supplement and later to more complete mechaniz-ation, will, however, require paid assistance, and hence further funds. Thanks to Bill Risoe and to his successor as Honorary Archivist, Edward Smyth, the Archives are now prepared for a major cataloguing effort, which will also require further fund-raising for completion. Fund-raising efforts with com-panies and grant-making bodies continue, but the response this year has been disappointing. Members' donations of books and money, and their covenants, are much appreciated. We also received a substantial bequest from the late Henry S Hall, who during his life was a frequent and most generous benefactor.

Michael Westmacott

ERRATA

The following errors in *AJ92* have been noted:
p206, line 4. The climbers were Sandy Allan and Rick Allen.
p208, line 6 up. Manirang was first climbed by Dr J de V Graaff, Mrs Clare Graaff and Sherpas Pasang Dawa Lama and Tashi.
p260, line 21. Melchior and Jakob Anderegg were cousins, not brothers.
p287. Tenzing Norgay did not take part in the 1933 Everest expedition, but did join the expeditions in 1935, 1936 and 1938. He was sirdar to the French expedition to Nanda Devi in 1951, himself climbing Nanda Devi East, and for the two Swiss expeditions to Everest in 1952. Angtharkay was Eric Shipton's sirdar on the 1951 Everest reconnaissance, and again in 1952 on Cho Oyu.
p301, line 30. For 1959 read 1956.

ACKNOWLEDGMENTS

Again I have to thank many people for their interest, moral support and practical help. Tribute should be paid to Phil Bartlett and W L (Robin) Robinson, who have 'retired from the fray' after five years' hard labour as Assistant Editor and index compiler (respectively). I express a particular word of thanks to Victor (Tony) Saunders, Phil's successor, and to Geof Templeman, Assistant Editor for many years past (and, I hope, to come), whose patient labour and sound judgement have been crucial. Johanna Merz has once again been a tower of strength, and has become a third Assistant Editor. Sheila

Harrison and Pat Johnson have quietly and efficiently produced much important information; and Peter Ledeboer has continued with the task of organizing the advertisements. We depend heavily on the information provided by our regular contributors who form a long and distinguished list: Chris Bonington, Evelio Echevarría, Lindsay Griffin, Harish Kapadia, Bill King, Paul Nunn, Edward Peck, C A Russell and Ted Whalley. We are delighted that they have been joined, this year, by Adams Carter, Zbigniew Kowalewski, Józef Nyka, John Porter and Andrew Wielochowski. Finally, a special word of thanks to Paddy Boulter for keeping the Editor in good repair, and to Janet Sondheimer for advice, support and forbearance. To all the above, and to many other helpers not specifically named, I express my gratitude and appreciation. At the time of writing, important changes are under way in the arrangements for producing and distributing the *Alpine Journal*. These – it is hoped – will give us an even better product and a bigger circulation, whilst preserving all that is best in the journal's tradition.

Ernst Sondheimer

CONTRIBUTORS

SANDY ALLAN is an offshore project engineer, married with one daughter. His mountaineering experience includes early Grade 6 Scottish climbs and ascents of the Muztagh Tower and Pumori S face direct. He has twice been to Everest's unclimbed ridge.

ANDREW BANKES was a barrister and an enthusiastic climber who made two expeditions to the Himalaya, in 1978 and 1984, and climbed regularly in the Alps. He died of cancer in 1987, aged 31.

PHILIP BARTLETT lives in Derbyshire. He increasingly prefers exploratory mountaineering to rock-climbing as he gets older and his arms get weaker. His other interests include physics and the violin.

ROBIN BEADLE is a Research Assistant at Bristol University. He previously lived in Derbyshire, and started climbing there nine years ago. He has had four Alpine seasons, and has also climbed in Peru, on Mount Kenya and in the Himalaya.

CHRIS BONINGTON, Britain's best-known mountaineer, crowned his distinguished career in 1985 by reaching the summit of Everest at the age of 50. His latest volume of autobiography was published in 1986. He continues climbing and writing at undiminished pace.

TREVOR BRAHAM is a Company Director. He has been on 14 expeditions to the Himalaya, Karakoram and Hindu Kush. He wrote *Himalayan Odyssey* and was Editor of the *Himalayan Journal* 1958–60 and of *Chronique Himalayenne* (SAC) 1976–86.

HAMISH BROWN has made 20 visits to Morocco. His recent books include *The Great Walking Adventure*, drawing on his world-wide expeditions, two poetry anthologies, and a volume of his own poems. He lives in Scotland.

H ADAMS CARTER is a retired schoolmaster who taught foreign languages. He has led expeditions to the Himalaya, Andes and Alaska, and has been Editor of the *American Alpine Journal* since 1959.

DAVID CHARITY is a solicitor. In his younger days he climbed extensively on British rock and had three successful Alpine seasons. More recently he has found it difficult to combine serious mountaineering ambitions with family holidays.

LT COL HENRY DAY's climbing with army mountaineers includes expeditions to Tirich Mir, Annapurna I, Indrasan, Everest, Trisul, Jiazi and Xixabangma. He reached the summit of the first three and reached 8400m above the S col on Everest.

KURT DIEMBERGER has lived with the world's mountains for many years. He has been on about 20 expeditions since going to Broad Peak with Hermann Buhl in 1957. A former high-school teacher, he lives now as a writer and film-maker.

EDWIN DRUMMOND, with many first ascents on paper and rock from 25 years of writing and climbing, hopes to be remembered as one who brought a little mountain to Mohammed: making peace with that misunderstood, maligned, non-climbing, five-star General Public.

MAL DUFF was born, of Scottish parents, below Mt Kenya, and his adaptation to risk and altitude was instilled at the age of two. His expeditions include the NE ridge of Everest, the Muztagh Tower, Lhotse Shar and Ben Nevis.

EVELIO ECHEVARRÍA was born in Santiago, Chile, and teaches Hispanic Literature at Colorado State University. He has climbed in North and South America, and has contributed numerous articles to Andean, North American and European journals.

MARIAN ELMES is a teacher. She began climbing in the late 1960s whilst studying at Bangor, and has had 14 seasons in the Alps and Norway. She also enjoys Scottish winter climbing, Welsh crags and ski-mountaineering.

JERZY GAJEWSKI was born in Cracow. He belongs to the Mountain Tourism Committee of the Polish Tourist Association. He has contributed many articles to tourist journals and has wandered through mountains in Eastern Europe, the Alps and in Wales.

TERRY GIFFORD organizes the Festival of Mountaineering Literature at Bretton Hall College of Higher Education. His collection of poems, *The Stone Spiral*, was published in 1987 by Giant Steps.

LINDSAY GRIFFIN, after early climbing in the Alps, nowadays specializes in 'exploratory mountaineering'. His trips are lightweight, alpine-style, and he has made many first ascents and quite a number of solo ascents and excursions.

BRIAN HALL works as a mountain guide, photographer, lecturer and climbing consultant. He has made many ascents in the Alps, and has been on expeditions to Patagonia, Bolivia, Peru, Jannu, Nuptse, Baltoro Kangri, Everest, Ogre II, Makalu/Chamlang and K2.

GORDON HAMILTON has extensive experience of mountaineering, climbing and skiing in his native Scotland, in addition to participating in three expeditions, to Arctic Norway, Iceland and the Pyrenees. He is currently studying geography at the University of Aberdeen.

JOHN HARDING is a solicitor. He served in the Welsh Guards (1952–4), in the Colonial Service in South Arabia (1959–65) and was resident in Australia (1969–70). He has been on 60 expeditions in Europe, Asia, Africa and Australasia.

GEOFFREY HATTERSLEY-SMITH DPhil, FRSCanada, FRGS (gold medallist), of the British Antarctic Survey, is Secretary of the UK Antarctic Place-names Committee. He is a glaciologist and mountaineer with many years' experience in the Alps, Antarctic, Canadian Arctic, Canadian Rockies and Greenland.

HARRY HILTON is a television writer and freelance journalist who has been climbing since the late 1940s. He has visited the Nepalese Himalaya and has made ascents (some 'firsts') in the Alps, Corsica, Algeria, South Yemen, Kenya, Zambia and Tanzania.

GEOFF HORNBY is an Industrial Safety Engineer who lives in Derbyshire. He has made many ascents in the European Alps and has climbed in Morocco, Kenya, Ecuador, Alaska, Yosemite, the Polish Tatra and the Kumaon and Garhwal Himalaya.

CHARLES HOUSTON, Professor Emeritus of Medicine, has climbed high in the Himalaya five times since 1936 and has carried out altitude research for many years. A third edition of his book *Going Higher* was published in 1987 by Little Brown.

TONY HOWARD, a founding partner of Troll Safety Equipment, took part in the first ascent of the Troll Wall in 1965. His expeditions include Greenland, N Canada and desert mountains in Morocco, Algeria, the Sudan, Iran and Jordan.

LUKE HUGHES is a furniture designer. He has climbed many new routes on Old Wardour Castle, Eric Shipton's climbing nursery, and has also climbed in the grown-up playgrounds of Europe, America and the Himalaya.

JOHN HUNT (Lord Hunt of Llanfair Waterdine) has had a highly distinguished career in the army, the public service and as a mountaineer. He was leader of the British expedition which made the first ascent of Mount Everest in 1953.

MICHAEL JARDINE is fluent in Chinese and Japanese, and works in Tokyo. He counts as his greatest achievement 'an epic winter ascent (and ski descent) of ice-bound Mt Fuji, in gale-force winds, a feat equalled only by several thousand Japanese'.

HARISH KAPADIA is a cloth merchant by profession. He has climbed and trekked in the Himalaya since 1960, with ascents up to 6800m. He is at present Honorary Assistant Editor of the *Himalayan Journal*, and Compiler of the *HC Newsletter*.

BILL KING works for Telecoms New Zealand. He has climbed extensively throughout New Zealand (with four routes on Mt Cook), and has participated in the NZ Antarctic Research Programme and in NZ expeditions to the Andes, Nepal and the Pamir.

WALTER LORCH, a ski mountaineer, served in the 6th Airborne Division and in the Mountain Warfare Establishment. He led the field-work for avalanche rescue transceivers, now standard world-wide, and is the author of *Snow Travel and Transport*.

ELIZABETH MARTIN lives in Sheffield and is a Management Trainee with the Department of Employment. She spent 1984–87 in her native Belfast, researching rock glaciers for her PhD. She has led expeditions to Alaska, Colorado and Iceland.

JOHANNA MERZ is a photographer specializing in audio-visual present-ations. A late-starter, at over 50 she has climbed in the Pennine Alps, the Mont Blanc Chain, the Brenta Dolomites, Bernina, Dauphiné and Apennines.

PAUL NUNN PhD is Principal Lecturer in Economic History at Sheffield City Polytechnic. His numerous climbs include first ascents of the British Route on Pik Shchurovsky and the SW Pillar of Asgard. He has been on nine Himalayan expeditions.

HENRY OSMASTON was a forester in Uganda, was President of the MCU, and wrote the Guide to the Ruwenzori. He is now a geographer at Bristol University and has recently spent three summers working in Ladakh and two in China.

JOHN OWEN is a general practitioner in Colchester, Essex. He has been climbing easy routes in the Alps since 1970, and has enjoyed several trekking holidays in Peru, Nepal and India.

ROGER PAYNE BEd (Hons) is a qualified mountain guide. He has not missed an alpine season since 1977 and has been on five expeditions to the greater ranges.

SIR EDWARD PECK was in the Diplomatic Service until 1975, when he retired to Tomintoul. He has climbed in the Alps, Turkey, Kulu, Borneo and East Africa. His object when serving abroad was generally to reach the highest point available.

JOHN PORTER is from New England, a Leeds graduate, now resident in West Cumbria. He has climbed extensively in America and Europe. Trips abroad include the Hindu Kush, Changabang, the Tatra, Andes, Everest, Annapurna, Mt Kenya, Alaska and K2.

LEWIS PRESTON is an architect. He has 16 years' mountaineering experience in Britain, and has explored areas of Norwegian wilderness. Climbs from his three seasons in the Swiss and French Alps have been documented in the *Alpine Journal*.

KEV REYNOLDS has climbed in the Atlas, the Alps and extensively in the Pyrenees. For many years a Youth Hostel Warden, he is now a freelance writer and lecturer.

C A RUSSELL, who works with a City bank, devotes much of his spare time to mountaineering and related activities. He has climbed in many regions of the Alps, in the Pyrenees and in East Africa.

MALCOLM SALES has been climbing regularly in the British Isles and other parts of Europe for the past 21 years. He has helped to run Scout expeditions to Norway and the Pyrenees. He frequently visits Scotland for the winter climbing.

A V SAUNDERS, an architect by profession, was taken up by alpinism at the age of 27, and remembers that Marco Pallis began in his thirties, and that Andrzej Zawada led his first Himalayan expedition when he was 40.

DOUG SCOTT is one of the world's leading high-altitude and big-wall climbers who has pioneered new routes on many of the world's most difficult mountains. He is firmly committed to the concept of lightweight, alpine-style expeditions.

GUY SHERIDAN OBE is a Lt Colonel in the Royal Marines. He commanded the Mountain and Arctic Warfare Cadre, 1972–74. He was a member of the British Olympic Biathlon Squad 1972, and has completed several long winter ski journeys worldwide.

ROBERT SNEYD is a hospital doctor currently engaged upon research into the control of breathing.

BELINDA SWIFT is a teacher of music, with 20 years' experience of mountaineering in Britain and the Alps. In the winter of 1978 she made a three-month overland trip from Teheran to Kathmandu, and she has visited Peru three times.

JOHN TOWN is a member of the Registrar's Department at the University of Manchester. He has a preference for little-explored mountain areas and has climbed in the Alps, Caucasus, E Turkey, Himalaya, Altai, Tibet and the Andes.

MARGARET URMSTON fell in love with the Scottish Highlands aged 13, but lost touch with the hills until she was 35. She has since been making up for lost time, climbing in Scotland, the Himalaya, the Caucasus and the Alps.

MICHAEL WARD is a Consultant Surgeon, interested in high-altitude and cold research. He took part in the expeditions which made the first ascents of Everest and Kongur, and his other expeditions include the Bhutan Himal and a Tibet Geo-Traverse.

CHARLES WARREN is a Consultant Children's Physician (retired). As a member of Marco Pallis's Gangotri expedition 1933, and of the Everest expeditions 1935–36–38, he made several first ascents, and he has climbed on Mount Kenya, Kilimanjaro and Table Mountain.

TED WHALLEY is a research chemist who works for the National Research Council of Canada. His extensive climbing experience includes many first ascents on Baffin Island and Ellesmere Island. He was President of the ACC, 1980–84.

ANDREW WIELOCHOWSKI is a past instructor for the Joint Services, with first ascents in Scotland, the Alps, Himalaya, Norway and East Africa. Publications include a guidebook to East Africa, where he has climbed and explored extensively; he currently guides there.

ANDRZEJ ZAWADA's notable climbs in Europe include a three-week winter traverse of the Tatra. His pioneering ascents in the Himalaya and Hindu Kush include the first winter ascent of a 7000m peak (Noshaq) and of an 8000m peak (Everest).

GUIDANCE FOR CONTRIBUTORS

The *Alpine Journal* has been published regularly since 1863 as 'A Record of Mountain Adventure and Scientific Observation'. The Journal has always been a record of all aspects of mountains and mountaineering and, although its main function is to record mountain adventure, articles on mountain art, literature, anthropology, geology, medicine, equipment, etc, are all suitable. Articles should be informative, and a good literary style is important. Scientific or medical papers should be of the general style and technical level of *Scientific American*.

Articles   Articles for the Journal should normally not exceed 3000 words (longer articles can be considered in exceptional cases). Please indicate the number of words when submitting your article. Papers should normally be written in English. Translation is usually possible from French, German and Italian, but papers requiring translation should be submitted at least 3 months before the editorial deadline.

Articles submitted to the Journal should not have been published in substantially the same form in any other publication. Authors are not paid for articles published in the Journal, but they do receive a copy of the issue in which their article appears. Please send articles direct to the Editor at 51 Cholmeley Crescent, London N6 5EX.

Typescript   The complete typescript including the text of the paper, list of references, footnotes and captions to illustrations should be typed on one side of A4 paper, at *double spacing* and with 20–30mm margins. Authors should keep a spare copy. *It will help the Editor greatly if authors could, as far as possible, adopt the Journal's house style for proper names, abbreviations, mountain features, etc (for which recent copies of the Journal should be consulted).* The Editor reserves the right to edit or shorten articles at his discretion.

Illustrations   The number of colour photographs which can be printed is extremely limited and only top quality photographs will be accepted. Prints should preferably be black-and-white, between 150200mm and 220300mm large and printed on glossy paper. Colour transparencies should be at least 35mm format and should be originals (not copies). A portfolio of up to 10 photographs should be provided. Maps and line drawings should be of a similar size to the prints and be finished ready for printing. Place-names appearing in the text, where relevant, should be marked on the maps also.

Each photograph should be clearly labelled with title, author and any copyright. This information should be typed on a separate sheet of paper attached to the photograph and not written on the back of the photograph itself. Routes of climbs should be marked on separate sheets of transparent paper.

Always take special care in sending prints through the post. Do include adequate stiffening to prevent folding and clearly label the cover: 'Photographs: Please Do Not Bend'. Do not include paper-clips or pins which could damage prints.

References   Details of other publications referred to in the text should be given in a separate list and should include the names of all authors; the title of the paper and publication as appropriate; the year of publication, volume number, and first and last page number.

Units   Metric (SI) units should be used throughout except when quoting original material which uses other units.

Biographies For the 'Contributors' section of the Journal, authors are asked to provide a 'potted biography', in not more than 40 words, listing what they consider to be the most noteworthy items in their career.

Deadline Copy must be with the Editor by 1 January of the year of publication. Space in the Journal is limited, and early submission improves the chances of acceptance. Articles for which there is no space may be considered for publication in a subsequent year.

INDEX

1988 Vol 93 Compiled by Marian Elmes

► *1970* – Imperial College Hindu Kush – British Women's Himalayan – Annapurna – British Patagonian – East Greenland – *1971* – East Greenland – Everest S.W. Face – *1972* – British Everest – Anglo/German Everest – Soviet Caucasus – Peruvian Andes – *1973* – British Fitzroy – Patagonia Icecap – East Greenland – British Torre Egger – *1974* – British Women's Nepal – Patagonia – International Pamirs/USSR – Indo-New Zealand Himalayan – *1975* – Norwegian Himalayan – British Everest S.W. Face – 2 man Dunagiri – Trango Tower – British East Greenland – Nuptse – *1976* – Changabang West Wall – Japanese Nuptse – Annapurna South Peak – Joint British/Nepalese Everest – Trans Karakoram – *1977* – British South American – International Makalu –

On top of the World
every year.

Approaching Summit Ridge, Norwegian Everest Expedition 1985.

British Kishtwar – New Zealand Everest – Greenland Kayak – *1978* – Mt. McKinley – Everest Canoe – Swiss Lhotse – Transglobe North Pole – Trans-Atlantic Balloon – Messner Everest without Oxygen – British Jannu – British K2 – Karakoram Canoe – American Women's Annapurna – British Women's Karakoram – *1979* – British Kantaiga – Barnaj 2 – British Kangchenjunga – Gauri Sankar – Nuptse/Everest – *1980* – Mount Kongur China Reconnaisance – Baltoro Kangari – British K2 – Nanga Parbat – Royal Marines Ellesmere Island – Makalu – Dhaulagiri – *1981* – Annapurna 4 – Karakoram – Mt. Kongur – Everest Winter – *1982* – Ogre – Everest N.E. Ridge – Transglobe – British East Greenland – *1983* – Xixabangma – Kangchenjunga – Gangotri – Imperial College East Greenland – Running the Himalayas – Anglo/French Karakoram – Japanese Nanga Parbat – Lhotse – Joint Services to Brabant Island – *1984* – In the Footsteps of Scott – Karunkoh – Indian Everest – Makalu – *1985* – Norwegian Everest – Pilkington Everest – China Caves – *1986* – Icelandic Canoe – Climb Aid Peak Lenin – American K2.

Mountain Equipment
SUPPLIERS TO 14 EVEREST EXPEDITIONS

FREE. Send for the latest Mountain Equipment full colour brochure.

MR/MRS/MISS/MS _____

ADDRESS _____

_____

_____ POST CODE _____

Send to: Mountain Equipment Ltd., Leech Street, Stalybridge, SK15 1SD. Telephone: 061-338-8793.   AJ87

Rowland Edwards
on Superjam E5 6B.
Photo: International
School of Rock Climbing

troll
FOR PEOPLE IN PRECARIOUS PLACES

Send for Troll '88 Colour leaflet or Complete Catalogue range:
TROLL SAFETY EQUIPMENT LTD.,
Spring Mill, Uppermill, Oldham OL3 6AA.   Tel: 04577 8822